John and Anne Spencer have been active researchers of the paranormal for over twenty years. John is Chairman of the British UFO Research Association, a member of the Ghost Club, the Society for Psychical Research (SPR) and the Association for the Scientific Study of Anomalous Phenomena (ASSAP). John and Anne are at the forefront of experimental work and research into many unsolved mysteries.

The Encyclopedia of the World's Greatest Unsolved Mysteries

John and Anne Spencer

HEADLINE

To Katie and Jenny.
Yours is the generation to solve these mysteries . . .
. . . and find the questions for the next generation.

Copyright © 1995 John and Anne Spencer

First published in 1995
by HEADLINE BOOK PUBLISHING

First published in paperback in 1996
by HEADLINE BOOK PUBLISHING

10 9 8 7 6 5 4 3 2

ISBN 0 7472 5013 8

Printed and bound in Great Britain by
Cox & Wyman Ltd, Reading, Berks

HEADLINE BOOK PUBLISHING
A division of Hodder Headline PLC
338 Euston Road
London NW1 3BH

Acknowledgements

Our thanks to the many individuals and organisations who have assisted with our researches many of who have patiently granted sometimes several interviews, including:

Alistair MacKenzie; Arne Groth; ASSAP; Brian Colliss (elder of the Borehamwood Baptist Church); Chris Walton; Dave O'Sullivan of the China Fleet Country Club; Dave Thomas; Department of Archaeological Studies, University of Bradford; Dr David Cross; Geometrics (manufacturers of archaeological survey equipment); Geophysical Survey Systems Inc and particularly Greg Mills; George Hamilton; Graham James and Julie Williams, of the House of Jupiter; Hakan Shah; Hasan Shah; Hazel and Warwick Spencer; Hilary Evans; Independent Television News Ltd; Jacques Vallee; Javier Sierra; Jenny Bright; John and Jayne MacNish; Kate Glass of Anglia TV's *Magic and Mystery Show*; Lena Norman; Leo Rutherford and 'Eagles Wing'; Manfred Cassirer; Maurice Grosse; Mrs Mary Murray; Mrs Pat Warner; Pam Tume; Paul Norman; Philip Walton; RAF Henlow; Reverend Geoff Bowyer; Simon Rose (for assistance with translation of Hebrew text); Ron Campbell and 1st Unit Fire and Safety; Stanley Conway and family; Stephen Gamble (for assistance with the Legend of Spring-Heeled Jack); Ted Harrison; The British Library (Oriental and India office collections); The Ministry of Agriculture, Fisheries and Food; The Natural History Museum; The New Jersey Police Department; The New York Department of Health; The New York Police Department; The Reverend Canon Dominic Walker OGS; The Science Museum (The National Museum of Science and Industry); Tony Wells.

None of these organisations or individuals is responsible for any of the views expressed in the book except where the text clearly indicates as such. If we have omitted any names we should have listed, we apologise.

ABBREVIATIONS USED IN THE TEXT

ESP	extra-sensory perception
EVP	electronic voice phenomenon
MIB	men in black
NDE	near-death experience
OOBE	out-of-body experience
PK	psychokinesis
RSPK	recurrent spontaneous PK
SLI	street lamp interference
SHC	spontaneous human combustion
SPR	Society for Psychical Research
UFO	unidentified flying object

Contents

Introduction	1
Airships of 1896	5
Alien Abductions	10
Altered States of Consciousness	15
Angels	17
Anomalous Faces	22
Apports	25
Atlantis	30
Auras	35
Automatic Writing	36
Banshee	40
Bermuda Triangle	41
Big Cats	46
Bigfoot and Sasquatch	51
Bi-Locations	55
Black Dog Phenomena	59
Close Encounters	61
Coincidence	66
Contactees	71
Crash Retrievals	75
Crisis Apparitions	80
Crop Circles	85
Crystals	90
Curses and Hexes	94
Déjà Vu	98
Dolphin Healing	98
Doubles and *Doppelgängers*	103
Dowsing	107

Dragons and Lake Monsters 111
Ectoplasm 116
Electronic Voice Phenomenon 117
Exorcism 120
Fairies 125
Firewalking 127
Flight 19 132
Flood Myths of the World 136
Flying Dutchman 138
Frogs, Fish and Other Falls 140
Ghosts 144
Hexham Heads 149
Incorruptibility 152
Incubus and Succubus 154
Levitation 156
Ley Lines 160
Luck 161
Map Dowsing 167
Marian Visitations 169
Martian Mysteries 174
Mary Celeste 178
Mediumship 182
Men In Black 187
Mothmen 191
Near-Death Experiences 196
Noah's Ark 202
Omens 206
Ouija 208
Out-Of-Body Experiences 211
Panic of 1938 216
Phantom Hitchhikers 224
Phantom Scenery 228
Philadelphia Experiment 228
Poltergeists 233
Possession 238
Premonition 243
Psychic Detectives 246
Psychic, or Spiritual, Healing 250

Psychic Surgery 256
Psychokinesis 259
Psychometry 263
Reincarnation 267
Savant Syndrome 272
Shamanism 275
Spectral Armies 277
Spontaneous Equipment Failure 281
Spontaneous Human Combustion 283
Spring-Heeled Jack 288
Stigmata 289
Street Lamp Interference 293
Telepathy 298
Thoughtography 302
Time Slips 303
Toronto Blessing 307
Tunguska Explosion 312
Turin Shroud 316
UFOs 321
Vampires 326
Vehicle Interference 330
Weeping, Bleeding, Moving Statues 333
Werewolves 336
Witchcraft into the Modern Day 340
Yetis 346
Zombies 351
The Value of Science, Scepticism and Commitment 355
Recommended reading and references 361
Index of Names 367

Introduction

We not only enjoy good mysteries, but we need them. Mysteries inspire our curiosity, and it is through curiosity that we develop as people and as a species. The mysteries in this book include one or two which endure in people's fascination; despite probable explanations on offer, they continue to arise even in current debate.

The world is not just a set of facts to be observed. We contribute to our world every time we observe something. When we observe it, we bring to that observation experience, interpretation and prejudices, all of which affect our responses.

This book contains not just a variety of mysteries, but a variety of types of mysteries. There are mysteries about the physical world; is there a large man-beast walking the Himalayas or the North American continent or virtually every other part of the world as so many have reported? There are mysteries which reflect our mythologies; is the Ark of Noah preserved in the mountains of Ararat? There are mysteries about the potential of people; can they move objects by sheer force of mind? Can they affect their own physiology by will?

Our society is not serving us well. The attraction modern technological man feels towards the less technological cultures, aborigines, North American Indians and so on, is not just romanticism. We recognise, perhaps subconsciously, that their societies have structures which support them. That support is not just material, food and shelter, but also spiritual, an inner conviction and belief in their history, legends and mythology. We have lost that. Our intuitive brain which feeds from, and into, these spiritual areas has been subjugated by a rational, calculating brain which may provide for our material needs but not our spiritual ones. Our religions have become diluted; more attention is given to not tripping at the altar and wearing the right hat, and too little to thinking about and concentrating on the spiritual focus.

Many of the mysteries in this book reflect that shortcoming in our Western society. For many shamans of less technological tribes these are not mysteries; they know – without any shadow of doubt – the truths about, say, out-of-body experience, near-death experience, mind power and so on, not because they have studied these things, but because they do them just as we breathe, walk and eat. They know which aspects of these mysteries have objective non-personal reality and which are aspects of the spirit and mythology.

Consider the quote by Plutarch which follows this introduction. Reading this book will not of itself answer questions, but if you are inspired to seek further into the mysteries, that journey of curiosity, rather than the destination, will be a valuable, exciting and enhancing experience for you.

John and Anne Spencer
April 1995

'The most beautiful and profound emotion one can experience is the sensation of the mystical. It is the source of all true science.'

Albert Einstein

'The mind is not a vessel to be filled, but a fire to be lighted.'

Plutarch

A

AIRSHIPS OF 1896

From late 1896 to mid 1897 the United States of America was subject to a wave of reports of airships seen over a widespread area. It is held by many that the objects seen could not have been airships as there were none at the time; but that is not so, and some of the reports were probably exactly what they claimed to be: the sighting of prototype airships. Others may have a more interesting origin.

The United States phantom airship wave arguably begins in the evening of 17 November 1896. Hundreds of witnesses, including the daughter of the Mayor, in Sacramento, California, some eighty miles northeast of San Francisco, watched a large glowing object drift over the city. The object was oblong, had tapered ends, propellers and a searchlight. Several people claimed to have seen a canopy. According to one witness, he shouted at the airship asking where they were heading and was told that the crew expected to be at San Francisco by midnight. That would require speeds of somewhere between thirteen and sixteen miles an hour, which was within the capabilities of airships at the time. The airship was also seen three nights later, in the evening of 20 November, above Oakland near San Francisco heading across the bay.

On 24 November 1896 a similar sight was reported by witnesses at Tacoma, Washington, over 700 miles to the north, a similar but not the same object. On 2 December 1896 two fishermen at Pacific Grove north of San Francisco watched an object land on the beach. As the fishermen, Giuseppe Valinziano and Luigi Valdivia, approached the crew of three, they were held at bay and never allowed nearer than fifty feet from the object. They described it as sixty feet long and cigar-shaped. The following evening an object fitting that description was seen in difficulty in the air near San Francisco; it crashed to the ground and two injured crew members were recovered. The propeller and the gas bags were damaged.

There were no known reports of the airship between late December 1896 and the end of March 1897. Perhaps it was under repair, or grounded due to the winter. On 1 April 1897, over Kansas City, Missouri, on the Missouri/Kansas border, an airship was reported over the city at approximately 8.00 that evening. Thousands of witnesses, including the Kansas City governor, watched the object which was described as approximately thirty feet long. The following night the object was seen above Omaha, Nebraska approximately 160 miles north to northeast. Airship speeds of the time would have allowed it to reach that location. The following night it was back over Kansas at Topeka approximately eighty miles to the west of Kansas City. A few nights later it was seen again over Omaha, apparently flying a circular route over the lowland valley of the Missouri River.

By 7 April the craft had ventured further north to Sioux City, Iowa, still over the lowlands of the Missouri River. On 10 April the object arrived over Chicago, Illinois on the shores of Lake Michigan. Many people saw it from the tops of skyscrapers. On 15 April there were reports of the airships in several states, including Missouri, Iowa, Tennessee, Kentucky and Texas which continued for several nights. On 18 April a similar object was seen over Sisterville, West Virginia and heading towards Ohio. The following day over 3,000 people at Cripple Creek, Kansas reported a sighting.

On 30 April 1897 the airship was seen over New York by many witnesses and on 6 May 1897 two law officers, Constable Sumpter and Deputy Sheriff McLenore of Arkansas, watched as an airship landed.

There is little in these sightings that cannot be explained by the technology of the time. In 1852 Henri Giffard, a French engineer, had succeeded in building a semi-rigid airship with a cigar-shaped gas bag 144 feet long and 40 feet wide holding 88,000 cubic feet of gas. On 24 September 1852 Giffard flew on a straight line against the wind at three miles an hour, though he gave up experiments as he found steering too difficult. Two French army officers in 1884 flew at fourteen miles an hour. In 1897, the year of the American airship wave, a German, Karl Schwarz, built the first rigid airship, with a gas bag made of thin sheets of aluminium rather than fabric stretched over a framework. It used an internal combustion engine to drive the propeller, but crashed on its first flight. Probably the first genuinely successful navigation of an airship was by Alberto Santos-Dumont who navigated a 108 foot long, 20 foot diameter airship around the Eiffel Tower on 19 October 1901. In the same year Count Ferdinand von Zeppelin completed his first airship in June and on its first trial achieved eighteen miles per hour.

There have been many attempts to identify the inventors of the airships seen over the United States. No firm conclusions have been reached but the names of E.J. Pennington who claimed, 'I have an airship over in Brown County undergoing some repairs' and A.C. Clinton (probably Omaha violin-maker Clinton A. Case) have been proposed. The one inventor everybody seemed to want to involve was the one who specifically denied any involvement. Thomas A. Edison announced, 'I am not, however, figuring on inventing an airship. I prefer to devote my time to objects which have some commercial value.' The fact that in Europe contemporary airship design matched what was being seen in the United States, and given that there were many inventors looking towards aeronautical machines at that time, it is highly probable that real airships were being seen. Given the numbers of witnesses to certain sightings that becomes almost a certainty.

One mystery remains however, which throws doubt on this. Where are the airships now? And what happened to the patents that should have been lodged, since evidently the airships seen were functioning reasonably well? Surely some of these early inventions would have found their way into private exhibitions and collections, but they appear not to have done.

In fact, the American airship wave stopped dead in its tracks, an abrupt end that is a usual characteristic neither of reality, nor of folklore.

But there were some very strange stories circulating about the airships amidst the reasonable reports.

- On 21 April John Barclay of Rockland, Texas, reported seeing an airship land while out walking his dog. Barclay approached the object, but a guard who identified himself as 'Smith' prevented him from getting to closer than within 100 feet of the craft. Smith asked Barclay for help in locating lubricating oils and tools and gave Barclay local currency with which to buy them. Nothing astonishing yet, but then Barclay was told that the object would be in Greece in two days' time, which was not possible for airships of the day. Furthermore, when it left, Barclay saw it leave like a shot out of a gun. No airship of the time could have done that.

- At more or less the same time, farmer Alexander Hamilton in Kansas was making a much more extraordinary report. He also described a 300 foot airship coming in low over his ranch containing 'the strangest beings I ever saw'. Hamilton apparently watched as the airship lassoed a heifer and flew away, taking the unfortunate victim with it. The following morning the heifer's fate was discovered; the skin, head and legs of the animal were found in a neighbour's field.

- Robert Hibbard, a farmer living near Sioux City, had reported seeing an airship in March. It was dragging an anchor which caught him and dragged him several feet.

- The 20 April 1897 edition of the *Houston Daily Post* contains a story of witnesses following a trailing object which snagged, of a small person climbing down a rope, cutting the object free and leaving the airship free to float away.

- In the 16 April 1897 edition of the *Saginaw Courier and Herald*, the newspaper reported that on Wednesday 14 April an airship had landed at Howard City, Michigan at 4.30 in the morning. The report described a naked entity emerging from the craft, a being over nine feet tall who used musical notes to communicate.

These claims seem a lot less likely to be realistic, and they are of some fascination when viewed in the comparative light of modern-day UFO reports (see 'UFOs', page 321). The claims by Hibbard and the *Daily Post* also need to be considered in the light of a claim from Cloera in Ireland – in the year 956 – that churchgoers had seen an anchor attach itself to the arch above a church door and men from a sky ship float down the cable to release it.

Alexander Hamilton's claim should be considered in the light of cattle and animal mutilations that are even in recent years forming a significant part of the UFO phenomenon.

Almost certainly, the fact that the 'real' sightings were ahead of public announcements of airship design at the time created some element of disbelief and mystery. Newspapers decided to boost their circulation by pandering to either the believers or the disbelievers. In fact William Randolph Hearst's papers took both lines on the same day, 28 November 1896: The *San Francisco Examiner* explained the sightings as 'probably due to liquor, the result of beer' while the *New York Morning Journal*, also owned by Hearst, claimed, 'The biggest problem of the age has been solved . . . a successful ship has been built.'

The folklore and hoaxes – probably partly generated by newspapers – were built on the real claims with a just sufficient blend of mystery and plausibility. In addition there would have been wishful thinking and outright hoaxes on the media by members of the public.

Interestingly, H G Wells's *War of the Worlds* was first published in serial form between April and December 1897 in *Pearson's Magazine*. His aliens from Mars arrived in cylinders, though projectile-like rather than floating. There may be little or no connection; certainly some reports pre-date the publication – and may even have inspired Wells – but the sudden upswell of reports in April 1897 might have created more attention and concern, given the fictional background available.

By making our best guess as to the reality of the airship wave, and examining the way speculation, folklore and a mischievous media distorted the truth, we can construct a better model that we have at present, through which we can look at more modern UFO reports, including reports of cattle mutilation, crash retrievals and alien contact.

ALIEN ABDUCTIONS

The alien abduction phenomenon, at least presented as such, is a very recent type of report. It is derived from the UFO phenomenon which came to prominence in 1947, though it was ten years later that the first abduction claim arose. In essence the claim is that a selection of people around the world have been 'kidnapped' by aliens and examined or used by them.

Claims have been made by people from all around the world: The United States of America, South America, the United Kingdom, Europe, Australia, Africa. Abductions have been reported by people of all ages from all cultures. Many of the reports have very similar components, but virtually every report also has unique components.

Many thousands of reports have been made, mostly in the United States. No one knows the number of incidents that have not been reported. Many researchers believe that the phenomenon is a repressed one; Professor David Jacobs, in his book *Secret Life* published in 1993, extrapolates from two surveys and concludes the possibility that fifteen million people in the United States alone may have had abduction experiences.

The first recorded UFO abduction was that of Antonio Villas Boas in 1957. He was abducted aboard a landed UFO while working late at night on an Argentinian farm. He claimed he was seduced by an attractive-looking female humanoid and that she was taking his seed back to the stars.

The vital question is, are these experiences really happening?

Abduction lore is much older than the UFO phenomenon. Edwin Hartland's book *The Science of Fairy Tales* refers to many missing time experiences. J. Evans-Wentz in *The Fairy Faith in Celtic Countries* refers to many stories of dwarfish fairies, fairy rings and time-shifts during time spent in the fairy realm. Just as UFO abductee Antonio Villas Boas attempted to steal a clock from a UFO as proof of the experience, and Betty Hill (see below) nearly got off a flying saucer with a book given to her by the aliens' leader (it was taken back from her), so Evans-Wentz recalled the case of a boy abducted by fairies who wanted to return to his mother and take her a golden ball he had been given. He was not allowed to take the ball when he left. The creation of hybrid humans perhaps has a forerunner in the stories of change-lings, the abduction of children and the substitution of a fairy child, that were common in Europe in the 1800s and already legend prior to that time.

Certainly any analysis of reports of people being visited in their bedrooms by aliens must consider the forerunner reports of the 'Old Hag' who sat on your chest crushing the life out of you, and of the visitation by incubi and succubi, demons which seduced or raped both women and men. Either alien abduction is a completely separate, but similar, experience, or it is new make-up on an old face.

At the time, the Villas Boas case was unique, and it was regarded as an isolated mystery associated with UFOs. Analysis of UFO literature and UFO reports clearly indicates that the starting point of abductions as a phenomenon in its own right, with its own parameters, is the abduction of Betty and Barney Hill.

The Betty and Barney Hill case arose in September 1961 during a drive to their New Hampshire home from a holiday in Canada. During several miles of driving they watched a light manoeuvring behind trees and mountain tops, and eventually they stopped the car to examine the light. Through binoculars Betty identified a huge craft. Barney shortly afterwards left the car and inspected the object at closer range, identifying windows and at least a dozen 'people' looking back at him. He panicked, and ran back to join his wife in their car, and they drove off. They became drowsy and aware of a 'beeping sound'. At a later point on the road their drowsiness lifted and they were still aware of the 'beeping sound' but believed the two sounds to be discontinuous. On arriving home they discovered that their watches were not working and much later it was pointed out to them that they had arrived home around two hours later than they might have expected to. Two days after the sighting Betty absorbed herself in UFO literature, most of which at that time emphasised the extraterrestrial hypothesis. Shortly after that she had frightening dreams of the abduction scenario, of being taken aboard the saucer, of being subjected to medical examination, of conversations with the aliens. She came to believe that these things had really happened to her during the 'missing time', the two hours for which she could not account. Her concern led her to see Boston psychiatrist Dr Benjamin Simon who, starting on 22 February 1964, used regression hypnosis to 'take her back' in her memories to the night of the experience.

Dr Simon recognised that hypnosis brings forward with conviction what the person believes, rather than what is necessarily objectively true. He pointed out that, 'It must be understood the hypnosis is a pathway to the truth as it is felt and understood by the patient. The truth is what he believes to be the truth, and this may or may not be consonant with the ultimate non-personal truth.' It should also be borne in mind that the suggestion that her dreams were actual memories was first made to Betty Hill by an authority figure in the form of her supervisor at work.

The Hill's story was published in 1966 in a best-selling book *The Interrupted Journey* by John G. Fuller. There is little doubt that the image of UFOs and aliens created by that book was a major influence. The stereotypical abduction was laid down in the minds of UFO witnesses and UFO researchers – particularly the new, enthusiastic influx of researchers – and the media.

What do these aliens want? The leading American researchers who are the enthusiastic proponents of this theory believe that the aliens are engaged on a programme of genetic manipulation using human DNA, ova and sperm to create hybrid human/alien children, possibly to replace some deficiency in their own physical make-up. Betty Hill and another abductee, Betty Andreasson, both believe they underwent probes through the navel, believed to relate to pregnancy testing. Kathie Davis, the principal subject of Budd Hopkins' book *Intruders*, underwent a series of abductions including presumed artificial insemination, an abduction during which time an unborn foetus was allegedly removed and a later abduction when she was allowed to see, perhaps it was intended she should 'bond' with, her nine hybrid children. British abductee Rohan Hinton reported one experience during which she felt her ovaries may have been 'tampered with'. Dr John E. Mack, MD, Professor of Psychiatry at Harvard Medical School has recently joined the fray, supporting such notions from his own researches.

There are now reports that go well beyond the isolated examination table on the flying saucer. In David Jacobs' *Secret Life* he reports, 'The abduction programme appears to be vast. Abductees routinely report rooms with as many as 200 tables holding humans in various stages of examination.'

Proponents of these beliefs point to the fact that many similar reports are received from around the world by people who have no connection with one another, and are unlikely to read UFO literature. But that overlooks the fact that most UFO researching is done by a small, homogenous group of basically white, middle-class people (mostly male) who come from a science-fiction influenced, technological background. They view the abduction phenomenon through that cultural setting, they transmit details of the stereotype between cases, either in their own interpretations or, of greater concern, by consciously influencing witnesses during hypnotic regression sessions, when the witness is in the most suggestible state.

The influence of hypnosis in abduction claims cannot be understated, although it is true to say that not all abductions are revealed or examined with the use of hypnosis. Hypnosis leaves the subject in a suggestible state and eager to please the hypnotist. If the hypnotist is known to be a UFO researcher, there is a subconscious pressure on the witness to provide a UFO story for the researcher. Researchers, in order to verify their facts, will ask over and over again for details of particular incidents; however, with hypnosis the effect of repeated questioning is to reinforce particular impressions, further creating as memories what may have started only as speculations or fears in the mind of the witness. This standardisation of reports using hypnosis is inevitable, given the situation described by Budd Hopkins and David Jacobs in the *MUFON UFO Journal* in February 1988 ('Abductions – a personal primer') where they suggest, 'The investigator and/or hypnotist should be well versed in the patterns of UFO abductions in order to pursue the investigation correctly'.

Many researchers point to the scars on the abductees' bodies, allegedly left by medical examination by the aliens. But far from being substantial evidence for a physical experience, these marks are highly likely to be a form of stigmata (see page 289). Like the traditional stigmata, they may well be the product of deep conviction on the part of the person displaying the marks that they have undergone a genuine experience. This is not the same as saying that they have physically undergone such an experience.

The most modern researches into abduction, pioneered largely by ourselves, have examined the personal effects of abduction on witnesses. One of the most common after-effects of abduction, and one that has been widely noted by researchers for some time, is that abductees enter a changed life style. Many become vegetarian, become concerned about ecology, and so on. Many turn to artistic expression to release their pent-up emotions, newly found following the abduction. We have many cases in our own files of abductees who have turned to music, to painting, to sculpture and other forms of art. We also have similar cases of such manifestations in people who have undergone religious experiences. This aspect of abductions, while arguably not central to the main experience, is a vital clue. It appears that the abduction – whatever the source stimulus, is either triggered by, or triggers, the so-called right brain functions of intuition, creativity and so on. Most people live day to day in their left brain, i.e. their scientific, rational, calculating brain, and in many cases never experience, except fleetingly, creative or intuitive urges. The abduction, possibly because it is frightening, forces the mind to search for explanations or solutions in areas it does not usually use. The by-product of that attempt to get to grips with unfamiliar and frightening imagery may be the triggering of right brain functions. By addressing the abduction experience in this light, it becomes an uplifting, developing experience for the abductee and not a frightening one.

Abductions seem to be less the product of an alien invasion and more a core human experience which is, because of its association with 'flying saucers', being reinterpreted. Abductions may have nothing to do with flying saucers; they may simply go together well, seemingly supporting each other in this modern twentieth-century version of an ancient mystery.

ALTERED STATES OF CONSCIOUSNESS

The question of altered states of consciousness, of switching into a different perception of reality, is one that arises frequently in paranormal research. Altered states may be part of the cause, or effect, of at least some claims of UFO encounters, alien abductions, visions of religious figures, perception of entities such as fairies, channelling, the passions that create stigmata, and so on.

The altered state is often recognised by a change in comprehension of the world around the subject.

Almost all altered states, whatever the trigger might be, will have certain commonalities; the main three are a loss of sense of self-awareness, distortion of time-awareness, and a lessening of inhibitions. Conditions also include seeing, or being engulfed in, strange light, and the realisation of the absence of sound.

During an altered state, a person's time sense may slow down or speed up. People threatened with, say, an impending road crash suddenly feel that time slows down and they can do much more in a few seconds than they would have imagined. A few claimants in these conditions have looked back on the road at the manoeuvres they have achieved without being able to believe the complexity of the result. One stated, 'I was conscious of every move, but I experienced them in slow motion.' Others have periods of 'missing time' where they are unaware that time has passed; typically this happens with those who channel automatic writing (see 'Automatic Writing', page 36).

Whether the altered state creates a hallucination that explains some paranormal experiences, or whether it allows for perception of a different reality to 'normal' is unclear. Many cases indicate that by the time the subjects realise they are in a strange situation, they may already be in the altered state.

Altered states vary in complexity. Sleep is an altered state, hypnosis can induce such a change, as can the use of alcohol or drugs. Certain altered states are sought, perhaps through meditation, but they can occur spontaneously, particularly when an individual is placed in a threatening situation. This may give some clue to what is happening in altered states; it may be that the conscious mind is accessing certain areas of the subconscious and memory not normally accessed, and that it 'closes off' other inputs in order to concentrate on that task. As most mechanisms of animal evolution have a survivalist base, the ability to use altered states may arise from that.

Altered states are not uncommon in claims of extraordinary survival and endurance. So perhaps the situation forces the altered state, rather than vice versa. In June 1964 Rob Schultheis was climbing the 13,000 foot Mount Neva in the Rocky Mountains. He became isolated on the mountain in increasingly poor weather, and worsened his situation by attempting to climb down by a difficult and unfamiliar route. He got into serious trouble and eventually slipped, bouncing off the mountainside and coming to rest on a narrow sloping ledge, bruised and bloodied. It was a painful and difficult experience to get himself to his knees, but as he began walking he found that his pain and fear had almost miraculously evaporated. He had heightened awareness; sharp vision, incredible dexterity and balance and a sense of euphoria. His appreciation of crystals in the rocks and of his surroundings seem to have been almost synaesthetic in quality. He got safely off the mountain after many dangers, once extraordinarily clinging to a fifteen foot sheer vertical face and making moves he believes were far beyond the normal range of his skills. As Schultheis said, 'There were no false moves left in me. I couldn't miss because there was no such thing as a miss. It didn't matter whether I fell or not, because I could not fall, any more than 2 plus 2 can equal 3. It was all sublime nonsense, of course, but I believed it, down in my very cells; if I hadn't believed it, I would have been hurled into the Pit below.' For a brief time Schultheis had achieved that heightened awareness often sought through meditation or occasional mind-altering drugs, but in this case forced on him by need.

ANGELS

Angels are most thought of as immortal beings, intermediaries between God and mankind. The term 'angel' is derived from the Latin *angelus* and Greek *angelos* meaning 'messenger'.

Angels belong to the same class of entities as demons. Satan, before falling from Paradise, was an angel. As such, therefore, they may be friendly or hostile, but modern, popular, interpretation particularly in the Western world, has tended to redefine angels as only the 'good version' of these beings.

Angels are not just a phenomenon of the Jewish and Christian faiths; they figure in many other religions. Islam, for example, has Jabril (the equivalent of Gabriel) and Mikail (Michael). The Muslim faith includes Azrail, the angel of death.

The angels of the Bible appear mostly in the Old Testament. The God of the Jews seldom spoke directly to his people, and therefore needed angels as intermediaries. In the New Testament (Luke i, 26–38) the Virgin Mary is the last named person to receive angelic announcements, regarding Christ's birth and death. She was visited by the archangel Gabriel who informed her that God had selected her to bring forth his son, Jesus, into the world. (The Gospel of Matthew has it that the angel appeared to Joseph in a dream to offer guidance while he dwelt on Mary's punishment for possible infidelity – i, 20–25). From that point on God works through Jesus, and the need for angels as intermediaries between God and mankind is reduced. In the Roman Catholic Church prayers are offered to Mary and she acts as mediatrix between God and the people. In the New Testament the angels' work is mostly confined to ministering directly to Christ; for example, while He is in the wilderness suffering the temptations of Satan (Mark i, 12–13). The last angelic encounter ministering to the needs of Christ was when 'an angel of the Lord descended from heaven and came and rolled back the stone . . .' announcing the resurrection of Christ after the crucifixion (Matthew xxviii, 2). This was witnessed by Mary Magdalene and Mary, the mother of Christ.

We interviewed members of the congregation of a Baptist church who believe that much of the Old Testament is superseded by the New after the birth of Jesus; indeed some of them were of the opinion that angels would never now be used by God, and that angels would only now be used by the Devil, though they cautioned that he would disguise them as heavenly messengers.

Hebrews xiii, 2, however, suggests that God might still use angels as messengers, 'Do not neglect to show hospitality to strangers, for thereby some have entertained angels unawares.' One congregation member pointed out that perhaps what is meant by this passage is that the angel might be near the human, rather than that the human was the angel. He was sure angels had no human form, and quoted several Biblical references: for example, Hebrews i, 7 'Who makes his angels winds, and his servants flames of fire.' and Mark xii, 25 'For when they rise from the dead, they neither marry nor are given in marriage, but are like angels in heaven.' (He believed this showed the angels in heaven were not, therefore, like the living.)

The influence of art on the imagery of angels has been strong. Angels are normally depicted in human form, often with large wings. The New Testament offers no such description. Gabriel, in announcing the birth of Jesus to Mary (or

Joseph) is never described, nor are the angels that assist Christ during the temptations. Of the angels that appear at the tomb after Christ has been resurrected, there are no descriptions of wings. Matthew and Mark refer to one angel, Luke and John to two angels; their descriptions are consistent in that the figures are described as dressed in brilliant, often white, clothing. None refer to wings. Almost certainly the wings are an artistic creation designed to indicate both the 'otherworldliness' of the beings and the ability of flight i.e. down from heaven or carrying Christ up to heaven. Artistic impression over the centuries has furthered the imagery; angels have become more and more unworldly, holy and blessed, depicted through visual ploys.

Drawing away somewhat from the religious origins of angels, before the eighteenth century it was felt that they played a major part in everyday life. They were credited with effecting cures, and prayers were directed to them. Between the fourteenth and eighteenth centuries they began to decline in significance, partly due to the rise in focus on the Virgin Mary, perhaps because it was thought that prayers were not being answered, but probably mostly because people claiming to be in contact with anything 'odd' would be open to a charge of witchcraft. The belief in the New Testament, the fear of witchhunts, and later the advancement of science, for a time relegated angels to the realms of poetry, art and romantic fantasy.

Much more recently, angels have been reinterpreted in a variety of ways that dilute the original definitions. They remain benevolent beings, but are seen less as messengers of God, and more as the 'beings of light' seen during near-death experience (see page 196); perceived by some as the 'spirit guides' that channel messages to mediums; and so on. In making this 'comeback' angels have changed their appearance and are often now described as human-like.

The angel which renewed the stigmata of Sister Jeanne des Anges of Loudun was described by her as 'a very handsome young man, about fifteen years old, just over a metre tall. His clothes seem white, very bright . . . a great light surrounds him . . .'

The major contemporary role of angels is that of a guardian; helping and guiding people. The idea that all people, or even all living things, have a guardian angel watching over them and guiding them through life is a very comforting thought. In the context of New Age thinking it creates a replacement mother-figure, and a means of transferring responsibility to others.

At times of danger, or need, people often report a guiding figure. People have reported giving up conscious control and allowing their bodies to be controlled by what they perceive is a separate intelligence. Edith Foltz-Stearns, a woman pilot, in 1928 stated that she was being watched over and protected by 'some "presence" (that) sits beside me, my "co-pilot" as I have come to think of it. In times of great danger some unseen hand actually takes the controls and guides me to safety.' Ernest Shackleton once reported that he had 'another person' with him on an expedition. Air Chief Marshal Lord Dowding apparently believed that during the Battle of Britain angels took over flying the planes when pilots were dead or incapacitated.

Billy Graham in his book *Angels – God's Secret Agents* confirms that he believes in angels because, 'I have sensed their presence in my life on special occasions.' He describes a case where the form of a dead daughter sought out a doctor to help her ailing mother. Graham asks, 'Could the doctor have been called in the hour of desperate need by an angel who appeared as this woman's young daughter?'

Kelsey Tyler, in her book *There's an Angel on Your Shoulder*, describes twenty-two angel encounters within contemporary American settings, all reflecting the modern belief that angels take a form indistinguishable from humans; as police officers, prison wardens, tramps, and so on. There is overlap here, and in the Graham report, between reports of angels and contemporary ghost sightings. Tyler makes the point that 'often the percipients only reflect on the divine origin of their helpers, guides and confidants with hindsight.' In one case a depressed woman who had suffered the loss of her father saw him and was comforted by his appearance. Rather than believing that she had seen his ghost – as many reports might have indicated – this witness believed she had seen an angel that had taken the form of her father. In a second case a child appealed to a motorist for help for a crashed school bus. While rescue workers were recovering the injured, one child was found dead – the one that had flagged down the motorist in the first place. The question is asked, 'Could the boy have been an angel, taking the image of the little boy who had died in the accident?'

One famous case of angelic intervention is that of the 'Angel of Mons'. During the opening battles of the First World War there were many reports of an angel being seen on the Belgian battlefields. The writer Arthur Machen pointed out that they could have been inspired by his fictitious story of the bowmen from the Battle of Agincourt appearing to the modern soldiers to guide and inspire them. Perhaps so; but whatever the inspiration, there were many unconnected reports from many areas. Either divine intervention was taking a form that would be easily recognised and followed, or a 'collectively agreeable' image – perhaps based on Machen's story – was created that was the image the subconscious mind could use for self-help and self-inspiration.

That percipients of angels, at least in modern times, see what they expect to see is clear. Although huge, feathery wings appear to be artistic in origin, they have become for many the 'real' image of angels. Several accounts, and witnesses we have spoken to, have described being ministered to by angels that have such features, and when questioned they have agreed that the angels were 'just as you'd expect them to look like'. The angel that appeared to a visionary in the Virgin Mary sightings at Garabandal in Spain had wings.

Perhaps the most modern interpretation of angels, harking back to the idea of angels and demons being one and the same, comes through in certain reports of UFO aliens. The principal division of such aliens is between 'Nordics' – tall, graceful, beautiful, with flowing blonde hair – and 'Greys' – short, cold creatures who exhibit little humanity or compassion in their actions or purpose. More than once we have heard the Nordics described as 'divine', or even 'angelic' and the Greys described as 'like demons'. Many Nordics are described as appearing in radiant and somehow unearthly light; one witness even started his description of seeing such aliens with the (perhaps subconscious) phrase, 'First, I saw the light'.

ANOMALOUS FACES

As ghost researchers, we have received many photographs containing apparently anomalous faces. In many cases the people taking the photograph did not see the face when they took the photograph, and only saw it when looking at the print later. We also noted that a high percentage of those photographs were taken in graveyards. For example in July 1993 Mrs Edna Barlow sent us a photograph taken the previous year, showing herself flanked by two other people next to a monument to John Myles, founder of the first Baptist Church in Wales. Just to the left of Mrs Barlow's head is what appears to be a face (see photo section).

A great many images either perceived by witnesses or recorded on film represent only the faces of subjects, dead and sometimes alive. This can make sense. If the image is being created or projected by someone else, the face of the person they are thinking about is most likely to be the part of them that will be projected, or at least it will be the most significant image in their mind. If the face is somehow projected by the person whose face is seen, the reason might be as identification of the 'sender'.

In many cases it is hard to confirm that the faces are actually there; they appear to be simulacra; 'accidental' images formed by leaves, shadows and so on. The fact that so many of them come from graveyards suggests to us that there is a higher expectancy of seeing ghosts in graveyards than in other locations. However, as an explanation that will not do for those images which have appeared on film and which clearly are definable human faces.

Faces were, of course, the primary image for faking of the 'spirit photographs' so common around the turn of the century. Photographs taken at seances would often include images of the dead who had 'come through', such as those taken by

William Hope and the famous images of spiritualist W.T. Stead taken by William Walker. These spirit photographs have not stood the test of time; they may have been impressive to a naive audience, but the manner of their making is all too clear in the modern day.

If we assume that a probably relatively small percentage of claims of spontaneous faces are genuinely paranormal images, the likeliest mechanisms would seem to be a projected thought form impressed in the film, generated by either the photographer, the person whose image appears or a third party (see 'Thoughtography', page 302).

But not all such spontaneous faces are photographic images; paranormal research is replete with a variety of spontaneous faces. Perhaps the most famous such faces are those which appeared on the kitchen floor of a small house in Bélmez in Spain in 1971 and for several years thereafter. The case is well reported in several books, including our own *Encyclopedia of Ghosts and Spirits*. Briefly, a mark was seen by Mrs Maria Pereira on her kitchen floor which over seven days developed into a face. Concerned by the image, her son destroyed it, but another face began to form. That image was cut out of the floor and put 'on display'. The floor was repaired, but new faces appeared. Over time many faces appeared, along with other images such as crosses. Perhaps most extraordinary, a face which appeared in June 1972 was later believed by many to have changed its expression. Certainly the almost predictable suggestion, that the faces were caused because the house was built over an old cemetery, is to be considered, but at least equal consideration should be given to the suggestion that the faces were the 'creation' of Mrs Pereira's subconscious. Certainly they appeared in her principal area of the house, where she is likely to have spent most of her time, and they appear to have moved with her to a new, replacement kitchen location. The faces may have been projected thought forms, representations perhaps of her prayers or fears.

The well-known psychic Eusapia Palladino, just before the turn of the century, could apparently project an impression of her own face into putty contained in sealed boxes.

The Society for Psychical Research (SPR) researcher Manfred Cassirer, in his privately published monograph *The Persecution of Tony Elms*, describes an anomalous face which appeared on the shop counter of the Kentish Garden Guild, a location that was the centre of poltergeist activity. 'The whole impression was skull-like and gruesome. It was subject to a gradual process of disintegration, rendering it even more macabre.' The face was made from falling fertiliser, though it appeared when no one was present and therefore the precise manner of its formation is uncertain.

Facial images of the dead are very common. In 1891 the face of a woman who had recently died appeared in the glass windows of her home in Indiana as if etched in the glass. No attempts to rub it off were successful until her son succeeded. In 1898 Dr Liddell, Dean of Christchurch, Oxford died; in 1923 what was reputed to be his face was seen in stains on the cathedral wall. Similarly, fungus caused by damp appeared to have created an outline of Dean Vaughan of Llandaff after his death, the image appearing in Llandaff Cathedral.

Perhaps a clue as to the production of the faces is offered by the case of the SS *Watertown*. If the report and photograph are to be believed, images of the faces of two dead crew members of the SS *Watertown* were not only seen by several members of the crew of the ship after their burial at sea in 1929, but were seen on two following voyages, and photographed. The images were 'viewed' on the waves and were always seen from the same point on the deck and always at the same angle of perspective. With faces in glass windows or on cathedral walls, it is fairly obvious that they do not move, because the structure they are impressed into does not move. There is therefore no reason to assume that movement would be part of the phenomenon. However, in the case of the SS *Watertown* the ship was moving and the faces apparently were moving with it, indeed maintaining exactly the same position and alignment during that movement. This case most surely suggests, if correctly reported, that the images, far from being literally impressed in the waves, were somehow 'constructed' in relation to the ship itself.

It is worth closing with a reminder that not all spontaneous faces are of the dead. W. Hudson tells in his book *A Hind in Richmond Park* how he saw the face of a girl he knew very well appear in the air in front of him, apparently fluttering as if in the wind, or as if impressed on an invisible flag blowing in the wind. He believed this was a telepathic message. Hudson, concerned for the girl whose image he had seen, wrote to the girl's mother but received an assurance that there was no problem. He remained unconvinced and visited the family, discovering that at the time he had seen the face, the girl had had a very serious argument with her family and had left the family home to seek out Hudson himself.

APPORTS

Apports are the spontaneous materialisation of objects without known origin. Such objects are generally small; stones, coins and jewellery being very common, but can include larger objects, elaborate ornaments and living creatures such as birds and flowers. In 1928 Mrs Agnes Guppy, formerly Agnes Nichols, a British medium, apported a variety of objects and large numbers of flowers. When she was asked to produce a sunflower, a six-foot specimen apported on to the table in front of her, complete with roots and clods of earth. Some years before a French medium, Madame Elizabeth D'Esperant apported a golden lily some seven feet tall.

Probably the most famous medium for producing apports is the Indian, Sai Baba. Born Sathyanarayana Ratnakara Raju, he announced as a teenager that he was the reincarnation of Sai Baba (*Sai* means saint, *Baba* means father). The former Sai Baba had been a middle-class fakir at the turn of the century, famous for astonishing miracles. Over the years the present Sai Baba has produced an incredible amount of apports witnessed by an estimated seventy-five per cent of his followers. His apports have included holy ash, gold statues, jewellery, photographs and even objects inscribed with his name. Most famous were astonishing apports of food, reportedly enough to feed hundreds of people at a time, including hot foods and a sticky, honey-like substance called amrith.

Under the observation of scientists such as Erlendur Haraldsson, Karlis Osis, Dr Michael Thalbourne and Dr Joop Houtkooper, Sai Baba was examined for many years. His refusal to become a subject of controlled experiment did not satisfy the scientist's requirements, but they were never able to prove fraud during their observations.

Sai Baba explained that he apported objects using powers from God, first by imagining the objects, and then transporting them from a place where they already existed. On one occasion, Haraldsson and Osis watched the materialisation of a sand-like substance. First Sai Baba waved his hands in small circles, and then a grey substance appeared in the air just below his palm. He closed his fist around it and poured granules from his hand.

This description is very similar to one given by Professor Arthur Ellison who watched a medium apport a rose. 'One time this chap (the medium) tottered up from his armchair, held his hands out to the man next to me . . . (our) host . . . I was right next to him. I stared at these hands from a foot away. The light was on, I could see perfectly clearly. Over the top of these hands appeared a sort of pink glow, it reminded me of the glow in a Crookes tube when you evacuate it . . . I had seen that in a physics lab. I stared at this, I looked up his sleeve, I couldn't see where the pink glow was coming from. I watched this and I could see something taking shape within it. Shadowy at first, then it solidified, then it dropped down onto his hands out of the middle of the pink glow, the pink glow died away and the medium, eyes still tightly closed, picked it up. It was a rose. It looked as though it had just been picked. He handed it to the spiritualist host next to me who thought it was from his deceased wife in the next world. I think it was much more likely to have been apported from a local flower shop, (actually) I have no idea where it came from. He put it in a vase. People asked, "Did you keep it?" What was the point – it was a perfectly ordinary rose. You couldn't tell it had been an apport.'

Of Sai Baba, Ellison stated, 'I really do think that Sai Baba understands the nature of physical reality and he can alter his thought forms wherever he wishes, and does so.'

Ellison was not sceptical of apports, indeed his attitude is highly enlightened for a scientist. He had seen others; one medium wandering around the room grabbing into the air, 'He got handfuls of daffodils out of the air, I couldn't see where they were coming from. I know they weren't there before he came in. He was in jacket and trousers, and an open-neck shirt, he didn't have any volume in a skirt in which he could conceal daffodils. I searched the room, I couldn't see where they were coming from. They had vases all around the room ready for them, with water in them.'

Apports are also part of the phenomenon of poltergeists. During the investigation of the famous Enfield poltergeist, conducted primarily by Maurice Grosse, Maurice had only been in the house a few hours when he saw a marble flying towards him, apparently from nowhere. He was certain it was not thrown by any of the children or other members of the household. Coins would drop from the ceiling as if they had materialised in mid-air or passed through the ceiling from above. A mug half full of water was seen in the middle of the kitchen floor where Grosse was certain no one could have put it without him seeing.

If spontaneous disappearances are the other end, as it were, of apports, we have two cases immediately to hand in our own investigation files, but both associated with poltergeist activity. In one case, a poltergeist activity associated with the Waldorf public house and restaurant in Maidstone, a cassette tape ejected from a cassette player which fell to the ground and clattered on the wooden flooring in front of several witnesses could not be seen when they looked down to pick it up. It never was located despite the barrenness of the surroundings and the thorough checks of the witnesses.

In the second case, one witness has been so plagued by spontaneous appearances and disappearances that she has been forced to change her life style to adapt to it. The poltergeist, it seems, will not allow her to have money on her, and if she ever leaves the house with money it will disappear. Spontaneous appearances of food in the fridge, articles under pillows and items all around the house – as well as movements of objects – are a major part of this particular case.

We were recently (1994) informed of an apport that arrived at the feet of a paranormal research group, the Plumstead Paranormal Research Group, an offshoot of one of our research teams. The team were investigating ghost reports and spending the night in a large public services building. The team had been in the building for some time and had already seen or heard some spontaneous happenings when, as our colleague and member of the team, Philip Walton, reported, they heard an 'almighty thud'. On turning towards the noise, they found a book had appeared and was sitting right in the middle of the floor. There was absolutely no doubt by any member of the team that it was not there earlier. The book was a hand-written address or telephone book, with all the appearance of normality. To date, the team have not been able to trace the owner.

Perhaps the most detailed research into apports was that conducted by SORRAT, the Society for Research on Rapport and Telekinesis formed by Dr J.G. Neihardt to study psychokinesis. In the history of SORRAT written by John Thomas Richards, he begins the section on apports with the same question we earlier raised relating to poltergeist activity. 'It is possible that the traditional apport is merely a PK target object that moves so rapidly that it only appears to flash into existence out of nowhere.' The SORRAT team members witnessed many apports over the years, often of known objects from known locations, including in one case the door handle of a team member's sports car which was at that time parked in a basement garage. They decided to attempt controlled experiments.

As the book states, 'The most convincing apports involved objects which entered or left locked or sealed containers.' The SORRAT team created the Cox Observation Box, a so-called mini-lab into which or from which objects could be apported under some observation and control. There were many experiments; for example on 25 May 1979 Cox placed a sealed container holding fourteen beans, seven white and seven blue into the mini-lab. The mini-lab had an automatic filming device. Richards heard the device operating and called Cox immediately to investigate. A green felt pen was lying in the mini-lab and it had written 'J. King' on paper in front of the coffee box in the mini-lab. Seven blue beans which had previously been inside the sealed container were lying on that paper. The white beans had not moved. Rice grains in the mini-lab had also been moved. Cox examined the mini-lab, confirming that it was still sealed and locked and that a booby-trap he had installed had not been disturbed. According to Richards the camera had not shown the movement of the beans or the rice, as these could not trigger the lights in the camera, but the camera had caught the pen in motion.

Incidentally, humour is rare in paranormal studies, but apports provided one small glimpse: at a seance conducted by the SORRAT team, they asked the agency with whom they were communicating what an apport was. They were told 'an apport is the place where the applanes land'.

The question of the energies or forces involved in apports is of course highly speculative. Quantum physics indicates that matter is made up of atomic particles in motion around each other, rather like planets in the solar system, and would therefore be theoretically capable of passing through one another if the atomic particles could be prevented from affecting each other. No even speculated laws of physics allow for this but apports may indicate that there is at least one more law of physics yet to be discovered.

It is easy to dismiss apports on the basis that stage magicians produce very similar effects. During the drafting of this chapter we were invited to an evening party to celebrate with our business related clients, one of whom happens to be an ex-member of the Magic Circle. During that evening, in a brightly lit room and from a distance of just a few feet, John Spencer watched him instantly make a lighted candle disappear to be replaced by a handkerchief and pour water into a newspaper which he then unfolded and displayed to us all, refolded and then poured the water back out again into a container. All the common stuff and staff of stage magic tricks, and all, of course, admitted to as such. No doubt there could be people who claim to perform apports using such techniques. However, there is a wide gulf between such observations and, say, Professor Ellison's close observation of the slow materialisation of a rose a foot away from his nose. If Ellison, and thousands of others like him who have witnessed such materialisations, are correct in their observation, and there is no reason to doubt that they are, until a stage magician can reproduce that 'slow materialisation' effect the question of apports must remain firmly open.

ATLANTIS

The legends and myths of the lost continent of Atlantis are probably among the most confused, elaborated and speculated upon in the catalogue of world-wide mysteries.

The most extreme legends have it that the Atlanteans populated a vast island continent from which they, or their offspring, civilised the world. They are credited with an idyllic society of equality, a Golden Age of Earth, an advanced global communication system, advanced transportation including air travel, X-rays, crystal power and more. Theirs was a society based more on psychic or mental ability than physical strength.

Most of the spiritual life of Atlanteans and the extraordinary inventions and abilities they possessed comes from psychic readings given in trance by Edgar Cayce, the so-called sleeping prophet who lived from 1877 to 1945. Cayce believed that in one of his own past lives he was an Atlantean. Cayce placed Atlantis in the Atlantic Ocean.

The psychic and mystic Helena P. Blavatsky believed that the Atlanteans were the descendants of another lost continent, that of Lemuria. Rudolph Steiner believed he could confirm this theory, he claimed, by access to the Akashic records, a kind of astral library of every event in the history of the world.

Whatever is believed about psychic readings, reincarnation and the like, we cannot enter such 'evidence' here as evidence for the existence of Atlantis; there is an obvious folly in trying to verify one unknown with another.

Therefore we need to see precisely what was the origin of the legend of Atlantis. For this we turn to the writings of Plato and the continuation of his political work, *The Republic*. In around 7,000 words, in two documents, 'Timaeus' and 'Critias', Plato describes Atlantis. It was apparently Critias who told the story, as a truth, relating what he had heard from Solon. He, in turn, had brought the story from ancient Egypt where it had apparently originated. In the 'Timaeus' writings Plato strengthens the authority of the description by quoting it as if directly from the Egyptian priests.

The 'Timaeus' document indicates that the island of Atlantis is situated in the Atlantic Ocean beyond the pillars of Hercules (at Gibraltar). Atlantis is described as being larger than Libya and Asia (Asia Minor: the known world at the time). The ocean beyond the pillars is described as a true ocean for which the Mediterranean was only a harbour, an ocean surrounded by continents on all sides.

In the 'Critias' document, the geography and society of Atlantis is described in some considerable detail. The island had an abundance of minerals, timber, domestic and wild animals and a wide variety of flowers and fruit which provided a balanced diet. The lands of the royal palace included a huge and excellent racecourse. The rest of the island had a beautiful array of forests, rivers and lakes which provided timber and transportation.

The Atlanteans worshipped the cult of the bull and pillar. Atlantis was ruled by ten kings, who between them had absolute sway over the population. They operated under a code of ethics which prevented them making war on each other, and allowed them to join forces against other oppression and to pass no judgements other than by a majority of their votes.

The downfall of the Atlanteans appears to have been that the gods mixed with 'mortal stock' gaining human weaknesses and desires. They acquired evil habits, sought materialism and led debauched life styles. They apparently moved from the spiritual to the physical and became obsessed with material gain and the pursuit of power; hence the wars of conquest against neighbours. Zeus, chief among the gods, decided to destroy this fallen race, which he then did in that one terrible day and night. Plato dates this destruction as around nine thousand years before the life of Solon, who lived around 600 BC.

So what have we in Plato's description of Atlantis? No X-ray machines, flying machines, crystal power or the like. We have a society which was basically one that would be recognisable to the Greeks of the time; horse racing, bull worship, acknowledgement of descent from the Gods and so on. This is, at least in one sense, the 'true' legend of Atlantis. It is at least the source document on which the rest of the myths have been built.

Plato was a philosopher, the pupil of Socrates, who appears in many of his poetically styled dialogues. Many of Plato's philosophical doctrines are voiced through Socrates as the leading character in his dialogues. He presented his philosophy in the form of questions. An aspect of his teaching is that none of his dialogues is presented as complete; the reader is made to question for him or herself. Plato covered all aspects of human condition: In *The Republic*, a ten-volume work, he discusses ideal government, in *The Symposium* love and beauty and in the 'Timaeus' documents Plato addresses the nature of the physical universe. As J.P. Kane, the lecturer in Hellenistic Greek at the University of Manchester, wrote, 'The philosophers did not totally reject myths as a source of knowledge. Plato employed them when argument could take him no further.' It seems highly likely that Plato was using the tale of Atlantis as a fable; asking his students to question the nature of the universe and steering them towards the conclusion that obsession with the material world was an evil to be avoided. Pliny, Strabo and Plato's most ardent student, Aristotle, all believed that Plato's story was illusion and questioned its historical basis. For centuries it appears to have been kept alive only by Arab geographers and Greeks who saw in the story their own superiority over this otherwise all-conquering race.

In 1882 the American writer Ignatius Donnelly published *Atlantis: The Antediluvian World* and produced a range of arguments to support a historical basis for Atlantis in the mid-Atlantic Ocean, at the site of the Azores. The Austrian physicist and engineer, Otto Heinrich Muck, continued in the same vein and produced a compelling argument for Atlantis being located at the Azores, based on geological and paleoclimatological evidence. Muck argued that Atlantis was destroyed in approximately 8500 BC by the impact of an enormous asteroid striking what is now the Charleston coast of the United States. He believed that the North Atlantic ridge was part of a lost continent. This argument has been superseded by current geological analysis, which indicates that the North Atlantic ridge is one of the points of extruding material from inside the earth, not a sunken landscape. Muck also argued that the evidence of the ice age indicated the submergence of Atlantis. He believed that it blocked the North Atlantic drift, turning it south. Once Atlantis had sunk, the North Atlantic drift moved north and freed the ice around the European plains, but not the American continent. His analysis of the terminal moraines of the ice age would appear to be correct, indicating that the ice age retreated in Europe earlier than on the North American continent. However, it is not clear what prevented the Gulf Stream from reaching Europe initially. A suspected mid-Atlantic continent is not needed: a huge mass of ice across the North Atlantic may well have had several 'knock-on' effects which could have changed the climate in prehistoric times.

Proponents of the ancient civilisation of Atlantis argue that Atlantis is needed to explain a common source for the civilisations around the Atlantic; that there has to be a connection between the ancient civilisations of the Mediterranean area and, say, the South American continent, given the similarities between these cultures. But the explorations of those such as Thor Heyerdahl have indicated that there probably was a greater flow of voyagers around the world than was once appreciated.

A civilisation with characteristics referred to by Plato as Atlantean existed in Crete around 1500 BC. In particular, the Minoan civilisation, named after King Minos of Crete, worshipped the bull. The most famous Minoan legend is of the Minotaur, the half-man half-bull killed by Theseus and Ariadne in the Labyrinth. The Minoan civilisation seems to have collapsed around 1500 BC, with its colonies and trading activities abandoned, a significant change in its artistic styles and a significant migration of its people to the Greek mainland.

Sixty miles to the north of Crete was the volcanic island Thera. In approximately 1500 BC the island erupted in much the same way as Krakatoa did in 1883. It is likely that the explosion of Thera was even more powerful. There would have been considerable local disruption from debris thrown into the atmosphere and deposited over an area which almost certainly would have included Crete. There would also have been destruction from tidal waves. Thera itself, which some analysts have suggested may have been the centre of Minoan civilisation rather than Crete, was devastated in the explosion. In the present day the remains of Thera are represented by Thira, Therasia and Aspronisi. Excavations on these islands have indicated an advanced civilisation and a bull cult.

From the point of view of location, if Plato got his description from the Egyptians, they might well have regarded Thera as being west; the way Plato described the position of Atlantis. For Plato, in Greece, the far west would have been in the opposite direction to Thera and out of the Straits of Gibraltar. Or Plato may have misheard a description; the Greek words for 'greater than' and 'between' are similar. He may have been told the island was 'between Libya and Asia' rather than 'greater than Libya and Asia'. However, we do not have to depend too much on Plato's historical accuracy. Rather than being confused about the location of Atlantis, he is more likely to have accurately noted the circumstances surrounding Thera's destruction and used it as the basis of a constructive fable. Plato may have deliberately exaggerated the size of his Atlantis in order to make his story more dramatic. Alternatively, he may have misunderstood the sizes he was being given; there has been a suggestion from Professor A. Galanopoulos that the translation into Greek may have exaggerated the numbers by a factor of ten; multiplying size, population, and even the length of time since destruction. If Plato erroneously believed the island so huge, or deliberately exaggerated it, he would have had to locate it outside the Mediterranean Sea; it could not have existed anywhere else.

If Atlantis is not totally myth, it is probably fable based on the reality of the eruption of Thera overlaid by New Age belief and wishful thinking. There may well have been civilisations in prehistory much more advanced, spiritually and technologically, than we currently appreciate, but Atlantis is not needed to embrace them. The civilisations of the Mediterranean basin and South America in particular, combined with the known probability that they can have contacted each other in distant prehistory, explains much, if not all, of what Atlantis is supposed to embody.

AURAS

An aura is a cocoon of energy surrounding all objects. It is deemed to be a psychic force, detectable by psychic sensitivity. There has been no experimental proof of the existence of auras, though a great deal of persuasive anecdotal evidence for their existence. Auras surround humans, animals, plants and inanimate objects (which produces for some the belief that nothing is inanimate – a belief in a 'Gaia' Earth, all part of one living force). One sensitive explained to us how he had seen the aura of the sea off Sweden going browner and browner, and heard later there were reports of depletions of fish stocks, suggesting an 'illness' in the sea.

Probably the best example of 'testing' for auras is described by Michael Crichton in his autobiography *Travels*. Crichton learned how to detect auras, though at first he couldn't see them. 'I moved my hand down towards Sarah's head, slowly, and suddenly I felt warmth. Surprised, I stopped my hand.'

But Crichton is thorough, which makes his reports so valuable. 'I got a little paranoid. Perhaps Judith was taking a visual cue from me, saying, "There," when she saw my hand. So the next time I stopped my hand above the warmth.' Judith (the psychic) castigated him, telling him the aura was not there. Crichton describes his feelings about the tests, 'I could feel this warm contour, just as distinctly as you can feel hot bath-water when you put your hand into it. You know when your hand is in bath-water and when it's not . . . Your hand will get warm and wet, even if you don't believe in bath-water.'

Psychics claim to see auras, and can 'measure' them with, for example, crystals. Auras are used by psychic healers to identify the general state of health of individuals, and to locate target areas needing special attention.

Arne Groth, a Swedish sensitive famous in that country for dowsing, described how he watched the declining aura of his wife as she became increasingly ill. He could detect the health of her aura even from his home when she was in hospital, and knew before being told that she had died. This is a claim made by many, often not those claiming to be psychic. Arne suggests that many people tune in to psychic aspects of the world when they need to without realising what they are doing, or how they are doing it.

Auras are reported in a variety of colours, the colour giving reference to the physical, emotional and spiritual state of the object it emanates from.

Some argue that Kirlian photography photographs the aura, others argue that it measures an electrical field that is not the aura, which they deem to be astral energy.

There have been scientific attempts to detect and measure auras, all without significant success. The nearest may be the work of Walter J. Kilner, of St Thomas' Hospital in London, who created 'Kilner goggles' to view the aura. He believed it could be seen if the subject was viewed against a dark background through stained glass. However, this work does not appear to have been continued, and it has been called into question since his death in 1920.

AUTOMATIC WRITING

There are many claims, associated with different areas of the paranormal, of channelled, or automatic, writing. Messages have been channelled from the dead, from aliens, from religious figures. The person receiving the channelled messages is acting as a medium. He or she enters an altered state and in that condition writes – often without apparent knowledge – what he or she 'receives'.

We studied in some detail the claims of one claimant, Heather Woods, whose automatic writing was part of a religious experience that included healing and stigmata.

She described one of her periods of channelling. 'I got this really strong urge to write . . . I went upstairs. Hazel (her sister) gave me some paper and I went in my bedroom and just let the writing come. Then I went through to Lucy (Hazel's mother-in-law) and asked her to witness that I had just done the writing.' When Heather went back downstairs, Hazel commented that she had not been long, and presumed there had been no 'receipt' of writing. Heather was surprised, thinking she must have been a long time; she was holding in her hands three sides of A4 paper completely covered in writing. In fact, she had been gone from the room only a few minutes. Lucy confirmed her own astonishment, 'I was in bed, and Heather came upstairs. In a matter of minutes she came into the bedroom and said she had just had this . . . prophecy, or whatever. I was absolutely staggered by the short time it had taken and how beautiful the writing was. It really was remarkable.'

Heather channelled tens of thousands of words of prose and poetry. Many of the poems she did not even recognise as such; it took us hours to find the line-breaks in the endless streams that she produced. Much of it was done at night, alone, or at other times with no witnesses. It is easy to be cynical and consider that Heather already had pages of writing pre-prepared. But we were able to speak to Helen, one of two people (the other was her late priest) who watched Heather, apparently in trance, receiving her writings.

As Helen described it, 'She wrote with her left hand, and using a red pen, which she'd never used before' (*Helen* gave her both the card and the pen, therefore Heather could not, in any case, have pre-prepared any of the writing.) 'She was writing quite furiously on this piece of white card – at an abnormal speed, I can definitely confirm that. Eric (her priest) and I sat with her in the lounge, ate sandwiches and drank tea, and watched her doing this writing. Then all of a sudden she dropped the pen, looked up and said, "Oh, tea." ' Heather had been unaware of the writing, and was astonished to see the card already filled with words.

The mechanism of channelled writing seems to be abnormal, but the witnessed accounts make it clear that it happens. The altered state presumably allows for applied concentration and strenuous muscle-movement. But what of the content? The majority of the writing received that we have studied from many such 'mediums' generally has few surprises. Aliens warn the Earth people to beware of nuclear misuse and to protect the ecology. The dead bring messages that are far from earth-shattering. The religious texts received, many of which Heather received and we examined, are rarely unexpected and almost always fit the predisposition and religious beliefs of the recipient.

Any analysis must consider that the person is channelling some part of his or her own mind; subconscious art, fears, dreams. That there are areas of learning and capability stored in areas of the mind that are rarely, or only under special conditions, accessed, is part of what the acceptance of paranormal abilities concerns.

But whether that is a fair analysis, or the whole picture, is arguable. There have been some striking receipts through 'automatic means', and not always in writing.

Medium Rosemary Brown is famous for having received channelled music from a variety of dead composers, including Beethoven, Liszt, Chopin and, more recently, John Lennon. She has no formal music training.

A Brazilian, Luiz Antonio Gasparetto paints pictures apparently channelled from, and certainly in the style of, many famous painters. He has been described as working at 'breathtaking speed'.

Rauni-Leena Luukanen-Kilde has written several books, channelled during meditation from extra-terrestrials. Her latest is called *The Messenger from the Stars* and was written in an extraordinary thirty-seven hours. She said, 'I was meditating and the pen started moving by itself.'

Francisco Candido Xavier spent over fifty years channelling books from deceased Brazilian authors, and Xavier accepted no money for his efforts, giving the books' earnings to the poor of his country. Quite often the language style was beyond his probable abilities, and he professed not to be able to understand much of it. One observer reported that he wrote as if his hands were 'driven by a battery'.

Heather Wood's writings also came as part of her mediumship. After her priest, Father Eric Eades, had died she channelled a message from him to his wife, Betty. Betty confirmed, 'It was actually for me and the family. And it was in his writing.' Heather had told her that she had a message for her, but was uncertain about some of the content. There were many small, but significant aspects that Betty felt were so personal it was unlikely that Heather would even have known about them, for example, the message contained a reference to 'Bet' which Heather was certain Eric had never called his wife. But Betty confirmed, 'In fact he always called me Bet when we were alone together.'

Betty confirmed to us that she had no doubts about the authenticity of the message. 'None at all . . . I have no doubts whatsoever about that message. Eric didn't very often write his sermons but when he did, the faster he wrote the bigger his writing; and this is exactly the same. The 'y's' are the same . . . it is all just the same.'

B

BANSHEE

One of the most famous of the 'omen ghosts' is the Irish banshee. The word 'banshee' comes from the Gaelic *bean sidhe* meaning 'woman of the fairies'.

The banshee is heard but not seen, and the noise of her wailing is said to be heard before a death, not by the person about to die, but by a family member or friend. Despite the association with death, the banshee is not held to be an evil spirit. According to legend the banshee is a protective spirit, watching over family members, giving guidance in its own way. The banshee, unable to express itself in human language, has to warn of impending death by wailing. The banshee is unable, by fairy law, to let her presence be known at other times. Some of the older Irish families still consider themselves to have a banshee as a guardian watching over them.

Sheila St Clair produced a radio show for the BBC on the subject of the banshee in the late 1960s. A baker from Kerry described how he and his workmates heard the noise of the banshee wailing outside the bakery. He described the wailing, 'It started low at first like, then it mounted up into a crescendo; . . . and you could make out one or two Gaelic words in it; then gradually it went away again slowly.' The next morning, when the 'change-over' shift arrived, one of the men coming on shift told the others that he had just received the news that his aunt had died.

The connection does seem rather vague, and those who heard the wailing were not family members, but the percipients felt the death of this man's aunt was the reason they heard the banshee 'keening'.

BERMUDA TRIANGLE

The Bermuda Triangle is a popular name for an area off the eastern coast of the United States of America, in which many planes and ships have suffered unusual effects and, more famously, many have been lost without trace. Although there are claims for other such areas around the world, the Bermuda Triangle is unquestionably the best known.

The author Martin Caidin reported in *Fate* magazine an extraordinary encounter that took place on 11 June 1986. It has the value of being a first-hand account (many Bermuda Triangle encounters are not) and it, as Caidin says, 'is real, detailed, recorded, witnessed and established beyond even the most tenuous shred of doubt'. He was flying, with others, from Bermuda to Jacksonville Naval Air Station in Florida, equipped with an array of navigational equipment. They were receiving satellite photographs of the area they were flying in. It was a clear, warm, perfect day into which they took off.

Suddenly Caidin was unable to see the outer portion of the left wing, and later the right wing, though he knew, according to the satellite readouts, that it should not be obscured by mist. Around him he then noticed that the blue sky had changed to a creamy yellow. They were now in a creamy yellow version of 'whiteout' and the instruments were 'going crazy'. As Caidin put it, 'two million dollars of avionics just up and died'. Even more extraordinarily, Caidin was able to see a tunnel-like hole straight up above the plane, through which he could see the blue sky and a similar hole pointing down to the visible ocean, yet these holes were pacing the plane exactly. Almost 'as if a long pipe extended from the surface to the sky above'. Fortunately Caidin, his wife and the whole crew remained calm and flew professionally and safely. This extraordinary phenomenon lasted for four hours and then suddenly it cleared and they were flying in 'perfect crystal clean clear air' again.

come from and the sky behind them was clear as far as they could see. Equipment immediately came back to life, and they continued the flight safely, landing at the naval air station without incident.

Of the planes that have been able to report their difficulties before being lost in the Bermuda Triangle, a great many have reported instrument failure or distortion. The yellow sky is another factor that has arisen in reports.

Caidin is only one recent witness of many; more people have survived difficulties in the Triangle than is usually appreciated. In 1928 Charles Lindbergh reported both his compasses failing while on a flight from Havana to Florida and a 'heavy haze' obscuring all vision. Jim Blocker in 1968 reported radio and navigational failure inside a bank of clouds while flying from Nassau to Palm Beach.

Ships have been similarly affected. In 1971 the USS *Richard E. Byrd* lost communication and navigation aids on a voyage to Bermuda and remained helpless for around ten days before it was able to regain contact.

Another witnessed case of a disappearance in the Triangle showing how swiftly ships can disappear comes from Captain Joe Talley, who in 1944 was in the *Wild Goose* being towed by the *Caicos Trader*. Talley woke to find the *Wild Goose* sinking and himself already under water. He was able to get a life jacket and get himself to the surface some sixty feet above. The *Caicos Trader*, itself in danger of being dragged under, cut its tow line and recovered Talley from the water. The ship sank within minutes, far faster than would often be supposed. No satisfactory explanation for the sinking has been confirmed.

The Bermuda Triangle is only one place where ships and planes have been reported missing in what appear to be strange circumstances. There are many reports of losses in the Bass Straits off Australia, losses in the waters near Japan in an area sometimes known as the Devil's Sea, around Cape Horn, off the Cape of Good Hope and even in the landlocked Great Lakes of the USA. Lloyds of London in April 1975 indicated that 'our intelligence service can find no evidence to support the claim that the "Bermuda Triangle" has more losses than elsewhere. This finding is upheld by the United States coast-guard.' There are genuine mysteries to be examined, but they are probably applicable across the world.

So why is it then that the Bermuda Triangle, above all other localities, is the focus of such extraordinary claim and counter-claim? The answer, not unusually, is that the Bermuda Triangle (as a name) became one of those popular catch phrases – like 'flying saucer' – that became its own advertising slogan. It is probably no coincidence that the Triangle lies off the American coastline; America has always taken such mysteries to its heart more readily than other countries.

Vincent Gaddis made first mention of the mysteries in his two books in the 1960s: *Mysterious Fires and Lights* and *Invisible Horizon*. He may have been influenced by an article on Flight 19 written by Alan W. Eckart in the April 1962 issue of *American Legion* magazine. Ivan Sanderson and John Keel appeared on television discussing mystery topics; Sanderson introduced the Bermuda Triangle which caused a massive viewer response. Sanderson published an article in 1968 in *Argosy* magazine and *Invisible Residents* in 1970 in which he also introduced the idea of the 'Vile Vortices'; twelve areas of mystery losses around the world. John Wallace Spencer (no relation to ourselves), in *Limbo of the Lost* pulled these various stories together, further promoting the mystery of the Triangle. In 1974 Charles Berlitz published *The Bermuda Triangle* which became a best-seller, bringing the Triangle to widespread public attention. The Triangle has further been promoted by fiction films and books. The latest ride at Florida Seaworld called 'Mission: Bermuda Triangle' centred around the loss of the USS *Cyclops* which disappeared in March 1918.

It is impossible to know how many ships and planes have been lost in the Triangle, for two reasons. Firstly, the Triangle is not a specifically delineated area and tends to vary according to the whims and wishes of particular theorists. (One fairly ludicrous suggestion we encountered put one apex of the Triangle at Liverpool, England!) Generally, the Triangle is an area of the Atlantic Ocean off the Florida, Georgia, and Carolina coasts of the USA mainland extending out to the island of Bermuda, the island of Puerto Rico and the northern coasts of the Caribbean, thereby including the Bahamas.

Secondly, that particular locality not only has an extraordinary high number of ships and planes crossing it, but arguably the highest number of illegal drug-related and immigration traffic, and inexperienced joy-sailors. That many of these losses, particularly the ones related to illegal activities, should go unreported is hardly surprising.

It hardly seems necessary here to list the major cases of loss associated with the Triangle which have been examined extensively in books on the subject for the past twenty years or so. It is worth, noting, however that some of the losses have been impressive. Six aircraft lost during the 'Flight 19' episode (see page 132); the aforementioned USS *Cyclops*, a 19,600 ton, 542 foot ship with a crew of over 300 lost in March 1918; the British South American Airways *Star Tiger* with a crew of six and twenty-five passengers lost in January 1948 and almost exactly a year later in January 1949 its sister plane, the *Star Ariel* with six crew and twelve passengers; in December 1948 a Douglas DC-3 with twenty-seven passengers; the *Marine Sulphur Queen* in February 1963, thirty-nine crew and a cargo of over 15,000 tons.

There is still considerable evidence that some of the losses in the Triangle area have been due to exceptional factors not fully understood, albeit they may exist in or above any body of water around the world.

That there is something unusual within the area of the Bermuda Triangle may be borne out by evidence from the Seasat satellite launched in June 1978. Part of its function was to measure the contours of the ocean surface. It is not generally appreciated that there are permanent contours on the surface of the oceans. The satellite Seasat mapped ridges and troughs on the water surface. When surveying the area of the Bermuda Triangle what was noticed was a virtually perfect circular depression some twenty-five miles across and fifty feet deep. One theory to explain this is that a large meteorite has buried itself at that location, creating a magnetic anomaly and gravitational effects. That this could in some way contribute to the reports in the Bermuda Triangle might be possible.

A most recent theory to explain sinkings of ships and effects on aircraft concerns deposits of buried gas. Dr Richard McIver has suggested that under the oceans, and possibly under the Bermuda Triangle, are large deposits of frozen methane, as methane hydrate, trapping large amounts of methane gas. If the hydrate breaks up, perhaps due to landslides, there could be massive gas releases which could account for sudden turbulence on the water surface and even large deposits of gas moving up into the atmosphere where they could affect aircraft. McIver notes that large gas deposits in water have sunk or destroyed drilling ships and rigs either by creating fire or explosion, as methane in the air is highly explosive, or by changing the buoyancy surrounding the ship, creating a swift sinking. One drilling rig sank in minutes and survivors even wearing life-vests, found they sank, so low in buoyancy was the water. If the density of the water was lowered, a ship would automatically float lower, possibly dangerously so.

Strange sea effects have been witnessed by several people in the Triangle. In 1954 Ray Clarke on the deck of the *Queen Mary* watched as two forty-five foot columns of water shot up from an area of the ocean which had minutes before unusually becalmed itself. In 1963 Captain R Shattenkirk flying from New York to Puerto Rico saw a huge white bubble of water form on the surface of the sea. A month later, a similar sighting was made by the crew of another airliner. These may be examples of the gas releases McIver refers to.

But the Triangle mystery involves the loss of airplanes also. The gas, being lighter than air, would rise into the atmosphere and if an aircraft flew into the cloud, its engines could fail from oxygen starvation. On the other hand, the aircraft could explode if the gas was ignited by heat or spark. Sudden changes in density in the atmosphere could also account for some aspect of the so-called 'clear air turbulence' reported by many witnesses. McIver also speculates that the turbulence in the water would cause huge clouds of ionised air that could affect magnetic compasses and other navigational instrumentation. The absolute disappearance of ships and plane debris is also accounted for: the water into which they sink is so lacking in buoyancy that the debris sinks unnaturally rapidly, and is then covered up when the disturbed sediments settle over it. One drilling rig that sank could not be found, so complete was the sedimentary covering. In December 1944, just a year before the ill fated Flight 19, seven Air Force bombers suddenly encountered clear air turbulence over the triangle. The planes were thrown backwards and fell abruptly 600 feet. Five of the seven planes crashed, two recovered, but no debris was ever found.

McIver's theory is compelling; it allows for many of the traditionally reported Bermuda Triangle features: white water (turbulence of gas release), strange lights (ignited gas), magnetic disturbances (ionised air), and so on. More research into this is needed within the Bermuda Triangle and around the world before the mystery of the Triangle, or part of it, can be regarded as solved.

Disappearances, particularly of small vessels, continue to the present day. For example, on 4 January 1993 the London *Daily Mail* reported the loss of a forty-two foot catamaran travelling from Rhodes Island to Martinique on 23 December of the previous year. A five day search located nothing of the craft which the newspaper reported as 'a complete mystery'. The newspaper noted that no storms had been reported in the area at the time.

BIG CATS

The big cats controversy started with the rumours of a puma at large in Surrey. The Surrey Puma made its first publicised appearance in the early 1960s; described as about five feet long excluding its long tail, dark golden brown, with a cat-like face and a black stripe down its back. Research has located reports of the animal going back into the 1950s.

Tracks of the Surrey Puma were found. A trail of footprints appeared overnight in freshly raked sand used by a near-by riding stable. These footprints were identified by experts from London Zoo as possible puma prints. The find triggered off a wave of 'I saw it too' but many of the other reported footprints turned out to have been made by dogs or foxes. Only one other footprint found at the time was thought to be that of a puma; a single print found at Hurtwood Common.

In 1964 puma reports reached their peak. A large cat was sighted many times. One report was of a frightful howling; on inspection cattle near by were found to be frightened, and one was found bitten and mauled. Police were sufficiently concerned to ask the public for help in locating the cat; they wanted sightings to be reported. They also issued warnings to people to be wary of certain areas because there was a puma on the loose. Sensible enough perhaps, but also guaranteed to put every oversized moggy in the country under scrutiny. By the time the police closed their file it contained 362 reports, and it is thought that there were also many unreported sightings and many that the police were unable to investigate.

The phenomenon of the Surrey Puma died as abruptly as it started. By 1968 the excitement was over. Rumours suggested that the puma had been shot, but this was never substantiated, and no body was ever discovered.

Some cats of unknown species have been found. A black cat was seen on the Kellas estate in Morayshire during 1984. In the next few years two were caught alive and cared for in a wildlife park. They were later given to the author Di Francis and while in her charge they felt secure enough to produce kittens. In 1988 a large black cat was killed by a gamekeeper in Duffdown, north-east Scotland. This was thought to be a Kellas cat, but Di Francis suggested that the cat had differences to her own, mainly in the skull shape. A jungle cat was knocked down by a car on Hayling Island in Hampshire in the same year. The following year another cat was knocked down by a car at Ludlow in Shropshire. In April 1988 a leopard was shot by a farmer near Widecombe on Dartmoor.

Many reports of such animals arose much earlier, in the 1700s. However the British wild cat was roaming free in the country until the 1920s so reports from earlier than that are not surprising.

There has been little produced in the way of physical

evidence. A skull was found by two boys near Newton Abbot in Devon that was identified as that of a big cat; perhaps a lion or a leopard. It was too large to be a puma. Even the finding of the skull, however, does not confirm that the animal was ever on the loose, it could have been a trophy from an overseas collection that was discarded, for example.

Since that first sighting large cats have been reported in several areas of the country. They are given local names, which have included: The Black Beast of Exmoor, the Beast of Bodmin, the Peak Panther, the Fiend of the Moors, the Durham Puma, the Leopard of Lanivet, and others.

There were many sightings in 1993 and 1994. Dave O'Sullivan of the China Fleet Country Club at Saltash in Cornwall gave us records of several reports of big cat sightings by golfers there. John Woodfield, a civilian police officer, described the animal he saw as 'bigger than a domestic cat, bigger than a domestic dog'. Retired headteacher Chris Ford confirmed the sighting. Members of the golf club were far from perturbed however; the cat was, they thought, keeping down the rabbit population and therefore doing the golf course some good. The course owners used night-vision equipment to hunt the cat through the night, but without success. Dave O'Sullivan provided us with copies of his own video-recording of the animal tracks on the course. Some of the prints are impressively large when compared to Dave's boot and a coin he laid next to the tracks for comparison. Chris Moiser, an authority on identifying wild cats, studied these recordings and considered they 'could be leopard' but admitted identification was difficult.

In January 1995 Dave confirmed to us that they had had twenty-one reports to date. They had also received a report on faeces that was thought to relate to a large cat. Analysis showed it full of crushed rabbit and rabbit bones; no domestic dog or cat food was present. The report stated that the faeces was consistent with 'a large feline predator'.

The question of whether a puma or leopard could sustain itself in the English countryside is part of the controversy. Rabbits and other small wild animals are certainly available, but one estimate of the feeding needs of big cats suggests several hundred pounds of food a week would be required by each animal. However, if the animal is relatively safe from predators it may be far less active than in its 'normal' environment and need less food. Such feeding would certainly come to someone's attention. Several sheep farmers believe that they have that evidence; Rosemary Rhodes, a Bodmin farmer, reported in December 1994 that she had had to give up sheep farming because of the high number of attacks on her livestock. Another farmer, John Goodenough, claimed to have lost 'a dozen sheep and three calves' in 1994 alone.

We interviewed Mrs Pat Warner who saw – and photographed – a big cat in her two-acre garden in Oxfordshire in 1994. Although she photographed the cat up a tree where it was relatively exposed, she described it as moving stealthily. And she was sure it was larger than the average domestic cat. We took comparative photographs, with Pat in the picture (see photo section). They were not perfect comparisons, as the cat was originally photographed up a 'double trunk tree', but one trunk had been cut down before we got there. The precise position of the cat, and the angle of the branch it was on, is therefore not certain. Based on the original photographs the cat appears to be somewhere between two and three feet long, unlikely to be a domestic cat.

The mysterious big cats were not reported in large numbers in the 1970s, the Black Beast of Exmoor made an appearance in 1987; in the 1990s there has been a surge of sightings. Why should the pattern of timings be such? Apart from the possibly single animal that was the Surrey Puma, the rest of the answer might lie in the Dangerous Animals Act of 1976. Prior to that time many wild animals were kept in private collections or as status symbols. Panthers were particularly popular. After the Act was passed, many owners had to get rid of their animals. It is possible that some owners could not afford the cost of compliance with regulations, and rather than face having their animals killed, or even angry at the law, might have released them to the wild. The 1960s sightings may have reflected a lone wild cat that eventually died or was killed. The widespread and frequent number of present sightings in 1994 suggest a breeding population which many think is sufficiently large to sustain itself and may now be difficult if not impossible to eradicate. If panthers (a form of leopard) are at loose there is cause for concern; unlike many of the suspected cats, leopards can become man-eaters.

Inevitably the focus on the big cats controversy has again brought 'I saw it too' claims from around the country, misleading police and others searching for the animals. Given media attention, there are people who will see something strange in sightings they would otherwise not feel significant. In one case an animal described as a 'small lioness' was hunted by thirty police officers and a helicopter in the North London suburb of Winchmore Hill. The culprit was named Bilbo – a large ginger tom cat.

Rarely do the cats show aggression, but like most animals the only substantiated cases are where the animal might feel cornered. Sally and Nick Dyke were hunting a rumoured black leopard in a graveyard in Inkberrow when they found it – all too close! The animal they encountered struck out, leaving Sally with severe scratches across the ribs on her right side. A clear confirmation for the couple of the existence of the animal, however. Rosemary Rhodes is concerned, as are many others, however, as to how long it can be before there is a real tragedy. She said in interview with Roy Kerridge; *Daily Mail* 31 December 1994: 'One of these days a farmer is going to find a sheep killed. He'll bend over it, not realising the cat is near by, and it could be fatal for him.'

Douglas Richardson, deputy curator of mammals at London Zoo, said in an interview for the *Sunday Mail* magazine *Night and Day*, 'If a big cat doesn't want you to see it, you won't see it. They're active at dusk and dawn, which makes them even harder to see. There are badgers all over the country: how many people have seen one of those?'

The Ministry of Agriculture has always taken a highly sceptical line on claims of big cats. They have pointed to a low incidence of official reports in comparison to the 'unofficial' claims. Farmers explained in contradiction, however, it is easier to get insurance compensation if you put a mauling down to a dog. However, in December 1994 the Exeter branch of the Ministry admitted it had more recently been inundated with reports and stated, 'There may be pumas and other big cats around . . . we have made a report, but it's an internal report, not to be released to the Press or public for a while.' In 1995 they announced that a study was being undertaken.

BIGFOOT AND SASQUATCH

The equivalent of the yeti (see page 346) on the North American continent is known as Bigfoot in the United States or Sasquatch in Canada. It is impossible to know how many reports of these creatures have been made, certainly more than 1,000 and probably something like 3,000. They appear to have arisen first in the early 1800s and have continued with frequency to the present day.

In 1851 two hunters in Greene County, Arkansas, witnessed a man-beast 'of gigantic stature, the body being covered with hair and the head with long locks that fairly enveloped the neck and shoulders'. Footprints of the creature measured some thirteen inches and the creature apparently had great dexterity, running at speed and leaping some twelve feet at a time.

President Theodore Roosevelt published *Wilderness Hunter* in 1893 which contained a story told to him by a trapper named Bauman who had apparently seen a tall man-beast when he and another had been camping on the Wisdom River. Bauman apparently left the camp one day and when he returned his companion had been killed, his neck broken and four huge teeth marks in his throat.

In fact, attacks by Bigfoot or Sasquatch are rare, and encounters are generally characterised by shyness on the part of the creature, which flees when discovered.

In 1917 Albert Fletcher encountered Bigfoot in a lumber camp in Washington State. While walking down the road one night he believed he was being followed and saw behind him a huge, approximately seven foot tall, creature walking upright. It was covered in hair and ran off when Fletcher cried out in alarm. Other workers on the camp had also reported the creature.

Probably one of the most extraordinary claims of encounters with Bigfoot comes from 1924 when Albert Ostman related that he had been kidnapped and held for several days by a colony of Bigfoots. He alleged he was picked up by an eight-foot Bigfoot in his sleeping bag and carried for several hours across country. The Bigfoot took him to what appeared to be its family group and held him captive but did not harm him. Apparently unwilling to harm the creatures, although he had a rifle with him, he escaped by overfeeding the leading creature, making him unable to pursue him when he ran off.

Perhaps Ostman's report is reflected by the report of O.R. Edmunds, who stated that he had encountered a man-beast in the Siskiyou Mountains during the Second World War. He saw the creature apparently carrying a man and running off away from him.

Probably the most famous evidence for the existence of Bigfoot is the film taken by Bigfoot enthusiast and hunter Roger Patterson in 1967 at the unfortunately named Bluff Creek in California. Roger Patterson and Bob Gimlin were hunting for Bigfoot when they allegedly encountered a female creature near the creek side. Patterson was able to take a short cine film of the creature as it ran away, looking back once directly at the camera. Patterson described the creature as approximately seven feet tall and, based on the tracks left behind, 300 pounds in weight. The Bigfoot was covered in short, shiny black hair, had pendulous breasts and a seemingly conical head. The neck was indistinct, the head seeming to come out directly from the shoulders.

Bigfoot is, of course, supposed to be man-like rather than necessarily ape-like, though in the case of this film the hair colouring and texture appears to be very gorilla-like. However, the movements of the creature, particularly its leg movements, are very human-like. There has been more than one suggestion that the creature filmed is a man in an ape suit, although some analysts of the film, for example Dr D Grieve of the Royal Free Hospital in London, have suggested that it would be difficult to fake. He estimates the creature to be six and a half feet tall, quite possible for a tall human in a suit. There is nothing which prevents the suit being padded to give the impression of extra bulk, though Dr Grieve indicates that the striding and arm swinging would be difficult for the person inside the suit. He stated, 'If it is a fake, it is a very clever one.' But there have been clever fakes before. We can speculate in any way we wish about the film, but it is fruitless; certainly the film appears to substantiate many of the Bigfoot reports, but if it were a fake then it would be expected to do so anyway.

Many suspected Bigfoot tracks have been located. There have been some trails with over 3,000 footprints going on for several miles. Some of these tracks have been in very remote locations. It is hardly likely a hoaxer would go to such effect for such little obvious reward.

Bigfoot and Sasquatch, however, present problems unique to the North American continent, compared to the reports of, say, the yeti in the Himalayas.

There have been thousands of reports, far more than reports of the yeti and other such man-beasts around the world. This is no doubt due to the fact that there are a good many more people around in America to report the Bigfoot than there are 16,000 feet up in the Himalayas or similar isolated locations. Certainly there are some parts of America probably equally isolated in their way, but Bigfoot has been seen in virtually every state including the flat and highly populated Florida.

Given the widespread reports of Bigfoot, it is also pertinent to ask why no bodies or skeletons have been found. It is also interesting that there are very few cases of sightings leaving footprints. The majority of sightings do not correspond with footprints, and the footprints that are found rarely relate to sightings.

There is no respectful superstition regarding Bigfoot that would prevent its being shot or captured as might be the case with the yeti in the high Himalayas. Indeed Bigfoot is roaming about apparently very visibly in a country where an enormous number of the population carry guns, and is being deliberately hunted by considerable numbers of people. There is a rumoured million dollar reward for anyone who captures a Bigfoot, presumably based on the likely media response it would generate, and there has been a certain $100,000 reward offered by a Canadian publishing company in 1973 to anyone who could produce a live Sasquatch. Yet in nearly 200 years no one has caught one yet.

Set against the objections to Bigfoot based on geographical and social circumstances is the fact that so many reports, if not true, ought to have the qualities of urban legend and myth. However, Bigfoot reports lack richness, social purpose, and fertility symbolism, as indicated by researcher John Napier.

Bigfoot hoaxes undoubtedly arise; there are several known fake films and people have made fake footprints in all kinds of elaborate ways. The argument that no one would risk dressing up as Bigfoot in case he was shot, while sensible, falls down when we realise that there has been at least one prosecution, in Pennsylvania in 1986, for impersonating Bigfoot. Craig Brashear was fined for dressing up in a costume of fake fur and a mask and jumping out in front of passing cars.

Bigfoot has also entered many American legends: claims of people being abducted; association with UFOs; apparent invulnerability to gunshots; and a few claims of empathetic or telepathic communication with such creatures have all added to the mystery.

Probably the most dramatic association of Bigfoot with UFO sightings arose during 1973. On 25 October, at Greensburg, Pennsylvania, Stephen Polasky saw a bright red UFO motionless over a field. He was in the company of fifteen other people two of whom joined Polasky in investigating the sighting. It was while they were watching the UFO that one of them saw two seven foot tall, bear-like entities covered in hair with green-yellow eyes. Apparently they were making whining sounds somewhat like a baby and smelt of burning rubber. Polasky fired over their heads. The Bigfoots kept coming towards him and eventually Polasky fired three bullets directly into one of them, causing only a mild reaction. The creatures returned into the woods and the UFO's lights disappeared. Approximately three quarters of an hour later Polasky was joined by State Trooper Byrne in investigating the report. While walking through the woods they again saw one of the Bigfoots approaching them and with the permission of the Trooper, Polasky shot at it.

Almost certainly, therefore, Bigfoot **is** an American myth, even if based on some real cases from the remoter regions. The existence of, or perceived existence of, Bigfoot almost certainly leads to a number of misidentifications and wishful thinking on the part of people who, seeing something somewhat unusual, attribute the most exciting possibilities to it. Whatever the truth, if Bigfoot were as widespread in America as the claims would suggest, it would almost certainly have been a solved mystery by now.

BI-LOCATIONS

In this section we consider those cases of doubles where the person seen as a double is seen at a distance from the 'original'.

Bi-location is commonly associated with religious experiences. Perhaps the most famous of such cases arose with the stigmatic and healer, Padre Pio. Chief of the Italian General Staff, General Luigi Cadorna, whose armies had just been soundly beaten by the Germans in Slovenia, sat in his tent in November 1917 contemplating suicide. A monk appeared to him, and told him, 'Don't be so stupid!' Then the monk vanished. Many years later Cadorna visited Italy and saw Padre Pio. He recognised him immediately, but it is said that it was Pio who first commented to the General, 'You had a lucky escape, my friend.' Padre Pio was known to have been in his monastery at Foggia at the time of the General's despair. On another occasion, in 1942, the Archbishop of Montevideo was woken up one night by a monk and told to attend the bedside of Monsignor Damiani, a devoted follower of Padre Pio. He found the Monsignor already dead, but by his side a note saying, 'Padre Pio came'. In 1949 the archbishop met Padre Pio, and recognised him as the monk who had awakened him. Padre Pio was aware of his bi-locations, when asked about them he replied, 'Is there any doubt about it?'

Bi-location is often a spontaneous experience, often unknown to the subject until he or she is later told. Ngaio Marsh related the case of Colin, a boy who often visited her. Marsh's mother saw Colin coming up their garden path and shouted to her to meet him. Her mother noted that Colin had been carrying a bunch of geraniums, and wearing a new jacket. When Marsh went to meet him, he was nowhere to be found. The following day Colin told her that he had been 'kept in' for being naughty, which was a pity because he had picked her a bunch of geraniums, and wanted to show her his new jacket. There is, however, no evidence in the narrative that Colin was ever aware he had bi-located.

Bi-location is not always spontaneous however, and it is probably from those cases that are not that we can learn the most. Consider the case of S.H.B., who reported his own deliberate bi-location in *Human Personality and its Survival of Bodily Death* by Frederic Myers.

'On a certain Sunday evening in November, 1881 . . . I determined with the whole force of my being, that I would be present in spirit in the front bedroom on the second floor of a house situated at 22 Hogarth Road, Kensington, in which room slept two ladies of my acquaintance, viz., Miss L.S.V. and Miss E.C.V. aged respectively 25 and 11 years. I was living at this time at 23 Kildare Gardens, a distance of about three miles from Hogarth Road, and I had not mentioned in any way my intention of trying this experiment to either of the above ladies. The time of which I determined I would be there was 1 o'clock in the morning, and I also had the strong intention of making my presence perceptible.

'On the following Thursday I went to see the ladies in question, and in the course of my conversation (without any allusion to the subject on my part) the elder one told me, that on the previous Sunday night she had been much terrified by perceiving me standing by her bedside, and that she screamed when the apparition advanced towards her, and awoke her little sister, who saw me also.

'I asked her if she was awake at the time, and she replied most decidedly in the affirmative, and upon my enquiring the time of the occurrence, she replied, about 1 o'clock in the morning.

'This lady, at my request, wrote down a statement of the event and signed it . . .

'Besides exercising my power of volition very strongly, I put forth an effort which I cannot find words to describe. I was conscious of a mysterious influence of some sort permeating in my body, and I had a distinct impression that I was exercising some force with which I had been hitherto unacquainted about which I can now at certain times set in motion at will.

(Signed) S.H.B.'

Both the ladies in question confirmed in writing their side of the account; they had seen S.H.B. and could distinguish him clearly. A third sister (who slept separately) confirmed that she had been told about the 'visitation' at the time and before meeting with S.H.B.

S.H.B. deliberately projected his image, or some part of himself, to a specific location. A case from 1889 suggests another aspect of such projection; an involuntary version perhaps caused by concentration or stress. The case comes from the SPR's *Report on the Census of Hallucinations* (vol. x, p.332). Mrs McAlpine, one day towards the end of June 1889, while waiting for her sister, rested by the side of a lake. She was enjoying the scenery as she reported.

'My attention was quite taken up with the extreme beauty of the scene before me. There was not a sound or movement, except the soft ripple of the water on the sand at my feet. Presently I felt a cold chill creep through me, and a curious stiffness of my limbs, as if I could not move, though wishing to do so. I felt frightened, yet chained to the spot, and as if impelled to stare at the water straight in front of me. Gradually a black cloud seemed to rise, and in the midst of it I saw a tall man, in a suit of tweed, jump into the water and sink.' After Mrs McAlpine met her sister, she told her and their brother of what she had seen; apparently both of them treated it with levity. But almost a week later a bank clerk, Mr Espie, was found to have committed suicide by drowning in that spot. In a letter Espie left to his wife he said that he had been thinking of, and planning the suicide for some time.

Here we have a number of possibilities. Mr Espie could have projected an image of himself to the spot during his deliberations, and Mrs McAlpine might have seen it in much the same way as the Verity sisters saw S.H.B. The Scandinavians coined the word *vardoger* (meaning 'forerunner') for a particular type of double that acts ahead of actual events, as is possible in the case of Espie. Alternatively, Mrs McAlpine might have had a precognitive vision; or perhaps telepathically picked up the intentions of Mr Espie. With the S.H.B. case it seems fairly certain that the image must have been generated by the subject; the people seeing his double had no knowledge of his intentions (though we might consider telepathy in this case, also). In the McAlpine case either she, or Espie, or perhaps even a third party, could have transmitted the image.

There is thought-provoking information in the work done by psychiatrist Dr Morton Schatzman with the subject, Ruth (in *The Story of Ruth* by Morton Schatzman). While perhaps not directly relating to bi-location, Ruth could create and project apparitions of other people that were recognisable to herself and third parties.

In one test Ruth was seeing the apparition of her daughter which she had created, while her responses clearly indicated to neurophysiologist Peter Fenwick that her brain 'behaved in the same way it would have if your daughter had actually been sitting on your lap.' On another occasion she created hallucinations that were seen by others, such as one of her husband sitting in her car which was seen, and identified, by her father.

Asked how she produced an apparition, she said, 'I stop paying attention to everything around me. I decide whose apparition I want to make. I remember what the person looks like . . . and I produce the person.'

As Schatzman tells of his continuing work with his subject, 'My relation with Ruth . . . had been impressing upon me that the human understanding of the mind is very limited and that much indeed remains unknown. What I now observed impressed that awareness on me even more.'

All of us reach out into the world in our minds before we take an action. It is called 'modelling'; creating an image of what we want in order to test the likeliest way in which we might achieve it. In these cases in this section, and perhaps the cases in the section on 'Doubles' (see page 103) we may see the possibility that perhaps all forms of doubles, and perhaps crisis apparitions (see page 80), may be self-generated by the subject for whatever purpose they may have at that time, even if sometimes the subject is not aware of what they have done, or the method their minds have used to do it.

BLACK DOG PHENOMENA

Black dog reports are essentially ghost reports. They may reflect sightings of real dogs and other creatures, but their interest to phenomenologists is in the spectral nature of the reports. The stories of black dogs followed emigrants to America and Australia etc, but they are primarily a British phenomenon.

The reports have local characteristics, according to local legends. For example, Barguest is a ghost dog with huge saucer eyes and shaggy hair. He drags a clanking chain, and is said to haunt the gorge Trollers Gill in Yorkshire.

In East Anglia there is Black Shuck, who has a single bright eye. He also features in legends in Suffolk and Norfolk. In Suffolk his appearance can foretell a death, in Norfolk he is a more sinister creature and no one who sets eyes on him can live. In the north of England, Padfoot has feet that point backwards.

The Isle of Man's best-known spectral dog is the Moddey Dhoo who frequents Peel Castle. Legend has it that a soldier sought to discover if the animal was 'dog or devil'. He returned gibberish and speechless and died three days later.

A few reports are less ghostly in nature. Sometimes black dogs are believed to leave claw marks, as for example on the church door at Blythburgh where the dog apparently sought entry in the sixteenth century. The discovered markings are, of course, highly likely to have been attributed to the spectral hounds after their appearances had been reported.

Phantom dogs do seem to have recurrent habits and have been known to haunt the same short length of road and others to appear yearly, in almost exactly the same way that phantom hitchhikers are often reported tied to a locality (see 'Phantom Hitchhikers', page 224).

Occasionally the black dog seems to be a guardian of some kind. The Church Grim of Somerset usually assumes the shape of a black dog and in this guise protects churches. Perceptive persons occasionally glimpse it at funerals.

A workman travelling home from Taunton in Somerset one misty night got lost, and became concerned. A black dog appeared in front of him and he followed it as much for company as anything else. Suddenly the dog disappeared, and the man discovered he was very near his home.

The legends will have some origin in the beliefs of early times, when it was thought that the soul of the first creature buried in a graveyard had the eternal job of guarding the site from then on. It was also believed that the devil would enter from the north. When a new graveyard was opened, a large dog would be killed and buried at the north end to protect the dead therein.

C

CLOSE ENCOUNTERS

Entities associated with UFO sightings go back to the first sightings of the modern era in 1947. It is interesting that they were not acknowledged at the time, however. When, in 1964, the National Investigations Committee on Aerial Phenomena (NICAP) published *The UFO Evidence* edited by Richard H. Hall, no mention of occupants was made. The document very carefully addresses the question of 'intelligent control' of UFOs, but only in the abstract. UFO research was suffering from the loss of credibility of revelations by people like George Adamski who claimed to have met aliens, and serious researchers did not want to be associated with such claims. In 1967 Ted Bloecher published *Report on the UFO Wave of 1947* in which he analyses 853 cases arising in that year over a two-month period. Not one of those cases refers to entity sightings. However, Ted Bloecher was one of the authors of the 1978 CUFOS publication *Close Encounter at Kelly and Others of 1955* (with Isabel Davis). The introduction states, 'At the beginning of the first contemporary wave of unidentified flying objects (UFOs) in this country in 1947 little was said about the possible occupants of these mysterious devices' and goes on to say, 'This does not mean that there were no reports of occupants in 1947'. The introduction goes on to list some of those sightings; clearly there had been a tide of change by that time. This document, referring to 1947, mentioned such sightings as Webster, Massachusetts 19 June when an elderly woman saw a 'slender' figure inside a UFO dressed in what appeared to be a navy uniform. The *News Tribune* of 8 July

1947 reported several 'little people' on the roofs of houses at the time of UFO sightings in Tacoma, Washington.

If contactee claims like those of George Adamski were damaging public perception of UFOs, one or two of the other stories circulating in the 1950s were doing no better. Frank Scully in *Behind The Flying Saucers* reported dead humanoids found near a crashed saucer; this account was based on information given to him by Silas Newton, who was later convicted of oil-stock fraud. The considerable tabloid attention that such stories generated drove entity reports out of the public eye; no investigator would risk credibility by associating him or herself with them.

In the years since, entities have become very much a part of the UFO subject, though we believe they should be divorced from studies of the objects if their proper perspective is to be understood.

The following cases, a tiny sample of the thousands of entity reports from around the world, show some of the variety that has been reported.

● *Papua, New Guinea*

During the summer of 1959 a wave of UFO sightings were reported over Papua, New Guinea by a wide variety of witnesses including doctors, missionaries, teachers, government officers, medical assistants, schoolchildren and several hundred village inhabitants.

On the night of 26 June, Reverend Gill, Stephen Moi and Eric Langford, and later many others, saw a bright light in the sky, apparently coming closer towards them. Contemporaneous notes indicate it was orange or deep yellow. Stephen Moi described its apparent size as 'a closed fist at arm's length would just cover half the object.' The report states 'All witnesses agreed that it was circular, that it had a wide base and a narrower upper deck, that it had a type of legs beneath it, that it produced at times a shaft of blue light which shone upwards into the sky at an angle at about 45 degrees and that the four human figures appeared on top. Father Gill is emphatic about the absence of sound throughout the whole activity.' The object disappeared at 7.20; it, or another like it, re-appeared approximately an hour later. Throughout the sightings other objects were seen in the sky around the main one, finally disappearing around 11 p.m. Altogether there were thirty-eight witnesses to the sightings of whom twenty-five signed the report.

The following night at about the same time, 6 p.m., a UFO was seen again. A crowd gathered and between 6.02 and 6.17 they watched the four figures on top of the object, 'There is no doubt that they were human'.

Father Gill raised his arm and waved and the figures waved back. Another witness, Ananias, also waved and two of the figures on the object waved back. Both Gill and Ananias waved their arms and all four waved back. The report states, 'There *seemed* to be no doubt that our movements were answered. All the mission boys made audible gasps.' (Of either joy or surprise, perhaps both.)

● *Kelly-Hopkinsville, 21 August 1955*
Just after sunset on the evening of Sunday 21 August 1955, an object was seen landing in a field behind the Sutton farmhouse at Kelly, some seven miles north of Hopkinsville, Kentucky. Shortly afterwards a group of 'little men' approached and besieged the farmhouse. The creatures were described as approximately three feet tall with oversized heads, huge, luminous yellow eyes, big ears, long arms and big hands ending in 'talons'. They all glowed with a silvery luminescence and they seemed to float rather than walk.

During the first visitation of the creatures, two of the witnesses, 'Lucky' Sutton and Billy Ray Taylor, engaged in a 'shoot-out' with several of the entities. Despite reports that up to fifteen creatures had been seen, in fact Mrs Lankford believed no more than one had ever been seen at one time; at the most two. The family alerted the police, who visited the ranch that night but could find no traces of the entities. The creatures returned later, after the police had left, and were finally gone by sunrise.

The farmhouse contained eight adults and three children, all but one of whom confirmed seeing the creatures. Investigators, including the police chief Russell Greenwell, found the witnesses varied in reliability and credibility, but both Greenwell and the initial researcher, Isabel Davis, were very impressed by Mrs Gleny Lankford. Greenwell stated, 'She was the most impressive witness. She is the type of person who wouldn't tell a lie if her life depended on it.' Davis reported, 'It was impossible to picture her taking part in a hoax; it was impossible to imagine her having hallucinations or going into hysterics.'

● *Isla de Lobos, Uruguay, 28 October 1972*

The only feature on the tiny Isla de Lobos just off the Uruguayan coast is the lighthouse manned by five people. At just after 10.00 Corporal Juan Fuentes noticed an object on a flat terrace next to the lighthouse. Fuentes could see three figures; one next to the object and two descending. The three figures confronted him, he raised a pistol to shoot at them, but was unable to do so. He felt paralysed and confused, unable to take action. The entities climbed back aboard the object which then took off, moving at tremendous speed towards the south-east.

Although a single witness case, researchers have placed some reliability on Fuentes' claim as he was regarded by many as 'a simple honest man incapable of inventing a story of this nature'. A leading American researcher, and expert on South American UFO cases, Dr Willy Smith, is a hard critic of UFO cases, but believes this case to be a valuable one, stating, 'The probability of the witness telling the truth is very great.'

● *Voronezh, Russia, September to October 1989*

A wave of sightings occurred in Russia in early 1989, going through to the end of that year. Many landings were reported in the September and October including the most famous of 30 September which reached the English newspapers. In all, over thirty witnesses are believed to have seen the landings and thousands of people witnessed the UFOs in the air. Many children saw the principal landing case; they drew and described a circular object similar to that seen at Socorro, New

Mexico in 1964, according to Jacques Vallee who personally investigated the sightings in the Soviet Union in January of 1990. Witnesses described 'giant' entities with no necks. The witnesses reported the height of the creatures to be twelve to fourteen feet. The case itself has been described by Vallee as 'one of the most important UFO events of the last ten years.' On the side of the craft was a symbol associated with the UMMO sightings (an alleged series of contacts from a planet fifteen light years away. It is a constantly on-going Spanish investigation which arose in Madrid in 1966.)

(The Socorro, New Mexico landing in 1964 was a single witness report of a landed craft and two entities seen by police officer Lonnie Zamorra at Socorro, New Mexico. Despite its being a single witness case, J. Allen Hynek concluded, 'It is my opinion that a real physical event occurred . . .' The Socorro object also had an insignia emblazoned on it, reported by Zamorra.)

Entities have been reported in virtually every country since the onset of UFOs nearly fifty years ago. There must now be many thousands of entity reports, many of which are highly credible, having many witnesses and long duration. In addition, there have been many cases where the witnesses have had all to lose in respect of their careers, credibility, social standing and so on, but even so, they have reported sightings. In most cases, witnesses have little to gain financially or otherwise from the reports they make. In the very many cases that we have personally investigated witnesses' responses vary from fear and seriousness to occasional levity; there is very rarely any apparent motivation other than to share an experience that they have genuinely undergone.

Given the numbers of witnesses and the long duration of some sightings, it is remarkable that there is not one single reliable entity photograph in existence. There are what seem to be notable fakes, such as the Cedric Allingham photographs (in the book *Flying Saucer from Mars*). There are what seem to be fakes that may have fooled witnesses such as the Falkville, Alabama photographs of what appears to be someone dressed in tin foil, there are photographs too vague to be of any use such as the 'Ilkley Moor Green Man' but there are no clear photographs, well witnessed and taken in ideal or near ideal conditions.

Whether photographs would necessarily help is debatable. The Gulf Breeze case which arose in America in 1987 is almost certainly the most photographed, and most photographically analysed, case in UFO history. The principal witness, Ed Walters, took many still photographs and some video footage of UFOs reported over a small area of northern Florida. But far from helping to solve the case, it has polarised viewpoints, created 'civil war' between believers and sceptics, and fractured the American UFO research groups. Those who accepted Gulf Breeze from the start found the photographs consistent with a large craft; those who believed the case was fraudulent found in the photographs evidence to support their contention.

But with the emergence of 'Camcorder Man' and high numbers of surveillance and other videos, we might expect the quality and verification of photographed images to change, if the entity experience is happening at the objective, non-personal level where it can be photographed. However, it is highly likely that at least part of the entity experience is happening at a deeper level of perception within people; photography may not be the evidence that is appropriate.

COINCIDENCE

Coincidence is a broad term used to cover a wide range of experiences of differing complexity.

The first category of coincidence might be regarded as those things which appear to be coincidental, but actually are well within the normal bounds of probability. Several people have made much of the fact that Sir Peter Scott's scientific name for his 'creature of Loch Ness with a diamond shaped fin', *Nessiteras Rhombopteryx*, turned out to be an anagram of 'Monster hoax by Sir Peter S'. But the limited number of letters available makes anagram-coincidence quite common. Political pundits have noted with glee for example, that,

Virginia Bottomley is an anagram of 'I'm an evil Tory bigot'.

The second category of coincidence might be regarded as those which seem coincidental, but which might have identifiable cause and effect. For example, Theodore Roszak and his wife were walking along Central Park West in New York when Mr Roszak began humming, 'I want to hold your hand', a song most famously sung by the 1960s group The Beatles. He had apparently never hummed the song before, it was not one of his favourites. However, Mrs Roszak noticed the coincidence; they were just passing John Lennon and Yoko Ono, who were walking on the same pavement. However, is this really a coincidence? Could it be that Mr Roszak recognised John Lennon, albeit subconsciously, and began humming the song as part of a random chain of thought triggered by the Beatle's appearance?

Perhaps the same applies to Eileen McCollum and Kathy Stone. In the *Daily Mail* of 7 January 1995, it was reported that the two women met each other, and spoke briefly, outside a bus-stop toilet on a US highway service station, north of Los Angeles. They did not recognise each other, but were attracted to each other's accent. They discovered that over fifty years ago Kathy had been maid-of-honour at Eileen's marriage, and they had had no contact with each other since.

Somewhere within the above two areas is probably a category of coincidence which occurs to most people; sending a letter to someone you haven't contacted for, say, a year and receiving one back in the post the next morning, obviously sent before yours arrived.

Telephones seem to play a prominent role in coincidence. We know of several cases of people near telephones that are not their own who have picked them up to find someone calling them, having misdialled the number. For example Mrs Glynis Shaw of Bough Beech in Kent was walking down the road when she passed a telephone box in which the phone was ringing. She found on the other end a person from her village who had been trying to ring her home number, but had misdialled. Another telephone case was reported by Barbara Doone of Highworth, Wiltshire who was in hospital waiting for an operation on the day her husband had to fly to Sweden. The operation was called off and Mrs Doone decided to get a message to her husband at the airport. She picked up the telephone and dialled Heathrow and immediately her husband's voice said, 'Hallo'. It appears that she had called the Heathrow enquiries number at the same moment that he had rung the hospital switchboard.

Beyond those areas of coincidence are the ones that seem to have deeper meaning or, conversely, absurd complexity and no meaning whatsoever. Famous in many books are the many coincidences between Presidents Lincoln and Kennedy, the dates of their assassinations, the names of their assassins, their vice-presidents, and so on. Similarly there is an array of fascinating coincidence surrounding the ship the *Titanic*: a fictional version of the ship called the *Titan* in the book *Futility* written years earlier with the fictional and real ships having many coincident factors. Then in 1935 William Reeves was aboard the *Titanian* on lookout and had been reading *Futility* when he felt an impending sense of danger, saw nothing, but stopped the ship. The ship came to a halt in front of an iceberg, indeed the *Titanian* was damaged, but not seriously, and was towed safely to Newfoundland. On 8 July 1975 a family in Dunstable in Bedfordshire was watching the film dramatisation of the sinking of the *Titanic* when a huge block of ice smashed through the roof of their house. All very complex stuff: but what can we learn from it? The answer seems to be nothing. There is nothing in this bizarre set of circumstances that could possibly make ship design or sailing safer, any more than the coincidences surrounding Lincoln and Kennedy could be used to lessen the likelihood of assassination for US presidents.

Another complex, but seemingly pointless, coincidence is that of King Umberto I of Italy in 1900. He dined at a restaurant in Monza on the evening of 28 July 1900 and met there the proprietor who looked and spoke exactly like him. The proprietor was called Umberto. Both the proprietor and the king had been born in Turin on the same day, the proprietor had married a girl called Margherita, the same name as the Queen whom King Umberto had married on the same day. On the day that King Umberto was crowned, the proprietor opened his restaurant. However, tragedy was to complete the chain. The King invited the proprietor to attend an athletics meeting with him the following day, but the proprietor died that morning in a mysterious shooting incident. The King himself was shot dead by an anarchist later that same day.

Cathy Mahalek was in class when her geography professor showed slides of his summer holiday, challenging the group to identify where the pictures had been taken. The first picture showed a group of people standing in front of a brick building with no identifiable markings. Ms Mahalek instantly announced the picture was taken in Russia. The professor was astonished and asked how she had worked out the answer. 'Well,' she explained, 'that man and woman in the picture are my Uncle Ron and Aunty Jean. They went to Russia this summer for their holiday.'

In *Fate* in 1985, a coincidence was reported when two people with the same surname (Baker), each owning a 1978 maroon Concord car, and each having an identical key, turned up at a shopping centre at Sheboygan, Wisconsin at the same time. Following confusion caused by one Baker taking the wrong car and the other reporting it stolen, American Motors Corporation spokesman Ben Dunn suggested that it was 10,000 to 1 against the keys fitting, but adding the factors of the cars being the same model and colour and in the same place at the same time, he felt that the odds could not even be estimated. And for those who believe that whatever force or gremlin arranges coincidences has a sense of mischief – this coincidence took place on April Fool's Day!

In the autumn of 1994, Cor Stoop, a sixty-year-old Dutchman was seasick during a pleasure cruise in the North Sea. Unfortunately he lost his false teeth overboard at the same time. Three months later a fisherman told the story on the radio of having caught a cod and finding a pair of false teeth inside! Mr Stoop heard the broadcast and was reunited with his teeth. The Ministry of Agriculture, Fisheries and Food confirmed to us that in 1993 (the last year for which they had figures) there were an estimated 199 million cod in the North Sea.

The last category of coincidences would seem to be those that might not be coincidence, but might suggest something paranormal in cause and effect yet to be understood. William Reeves stopping the *Titanian* might be regarded by some as a premonition. A coincidence that might have similar origins arose in 1971 when an architect suffering a nervous breakdown attempted suicide by throwing himself on to the rails ahead of a London tube train. The train stopped just before killing him and he survived. However, it transpired that the train stopped because a passenger had pulled the emergency stop handle without apparently knowing why he had done so. (It is worth pointing out that the construction of London Underground tube trains – unlike many of their foreign counterparts – prevents passengers seeing forward down the track.)

Whether there is cause and effect in the more complex coincidences is, of course, arguable. Many philosophers and philosophical arguments have been based on the assumption that they are. Arthur Schopenhauer believed coincidences reflected the 'wonderful pre-established harmony' surrounding all of us. Arthur Koestler who has dedicated much of his research to coincidence, uses the phrase 'puns of destiny'. Wolfgang Pauli and Professor Carl Jung's *Synchronisity, and a Causal Connecting Principle* was described by one reviewer as, 'the paranormal equivalent of a nuclear explosion'. Brian Inglis created an analogy of coincidence which is compelling; he described the effects that we see as being like the islands of an archipelago, where we are unable to see the connection on the seabed below the surface. The implication of course is that there is a connection.

If there is a connection, the cosmic gremlins seem to have mischief in their minds. In *Strange Deaths* John Dunning reports that a vegetarian jogger was killed when an eight-pound leg of lamb fell on him from a third-floor window. And a newspaper reported that in April 1994, Reginald and Kathryn Turner of Cumbria flew to Florida, having won a free flight as part of the catastrophic sales promotion by vacuum cleaner producers Hoover. While they were there, burglars broke into their house; the only thing they stole was the vacuum cleaner that the couple had bought to qualify for the trip.

CONTACTEES

It was not until George Adamski came forward to say that he had had meetings with the occupants of flying saucers that any real interaction was reported between witnesses and aliens associated with UFOs. Adamski's claims were not modest. He claimed that on Thursday 20 November 1952, he met an alien at Desert Center in California. The alien was tall, graceful, beautiful, with long blond hair. He was dressed in a brown uniform with no visible fasteners or seams. Adamski and he communicated telepathically, the alien mostly warning Earth through Adamski of impending problems with its newly emerging nuclear technology. Adamski published a book of his experiences, *Flying Saucers Have Landed*, which became an international best-seller. That book recounts the initial meeting in some detail, and similarly the return visit on 13 December 1952. Adamski later went on to take trips in the flying saucers into space as recalled in his follow-up book *Inside the Spaceships*. His commentary was a mixture of absurdity and what his co-author Desmond Leslie described as 'lucky guesses'. He described Venus as habitable, yet later space probes proved it to be quite uninhabitable for an Earth man. Yet he also described 'fire-flies' in space similar in description to those reported by John Glenn on the first American orbital Mercury flight. Adamski described bands of radiation before the Van Allen belts were discovered and air glow in the atmosphere reported by several Gemini flights.

The Adamski stories opened up a floodgate of contactee claims. Truman Bethurum wrote the story of his meetings with aliens in *Aboard a Flying Saucer* in 1954, Daniel Fry wrote *White Sands Incident*, setting out his contacts, in the same year. In the following year Orfeo Angelucci wrote *Secret of the Saucers* and in 1959 Howard Menger wrote of his encounters of extraterrestrials in *From Outer Space to You*. The contactee stories gained in complexity and astonishing contents. Bethurum's almost romantic interlude with the captain of a flying saucer, Aura Rhanes, whom he described as 'tops in shapeliness and beauty', Angelucci's meeting with Jesus and so on.

Another early contactee was George W. van Tassel who was working for one of Howard Hughes's companies as an aircraft safety expert. He began experiments with telepathy and in 1951 claimed contact with 'The Council of the Seven Lights' who apparently occupied a spaceship near the Earth. Van Tassell published his stories under the title *I Rode A Flying Saucer*.

There is little evidence that the contactees' claims are genuine, though some of them may have been doing their best to interpret novel experiences, perhaps similar to religious experiences, within the background of the newly emerging UFO phenomenon. What is apparent is that many of the contactees enjoyed their status as 'special people' whom others would look up to.

A contactee without such a message was the late Elizabeth Klarer. She reported meeting an alien called Akon in South Africa, where she lived in the Drakensberg Mountains. She related flying with him to his planet, Meton, and having a child by him who currently lives on that planet. Her book, *Beyond the Light Barrier* is written in a highly romanticised way. It seems apparent that she was writing a personal fantasy that reflected her wishful thinking, whether or not it also embodied any genuine experiences.

Personal needs aside, the contactee claims mutated very quickly into cults that placed the contactee as a very special person indeed, the central channel between higher intelligences and the rest of the people. The contactee cults were religion by any other name, with the contactees adopting the role of chief priest.

Probably the most famous UFO-related contactee group is the Atherius Society, started by George King. One morning in March 1954, King was washing dishes in his bedsit in Maida Vale when he was, he says, appointed 'the voice of

Interplanetary Parliament'. There can be little doubt, particularly when talking to members of the Atherius society, that the charisma and dynamic personality of King is a major force in what they see as the credibility of the Atherius Society.

The Atherius Society may be the most successful and enduring of the contactee cults, but is by no means the only one. Allen-Michael Noonan created the One World Family after apparently travelling to another planet to meet angelic creatures. Noonan was chosen to be 'Saviour of the World' and has travelled to Venus. Unlike King, who presents himself as a channel for a higher entity, Noonan believed himself to be the Messiah and rewrote the Bible. Robin McPherson, who took the name Estelle at the behest of an alien contact, created Light Affiliates, channelling messages from an alien called Ox-Ho. And there have been many others over the years, each with his or her particular message and method of delivery.

Surprising in the galactic context, but perhaps not if the contactee claims are of a more individual basis, is that none of the contactees or their higher beings ever seem to know each other, and all claim to be the only chosen channel.

Contactees as a phenomenon are not new of course. Arguably Joan of Arc was a contactee taking divine guidance from voices she heard and going on to lead her armies. Mediums channelled messages from beyond, often messages offering guidance and so on. The phrase 'contactee' has become associated with the UFO-related experiences of a similar nature only in more recent years.

The method of control by cult leaders is classical. First there is the suggestion of promise; that there is a better world to be had by following the leader than by following your own path. Then there is the reinforcement of ostracization. You have to obey the rules in order to be part of the group, and if you do not the group does not want you. There is no better salesman's trick than telling someone there are reasons why they cannot have something, to encourage them to seek it and demand it for themselves.

The contactee always 'holds a little back' as a promise of

something further to come or of some further revelation that can be offered to particularly devoted followers. In *Flying Saucers Have Landed* Adamski states of his communication with the Venusian, 'He answered this question for me, but warned me not to mention it further. In fact, I might add right here that he told me a number of things which I must not reveal at this time.' When John was given a day-long interview with one contactee, he was told that he was only being given ten per cent of the information the contactee had to offer; John had to prove himself before more could be given.

It is astonishing how many people can slavishly accept the word of the cult leaders, without a degree of critical analysis that they would employ to a salesman in a shop trying to sell them a vacuum cleaner. Of Adamski's charisma, Desmond Leslie said, 'George . . . has the kind of will power that makes you instinctively comply with his requests.'

Probably the most current and disturbing feature within UFO research circles is that the new cult groups are not so likely to emerge from contactee claims, though that will undoubtedly continue, but that certain abductees in trying to take control of their own experiences are seeking to influence others, in much the same way as the cult leaders of old have done. Although we believe it is right and proper for abductees to take control of their own experiences away from manipulative, albeit well-intentioned, researchers, it is of no service to other abductees to simply replace the frying pan with the fire.

One abductee has made all the usual moves towards forming a cult: Isolating devoted followers from the rest of a group meeting of witnesses; personally financing and running a newsletter, thereby taking control of communication between the group entirely into their own hands; and using all the influencing techniques mentioned earlier to maintain a central and important position as they emphasise their own special chosen position. Like many cult leaders the individual in question is of limited formal education, but has high natural intelligence and considerable charisma.

Arguably this last twist in the tale is the most sinister of all. If one thing characterises the majority of the contactees, it is the absence of anger, either because that was in their nature or because, more cynically, it was the right image to project. However, the abductees sometimes exhibit anger and they can talk about it freely, as the abduction phenomenon as presented is one that does not make anger unreasonable. Given charisma, influencing skills and anger, it is highly possible that we will see an abductee cult emerging. Given the perceived predisposition of flying saucers to land in isolated places, it will not be difficult to gather a group in an isolated, perhaps American desert, location. We think this may be several years in the future yet. But such cults can become destructive, as history has shown.

The contactee era in UFOs presented the media with the best 'silly season' stories it could have had, and tainted the image of UFOs as a serious subject for many years; should the worst possibilities arise out of an abductee-led angry cult the image of UFOs will suffer a far worse decline.

CRASH RETRIEVALS

A relatively modern phenomenon associated with UFOs is the belief that flying saucers have on occasions malfunctioned or crashed on Earth and been recovered by government or military units. Rumours have included the recovery of dead alien humanoids, and even most recent rumours that live aliens and government scientists are working together on clandestine projects. Such rumours suggest that stealth technology, the speculated Aurora plane, etc, are spin-offs from such work.

Despite rumours of retrieval of fragments from around the world, crash retrievals are essentially an American phenomenon, and it is from America that the bulk of rumours persist of recovery of whole discs and humanoids.

The most famous of those incidents is the so-called Roswell Incident of 1947. In the *Roswell Daily Record* of Tuesday 8 July 1947, the headline announced that 'RAAF [Roswell Army Air Field] captures flying saucers on ranch in Roswell region'. The report was based on a press release from Roswell Army airbase issued by Lt. Walter Haut. Very quickly the release was retracted and a story put out that the disc that was recovered was the reflector dish of a weather balloon. Whatever was actually recovered, and something was whether it belonged to the military, rocket development or extraterrestrials, no sensible explanation has ever been given as to why such a provocative release should have been made by the Army Air Force. Ted Bloecher's 1967 publication *Report on the UFO Wave of 1947* says of the announcement, 'Through a series of clumsy blunders in public relations, and a desire by the press to manufacture a crashed disc if none would obligingly crash of itself, the story got blown up out of all proportion . . .'

It is worth bearing in mind that crash retrieval research did not start until the 1970s. One ardent researcher of crash retrievals, Leonard Stringfield, published his first book *Situation Red, the UFO Siege* in 1977. The first real book on Roswell, *The Roswell Incident* by Charles Berlitz and William Moore, was published in 1980. In the book *Crash at Corona* by Stanton Friedman and Don Berliner it is pointed out that Friedman was offered his first significant lead into Roswell on 20 February 1978. As the book states, 'This wasn't the first crashed saucer tale Friedman had heard in his eleven years of lecturing and listening . . . But none had turned out to lead to any valuable evidence. In 1978 claims of the recovery of crashed saucers bordered on the disreputable . . .'

Crash retrievals can be directly linked back to the change of attitude caused by the Watergate crisis in America. That incident, corruption which led to the office of the President of the United States, changed people's perception of their governments, probably for ever. Prior to that time governments and high officials were regarded as trustworthy, with the occasional bad apple. The scandals of the 1960s were so dramatically etched in history precisely because they seemed to stand out against a background of honesty. After Watergate beliefs reversed; all leaders were thought probably corrupt and capable of any form of deception.

The Roswell Incident, in summary, suggests that one, or possibly two, crashes occurred in New Mexico in July 1947.

The recovered debris and bodies were taken to secure military locations such as Wright-Patterson Air Force base where they have been retained ever since for study.

Many witnesses have been located. For example, one witness close to the action, Bob Lazar, stated of his examination of the discs while working for the government, 'Inside, there were tiny little seats, much too small to comfortably handle an average sized human . . . the ceiling curved down to below five feet eleven inches inside.' Many of the witnesses have told stories of being on the crash site, of doing autopsies on the alien bodies, of being threatened with sanctions and even death if they revealed anything to anyone. Testimony cannot be ignored, but it should be challenged. Claims of autopsy of dead aliens could be questioned as possible misidentification of humans incinerated in a plane crash, or even of dead monkeys used in experiments as they were in the early Mercury space capsules. But it will reach no conclusion without some physical evidence for both sides to examine. The witnesses can only state what they believe, and of that the researchers will believe what they want to believe. The problem is that there is little of substance to challenge. No reliable artefacts, no reliable photographs, no highly corroborated evidence.

In December 1984, just when it seemed the interest in crash retrievals was on the wane, an incredible package was sent to TV producer Jamie Shandera, who shared it with mysteries researcher William Moore and UFO enthusiast Stanton Friedman. The package was a film of documents from 1952, exposing details of the retrieved flying saucer and including documents which tied President Eisenhower to the crash retrieval. Rumours that these MJ12 documents, as they were known, were fakes have abounded. There are those who suspect that the hoaxer decided to fool the UFO community and those that believed that the UFO community itself faked the documents.

In more recent years crash retrieval lore has moved on. The allegations of Area 51 suggest that live humanoid aliens are working with humans in huge underground locations on top-secret military operations. Area 51 is supposedly a top-secret location at Groom Lake, Nevada, near Nellis Air Force base. Buried deep in the desert, the base is alleged by some to be the size of Manhattan and to house over 600 aliens. Part of the work the humans and aliens are said to be doing relate to genetic studies, for which cattle mutilation was an integral part of the work.

It would be very convenient if we could list here ten main reasons why crash retrievals were true, or alternatively ten main reasons why they were blatantly false. The fact is that this particular mystery does not work like that. The complex beliefs in conspiracy and cover-up which are disguising crash retrievals rely on no authoritative documents whatsoever, but on a good many bar rumours and much hearsay. The documents which are of proven authenticity are ambiguous or vague; the documents which are specific have a dubious and unlikely history. It is only by weaving a combination of the two that a meaningful story emerges, but meaningful does not necessarily mean credible.

In our view, crash retrievals represent the worst of UFO journalism and the clearest confirmation that many UFO researchers apply the 'ratchet effect' to their research, i.e. they accept the evidence they want to accept and ignore the contrary evidence.

So many important questions are skirted over by researchers when confronted with them:

- Given that several large military bases are alleged to have housed a considerable quantity of highly classified extra-terrestrial material over a period of fifty years, just how many thousands of people would, accidentally or deliberately, have had access to that material, any one of whom could have made themselves multi-millionaires by arranging with a serious investigative journalist to provide an unarguable path to the truth? It is not just military people involved here; how many doctors, cleaners, nosy politicians and civil servants and so on would have had access to the material?

- In a decade or more of revelations by spy masters and others in best-selling books not one mentions involvement with crash retrievals.

- While there are possibly regimes around the world that might be able to hide a city the size of Manhattan under a desert without anyone noticing it, is it likely to be successful in a country where even the President could not lie well enough to keep himself in office?

- What precisely is it that humans offer a superior alien technology that they could not take by force?

- What is the pay-off? What is it that the aliens are offering the humans who are helping them? Money? Political power? Salvation when the end of the world comes? Whatever promises a group of extraterrestrials would offer, is it credible that a huge number of people would all unwaveringly believe them?

These are significant questions, to which researchers offer no clear answers. In *Revelations* Jacques Vallee shows the results of his sharp thinking very clearly. Confronted with a description of 600 aliens in a city the size of Manhattan his question was, 'Who takes out the garbage?' And it is a good question; there are a whole host of practical considerations relating to such an installation that need to be answered which, even if they are answerable, have not been addressed by the UFO community. Vallee states, 'There is a certain unwritten etiquette one is supposed to follow when crashed saucers and government secrecy are discussed; you must not ask where the information comes from . . . you are not supposed to point out contradictions in the stories . . . questions must always be directed at the higher topics, such as the philosophy of the aliens, or their purpose in the universe – not the practical details of their existence. In other words, *it is not done* to ask any question that has a plain, verifiable answer.'

Governments do lie about their involvement in UFO

research. That much is clear. Documents released under the Freedom of Information Act indicate that governments were doing UFO research at precisely the time when they were making public statements that they were not doing so. However, there is nothing, in our view, which indicates that governments are covering up anything other than their own ignorance and the level of knowledge not dissimilar to that of civilian UFO researchers, rather than their incredibly complex knowledge.

We might consider that governments are using crash retrievals for disinformation purposes. This would allow governments to carry out clandestine military operations and then, when they have, for example, to recover their own crashed hardware, they can suggest they are recovering UFO material. To this end governments might well be working towards discrediting UFO research so that UFO researchers who stumble across military operations are ignored by the majority of the public. Vallee in *Revelations* suggests (of MJ12), 'If the objective of that particular piece of disinformation art was to destabilise the few groups that are still seriously doing UFO research, to place the few competent investigators in a ridiculous light, and to disseminate spurious data, then they have succeeded beyond their wildest dreams, as the disintegration of American UFO research over the last few years demonstrates.'

Until there is more substantial evidence in support of the claims, crash retrievals must be regarded as highly likely to be a modern mythology and a reflection of distrust in governments.

CRISIS APPARITIONS
In 1886, Edmund Gurney, Frederic W.H. Myers and Frank Podmore published *Phantasms of the Living*, a summary of research into apparitions and telepathy. It detailed 701 accounts of apparitional sightings. The tentative conclusion was that these so-called crisis apparitions were some form of telepathic cry for help or recognition.

The crisis apparition appears to be some form of message

perceived, usually visually, by a person at some considerable distance to a person in difficulty or near death. Many people seeing apparitions often report 'knowing' that it means a relative or friend has died, even before they are acquainted of that fact in the normal way.

In a census of hallucinations conducted by Professor Henry Sidgwick, he defined a crisis apparition as a phantom seen within twelve hours before or after a crisis in the life of the person whose image was seen. On that basis the census indicated that crisis apparitions were 440 times more likely to occur than any other form of apparitional sighting.

On 15 October 1785, Captain Sherbroke saw in his sitting room a stranger, some twenty years old, looking very ill and wearing clothing not suited to the cold Canadian climate. Sherbroke called to his companion, George Wynyard, who recognised the figure as that of his own brother, John. Together they watched the apparition move into the bedroom, but on following it found the bedroom was empty. George was certain that this boded ill for his brother. Some days later they received a letter from England reporting that John Wynyard had died on 15 October.

On many such occasions an apparition is seen, but it is only later, when the sighter is told of a death, that he or she realises the sighting occurred at the same time. An example of this is the case of Admiral Sir George Tryon. On 22 June 1893, Lady Tryon was entertaining at her house in Eaton Square, London when a small number of the guests noticed her husband enter the drawing room and walk across it, without acknowledging those present. If they were surprised at his rude behaviour, they were probably equally surprised at his presence, as he was supposed to be in the Mediterranean, conducting manoeuvres off the Syrian coast. In fact at the time of the sighting in London, Admiral Sir George had just died in an extraordinary naval fiasco of which he himself is reputed to have stated in his last words, 'It's all my fault.' The suggestion is that the extreme stress and anguish suffered by Sir George caused the apparition.

A similar story is offered in *Phantasms of the Living* in the section 'Dreams which may be reasonably regarded as telepathic.' R.L.M. wrote an account of the death of H.'s wife's sister Maggie.

H. and his wife R. had been visiting R.'s younger sister Maggie and returned home on 9 November. Very early on the morning of 21 November 1885, Maggie felt violent pains which continued until 5.15 p.m. when she died of 'perforation of the stomach', all unknown to H. Later that night H. dreamt that Maggie had been taken dangerously ill. The following night, he saw an apparition of Maggie in his dining room. R.L.M. comments that H. was not the sort of person likely to receive such a 'message', 'for he was not in the least superstitious, nervous or fanciful'. However, R.L.M. reasons that, 'The only way we can account for it is that the telegram which (the family) sent off on Sunday never reached us, and it was actually Wednesday, the day of the funeral, before we heard the sad news, and she might have known this and come to tell us that she was gone.'

Here, then, is the suggestion of a deliberate message being transmitted by the person dead in order to inform her relatives of her death, knowing that attempts to tell them through normal channels would not be successful.

Is it that the percipient somehow receives the message by psychic means, perhaps projecting the visual image him- or herself without any part played by the person in crisis? Or is it that at times of crisis, a burst of 'a psychic something' rather akin to adrenaline in the physical body allows or forces some method of broadcasting a message or an SOS? If this is the case, perhaps the broadcast is either fine-tuned to a specific target or is an open broadcast that can be picked up by anyone, but only if they are in the right frame of mind. If we accept that telepathy, or even intuition, are genuine phenomena, these may play a part in the answer.

Assuming that the crisis apparition is generated by the person dying or in crisis, rather than by the percipients, what mechanism is being used? Since we have a number of claims of out-of-body experiences (see page 211), we can at least consider that that is the vehicle or mechanism by which the message or communication is transmitted. In short, the person in crisis 'leaves their body' and goes to someone who can assist them. In the case of someone who knows they are dead or dying their out-of-body experience might be a last way of saying goodbye.

Similar is the case of Mary Goffe. Dying, she expressed a desire to see her children one last time; they were being cared for some miles away. She could not be taken to them however. During her last days she fell into a coma, and on reawakening told those around her that she had visited her children. They dismissed it as a dream, and she died shortly afterwards. Later, the nurse looking after the children confirmed having seen Mary's form standing over the children's beds at the time she had been in the coma.

On 7 December 1918, Lt. David M'Connel was flying from Scampton in Lincolnshire to Tadcaster sixty miles to the north when he encountered fog. He continued, but just outside Tadcaster crashed and died, presumably at around 3.25 p.m., the time his watch was found stopped. At some time between 3.15 and 3.30 p.m., back at Scampton, Lt. James Larkin looked up to find his friend M'Connel standing in the doorway. M'Connel was dressed in full flying clothes, cap pushed back on his head as usual, casually holding the door knob, smiling and announced himself with his usual 'Hallo boy'. Larkin asked M'Connel, 'Back already?' M'Connel apparently replied, 'Yes. Got there all right. Had a good trip.' Then he said, 'Cheerio,' closed the door and left. It was later that evening that Larkin learned of M'Connel's death at the time he had seen him.

As a crisis apparition M'Connel is a fairly classic case, but here we can be reasonably certain that if the apparition was generated by M'Connel himself, M'Connel had no idea of his own true fate. Indeed more strangely than his being confused, as is sometimes suggested with recently dead ghosts, M'Connel seems to have been completely wrong. He actually believed he had completed a mission when in fact he did not.

Philip Steff, a rescue medium, told us of a crisis apparition he had seen in 1994. He had been comforting a dying friend in the Bath area, but a few days later was enjoying a concert of classical music in London. Suddenly he saw his friend's face. Philip turned to his companion and told her that his friend in Bath had just died. On returning home Philip checked up on his friend's condition, and confirmed that he had died more or less at the time his face had appeared in London.

The case of Bonnie Mogyorossy was self-reported in *Fate* magazine of January 1993. She was engaged to a soldier, fighting in Vietnam in 1970. While watching television with friends, she described the picture dissolving to 'a distinct image of a jungle on the screen. Right in the middle of it was my fiancé, shot dead on the ground'. She could hear a voice inside her head telling her that her boyfriend was dead. One week later she was told her boyfriend had been killed at the time she had seen the image.

Sometimes the form of the apparition is such that information is transmitted that could only be known to the person in crisis or someone with them at the time. On 3 January 1856, Mrs Collier woke up to find her son, Joseph, standing in her bedroom looking at her. She knew that he should have been 1,000 miles away, commanding a Mississippi river boat. His face and head were disfigured and wrapped in a bandage. Two weeks later, she discovered that her son had indeed been killed in a collision on the boat. His skull had been smashed by the falling ship's mast at more or less the exact time his apparition had been visible to his mother. Although it could be argued that a mother could project an image of her son if she feared for his safety, the precise detail of projecting an image of the injuries to his head seems improbable.

Precisely who is generating these images? Gurney and Podmore believed that they were due to telepathy on the part of the sighter. Their reasoning was that psychic powers needed a living mind and they believed that ghosts were remnant energies without purpose. However, Myers believed that the person seen as the ghost was the person generating the image. Although many others have joined the debate, it is clear that it is not one likely to reach a definite conclusion, not least because all of the possible mechanisms being considered are themselves not understood.

Nor are their parameters accepted by any consensus with different psychic researchers. Dr Charles Honorton, a modern-day researcher, came down on the side of Gurney and Podmore, believing that psychic powers in the living can explain all paranormal phenomena of this kind. Professor Erlendur Haraldsson, a parapsychologist, came down in favour of the Myers theory, having concluded that many of the apparitions seen were of people who had died violently and suddenly. He stated, 'This finding gives considerable support to Myers' theory and the popular belief that the apparition of the dead person played an active role in the encounter.'

CROP CIRCLES

In the *Wiltshire Times* of 15 August 1980, two simple crop circles were reported at Westbury. In the years up to 1990, patterns of circles appeared predominantly in the south and west of England, peaking, according to the best estimates, in 1988 with fifty patterns. However, in 1989 the media attention focused on the subject; it was making national news broadcasts and spreads in a great many newspapers. The number of patterns in the following year, 1990, rose to an estimated 232, 181 in the year after that, and a similar number in 1992.

Crop circles had a clear evolution. They started as simple circles, evolved into slightly more complex patterns, until eventually they displayed elaborate patterns involving rectangles, triangles, swirls, curls and more.

Flattened areas of crops are no mystery. Wind damage regularly flattens grasses; circular winds flatten circular areas. Add to that the rarer, but common enough, circles caused by wildlife such as rooks. These patterns have of course appeared for decades and there are a few photographs to show this. But there was always a significant difference between these fairly 'untidy' flattenings and the 'cookie-cutter' precision of the more elaborate, and later very elaborate, ones.

Claims that the crop was somehow genetically mutated or affected were spurious at best. Many of the so-called 'special attributes' of the circles were almost certainly wishful thinking on the part of the observers. Dr Robin Allen, having completed a fake, which was surveyed by believers confirmed that 'mistakes we made were actually ascribed significance . . . so even when you make errors, it's presumed to be significant'. The only real differences were in the precision. Researchers rightly kept open minds on all possibilities, but the evidence now strongly indicates that the most complex formations were all man-made.

But it was not the scientists, the believers or the sceptics who found the answer. The answers were found by ruthless investigative journalism. John MacNish, a BBC producer, together with his wife, followed the trail that led to the solution. What makes his investigation of further significance is that John started convinced the circles were paranormal. His book, *Crop Circle Apocalypse*, describes the transition as John began to realise that they were not. John managed to keep a balance between an eye on the facts and a mind open to possibilities.

An article published within the UFO in-house literature, written by John Spencer (*UFO Times* No 7, July 1990, published by BUFORA) set out the difficulties of that balancing act, 'In the circles we have a tremendous potential resource. Not to solve the UFO mystery or even the circles mystery (though of course that too) but mainly the resource we have here is proof of ourselves. Proof that we can research scientifically. Proof that we are not cultists seeing only what we want to see. Proof that when given the evidence we can deal appropriately with it. Proof that we are not self-perpetuating myth makers but ready to say "job done and finished" when the time comes. Proof that we are "in the business" to find answers, not to pander to our own fantasies. The circles are a phenomenon that – because of their obvious physical existence – can be shared by non-UFO researchers. They are evidence that even the most hardened sceptic cannot say "it's all in the mind" . . . Others not sympathetic to our views can do their own work; and can tear our approach to shreds if we do defective work. We are – for the first time in the forty-three years of modern ufology – threatened with external audit.' The article went on to summarise the circles phenomenon in what was then, and probably still is, regarded as a novel way, 'Doesn't it all sound familiar: an intelligence with purpose, increasing in its complexity (presumably its meaning), targeting certain areas, understood only by certain people who have the ability to see the Real Truth (so we must depend on them to translate the message to us mere mortals); defying even basic scientific reason because They are Special. *It's the contactee cults all over again!* Those friendly old, innocent Circles are mutating into the new Contactee Era. And the consequences look like being very 'Californian'; with new high priests to bring the message of the High Intelligence to the Masses.'

The article ended, 'If we fail, the circles will become a mirror which the world will hold up to us, as the Knight of the Mirrors did to Don Quixote, to show us how foolish we all really are.'

The mirror started to be raised when two 'artists', Doug Bower and Dave Chorley confessed to having started carving out circles in 1978 (their first attempts had not been discovered) and had carved out all the patterns which many of the 'believers' had established as genuine. John MacNish put Doug and Dave through tests to confirm their claims. At night (photographed and filmed through night-vision equipment), and in daylight, Doug and Dave passed all John's tests, carving out huge pre-designed pictograms containing all the features professed by so many to be the signs of a 'genuine' circle.

Proving that an effect can be replicated does not mean that it cannot arise naturally. But 'natural' was never the issue with crop circles. Quite the opposite; the supporters of exotic theories argued that the elaborate patterns, and the details of the crop manipulation, were of a nature that could *only* be achieved by a higher intelligence than humans. That Doug and Dave, taking all and any instruction from MacNish, could show that there were no features of crop circles that they, and presumably others, could not reproduce, cut the argument away from under them.

But if the crop circles are now seen for what they always were; artistry, possibly inspired by rough natural flattenings, there are disturbing – but fascinating – developments to follow that require study.

In 1964 Leon Festinger (with Reicher and Schacker) published *When Prophecy Fails*. It was an analysis of the collapse of a contactee cult when the promised arrival of 'The Guardians' who were to save mankind failed to happen. A great deal was learned about dependence on belief when the belief was taken away. A great deal will be learnt by studying the way in which crop circle mysticism collapses. Those who walk away, those who change their views, those who hold on to their views despite the facts and those who try to mutate the facts to suit new views they might hold.

Those who walk away will show their objectivity. They do not have to walk away from all their beliefs; one of the fears that has been voiced to us is that 'if crop circles were all faked, maybe all the paranormal is'. Perhaps, but probably not. It would be absurd to argue that because crop circles were faked there is therefore no such thing as, for example, telepathy.

But those fears are justified. Sceptics are saying just that and making unfounded associations between differing subject areas without any reasoned evidence; precisely the kind of 'bad science' that sceptics chastise 'believers' for.

And there is a huge body of people who refuse to examine the evidence dispassionately. They are the vested interests that have arisen over the past few years. No magazine editor seems prepared to issue his final magazine, no lecturer to attend his farewell lecture, or researcher to give up the position of importance that was bestowed on him by the circles. The rear-guard action is almost embarrassing to watch. Periodically there are new patterns passed around 'proving' that *this time* no human could have done 'that one', or some new idea proposed that 'proves' there is a special characteristic in the crops that cannot be accounted for in normal terms. Some are taking refuge in the plain circles as evidence of something not man-made, rather in the nature of a face-saver. Perhaps so, but that is still not evidence of higher intelligence which was, for many, their original claim. Whether they would recognise the term or not, these people are acting with all the characteristics of cult belief. When one American cult collapsed, one shocked member said, 'But I can't afford not to believe, I've invested half my life here. I have to go on believing.' That is what is being heard from crop circle cultists at the present time. Sometimes it gets a little more vicious; at a recent (1994) crop circle conference there was a mood of Churchillian defiance when the declaration was made, 'We shall see these hoax theorists off!'

The attitude towards MacNish is telling. Many of the protagonists will not speak to him or his wife any more. We suggested to one entrenched believer that he should look at MacNish's video and read his book and were met with derision. It wasn't necessary to look at MacNish's evidence, it wasn't worth it, we were told. MacNish (and Doug and Dave) are probably government agents sent out to disinform people about the government's involvement in crop circles, we were confidentially informed!

A second continuing area where we can learn a great deal from crop circles is in what it has done for people. John Spencer has presented the case (in *Gifts of the Gods?*) that we must never lose sight of the enhancement and development of people that curiosity offers. *Gifts of the Gods?* made the point that, 'The circles may all be man-made; they may be natural and still a puzzle to be solved, there may be new energies we have yet to discover . . . They might be a message from Gaia-Earth telling us to take care of our planet; they might be a message from the stars . . . but it is the journey to the answer – not the answer itself – that is helping mankind to learn new ways of thinking.' People who had no other way to exercise their curiosity, stretch their thinking and no other 'totem pole' with which to look in on themselves used the crop circles for just that purpose. Ironically, even Doug and Dave in the videos *Crop Circle Communiqué Two – Revelation* make the point, 'The most valuable experience that we have learned from the whole thirteen years of circle making has been the wonderful feeling that we have got in the world that we live in. And I don't know what it is, I can't explain it . . . When we are both sitting in the field together and looking at the whole thing that sort of feeling comes through us, that feeling of mystery. Why we did it I can't explain . . . Were we being told almost to go out and do them?'

The greatest mystery we face is that of ourselves and the workings of our minds. An analysis now of what we can learn from the crop circles offers real value.

CRYSTALS

Crystals have become a favoured tool in many modern, alternative beliefs. Their use in science; in precision time-pieces, in focusing artificial light such as lasers, and their suspected use in data storage, have brought them to the fore. They were a pillar of 'New Age' development and since then have been applied in a wide variety of uses.

Healing

Crystals, minerals and magnets are used in complementary healing in perhaps the same way as they were used in ancient times. Healers are said to use crystals or other stones to amplify and direct their own healing energies into the body.

Graham James, a former paramedic and presently a psychic healer, described such a usage, 'I had one patient with sciatica, a young chap of nineteen years of age. He'd been under the medical profession for a year, without relief. I treated him with lodestone therapy and healing. Lodestone has its own natural healing energy. By putting one lodestone, for "male" or "positive" energy at the sciatic nerve at the base of the spine and then the other one, "female", down behind the back of the knee – this is where you get the shooting pain going down the buttock – you then use your energy and the electricity involved with the magnetite to re-normalise that channel. Within a few sessions the patient felt the pain diminish and now no longer suffers from it.'

Different crystals are said to hold different properties. For example, quartz crystals are held to be useful in cleansing blocked *chakras*. The crystal is held in the hand of the healer and placed over the chakra to be worked on. Healing energy is passed from the palm of the healer through the crystal and thereby focuses into the chakra in need.

Healing can be done with one stone, but it is more common to use the crystals around the patient, perhaps to have the patient hold certain crystals as receivers. It is sometimes suggested that the healer should tape a crystal on his or her forehead in the place of the Brow Chakra, or third eye.

Crystals can be used to complement other forms of healing. For example, crystals can be placed around the patient when he or she receives aromatherapy; the therapist seeks to balance the crystals with the work he or she is doing.

The believed qualities of certain stones:
Amethyst: stimulates intuition, and also has a calming effect.
Quartz: a healing stone that works on the heart and spine.
Rose quartz: works to reduce fears and vulnerabilities.
Emerald: stimulates the brain, and aids fertility.
Opal: the stone of emotion, assists in developing psychic awareness.

Ground crystals are sometimes ingested as medicine to effect the same cures and development.

Protection
Crystals can also be used to block, or ward off, unwanted energies or intrusions. Some practitioners ask their patients to wear necklaces or other ornaments of crystal in order to prevent them getting ill, or being affected by the moods of others.

One couple we interviewed used crystals placed strategically around their house to try to eliminate poltergeist activity. Another case of 'exorcism' was conducted in an inn (where we had done some investigations into hauntings) with success. Despite the fact that the owner had no confidence in the procedure whatever – and was quite scathing of it – the hauntings stopped immediately the crystals were positioned.

Scrying
Crystals are used for scrying. Most people are familiar with the traditional use of the crystal ball, this can be a glass sphere, but

true crystal is often preferred. A crystal used for scrying must have reflective qualities and depth. Turn of the century occultist, Aleister Crowley used a gold-coloured topaz.

Scrying is the traditional method of divination used by practitioners of Wicca. It is a form of clairvoyance. The crystal ball is a focus for the scryer.

The scryer looks into the crystal, rather than on to its surface. By entering a trance, or altered state, the scryer sees in the crystal images or symbols that allow for prediction.

Scrying is also used to develop psychic powers and awareness. Concentration on the user's own reflection in the crystal develops the ability to enter a trance. One of the first lessons of using crystals in this way is to watch your own face change, often appearing very young, very old, or quite different. Some believe the different faces that are seen are past life memories of previous physical appearances.

Dowsing

Crystals are often used, suspended on a thread or fine chain, as a pendulum for dowsing (see page 107). As such they are used in map dowsing (see page 167) or for locating areas on the body in need of healing.

Crystals are not usually used in field dowsing for the simple reason that they are light and subject to getting blown about in the wind. If they are used, they have to be large and heavy, which often makes them expensive.

Choosing a crystal

Users of crystals believe that the crystal focuses energy within the individual's own body. They believe that there is a natural match between a crystal and an individual. The suggestion is that you 'let the crystal find you'. Go to a shop or other place where there is a selection of crystals and pass your hands over them, rather as if healing. At some point you should 'know' that this or that particular crystal is the one for you. Some describe – as with healing – your hand gets warm or cold, or tingles, or reacts in some other way, when the 'right' crystal is located. This implies a need for some psychic awareness or development in the first place in order not to select the wrong one based on rationale rather than intuition. If in doubt, a developed psychic can assist in 'matching you' with your natural crystal partner.

Does it work?

There is no known scientific basis for many of the claims of crystal usage. Those who believe there is an unknown science of crystals yet to be discovered base most of their beliefs on vibration. All matter has certain vibrations and the crystals can be 'tuned' to certain uses by using these vibrations. In many ways the attention given to both vibrations and crystals seems to be almost a totem, or even distraction, from the real abilities. The crystals seem to be used to focus the attention and concentration of the healer, scryer, dowser or other users and may play no actual part in the work. Rather as Dumbo in the Disney cartoon believed he could fly if he held a magic feather, but discovered that he could fly anyway, so many who use crystals may only be giving themselves confidence to do what they could do anyway.

To that extent at least it does work. Map dowsing can and does produce positive results, scryers can produce accurate prediction or premonition, healers unquestionably effect healing. But quite how any of these mechanisms work is not known, even by the practitioners, most of whom will admit this, and whether the crystals play an integral part in it is therefore equally unknown.

One anecdotal story we were told by a friend who works in complementary therapy and uses crystals does give pause for thought, however. She went to a therapist to seek assistance in emotional development. The therapist used crystals 'targeted' at her heart, solar plexus and sacral *chakras* apparently to no effect. The therapist recognised she was not making 'contact' and our friend felt no effects. Not, at that time, being knowledgeable about the use of crystals, our friend just accepted that 'it wasn't going to work for her'. The therapist touched her lightly, and realised that she was wearing a pendant containing a large crystal under her blouse. She asked her to remove it, which our friend did, though not knowing why. Suddenly our friend felt a surge of energy in her chest, to the point of almost startling her. From that point on both the therapist and she made progress. The dynamics of the pair together make it impossible to know if any subconscious suggestion played a part in what happened, but the implication was that something was genuinely blocked, and then released, by the crystal.

CURSES AND HEXES

Aleister Crowley cursed a doctor who would not prescribe morphine for his addiction. Crowley claimed that when he died he would take the doctor with him. The day Crowley died the doctor was killed by an injury to his head. Curses in various forms exist all around the world. But can they have effect? Did Dr Thompson die by coincidence, or did Crowley really exert some sort of influence?

The most famous curse to which people attribute significance is probably that of Tutankhamun. The Pharaoh's tomb was discovered and first opened in 1922, in an expedition by Howard Carter and Lord Carnarvon. That the tomb would be found was thought likely because Carter had brought a canary to the site; this was thought to be lucky.

After the tomb was opened the canary was eaten by a cobra.

Within three months of the excavation Carnarvon fell ill; he died two months after that. At the moment he died, all the lights in his hotel plunged into darkness. At allegedly the same time in England, Carnarvon's dog died.

Several of the excavation team died shortly after the discovery; two visitors to the tomb died on the same day as their visits.

Fifty-two-year-old Dr Gamal ed-Din Mehrez, Director of the Department of Antiquities dismissed the curse, 'Look at me. All my life I've been involved with tombs and mummies. I am surely the best proof that it is all coincidence.' Four weeks later he dropped dead.

Once the curse snowball was moving, it ran downhill fast;

everything that could be attributed to it was, even a workman who broke his leg two years later!

Interestingly, it was later suggested that the curse was a rumour started by Carter to keep tourists away.

If so, then either people created the connections of incidents by association, or they made the curse come true. If we believe what we are told, can we curse ourselves? Perhaps those who believe in curses and hexes make them self-fulfilling prophecies. If you believe a curse that says you will fall down and break your leg, you will walk in a cautious way; walk unnaturally and you increase the chances of falling over and breaking your leg.

It is known that many peoples of non-Western or primitive societies will die or suffer if hexed or cursed, particularly if the curse is placed by an authority figure such as a witch doctor.

Dr Herbert Basedow described the agonies of an Australian aborigine he watched 'boned'. The man had a bone pointed at him; a sign of death. Basedow reports how the man who was cursed stared with fear, his cheeks lost their colour and his whole face became distorted. His whole body started to shake; finally, he collapsed in agony. After this, he may have recovered enough to return to his abode, but would possibly still fret and sicken. If so, he might not eat; and would soon die.

The only way to avoid death after being cursed is to call on the aid of a more powerful magician. There are rare cases of Western doctors defeating curses; for example, convincing a patient that a particular treatment has lifted the curse. On most occasions there is little that can be done.

It seems that the victims of the hex die of fear. Their internal body responses possibly cause the heart to slow, blood pressure to fall or the lungs to become paralysed. Perhaps there is little difference between the Western man who believes he has a fatal illness and the non-Western man who believes he is cursed.

Speed-ace Donald Campbell was very superstitious; he surrounded himself with the colour blue which he felt brought him luck, and he had several rituals which he observed religiously, such as always taking his teddy bear, Mr Woppit, with him on speed runs. But if anything in these rituals went wrong, he could create his own bad feelings. On the night before the water-speed attempt on Lake Coniston in which he died it is rumoured that he drew the 'death card', the ace of spades, in a game. If so, it would quite likely have weighed heavily on him.

Can one person make another do something by sheer force of will?

Brad Steiger, in *Mysteries of Time and Space* includes a note of Sidney Porcelain's attempt to do this. He was in a Roman Catholic church and sent the priest the somewhat mischievous message, 'Spill the wine. Spill the wine.' Apparently the priest did just that. Porcelain comments that he believes it is easier to use PK on another mind than on an object.

If it is possible to affect circumstances, we should consider those situations where, far from cursing, the outcome is beneficial. The principles may be the same. Dave, described below, uses visualisations to achieve his needs.

He told us that he could always get a parking place when he wanted one; he just visualised the parking space and it would be there. Considering that at the time his office was in Mayfair, just off Oxford Street in Central London, where parking is an extreme difficulty, that represents some achievement. Yet John (Spencer) witnessed him planning and achieving what he claimed. Twice, John has been in Dave's car with him when he has driven to his office and on both occasions cars parked within a few yards of his office door pulled away as he turned into the road, leaving parking spaces clear. On the second occasion, John deliberately watched to see how frequently traffic moved; one car moved within a few minutes, nothing else moved for nearly an hour. Any time we visited his office, his car was parked right outside.

Dave is a believer in the power of positive thinking. He built his business up on the basis of envisioning what he wanted, then getting it. For a time it looked as if he had stumbled; one of his businesses collapsed and he was near bankruptcy. But he was of the opinion he was in the wrong business anyway and needed to be more creative. Now he is a highly successful scriptwriter for TV, in one year alone earning over £60,000.

People, predictable in sufficiently large numbers, are very unpredictable individually. It is easy to attribute their actions to your own efforts, or to attribute your own actions to outside forces. The common wisdom, supported by many, is that we are all masters of our own destiny.

Yet there is a hint of evidence that intrusion into other people's perceptions may be possible. Dream telepathy experiments have indicated the possibility that we can transmit pictures and thoughts to other people. Given that one person can create the dream images of another, there is the suggestion of influence. How far that influence can extend is uncertain. But one fact is suggested by a whole range of paranormal phenomena; that spontaneous bursts of most effects are more powerful than the planned ones.

On that basis the power of passion in thought could be an influencing factor, and curses may have more validity than we often suppose.

D

DEJA VU

The odd sensation of having been in the same situation at a past but unknown time is known as '*déjà vu*'. Most people have some sense of this at some time, yet what is happening is still a mystery. Some have suggested that we may be accessing a memory and confusing it with the present situation because of similarities of geography, the people we are with, etc. Another suggestion is that the memory comes from a past life, telepathy or even a memory of an out-of-body journey.

One possibility is that a malfunction, or 'over-function', of the temporal lobe area of the brain causes it to store a memory before it is registered in the conscious. Then, when the conscious mind registers the scene moments later, it finds it has a memory of that scene already coming up from the subconscious store.

Also put forward is that the mind adapts its sense of time to avoid a disturbing experience. By professing that we have had the experience in the past may lend some comfort. This theory may have validity, but most experiences of *déjà vu* seem to occur at times of no danger whatsoever, and it does not seem to answer all the questions raised by this phenomenon.

The question must concern precognition and whether or not these two phenomena are from the same base. If premonition is a valid ability, then is the experience of *déjà vu* a glimpse of that power?

DOLPHIN HEALING

Many observers of dolphins believe that their intelligence,

while on a different plateau and structure to human intelligence, may be at least as high as human intelligence.

The most common image of the dolphin is the bottlenose dolphin made famous by TV series such as *Flipper* and appearances at dolphinariums around the world. Bottlenoses, more than other dolphins, seem most receptive to human contact and adaptable to confinement. It is also the bottlenose dolphin with which non-scientific human contact is most achieved. Indeed many contacts are with lone dolphins who may be rogue animals expressing, as it were, their own individuality or they may be outcasts from their own social groups. For example, near the Turks and Caicos Islands, near Cuba, one wild, lone dolphin – Jo-Jo – has had a ten-year relationship with marine biologist Dean Bernal. It appears they bring each other 'presents' during long swims together.

There is evidence of complicated social interaction also suggestive of intelligence. Studies of several dolphin groups around the world indicate that they use 'signature whistles' as names which enable individuals to identify each other. Not only can they 'speak' their own names, but they can imitate the sounds of each other's signature whistle, therefore like humans they can call each other by individual names, one of few creatures known to do so. As the social behaviour of the groups increases in complexity, so does the complexity of the sounds, suggesting not only a wide vocabulary, but possibly an exchange of information.

Dolphins are well known for their warm relationship with humans, and this has been used to good effect in therapy. James Woods, who has an enlarged brain and suffers from a condition affecting his speech, went to the Dolphin Research Centre in Florida and was shortly able to speak for the first time in his life. He would look at and touch picture cards and then be rewarded by a swim with dolphins. At the end of a fortnight he had taken the first steps on the road to speech. The director of the research centre, Dr David Nathanson, indicated that he believed the dolphin was only a carrot to spur James's learning. 'Often disabled children withdraw, they don't try very hard. But here they try harder, because they want to be in the water with the dolphins.'

Nigel Mansell, the Formula 1 champion, who swam with dolphins at the Gold Coast Seaworld Centre claimed, after the IndyCar race in Queensland in 1993, 'They put me in such a relaxed mood that I owe that victory to them.' He planned a similar swim prior to the 1994 race stating, 'I thoroughly recommend this to anyone who wants to forget the world's tensions.' Not that dolphins are above assertive criticism; Robin Williams, swimming with one dolphin for the making of a documentary, got at least two hard butts to move him away, 'I guess I'm one of the only human beings on the planet who can piss off a dolphin,' he said ruefully.

One of the most frequently reported claims for dolphins arising from New Age beliefs is that they have the ability to heal.

Arlene Murray was injured in a car crash and forced into early retirement. At the age of fifty-three she went to Israel and swam with five dolphins for an hour and a half a day. She said, 'Being in the water with them, you feel peaceful, yet ecstatic at the same time. They are very intelligent creatures and they are interested in you. It's a very special feeling, unlike anything I have ever experienced . . . I am not saying I am cured, or that the dolphins cured me, because I still can't work. All I can say is that after my experience I have far less pain and I am much more mobile.' Arlene does, however, suggest that there may even have been some physical attention offered by the dolphins; one knocked her gently on her back and, she implies, 'reset' one of her vertebrae relieving much of her pain.

There are many who have worked with dolphins from a New Age perspective who believe them to be telepathic, to have healing abilities and who believe that our thinking towards dolphins should be radically altered. Perhaps the most famous of these is Dr Horace Dobbs, the founder of International Dolphin Watch, who has promoted this view of dolphins. Author Timothy Wyllie in his book *Dolphins, Telepathy and Underwater Birthing* states of a film made by Dobbs, and showing apparent telepathy, 'it was one of the things that so intensely provoked my interest . . .'

Jemima Biggs suffered from anorexia, but is on the road to cure following swimming with Freddie, a lone dolphin who took up residence in the North Sea off Amble and has been the subject of many British attempts at healing, with several people swimming around him.

Ruth suffers from ME, also known as chronic fatigue syndrome, or somewhat cynically as 'yuppie flu'. She also swam with Freddie, and after he left with Fungie in Ireland. She believes that swimming with these animals has relieved her condition and made her feel better.

There have been similar claims of relieving the conditions associated with multiple sclerosis, arthritis, brain tumours, Dudewitz Syndrome and so on.

Robert Barnes swam with both Fungie and Freddie and felt he had an emotional contact with Fungie. He believes dolphins have open hearts and a catalytic effect on those who swim with them. He has become a 'green' person, having had no such tendencies prior to his dolphin encounter.

Jason Smith, a musician and artist, sparked off his interest in cetaceans when he dreamt of humpback whales' songs and later met Fungie. He stated, 'At eye to eye, it was the most beautiful feeling I have ever experienced. I cried from the feeling of euphoric life, freedom – hard to explain in words.'

Jean-Luc Bozolli is a French artist who was apparently inspired to art for the first time by being 'taught' to paint by dolphin encounters.

The BBC's *Travel Show* presenter, Matthew Collins said, 'The experience did bring about changes within me, the greatest change being that my awareness of ecological issues has become heightened,' following swimming with Freddie. His contemporary, John Craven, of *Newsround* claimed after close contact with dolphins that he felt 'privileged'.

There is certainly evidence that people project into their encounters with dolphins their own beliefs. One woman swimming with dolphins indicated that she believed they had told her that they were from another planetary system. Many have 'given' messages relating to the ecology, a popular human theme. One contactee, Lennart Lidfors, claimed channelled messages from three entities, two extraterrestrials and one dolphin called Venus.

However, are dolphins actually healing or are they acting as catalysts for people to heal themselves? There is a great deal of evidence to suggest that many alternative healings represent ways in which people can refocus their own attention on themselves and cure their own ills. Swimming with a large, intelligent mammal in circumstances quite different to those usually encountered and in a new environment could itself be a catalyst helping some people to change their own attitudes towards their illnesses and cure themselves. The circumstantial evidence of those swimming with dolphins being genuinely cured is still ambiguous. Even many of the individuals cured have indicated that the dolphin has acted more as a focus for themselves than in any other capacity. Just as the totem pole of the native American Indians represents those animals with which the Indian believes he has an intimate and mysterious connection, so the dolphin has become a modern totem.

That a healing process takes place seems indisputable; whether it relates directly to dolphins is more of a mystery. However, there is one aspect of dolphin ability which at least suggests the possibility of physical change in the human body when swimming with dolphins, and research in that area may one day indicate whether or not some genuine healing process may have been at work.

Salt water carries sound waves much more efficiently than air and it is hardly surprising that creatures evolving in an ocean environment have also evolved the use of sound waves for communication and environmental sensing. Dr Kenneth Norris, a professor of Natural History at the University of California and Santa Cruz, has described what he calls 'ensonification'. The same or a similar mechanism in a dolphin which creates its echolocation signal for sensing can, he speculates, be focused into a 'stun gun' beam, disabling fish prior to attack. The ensonification beam is apparently long, low-frequency pulses, much stronger than the echolocation 'clicks' and lasting some 800 times longer. Norris believes that the sound builds up an overload in the fish. There is very little observational evidence available of Norris's theory; however, one experiment that took place in Santa Cruz mimicked the 'ensonification sound' and successfully killed anchovies, suggesting substance to the theory.

These sounds pass physically through the water as a wave, and must therefore pass into humans if they are swimming with dolphins. Little is known as to what the effect would be on the human body, which is itself largely composed of water. Certainly sound of a quite different nature is used medically, for example sound waves used to break up gallstones, and it is known that some sounds affect the chemical and electrical operations in the brain. What these unknown sounds may be doing to those swimming with dolphins is therefore a field for research in the future which may offer some more insight into this current mystery of the human interaction with dolphins.

DOUBLES AND *DOPPELGÄNGERS*

Apparitions of living people are seen as often as, or even more often than apparitions of the dead. Because of possible differences in the characteristics of these types of reports, we have restricted this section to those doubles seen by the self, or where the self and double are seen in close proximity.

There are many reports of *doppelgängers* mimicking the self. In one case, a man mowing his lawn watched an identical version of himself walking up the lawn next to him, copying his every movement. The only difference was that the *doppelgänger* did not have a lawnmower. In another case a man eating his dinner watched his double sitting at the table opposite copying his every move.

The appearance of a double is sometimes considered to be a bad omen and a foretelling of death. For example, both Lady Diana Rich and her sister Lady Isabel Thynne saw their own doubles and both died shortly afterwards. Perhaps more in the nature of premonition was the case of Sir William Napier who, in perfect health, stayed at an inn overnight and saw his own corpse lying on the bed when shown to his room. He died shortly afterwards. Percy Shelley is alleged to have seen his own double shortly before he drowned. Empress Catherine of Russia saw her double sitting on her own throne. She had her guards fire at it. She, too, died shortly afterwards.

Not all such sightings follow the pattern however. Sigmund Freud, in 1905, saw a man who looked like himself and believed it an omen of his own death. He went on to live until 1939.

Doppelgängers are rarely harmful, though the fear generated by a belief in them as an omen of death may play some part in deteriorating the health or state of mind of those who see them. For the most part they are non-interactive. The cases mentioned above of the man mowing his lawn, or the man having dinner, suggest no interaction on the part of the double. Sometimes there is, however, the suggestion of evil, of even a split in the personality of the self.

Hilary Evans in *Visions, Apparitions, Alien Visitors* describes the case of a young woman admitted to hospital with a cut in her tongue, and her face was swollen and congested from what seemed like a strangling attempt. She apparently explained that she had met her double while shopping, but a double with a 'sharp, unkind expression'. The following day the double visited the woman at her home and attacked her, trying to strangle her and cut her with scissors.

This case seems to suggest that the *doppelgänger* might be the embodiment of some particular part of the self; the Mr Hyde released from the otherwise balanced Jekyll and Hyde combination. If so, then the entity, or perhaps thought-form, that was the *doppelgänger* took on a dangerous life of its own. However, there was nothing in the mutilation of the woman that could not have been done by herself. In fact, on examination, the wounds were deemed to be self-inflicted. The medical examiner attributed the attack to an exteriorisation of her personal problems. Perhaps her image of the evil *doppelgänger* was a hallucination that 'allowed' her – gave her permission – to do what she did to herself.

The person most reported to have been seen as a double is Emelie Sagee, a teacher in 1845. She was working in a school for girls in Livonia. Pupils there saw her on numerous occasions to be in the company of her own double. One pupil, Antonie von Wrangel, fainted after looking into a mirror where she saw both Emelie and her double fixing her dress. When the school lost the majority of its pupils over concern about her manifestations and she was asked to leave, Emelie confessed that this was the nineteenth position she had lost in sixteen years.

The suggestion by those who 'touched' Emelie's double was that it was somehow insubstantial. One case reported to us suggested more physical substance. Fleur Conway was painting in an upstairs playroom when she looked out of the window and saw herself hanging up the washing in the garden below. We note in this case that both 'bodies' were physically moving objects, suggesting a physical split.

In 1982, Henry J. Purdy in Middlesex awoke one night to see his wife looking out of the window. This he had seen before and did not feel it was unusual, but when he moved in the bed he felt his wife with him. He realised she was sleeping peacefully. Looking back to the apparition, he then watched it fade away. His wife was apparently not aware of anything unusual.

We note from this that the image faded when Mr Purdy realised what he was seeing. Whether this is significant or not is uncertain. Whether the seeing, or the realising, is part of re-adjusting the brain to alter the conditions that allow for – depending on your belief – creation or perception of the double is uncertain. We must also consider who was generating the double; Mr Purdy or his wife. If his wife, then she was apparently unaware of it, but perhaps some part of her was contemplating her garden, or some such scene.

Occasionally the *doppelgänger* does not appear as a warning or omen, but does seem to show future events, as in the case reported by Goethe. Goethe wrote of his experience, 'I rode on horseback over the footpath at Drusenheim, when one of the strangest experiences befell me. Not with the eyes of the body, but with those of the spirit, I saw myself on horseback coming towards me on the same path dressed in a suit such as I had never worn, pale-grey with some gold. As soon as I had shaken myself out of this reverie the form vanished. It is strange, however, that I found myself returning on the same path eight years afterwards . . . and that I then wore the suit I had dreamt of, and not by design but chance.'

Goethe refers to using 'eyes of the spirit'; quite what he means is unclear. He might be referring to the 'third eye' of psychic perception. Alternatively he might be making a poetic reference to premonition. It seems he is telling us that he perceived the double through senses other than the usual five.

The *doppelgängers* seen by Kathryn Reinhardt represent another case that seems to be a vision of a future time, and perhaps a version of precognition. Her *doppelgängers* were always approximately five years older than she was at the time. The most extraordinary experience came when she was twenty-eight and saw her double at a cocktail party. The 'older' double walked with a slight limp. Four years later, Reinhardt was in a serious car crash that killed her husband and left her leg badly injured. From that time on, she always walked with a limp.

At least part of the explanation for doubles may be in the possibility that the double is a projection from the sighter's own mind for a purpose. Just as in 'Crisis Apparitions' (page 80) we consider the possibility that those in danger (say, on a lonely mountain) may 'create' an image that guides them from their own subconscious, so doubles may serve a similar function. They may be a complex way of talking to, or communicating with, oneself – perhaps the subconscious talking to the conscious. Why the brain might need to circumvent its normal channels of communication is unclear, but there is evidence that it does in many situations. The case of the French writer Guy de Maupassant appears to be such a case. In 1885 he was suffering writer's block while working on his horror tale *The Horla*. A figure entered his room and sat down opposite him. The figure dictated passages of the book. De Maupassant was worried; he could not understand how the individual had got into his rooms, nor could he understand why the figure knew so much about the book he was writing. Only then did he realise that the figure was his own double, which shook him somewhat, but provided him with a cure for his writer's block.

There is one case of a person who deliberately set out to do what de Maupassant may have done accidentally. Psychiatrist Morton Schatzman worked with 'Ruth' who had been troubled by apparitions of her family. With Schatzman's help, she learnt to control them, but also managed to produce an apparition of herself. Ruth wrote of this, 'It took about two hours of continuous trying to produce an apparition of myself. It was so hard. At first I couldn't see her but for a moment or two at a time. Finally I did learn to do it. I decided to experiment and play some games. I had the apparition sit across the room from me. I felt I was looking at someone who knew more about me than I knew about myself. I watched it closely. I tried to see if it was breathing, but I couldn't tell. The eyes fascinated me. Could I be looking through them into myself? A calm seemed to flow between us, from one to the other. It was very tiring and before long I had to take a nap.'

DOWSING

Dowsing is best known and most frequently used to find underground sources of water. Nomadic groups, particularly from so-called primitive cultures, use dowsing to locate sources of water during long treks. Almost certainly, dowsing is an ancient and probably inherent ability in people which would have been instinctively, and frequently, used by our less technological ancestors. It is known that both the ancient Egyptians and the ancient Chinese used dowsing. The use of technology such as metal detectors, coupled with a belief system that puts scientific measurement above human intuition, has probably made dowsing largely redundant, particularly in the Western world. Its current come-back is still confined to what might be regarded as the New Age disciplines.

Water is not the only substance that can be detected by dowsing, indeed many dowsers believe that there is nothing that cannot be detected with sufficient application. It is regularly used to find metals, oils, lost objects and even lost people (see 'Map Dowsing' page 167). Dowsing is used over the body by healers to identify the areas in which to apply healing.

Dowsing is proved to be a real ability beyond any reasonable doubt, which is why it has been engaged by emergency services, police forces and large corporations all around the world. This does not mean that we have yet understood how it works. The mystery, and the challenge to real scientists, is to learn what forces are at work and to understand them more fully.

In the 1930s dowsing was known as radiesthesia, based on Latin and Greek roots for radiation and perception. It was believed that what the dowser picked up was a radiation emanating from the ground.

T.C. Lethbridge, famous for his personal researches into dowsing, ghosts, etc. spent a great deal of time studying dowsing, believing it to be a measurable science. He wrote up the results of many experiments with a pendulum, even to the point of identifying pendulum lengths for certain elements and objects. He concluded that the tables of pendulum length to object would vary according to the person using the pendulum, but not according to the pendulum used. Other dowsers, following his work, have written up tables using rates of rotation for the pendulum, suggesting that certain speeds of rotation would identify certain elements and so on.

More modern interpretations of dowsing suggest that Lethbridge and those like him were more likely needing and finding a rational explanation which 'felt' scientifically correct to support an ability they inherently had and could use. It is not believed by all dowsers that length of pendulum is crucial. It is most widely believed nowadays that dowsing is more to do with inherent abilities in the mind. However, if the mind needs a way of concentrating on the substance being sought for, perhaps those who believe pendulum length is crucial use it as their way of focusing that concentration. For those who believe that a scientific principle is needed before something can work this is arguably their 'prop'.

The tool of dowsing is traditionally a forked stick of willow, hazel, elm or other wood, but dowsing rods can be made of metal or plastic. Many dowsers use rods cut from a wire coat hanger. One method of using the rods is to hold two rods out in front which will cross over each other when a positive result is achieved. Another method is to hold a forked stick out in front which will dip downwards or rise at a positive result. Other 'tools' used include pendulums of various materials (crystal is very popular), sticky rubber pads, or simply open hands.

Our own experiments with, and exposures to, dowsing have reinforced what we have learned from others; that dowsing is essentially an ability of the mind. What we know from dowsing is that certain items or energies can be detected by people who are not apparently using their normal five senses.

The five senses may be used to analyse, even at a subconscious level, the topography of a site and to that degree dowsers might be doing some geographical version of 'psychological profiling'. But this does not seem to be the whole answer.

It may be that a part of the human brain recognises more than it can communicate in language. This ability would be a part of the more intuitive 'right brain' (or older brain stem) functions. This non-conscious response may cause a muscle movement that the conscious is unaware of, but the dowser will see the movement amplified and infer that the movement is produced by the rod's diving powers. This might create a 'feed-back loop' with the rod movements acting as a 'reward' for the dowser. Seeing the dowsing rod move further builds confidence in the dowser's abilities.

Those abilities, however, may be psychic ones nevertheless. No one feeling the movement of a dowsing rod could be fooled into thinking it is a product of imagination, even if the feed-back loop makes the sight of the movement encouraging. Based on our own observations of many dowsers, and our work with one of Sweden's leading figures in the field, Arne Groth, we would compare dowsing to ground-penetrating radar, which recognises that all substances produce a different electrical response. A signal is sent into the ground and the return indicates the substance buried. Dowsers may be doing nothing different, except that the signal being sent out – and the interpretation of the return – is one of the little understood psychic abilities of the mind.

All psychic powers may be inherent abilities in the subconscious mind that the conscious mind misperceives. Using tools to give a visual response encourages and motivates the dowser. In that sense dowsing becomes a very effective way of getting in touch with these psychic abilities.

Dowsing is widely used with many successes. One of the most spectacular was probably Colonel Harry Gratton, CBE, of the Royal Engineers who in 1952 used dowsing to solve the problem of siting the headquarters for the British Army in Germany. The headquarters would house 9,000 people, who would need some three-quarters of a million gallons of water a day, which would have been extremely expensive coming from existing water-supply companies. Gratton used dowsing to locate the appropriate water reserves; test bores indicated his findings were correct. Today the area, Mönchen Gladbach, has a population of 10,000, receiving a million gallons of water a day from the Colonel's work.

A. Gotowski was engaged by the Fox Brewing Company of Chicago to search for oil; using a pendulum he discovered the largest oil field for many years. In a similar way Clayton McDowell located oil for the Edwards County Senior High School, a field which now produces over 100 barrels a day.

The army has a long association with dowsing. Dowsing was used to locate mines in the Second World War and indeed was being used in Vietnam for the same purpose more recently. The Royal School of Military Engineering at Chatham had courses and demonstrations in dowsing. However, in 1970 the British Ministry of Defence conducted experiments on field dowsing and map dowsing which were not successful. In one case a dowser missed 142 of 160 buried mines. While such results cannot be ignored they should not cloud the many successes. It may simply mean that the test conditions were inappropriate or that the dowsers engaged were no good at the job. There are bound to be incompetent dowsers who only think they know what they are doing, just as there are incompetent doctors, dentists, accountants, car workers, or painters.

We believe that dowsing is one of the easiest ways to begin

to discover faculties of the mind not usually used, and our suggestion is that readers of this book might try some simple dowsing for themselves, preferably in the company of someone who can already do it, as being their contribution to this subject.

DRAGONS AND LAKE MONSTERS

'The dragon is a most terrible animal, but probably not of Nature's formation,' according to *Natural History* published in 1776.

Legends of dragons can be found in mythologies the world over: in the legends of the native Americans, the peoples of the Eastern world, the Indians, Chinese, and so on. In Britain there are the Welsh dragons, and, of course, the story of St George.

In the Far East dragons are regarded as benevolent; the scaled, horned and clawed Chinese dragons are mostly associated with good fortune, only a few are evil. Yellow dragons symbolise luck, azure dragons herald the birth of great men.

Western dragons, usually depicted with short, leathery wings, are generally regarded as evil; they are foes to be beaten. In Christianity they are symbolic of the powers of Satan, defeated by Christ. According to 20 Revelations, 'Then I saw an angel coming down from heaven, holding in his hand the key of the bottomless pit and a great chain. And he seized the dragon, that ancient serpent, who is the Devil and Satan, and bound him for a thousand years.' The passage goes on to add, ominously, 'After that he must be loosed for a little while.'

For many of the races that invaded Britain such as the Vikings and Romans, the dragon was symbolic of strength and usually featured on their war-banners. Slaying a dragon gets at least some of its origins from these early battles. Such symbolism also appears in more recent history. For example, in Suffolk it was said that two dragons were seen fighting on a hill at Little Cornard on 25 September 1449. Almost certainly this refers to the banners of two feuding factions. It may also be a local legend which reflects the fight at that location between Boudicca and the Ninth Roman Legion.

An allegedly more specific sighting is attributed to the St Leonard's Forest area of West Sussex, though almost certainly this has a basis in the legend of the sixth-century St Leonard who slew a dragon in that area. In 1614, three local villagers saw a 'strange and monstrous serpent' just over nine feet long, thick in the middle and thin at the ends, with red scales on its belly, black scales on its back and a ring of white markings around its neck. It had large feet, could run as fast as a man, and had on its flanks 'two great bunches as big as a large football, which (as some thinke) will in time grow two wings.' Wherever it went, it left a trail of slime, and it killed at least two people by spitting poison at them. Its eventual fate is not recorded.

In what seems to be a good example of how to construct a theory based on a desired result, Peter Dickson in his book *The Flight of Dragons* has worked out some of their practical points. He believes they fly because they are essentially gas-bags filled with hydrogen, not unlike airships. They manufactured the hydrogen naturally. This gets over the problem of their wingspan not being sufficient for 'lift' in a normal animal of their reported size. The stories of their 'breathing fire', he reasoned, arose because they vented the gas and ignited it occasionally, as a means of descending or staying on the ground.

Dinosaurs almost certainly play a major part in dragon legend. Dragon bones were a major part of early Chinese medicines and were almost certainly fossilised dinosaur bones. Such skeletons must have been discovered at various times in history, but without a framework in which to fit them, and without a consideration of the length of pre-history, the dinosaur skeletons were almost certainly regarded as the remains of contemporary, huge creatures; hence a belief in living dragons.

During the late eighteenth and into the nineteenth century the discoveries of large skeletons were identified as dinosaur fossils and a history of them, currently evolving almost daily, incidentally, was created. It was palaeontologist Sir Richard Owen (later director of the Natural History Museum of London) who in 1841 created the term 'dinosaur' to describe these creatures; it quickly became popular parlance.

In addition to dinosaur bones, belief in contemporary dragon sightings has almost certainly included the misidentification of large snakes, of which the world has plenty. Twenty-foot-long snakes are not unknown. In the seas and lakes there are equally impressive eels, and possibly other large creatures that, if seen on the surface, would easily support dragon and serpent legends.

It seems likely that dragon mythology has come forward into the twentieth century in well-known reports of sightings at such places as Loch Ness, in Scotland. The famous 'Loch Ness Monster' has been seen too often not to have a basis in truth, but what is being seen is almost certainly – at least sometimes – misidentified eels, otters and birds. Some photographs of the 'Monster' are so vague they may only be waves, and many sightings consist only of 'bow waves' that could be caused by any underwater swimming animal. Large eels such as *Anguilla anguilla* inhabit the loch. The most impressive-looking photograph of 'Nessie', the so-called 'Surgeon's Photograph' (see photo section), has been confessed to as a hoax. But the point about the tales of Loch Ness is that the Monster is almost always thought of as a dragon-like shape (long neck, fat body, stubby flippers).

The rational support for this particular dragon is in the implication that it is a preserved or surviving plesiosaur from the dinosaur era. The myths begin to merge! The photographs and reports from Loch Ness and other sites, equate well with a plesiosaur, but that may reflect expectancy on the part of witnesses. When alternative suggestions are offered, the images acquire a new ambiguity; what looks like the hump on the back of a dinosaur can quickly look like a bird diving below the waves when that suggestion is put forward.

Loch Ness is the most famous water monster location, but it is only one of many. In the Swedish publication The *Gentleman's Magazine* of 1765 it was stated, 'The people of Stockholm report that a great dragon, named Necker, infests the neighbouring lake . . .' In central Sweden, in Lake Storsjo, there were twenty-two reports of a creature between 1820 and 1898. One report described the creature as resembling an upturned boat. In 1860 the Reverend Sabine Baring-Gould reported his conversation with two fishermen who had seen the Skrimsl in Iceland; they described a creature with the head of a seal, behind which was a large hump. They estimated its length at forty-six feet. In North America monsters have been reported in Lake Erie, the various Wisconsin lakes, and many others. In Lake Payette in Idaho there were several sightings in 1941; over thirty people reported the creature. One description was of an animal thirty-five feet in length slowly undulating up the lake. In Flathead Lake in Montana, in 1963, Ronald Nixon reported a twenty-five-foot creature. Lake Okanagan in British Columbia has the Ogopogo, reported sometimes as a series of black humps. In 1914 a strange carcass was washed up on the shores of the lake; debate goes on as to its identification, the manatee (sea-cow) was suggested. In 1960 three priests fishing on Lough Ree on the Shannon in Ireland saw a large creature; a snake-like head being followed by a semi-submerged hump. A similar creature was reported in Lough Bray, south of Dublin, in 1963.

Nor are all such creatures freshwater inhabitants; there are many reports of similar creatures at sea. Captain Christmas, from Denmark, reported a long-necked creature apparently chasing a school of porpoises in 1846, near Iceland. Captain Cringle, on the *Umfuli*, sailing near Mauritius, reported an eighty-foot-long creature with a long neck and three humps.

In April 1907 Arthur Rostron, on the *Campania*, saw a creature as the ship headed for Cobh harbour. Its neck rose eight or nine feet out of the water. If ever there was a level-headed witness it was this one; in 1912 he captained the *Carpathia*, and was awarded the Congressional Medal of Honour by the American Senate for his clear thinking and precise handling of the rescue of survivors from the sinking *Titanic*.

Lake and sea creature reports run into hundreds around the world, from the distant past to the present day.

However, if it is wise to consider the mythological backgrounds to the way people view unknown objects, it is equally important not to be blinded by them. There could be an unknown species of animal in Loch Ness and other locations around the world. Photographs taken by Robert H. Rines in 1972 and 1975 did seem to show a diamond-shaped fin very like that attributed to the plesiosaurs, and another picture – while ambiguous – is very reminiscent of the shape of that creature. Dr C. McGowan of the Department of Vertebrate Palaeontology of the Royal Ontario Museum assessed the photographs and stated, 'I am satisfied that there is a sufficient weight of evidence to support that there is an unexplained phenomenon of considerable interest in Loch Ness; the evidence suggests the presence of large aquatic animals . . .'

It would be ironic if instead of our interpretations of what is seen in lakes such as Loch Ness, Loch Shiel, Lake Manitoba, Lago Lacar in Argentina, and probably a hundred other locations around the world, being coloured by mythology, the mythology was itself based on a contemporary living creature that had survived sixty-five million years in its present form. There is precedent for such unexpected survival. Many people know of the coelacanth, a fish believed extinct for seventy million years that swam up to a diver off the coast of Africa. Lesser known perhaps is the neopilina, a snail-like creature thought extinct for three hundred million years; one turned up alive in 1957. Our view of dragons and serpents might have to be reviewed.

E

ECTOPLASM

In the later part of the nineteenth century, when the physical medium was popular, ectoplasm was said to be a common phenomenon. Virtually all mediums were expected to perform using the substance.

In *A Dictionary of Modern Spiritualism* by Norman Blunsdon, ectoplasm is defined as, 'A subtle living matter present in the physical body, primarily invisible but capable of assuming vaporous, liquid, or solid states and properties. It is extruded usually in the dark from the pores and various orifices of the body and is slightly luminous, the more so when condensed. The temperature of the room is usually lowered when ectoplasm is produced; it possesses a characteristic smell and is cold to the touch. This substance is held to be responsible for the production of all phenomena classed as "physical" '.

Ectoplasm has been described in many different ways, ranging from a gentle, misty type of substance to something akin to a revolting, clotted mucus. Ectoplasm was responsible not just for the materialisation of spirit limbs and bodies, but was also the 'force' used to cause levitations, and other effects.

During the early days of spiritualism there was a great deal of competition to be accepted as the 'best' medium; inevitably many mediums resorted to fraud, and the ectoplasm they produced seems to have been created from such things as gauze, melted butter, and so on. This was detected by sceptics who then wrote off much of physical mediumship. William Crookes said of the more than one hundred mediums he knew, all resorted to tricks at some time. But this probably does not explain all ectoplasm; some was produced under very strict conditions.

There are now very few physical mediums, and the ones who are working are not inclined to feel the need to prove themselves. Mental mediums are now much more popular. To some extent this reflects the fact that certain aspects of the paranormal seem to be 'in vogue' at certain times. Physical mediumship, and the production of ectoplasm, are currently 'out'.

If ectoplasm is a naturally produced substance (i.e. not faked), then it is unusual that none ever appeared spontaneously; virtually all paranormal effects do, and it is often the spontaneous ones that are the most spectacular.

ELECTRONIC VOICE PHENOMENON

It is believed by many that the dead can speak to the living through a medium and the medium's spirit guide. According to the subscribers to the electronic voice phenomenon (EVP), the medium's place is taken by electronic equipment; a radio and a recorder. The spirits of the dead are thought able to manipulate the equipment and produce an audible sound.

Friedrich Jurgensen, in 1959, after playing back birdsong he had recorded, heard amongst the singing a voice speaking in Norwegian. At first Jurgensen believed that his recorder was picking up radio signals. But on later recordings he realised the messages were personal; indeed he believed that he could recognise his mother's voice. He would then tune his radio between stations and listen for messages. A radio 'off station' produces a 'white noise' background (a hiss) which some believe provides the 'building blocks' with which the spirits create the words.

Dr Konstantin Raudive, a Latvian living in Germany, had worked with Jurgensen and continued the work. Raudive would link his tape recorder direct to his radio, tuned between stations, and from this he would record his anomalous voices. The obvious drawback of this method is the possibility of picking up a radio broadcast, which sometimes happens. But Raudive's messages were often personal and relevant. Throughout his work he amassed an incredible 70,000 recordings. His account was written up in his book, *Breakthrough*.

Some testing was done in 1969 and although there was difficulty picking up the voices at first, a few minutes after starting to record on the fourth new tape, Raudive asked for the tape to be played back. The investigators heard 'clear and without a shadow of doubt, a rhythmic voice, twice the speed of the human voice said, "Raudive there" . . . there was a voice and it called the name of the one person who was most concerned with it all.'

Although credited with the origination of EVP, Jurgensen was not the first to notice the phenomenon. In 1938 an American psychic, Attila von Szalay, heard the voice of his late son calling out his own name. In 1941 he was experimentally trying to record the voices he had been hearing, using a 78rpm record cutter. This was unsuccessful, but later working with investigator Raymond Bayliss in a Hollywood studio he found they were able to hear voices and whispers. Later, in 1956, they also found more voices recorded than they had heard over the loudspeaker.

Many others have continued with the work. One of those is George Bonner who studied the phenomenon for twenty years. Bonner wrote of his experiences, describing that the first experiments were to confirm to himself that the voices received were paranormal and that a genuine phenomenon existed. After many years of practising Bonner was able to hear and record not only words but sentences and conversations. Bonner starts his sessions by introducing himself, for instance, 'This is Gilbert Bonner calling,' a voice might respond, then Bonner asks, 'Can you say my name please?' and receives back, 'Calling George Bonner.' Amongst the voices he has heard, Bonner believes he has that of the now-dead Raudive.

We recently received a tape-recording from Delilah Rohman of Birmingham made during a sitting with a medium. She had recorded the sitting out of interest, and with the medium's permission. At one point in the tape the medium describes a young boy 'in spirit' who the medium believed was Delilah's child growing up in the spirit world. He believed that the child had never been born, either a miscarriage or an abortion. Delilah confirmed that she had had a miscarriage. The medium described the boy as 'pulling at her skirts while you're sitting there'. The medium said he heard the boy saying, 'Mum'. When listening to the tape, just at that point there is a rushing build up of static and a voice can be heard faintly saying, 'Mum'. Delilah was certain that there was no one else in the house, and that she had not heard the voice at the time, or in fact until she replayed the tape the following day.

EVP research has been far from conclusive. There are many who doubt that any voices are being recorded other than spurious radio signals and misinterpreted sounds. Certainly most recordings require a great deal of listening to in order to pick out the words, and many are ambiguous. But even if the voices are being recorded, they do not prove the existence of the survival of spirit. There is a quality to many of the presumed messages that could be projections from the mind of the experimenter, or of telepathy from those near by. While that would still constitute an impressive paranormal effect by our current standards, it would not represent the proof of life after death that proponents of EVP are seeking.

There have been suggestions that the voices on the tapes could have originated from another 'personality' within the experimenter. Multiple-personality syndrome has been suspected as a contributing factor in several areas of paranormal research. The suggestion is that the sub-personality speaks the words, unknown to the main personality, which is then surprised to hear the voices on the tapes. The conditions releasing the sub-personality might also account for the 'speeded up' speech sometimes recorded.

If EVP does represent contact from the spirit world, then perhaps one day someone will invent the machine that Edison spent much time on, 'an instrument so delicate as to be affected or moved or manipulated by our personalities as it survives in the next life'.

EXORCISM

Exorcism is the casting out of non-physical entities; demons, spirits, and so on that are said to have invaded their victims. The rites of the exorcism depend upon the belief system of those involved; the priest, the victim, and the family and friends of the victim.

Exorcisms are performed around the world wherever there is a belief in possession. The exorcist is normally a priest, shaman or magician using rituals that date back to the beginnings of religion.

In the Bible demonic possession and exorcism by Jesus is described (Luke 8, xxvi), '. . . as he stepped out on land, there met him a man from the city who had demons; . . . When he saw Jesus, he cried out and fell down before him, and said with a loud voice, "What have you to do with me, Jesus, Son of the Most High God? I beseech you, do not torment me." For he had commanded the unclean spirit to come out of the man . . . Jesus then asked him, "What is your name?" And he said, "Legion" for many demons had entered him. And they begged him not to command them to depart into the abyss. Now a large herd of swine was feeding there on the hillside; and they begged him to let them enter these. So he gave them leave. Then the demons came out of the man and entered the swine, and the herd rushed down the steep bank into the lake and were drowned.'

Exorcism nowadays is a 'last resort'. Canon Dominic Walker, the Church of England's chief deliverance minister has only performed six exorcisms in over twenty years in the job; most cases are dealt with through less extreme methods. Indeed, Canon Walker was clear that using the exorcism rites where it is unnecessary can make a situation considerably worse. It can lead to suicide, where for example the person feels that the demons have not been removed, or to murder. In the Barnsley case of 1975 (reported in *The Times* of 26 and 27 March) a man murdered his wife following a ceremony of exorcism by a charismatic Christian group; he believed not all the demons had been removed. In 1976 both the Methodist Conference and the General Assembly of the Church of

Scotland pronounced on exorcism, instructing that the greatest care should be taken in its use. A working party set up to examine the question concluded, 'We believe that it effects nothing that cannot be accomplished by the expeditious use of medical skills and pastoral skills . . .'

Many spiritual mediums use deliverance ('sending to the light') and 'rescue' rather than exorcism, which is a form of banishment. This would seem to depend on belief about precisely what is being exorcised. Some mediums believe in a world beyond death occupied by former living humans who can be 'rescued' and 'lower level' entities that need to be banished.

In many cases the ritual may be long, involving considerable symbolism. In voodoo it is believed that the spirit of a dead person can be sent to possess another as a curse placed by a sorcerer. To remove these spirits the subject needs the services of a more powerful sorcerer. Felicitas D. Goodman in her book *How About Demons*? describes the exorcism of a man called Antoine, sought by his family because following such a curse he was now ill and wasting away.

The priestess Lorgina, after deciding that the man was possessed by three 'dead', had Antoine's body prepared as if it were a corpse. She then performed a ritual which included the use of a hen and rooster that were then buried alive as a sacrifice, fire and water, and prayers to 'God the Father, God the Son and God the Holy Ghost, in the name of Mary, in the name of Jesus and all the Saints and all the dead'. During the ritual, the priestess called for help from her personal deities (*loas*) and also the *loas* of the possessed man.

The ritual included symbolic death and rebirth 'complete with reducing him to a corpse, burying him, and then having him be born from the depths of the ditch-womb, and finally giving him his first bath and making him drink like a new-born infant.' This is reminiscent of New Age rebirthing, which allows for 'out with the old and in with the new'.

Some religious beliefs about exorcism need consideration because of the dangers to both the exorcist and the subject.

In October 1994 it was reported that a twenty-two-year-old woman, Farida Patel, was beaten to death in Essex by her exorcists. A 'holy woman', Mona Rai, had been instructing Farida and her sister Rabiya in the ways of their religion, Sunni Islam. After Rabiya had reported a dream, and strange behaviour by Farida, it was decided that Farida was possessed and an exorcism was thought necessary. Farida was thought to be possessed by a djinn (a middle-Eastern entity created by fire). They believed that traditionally the only way to remove a djinn was to beat it out of the person. On the first night, 8 December 1993, Farida was beaten by Rai wielding a part of a vacuum cleaner. 'I am not hitting Farida, I am beating the evil spirit,' Rai insisted when she was asked to stop. The next night Rai came again, bringing a friend, and beat Farida with a stick asking for help from her friend, and from Farida's brother and sister. Rai then jumped up and down on Farida, breaking nine of her ribs until at last Farida was quiet. Rai announced that the djinn had left her. But Farida was found to be dead. On 20 December 1994, Rai was jailed for seven years for manslaughter.

On 4 September 1980 *The Times* reported the case of a preacher who kicked a woman friend to death trying to exorcise the spirit of Judas Iscariot.

Exorcism, or some form of service, is used not just to drive spirits out of people, but also out of places. Without surrendering too much to semantics, it is fair to point out that there are priests who believe that exorcism only applies to people. For example, Jesuit Father Thurston has pointed out that the Catholic rite of exorcism contained in the *Rituale Romanum* only applies to people. (The *Rituale Romanum* also contains blessings and consecrations that can be used to cleanse buildings.) The *Rituale* reminds the priest to be aware he is dealing with an ancient enemy, strong and cunning. The priest must be prepared to continue the exorcism until the end, and this can take weeks, even months. Therefore the priest must be devout and confident in his faith.

Before exorcism will be performed, the Church must be certain a possession is being dealt with. The signs looked for include speaking in tongues, understanding strange languages, levitation, claims and demonstrations of psychic abilities, unusual strength, and a revulsion towards holy objects and holy water.

Nevertheless, exorcism in some form is used by many to banish poltergeists. But there can be dangers here for the exorcists. Consider the case of three priests attempting to exorcise a poltergeist in Ireland, in 1914. They were – along with the family – driven from the house they were working in and suffered nervous breakdown, spinal meningitis, and facial paralysis. Perhaps for that reason exorcism is not taken lightly within the Christian churches; priests are warned to take care and not to approach the problem alone. The priest and the possessing demon engage in battle for the possessed's soul. The devil will mock, blaspheme, and lie in order to distract the priest and force him to give up the struggle.

Some researchers of poltergeists, such as Maurice Grosse, a leading authority on the subject, have suggested that the approach to take towards 'casting out' is non-religious and based on stress management. He has identified that most poltergeist activity occurs in families where significant stress situations are apparent, even before the poltergeist manifests. Grosse believes that by reducing the stress, the poltergeist often diminishes in strength and dissipates.

In one case from our own research, we took Maurice's advice to 'bring the family into the work'. At his suggestion we asked the family to re-evaluate their feelings towards the poltergeist by 'coming on board our team'. Instead of regarding themselves as victims, they regarded themselves as researchers. Every time an event occurred, instead of being frightened or annoyed they became pleased because they knew we would be pleased to have another 'item' for research. Within a very short time they reported to us their first period for months without any poltergeist activity.

We believe that part of the reason might be the areas of the brain that are at work, particularly if the poltergeist activity is linked to PK or other paranormal abilities. Those who learn to develop their psychic powers are taught to exercise their right-brain thinking; creativity, intuition, artistic appreciation, and so on. When the 'victims' become researchers we are encouraging them to use their left-brain functions; they become analytical. Switching to this mode of thinking may be what assists in diminishing the poltergeist presence.

Poltergeist activity, and more importantly possession (often now called possession syndrome), may reflect conditions of the mind. There is some debate as to what part is played by multiple personality syndrome in cases of possession and exorcism. This point is examined in the section on 'Possession' in this book (see page 238). Canon Walker commented in an interview with us that although he believes in spiritual powers it is important 'not to turn them into "magical" beings'. He confirmed the position set out in Terry White's book *The Sceptical Occultist*, 'My own view of exorcism is that it is not driving out spiritual entities from outside a person but exorcising deep unhealed parts of the unconscious which manifest themselves in unusual ways.'

F

FAIRIES

Cultures around the British Isles have legends of little people; Irish leprechauns, Cornish pixies, Scottish kelpies, and so on. The English tend to use the term 'fairies' for their 'little folk', though the term is misleading in that context, since it is also used to embrace a whole range of good and bad entities, many human sized, some even giants.

The little people are said to inhabit the earth, invisible to all but the clairvoyant. It is argued that others may see them sometimes, when they are 'tuned in', or when the little folk want to be seen.

Prominent researcher Hilary Evans described fairies, 'Fairies are real entities with at least a quasi-physical nature and possessing the capability of autonomous action; they are, however, dependent for their capability of being perceived – and perhaps for the physicality of their existence altogether – on some subconscious mental process on the part of the percipient.'

The majority of fairy folk are said to be beautiful and helpful to humans. But the folklore includes that of changelings; some fairies have a liking for human babies, which are much prettier than the fairy babies, and they are substituted just after birth. In earlier centuries, unfit or ugly babies may have been believed to be fairy changelings, and left to die.

Fairies are often said to help around the home and in return are grateful for small gifts of food, and the like. The folklore changes from one area to another however; for example, brownies are said to leave a house immediately if clothes are given.

Some folklore holds that sightings of fairies can be a

foretelling of death. The Washer-by-the-Ford, an ugly buck-toothed hag seen washing bloodstained clothes, is reputed to be seen before a violent death or deaths. The Irish banshee's keening foretells of tragedy.

Reports these days are more likely to be of nature spirits or elementals. Nature spirits were seen by the Findhorn settlers. These spirits gave botanical advice and help that enabled vegetables to be cultivated, such as forty-pound cabbages. A similar report comes from Perelandra, south-west of Washington DC. This site of the Center for Nature Research was set up in the 1970s by Machaelle Small Wright, who also claims to be in touch with nature spirits.

The Cottingley Fairies
No item on fairies would be complete without mention of the Cottingley fairies, which were photographed in 1917.

Two children in Yorkshire, Elsie Wright and Frances Griffiths, claimed they had photographed fairies. The pictures were sent to Arthur Conan Doyle. He never met the two girls, but he sent a friend to interview them and on examining the photographs he published, in *The Coming of the Fairies*, a confirmation that he believed the pictures were genuine.

Both girls claimed they had seen fairies several times in a beck at Cottingley in Yorkshire. Unable to convince their parents, they set out with a camera to photograph them. The first pictures were taken in 1917. Further photographs were taken in 1920.

Eastman Kodak's spokesman claimed the photographs were visibly faked and noted that the fairies were dressed in contemporary Paris fashions.

In 1977 a researcher Fred Gettings came across pictures of fairies in *Princess Mary's Gift Book*, published in 1914, which looked very similar to the ones photographed by the girls. The arrangement of limbs and body posture of one figure in particular matched one of the Cottingley fairies very closely.

In 1981, sixty-four years after the photographs were taken, Frances admitted that the photographs were faked; saying, 'From where I was I could see the hatpins holding up the figures. I've always marvelled that anybody took it seriously.'

However, she added, 'The last one's genuine.' Although Frances admitted the photographs were faked, she always insisted the fairies were real, the fake photos being produced only to satisfy the grown-ups!

In the present day . . .
Fairy-folk are not only a thing of the past. Researcher Wesley Downes published a trio of contemporary reports in *Essex Ghosts and Hauntings* (Spring 1994). One such report was of a woman in Lawford, in Essex, who saw on the path ahead of her a 'perfect figure of an elderly lady, standing just over one foot in height'. She was dressed in a bonnet and button-up boots and carried flowers. After smiling at the witness the figure floated away, waving goodbye.

FIREWALKING
Firewalking is an ancient practice usually associated with religion. Pliny the Elder noted it in writings in Rome in the first century as part of the religious observance of the god Apollo. Although found all around the world, it has been prominent in the South Pacific, India and the Far East. In a religious context, firewalking is often used to test the degree to which the firewalker is looked on favourably by the gods. In Hawaii firewalkers are protected by the goddess Pele, for example.

Fire is one of the primary elements involved in ancient religious rites. The Celts used it as part of purification. Ordeal by fire, usually holding red-hot iron, was a form of test for innocence or guilt in Europe during the Middle Ages. Fire in various ways usually forms part of mystic ceremonies. Firewalkers stepped through beds of stone, coals, burning wood or ashes with temperatures measured between 1,000 and 1,500 degrees Fahrenheit.

The Bible contains a description of firewalking. To punish the disrespectful Shadrach, Meshach and Abednego, Nebuchadnezzar threw them into a furnace. The furnace was so hot that those who took the trio to the furnace perished from the heat. But the trio came to no harm; the king watched them walking safely in the furnace and saw that 'the fire had not had any power over the bodies of those men; the hair of their heads was not singed, their mantles were not harmed, and no smell of fire had come upon them'.

A more modern religious festival is the firewalk that takes place in Langadhas in northern Greece each May. The firewalkers fast, preparing for several days before the event, placing themselves into a hypnotic trance or other altered state. The actual firewalk is preceded by a long ceremonial dance involving the ritual sacrifice of animals, which presumably enhances the state of mind of the firewalkers. Firewalkers spend up to twenty minutes walking on and off the 'fire' with no apparent harm.

In 1980 some research was done into the Langadhas firewalk by German scientists from Tübingen. They noted that the fire was around 1,000 degrees Fahrenheit surface temperature. Devices recording the temperature on the soles of the walkers' feet showed only around 350 degrees Fahrenheit though no explanation could be found for this. Another noted phenomenon was that theta activity in the brain increased in one of the firewalkers, suggesting that there was some mental process blocking the pain. (The same team had recorded similar theta activity when a fakir had penetrated his own body with spikes.) This may have been that particular firewalker's personal method of dealing with the firewalk. Two of the German scientists decided to test it out for themselves and walked on to the coals, immediately suffering third-degree burns.

Probably the most famous firewalk recorded in Britain was that of Kuda Bux, an Indian firewalker, in 1935. The psychic researcher Harry Price set up a firewalk in Carshalton in Surrey, aided and supervised by a physicist from the University of London. A twenty-four-foot fire pit was heated to a temperature of some 800 degrees Fahrenheit and Kuda Bux walked through the pit four times. Observers indicated that Kuda Bux took no special precautions, used no artificial aids and cleaned the ash off in between each walk, preventing it acting as an insulation. Throughout the whole event, and afterwards, Bux's feet showed no signs of injury or blistering, nor in fact did they record a rise in temperature. Two spectators – Digby Moynagh and Maurice Cheepen – decided to copy Bux; both ended up badly blistered.

Price later invited another Indian, Ahmed Hussain, who successfully repeated the feat. Price commented, 'Any person with the requisite determination, confidence, and steadiness can walk unharmed over a fire as hot as *800 degrees F*. The experiments proved once and for all that no occult or psychic power, or a specifically-induced mental state, is necessary in a fire-walker'.

One of the observing physicists of Bux's walk, Charles Darling, decided that 'firewalking is really a gymnastic feat' and was sure that Kuda Bux moved at such a pace and in such a manner as to reduce contact with the fire to the bare minimum.

This belief was echoed by magician Ian Rowland when he performed a firewalk for Anglia Television's *The Magic and Mystery Show* in April 1994. Rowland used no tricks, not covering his feet beforehand in any substances. He said, 'You don't need to concentrate the mind to firewalk, you just have to walk quickly enough to make sure the heat doesn't transfer to your feet. If you walk too slowly you get burned.'

Dr Jearl Walker, Professor of Physics at Cleveland State University, also did several firewalks, because he believed he knew the 'trick'. But he attributed his successes to the 'Leidenfrost effect'. Johan Leidenfrost noticed that water on a very hot surface evaporates more slowly than that on a cooler surface. Walker discovered the change took place at just over 200 degrees and he decided that was the explanation for firewalking. Sweat forming on the foot of the firewalkers or water picked up from wet or dewy grass prior to walking into the pit formed a cooling insulation which did not evaporate quickly and protected the soles of the firewalkers' feet. Walker took his devotion to physics seriously, walking across a fire pit holding the book *Physics* in his hand. His firewalk was successful, though later attempts were less so.

What do all these people have in common?

The firewalkers at Langadhas have their religious faith, Ian Rowland had faith that he had worked out the 'trick', Dr

Walker had faith in physics. The common denominator was that they all believed that they would be safe for whatever reason; their belief in something is the common factor. Contrast with that the various observers who have decided to 'have a go' themselves, all of whom had got themselves burned. They had no reason to believe that they were going to succeed, and they did not.

It is possible that a firm conviction in the ability to firewalk sets up the mental processes that change the body's physiology sufficiently to protect it. An extreme claim, but one that we feel can be supported, at least by circumstantial evidence at present, from a subject assisting us in experimentation in this area.

Philip Walton was injured in a school chemistry lab experiment, with the result that he lost the ability to sense pain in his palms. His work involves him in situations where he frequently receives burns to the upper arms but he does not blister. His belief is that blistering is psychosomatic, that if you believe you will blister, you do. He even conducted one experiment following a programme on the radio which told people how to respond if they were burned. He followed the advice exactly, for the first time treating his burn in the way other people would do, and blistered very badly. However, normally his skin just goes a bit red despite contact with some very high temperatures. 'Because I had concentrated on it, I felt it more,' he said. Philip commented, 'The pain bit isn't really there. It's not a matter of turning it off, it just isn't there. If I think about it it turns on more, but as long as I don't think about it, I think I have overcome my fear of pain, and therefore pain itself.'

The question is one of when the tissue damages. Philip has held his hands motionless in a red-hot fire for several seconds but skin damage does not occur. He has even been forewarned on some occasions by smelling the burning of his flesh, but even then has found it only 'mildly singed', not blistered. So if the firewalker is sufficiently protected from fear by his belief and can anaesthetise himself to the pain using some kind of hypnotic or altered state, the firewalk becomes relatively safe at even a moderate pace of walking. (One individual blocked pain by self-hypnosis prior to an un-anaesthetised vasectomy operation, and even, according to his surgeon, controlled his blood flow.) The severe blistering which has been reported in the case of people tentatively 'trying their hand' at firewalking would, according to Philip's logic, be psychosomatic; they blister because they expect to blister.

In Father Herbert Thurston's *Physical Phenomena of Mysticism* published in 1952, he relates the account of a firewalk in Mysore, southern India, in 1921 or 1922, which was witnessed by a Catholic bishop who recorded the story. The bishop, Mgr. Despatures, took pains to ensure that there was no trickery. At the designated time the Mohammedan in charge of the occasion physically pushed a reluctant servant into the pit. No doubt frightened and horrified, the servant struggled to get out of the pit and then 'suddenly the look of terror on his face gave place to an astonished smile, and he proceeded to cross the trench lengthwise, without haste and as if he were taking a constitutional, beaming contentedly upon those who were standing round on either side of him. His feet and legs were perfectly bare.' Encouraged by this, 200 people walked over the embers. The head of the Maharaja's police force and a civil engineer went through, commenting, 'We felt we were in a furnace, but the fire did not burn us.' Mgr. Despatures concluded that the fire was real but had somehow 'lost its power of injuring those who crossed it' and concluded, 'I am forced to believe in the influence of some spiritual agency which is not God.'

It is tempting here to consider that the people who actually did the firewalk had no belief or faith that would protect them. However, the charismatic personality of the Mohammedan may have been sufficient for them to believe and trust in him enough to create their mental protection. Arguable, but consider the outcome of a repeat performance two weeks later; the Mohammedan warned that no others should attempt the firewalk, but three pushed their way in. All were badly burned.

The most modern 'use' of firewalking is as a positive enforcement technique for self development and consciousness-raising courses. In 1985 one such group completed a firewalk chanting the *mantra*, 'Cool, wet grass, cool, wet grass . . .' Most had no ill effects and a few only slight blistering. John McElrow, who did a firewalk in 1969, commented, 'It was exhilarating in a way that cannot be compared to any other experience I have ever had.'

FLIGHT 19

In May 1991 a team of explorers in the Bermuda Triangle area located five TBM Avengers in 750 feet of water some ten miles off the Florida coast. It appeared for a time that a forty-five year mystery was about to be solved. Flight 19 had been located. However, it was subsequently discovered that these were not the planes of Flight 19 but five of the other 100 Avengers to be found sunken in the area, the result of military target exercises. Flight 19 therefore remains lost; one of the most enduring mysteries of the Bermuda Triangle.

Those who believe that the Bermuda Triangle is an area of paranormal mystery, of strange forces and alien intelligences have anchored much of their argument on the loss of Flight 19 and a series of 'quotations' from radio transmissions from the crew which are very difficult to substantiate and which are, if not downright fiction, probably the result of hearsay and Chinese whispers rather than specific research.

By the same token, those who seek to demolish the Bermuda Triangle as any sort of mystery at all have also anchored their arguments on Flight 19.

Flight 19 consisted of five Navy Grumman TBM-3 Avenger torpedo bomber planes. They were on a training flight which left the US naval air station at Fort Lauderdale in Florida at between 14.00 and 14.10 Eastern Standard Time on 5 December 1945. The flight instructor and leader of Flight 19 was Lt Charles Taylor. Four of the planes had a full crew complement of three, one plane had only two, as one assignee to the flight pulled out at the last minute. Although it was a training mission, the pilots and crew were experienced aviators. Each had logged around 350 hours, including over 50 in Avengers. Taylor had over 2,500 flying hours to his credit. We contacted the RAF at Henlow to confirm whether 300 hours represented adequate experience for such a flight. We were assured that it did.

The flight was to be a routine training exercise to fly a

triangular route from Fort Lauderdale towards the Bahamas and returning to Fort Lauderdale naval air station. The planes carried sufficient fuel for a flight of approximately 1,100 miles, far longer than the anticipated flight duration of just over 300 miles. At average flying speed in average conditions the fuel supply should have allowed Flight 19 to stay airborne until 20.00 hours Eastern Standard Time, a total potential flying time of six hours. The flight should have taken approximately two hours.

Weather conditions at take-off were clear. The first part of the mission is known to have been successful. The first sign of problems arose at approximately 15.40 to 15.45. Lt Robert F. Cox, a Senior Flight Instructor at Fort Lauderdale naval air station, was flying with his own students near the base when he overheard on the radio frequency reserved for training flights what appears to have been communication between Lt Taylor and Captain Powers, one of the pilots, indicating that they were lost. Cox heard, 'I don't know where we are, we must have got lost after that last turn.'

Cox asked what was causing the problem and Lt Taylor indicated, 'Both my compasses are out.' Here we have one of Flight 19's genuine mysteries, and one that has been glossed over by its detractors. There was no indication in the conversation between Taylor and Powers that Powers' compass was working either. On being asked specifically for a compass reading Powers admitted they were lost. That both compasses on Lt Taylor's plane should malfunction may be coincidence enough, but it appears no plane on the flight was able to offer a compass reading, suggesting that some external force may have affected the compasses. Such a force is not unknown in the Bermuda Triangle or elsewhere, and indeed instrument failure features in a large number of Triangle reports. There has been a suggestion that Taylor handed over the navigation of the flight to a plane with an effective compass and this may be so; certainly he handed over the flight, at one point asking Powers what course he was taking.

Cox gave Taylor instructions for locating Fort Lauderdale by putting the sun over the port wing and flying up the coast. Cox also indicated he would fly south to meet Flight 19. But Cox soon noticed that transmissions from Flight 19 were fading, though they should have been getting stronger as the planes approached each other. The problem is almost certainly that Lt Taylor believed himself to be over the Florida Keys and, flying north, should have been approaching Cox's plane at Fort Lauderdale, but in fact Taylor was probably over the Bahamas, and flying north was taking him directly away from Cox. (A later fix established the flight at this location.) This fading transmission is the strongest clue that Taylor and the others were totally lost.

The planes were therefore flying over open ocean probably parallel to the Florida peninsula off to the left. Taylor instructed the planes to fly east which would take them directly away from the Florida peninsula into the Atlantic. Taylor apparently did this because he believed that he was in the Gulf of Mexico with Florida to his right. He had been flying without compass, without clocks, possibly without a watch, without a flight plan (he had apparently regarded the training exercise as so simple he had not even taken his plotting board with him). He had clearly become very disoriented.

Several of the phrases attributed to Flight 19 which have become the cornerstone of the mystery are explainable, given the nature of the disorientation. For example, 'the ocean doesn't look right' may only refer to Taylor expecting lighter blue coastal waters rather than the deeper blue ocean water he was seeing. The more extraordinary statements of which the most famous is the ending of the last known broadcast, 'Don't come after me', with, 'it looks like they are from outer space', appear to have been introduced by speculation at a later date and there is no evidence of this in the actual transmissions from the flight.

It is held that Taylor acted calmly throughout, and indeed the official report blames unexpected weather conditions and praises his attempts to save the flight despite adversity. However, the fact that he made many bad decisions, including zigzagging around trying to find the Florida peninsula, are perhaps more suggestive of a person under stress than is generally acknowledged.

Almost certainly the flight either voluntarily ditched or

1. Alien abduction, kidnapping by 'greys', extra-terrestrials, such as depicted in this reconstruction, is reported from all around the world. *Credit: John and Anne Spencer*

2. Spontaneous faces are reported appearing in photographs around the world. In this photograph the 'face' appears to the left of the centre figure's head. Ghost or trick of the light? *Credit: Edna Barlow*

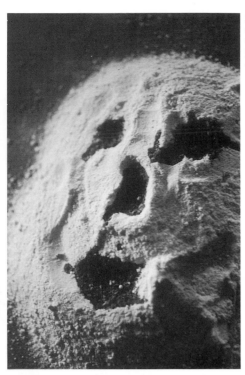

3. 'The face' that spontaneously formed during the Tony Elms poltergeist case. *Credit: Manfred Cassirer*

4. Tony Elms (left) who was 'persecuted' by a poltergeist pictured at the Kentish Garden Guild, where the activities occurred. *Credit: Manfred Cassirer*

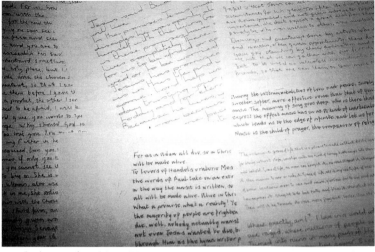

5. Automatic writings. The picture shows a sample of the wide variety of handwritings all channelled by one person – the stigmatic and healer Heather Woods. One witness described watching her writing at 'abnormal speed'. *Credit: John and Anne Spencer*

6. A big cat photographed in a garden in Oxfordshire. *Credit: Pat Williams*

7. Comparative photograph of Pat Williams taken at the location where she photographed the big cat some months earlier (part of the original tree had been removed). *Credit: John and Anne Spencer*

8. Rumours of crash retrieved flying saucers held in secret American military locations have abounded throughout the fifty years of the 'Flying Saucer' mystery. *Credit: Martin J Bower (sci-fi model maker)*

9. Doug Bower and Dave Chorley, who claimed to have created many of the major crop circle pictograms in the UK, photographed at night by night vision equipment. *Credit: John MacNish*

10. A huge crop circle pictogram. Froxfield 1994. The size of the formation is shown by the people riding bicycles within the flattened area of crop at the foot of the picture. *Credit: John and Jayne MacNish*

11. Crystals. The 'new age' brought claims of crystal energy, crystal healing and other properties to the fore. *Credit: John and Anne Spencer*

12. Dolphins. Believed by many to display spiritual and healing effects on humans. *Credit: John and Anne Spencer*

13. John Spencer (right) being instructed in the art of dowsing by Swedish dowser Arne Groth during a UFO-abduction investigation north of Stockholm. *Credit: John and Anne Spencer*

14. The Loch Ness Monster 'Nessie'. This 'surgeon's photograph', now an admitted hoax, is still the best known image of a type of creature said to inhabit lakes the world over. *Credit: The Official Loch Ness Monster Exhibition Centre*

15. Philip Steff, a rescue medium from Bath, who has 'cured' poltergeist activity by sending troubled spirits 'into the light'. *Credit: Philip Steff*

16. TV Reporter Kate Glass starting out on her firewalk during the filming of Anglia TV's 'Magic and Mystery Show'. 'It was mind over matter,' said Kate, 'I didn't mind so it didn't matter.' *Credit: Kate Glass, Magic and Mystery Show, Anglia TV*

crashed into the ocean when it ran out of fuel somewhere in the Atlantic north of the Bahamas, well off course. They would have ditched in the dark in bad weather and rough seas, and within a short space of time the planes would have sunk. That no trace of the planes was ever found is unfortunate, but probably not a mystery. Most of the search was almost certainly conducted in the wrong place and in any case the sea often does not offer up its clues. There are many cases of known sinkings where debris has not been found.

It is in the search that we discover yet another mystery. One of the search planes sent out was a Martin Mariner seaplane known as Training 49, piloted by Lt Walter Jeffrey. The plane took off shortly before 19.30 hours Eastern Standard Time, but failed to report in one hour later as it should have done. At 19.50 hours crew members of the SS *Gaines Mills* saw an explosion in the air and a plane crashing into the sea. That location ties up quite accurately with the presumed position of Training 49 at that time, and almost certainly the explosion reflected the end of that rescue mission. Unlike the lost flight, therefore, its end does not appear to have been caused by the same difficulties.

However, what did cause the loss of the Martin Mariner? It has been pointed out by some writers that they are unstable planes known as 'flying gas tanks', at risk of ignition from a spark or smoking by a crew member.

Since there were many other search planes in the area before, during and after the Training 49 explosion and indeed other planes in the area at the time of Flight 19's hopeless wanderings, there seems little ground for assuming that the more extreme suggestions of authors such as extraterrestrial kidnapping, trans-dimensional corridors and so on were to blame.

However, the theory outlined in this book in 'Bermuda Triangle' (see page 41) that released deposits of gas could affect both ships and planes could apply here. We know that such deposits could cause instrument disturbance and it appears to have been the loss of his compasses which first caused Lt Taylor's difficulty; we also know that such gases are highly inflammable and if the Training 49 flight went through such a cloud it could have caused the explosion.

Flight 19 and the loss of its rescue plane is therefore probably a mystery solved; but one that cannot be finally put to rest until the remains of the planes are located.

FLOOD MYTHS OF THE WORLD

Probably the most widely known version of the flood story is that of Noah and his Ark. The Lord decided to punish a wicked mankind with a great flood which would engulf the earth. Noah, however, was a righteous man and God chose him to be saved along with selected examples of other living things in a huge Ark. God gave specific instructions for the building of the Ark which then rode out the floods and, when the water subsided, came to rest 'upon the mountains of Ararat'. Noah, his wife, his three sons and their wives, together with pairs of animals, were then instructed to begin restocking and re-populating the earth.

In fact the most ancient version of the great flood story in that locality comes from the ancient myths of Mesopotamia and is so similar to the story in the Bible that it either has the same historical roots or was the foundation for the biblical tale. In Mesopotamian mythology four gods planned the flood and a fifth god, Ea, revealed the secret plan to a man named Ut-Napishtin. Ut-Napishtin was told to build a boat in order that he should be saved. He built the boat according to precise measurements that the god gave him. The boat was to contain provisions of silver and gold, wild animals and his own family. Then there was a storm which lasted for seven days and seven nights. At the end of the storm the boat came to rest on a mountain. Ut-Napishtin first sent out a dove, then a swallow and then a raven. It was when the raven did not return to the boat that Ut-Napishtin decided the waters must have subsided. Ut-Napishtin made a sacrifice to the gods thanking them for his salvation, rather in the same way that the Old Testament of the Bible indicates that Noah built an altar to the Lord as one of the first things he did on leaving the Ark.

Greek mythology from the same general area has a similar tale where the Greek hero Deukalion and his wife Pyrrha survived a flood sent by Zeus to destroy all mankind.

A wide variety of ancient cultures have a great flood story associated with their origins or with the origins of the world as they understood it: Native Australian aboriginal legends contain the story of the rainbow snake that swallowed and drowned people during a great flood; ancient Chinese writings such as the 'hill and river classic' tell the story of a great flood arising from a battle between the fourth emperor Yao and the monster named Kung Kung; the Tango people of Mandang Province, Papua New Guinea, have a myth of a brother and sister pair of orphans saved from a gigantic flood by climbing into a coconut tree, leaving all of humanity to die and these two to mate to re-populate the earth.

The widespread legends of Mithras (his Roman name; he is Mythra in Iran and Mytra, a Vedic God of Light in Hinduism) holds that he came from the east, from Persia, in the first century AD, and relates that he saved mankind from a great flood.

Hopi Indian traditions contain a story with certain parallels to the biblical story of Noah and his Ark. In Hopi tradition, when mankind had become licentious a great flood engulfed them and people escaped by following the Spider Woman up reeds, pine trees and a sunflower to reach above the flood. As the people reached safety, so the Mocking Bird assigned each to a specific tribe. In the aftermath of Noah's voyage his descendants formed one race and one language, but the Lord scattered them over the face of the earth and gave them all different languages.

In Aztec legend the first of the ancient ages was the age of water; men were invented by Toltec and Quetzalcoatl and then, when everything was overtaken by water, the people were turned into fish.

In Hinduism Manu, a son of the Sun and the ancestor of the human race, was saved in a ship from a deluge which swept away all other creatures. During the flood his ship was towed to safety on a mountain by a fish (later identified as Vishnu).

A close parallel of the great flood story of Noah and his Ark comes from an area far from the Middle East; it is a legend from South American Inca tradition. The traditional place of creation in Inca mythology is the locality around Lake Titicaca. The god

Viracocha created the earth and the people on it, but when they disobeyed him he destroyed them in a great flood which engulfed the entire earth. Only two people survived the flood, a man and a woman who remained in a box and who, when the flood subsided, were carried by the wind to nearby Tihuanaco where Viracocha lived. There Viracocha created all the peoples of all the nations, giving each their own language and songs.

That the flood story should be so widespread around the world suggests two main possibilities: either there was a general, severe raising of water levels at some time in the ancient past (and the last ice age may have ended not much more than 15,000 years ago) or the story is pure mythology, told and retold as people travelled about the world. The similarity of details in widespread accounts such as the biblical and Inca stories indicates the probability of some re-telling of traditions. Certainly the work of explorers such as Thor Heyerdahl has indicated that there may have been more cross-pollination of peoples and their mythologies than was once believed.

FLYING DUTCHMAN

The ghostly ship the *Flying Dutchman* was seen in 1923 by four seamen, one of whom made this report. 'About 0.15 a.m. we noticed a strange "light" on the port bow; . . . it was a very dark night, overcast, with no moon. We looked at this through binoculars and the ship's telescope, and made out what appeared to be the hull of a sailing ship, luminous with two distinct masts . . . no sails were visible, but there was a luminous haze between the masts. There were no navigation lights, and she appeared to be coming close to us and at the same speed as ourselves. When first sighted she was about two to three miles away, and when she was about a half mile of us she suddenly disappeared.

'There were four witnesses of this spectacle, the second officer, a cadet, the helmsman and myself. I shall never forget the second officer's startled expression – "My God, Stone, it's a ghost ship." '

In 1939 the *Flying Dutchman* was seen off the shore by sixty people relaxing on the beach of Glencairn in South Africa. The ship reportedly had its sails full, although there was no wind felt. The *British South Africa Annual* of 1939 reported, 'With uncanny volition the ship sailed steadily on as the Glencairn beach folk, shaken from their lethargy, stood about keenly discussing the whys and wherefores of the vessel which seemed to be bent on self-destruction somewhere on the sands of Strandfontein. Just as the excitement reached its climax, however, the mystery ship vanished into thin air as strangely as it had come.'

It was speculated by some that what was seen was a form of reflection, the image of another ship perhaps hundreds of miles away, refracted in the light. But to the sighters this was no answer for they had seen a ship from the seventeenth century, not at all like the ships of the nineteenth century.

The phantom ship was seen again round South Africa in 1942, when four people saw it sail into Table Bay and disappear behind Robben Island.

The most famous sighting is surely that which took place in 1881 when the then Prince George (later King George V) was serving as a midshipman on HMS *Inconstant*. The *Inconstant* was near Australia when the Prince and other crew members saw the *Flying Dutchman*, and noted the vision in the ship's log.

'At 4 a.m. "The Flying Dutchman" crossed our bows. She emitted a strange phosphorescent light as of a phantom ship all aglow, in the midst of which the masts, spars and sails of a brig 200 yards distant stood out in strong relief as she came up on the port bow, where the officer on watch from the bridge saw her, as did the quarter deck midshipman, who was sent forward at once to the forecastle, but on arriving there no vestige nor sign whatever of any material ship was to be seen either near or right away to the horizon, the night being clear and the sea calm.'

The first seaman on the *Inconstant* to witness the phantom ship died the next day when he fell from the rigging.

The original ship on which this legend is based has not been identified, and different early stories can be found. The most commonly held origin is that of a ship sailing round the Cape of Good Hope. The ship sailed into a terrible storm, the crewmen wanted to head for the shore and find a safe port, but the stubborn captain would not allow this and refusing to give in to fear, he ordered the sailors to continue. As the storm grew worse the captain challenged God to sink his ship (the builders of the *Titanic* did much the same!). For this blasphemy the captain was condemned to sail the seas forever with his phantom crew.

The captain is said to have been a Dutchman, Hendrik van der Decken, but other names too have been put forward and these include another Dutchman, Bernard Fokke, who was said to have supernatural aid on his most remarkable voyages. Both captains were known for their seamanship and both seem to have disappeared along with their ships without trace.

FROGS, FISH AND OTHER FALLS

1983 was a good year for falls. There were crabs in Sussex, small chunks of coke in Dorset, and pennies in Norfolk.

It seems that anomalous small objects, live or dead, have been falling from our skies since records began. The earliest report comes from Greece in the year AD 200, when a heavy fall of frogs polluted water supplies and blocked walkways.

Many small animals have been reported. Frogs and fish are probably the most common, other creatures have included an alligator that fell in Indiana in May 1911, and an ice-wrapped turtle in Mississippi which was noted in 1894. That creatures fall from the skies is not in doubt; one frog fall was described as bounding off umbrellas, and men were described shaking them from their hat brims. It does not seem that they could have been thrown from buildings either; many were found on the roofs of buildings.

In Bournemouth in 1948 golfers found herrings showering onto a golf course after a storm. On the other hand, in September 1969 the streets of Punta Gorda in Florida were filled with hundreds of golf balls that had apparently fallen from the sky.

Perhaps more bizarre were the flakes of meat that fell slowly on to a field in Kentucky in 1876. One investigator was brave enough to taste the meat and described it as 'mutton or venison'. Other meat fell in Brazil in 1968.

There are many reports of seeds and grain falling, but also other small objects, and money. Charles Fort, who collected reports on curious phenomena, listed coins falling in Trafalgar Square. In December 1968 between forty and fifty pennies were reported to have fallen in Ramsgate.

Theories are lacking, and phenomenologists tend to end up with fascinating lists that offer very little in the way of understanding or meaning. The most popular explanation is that the items are being picked up by whirlwinds and later dropped as the wind speed dies down. This would account for such reports as the pink sand which covered north London in the early 1970s. It was traced to the Sahara and had been carried on fierce winds. Such a theory might also account for the straw that fell all over Orpington High Street. Many of the animal reports may be accountable this way, some believe frogs and fish could be scooped up by fierce winds and then disgorged. The aerial journey cannot have been long in all cases; some of the fish were still alive when found.

On the other hand since many items, such as coins, could be of a personal nature, it is surprising that there are no reports of anyone having items 'lifted' by the whirlwinds.

The whirlwind theory would seem to fit in certain respects; the animals that are reported falling do tend to be those that live in large clusterings. The falls also appear to happen at times of storms and electrical atmospherics. Against the theory is the fact that each fall seems so discerning; all frogs, all fish, and so on. There is no sign of debris, branches, seaweed, etc.

It is just possible that if a variety of items were picked up, the motions within the whirlwinds might 'sort' the objects into sizes in the same way that a variety of sizes of sand grains dropped in oils will sort themselves out as they drift downwards, and settle in order.

Reports of metal falling from the skies sound reasonable enough; there are thousands of objects and bits of debris floating around in decaying orbits, all of which will re-enter the earth's atmosphere sometime and some of which will remain intact to the ground. When Skylab broke up in 1979, fragments hit the Australian mainland. But what of the fall of copper fragments in New Haven, Connecticut? They fell in 1953, pre-dating the first object in orbit by four years.

The substance most often reported to fall from the sky is lumps of ice. These may have some simple explanation. It is possible that some are the remains of meteorites. Ice can form on the outside of, and fall from, aircraft. Aeroplane toilets have been known to leak, the resultant fall is identifiable by the ice that lands being stained by chemicals. But there are also many other falls of ice that test the imagination; one report is of perfect 'household-refrigerator-shaped' cubes.

The whirlwind theory might explain the peaches that fell in Louisiana in 1961, but not the hazelnuts that fell all over cars in Bristol, England in 1977. Hazelnuts were not in season at the time.

There are many stories of stones and small rocks, in one case no less than 14,000 bits of rock fell in one area of Arizona in 1912. Some of these reports may represent rocks that have been 'picked' up; others could be meteorites. Apparently 1,000 tons of meteorite material falls to the earth every day, a proportion of it over land.

There are reports of dead birds that have fallen. Clearly there is no mystery about birds being in the sky. But that a whole flock can be flying along and all die at once is mysterious. In 1896, at Baton Rouge, Louisiana, hundreds of dead birds fell to the streets.

Nevertheless, there are eyewitness accounts of the whole process from English reports. During the Warminster UFO reports of the 1960s and 1970s a gamekeeper on the evening of 11 April 1964 saw a flock of wood pigeons roosting in Southleigh Wood. They were disturbed by a loud sound (often reported; it came to be known as the 'Warminster Sound') and flew into the air. Suddenly several of them dropped dead with no visible signs of injury. During the same 'flap' Mr and Mrs Bill Manson in Hillwood Lane, Warminster heard noises beating against the roof; in the morning they found the garden littered with several small mice all burned and riddled with holes.

Reports get into the bizarre end of the scale when we hear of one fish fall where the fish were ready cooked. Blood, slime, 'goo' and glue-like substances have all fallen. Birds regurgitating material have been offered as an explanation. A substance described as 'warm, sticky and somewhat like blood' burnt the hand of a Mr Mootz and apparently caused his peach trees to die.

Discounting the whirlwind, there have been attempts to tie in these spontaneous falls with apports, or poltergeist attacks. Nails, stones, and other small items have been reported bombarding houses. In February 1979 just three houses in a road were all covered in sticky mustard-and-cress seed from no obvious source. But not only were only the three houses 'hit', but one of them had been 'hit' the previous year. Perhaps investigation should look less at what falls, and more at who it falls on. To date, no such structured research – if any is even possible – has been done.

One explanation probably will never suffice, yet there can only be a limited number of explanations for a myriad of strange things appearing from the sky and then falling out of it. No subject ever seemed better equipped to demonstrate what Johannes Kepler meant when he said, 'The diversity of the phenomenon of Nature is so great, the treasures hidden in the heavens so rich, precisely in order that the human mind shall never be lacking in fresh nourishment.'

G

GHOSTS

Ghosts or apparitions are arguably the most commonly reported form of paranormal experience; almost everyone knows someone who claims to have seen a ghost, even if they have no such experience of their own. Certainly ghosts are the best known of paranormal manifestations in the general public's mind.

The most popular view of ghosts is that they represent the spirits of dead people. While that may be the explanation for many ghosts, there are many other explanations needed to encompass the whole of ghost phenomena.

The term 'ghost' is a very loose one, covering a wide range of phenomena that may or may not be related. Ghosts, apparitions or similar phenomena may be conveniently divided up into 'groupings' with identifiable characteristics. Many of these are separately examined in other sections of this book: see 'Bi-locations', page 55; 'Crisis Apparitions, page 80; 'Doubles', page 103; 'Phantom Hitchhikers', page 224; 'Poltergeists', page 233; 'Spectral Armies', page 277; 'Time Slips', page 303. In this section we examine the basic reports of ghosts.

The ghost of Sir Walter Raleigh is frequently seen walking in the Tower of London. In 1983, for example, a yeoman in the Byward Tower saw him for a short period of time, after which Raleigh vanished.

This is an example of a 'recordings-type' ghost, so called because such images appear to be only recordings of past images being replayed. There is no sense of interaction with the surroundings, or with the observers. Whether or not certain types of ghosts and apparitions actually are recordings or not is debatable, but certainly there are many ghosts that demonstrate such characteristics.

A good example of such a ghost is the 'New Year's Eve Nun' who was first reported in the late 1930s at a (then) girls' school in Cheltenham, Gloucester. A nurse, Margo Smith, and the headmaster together saw the image of a nun at the edge of the playground. The nun sat down, though there was no chair, and remained in the seated position for some time. The following year they saw her, again on New Year's Eve; she was sitting down again. On this occasion the headmaster got close enough before she disappeared to determine that her image was three-dimensional and well-defined. The fact that she was in a sitting position where there was no chair suggests, though, that if events can be embedded in some way then this was such a case. Perhaps there had once been a chair or bench there that the nun had used and somehow 'left' a trace of herself that reappeared periodically. There is no suggestion that her 'presence' was there; merely a replay of an earlier occurrence.

Something of this type of definition appears to have been in the mind of Frederic W.H. Myers, a founder of the Society for Psychical Research during his researches. He defined a ghost as 'a manifestation of persistent personal energy, or as an indication that some kind of force is being exercised after death which is in some way connected with a person previously known on earth' (from *Human Personality and Its Survival of Bodily Death*). But Myers did not believe there was any purpose to the ghost; it was just a fragment of energy left 'floating around'. Researcher Hans Holzer, similarly, defines ghosts as 'surviving emotional memories of people'.

T.C. Lethbridge had a slightly different suggestion, but one which is compelling in certain cases. He suggested that a ghost may be a projection from a sighter which then becomes recorded in the landscape and is later 'played back' when it could be perceived as a ghost. In this situation the recording is not 'laid down' by the person now being perceived as a ghost, but rather by someone acting as a 'camera' who sees the individual and 'embeds' the image in the environment. Such a suggestion would offer a tentative explanation of why certain ghosts 'switch off' or disappear at certain points – perhaps the sighter just stopped looking, or walked away. The theory could even be extended to auditory 'hauntings'; perhaps the 'camera' in that circumstance was not watching the scene, but hearing it and embedding an audio-recording. For example, when Detective Elvet Price stayed in a Welsh hotel in 1969 he awoke in the night to hear banging, choking and gasping noises, but he saw nothing. The noises stopped when he switched on the lights. He discovered that in 1920 the landlord's wife had been murdered in that room; throttled and beaten to death. Had the murder been heard by someone, but not seen?

The theory of recordings to explain unresponsive ghosts does not take into account one problem. There are occasions when a ghost of a relative, say, appears to be acting without purpose or interaction, but is in a location that person never occupied. For example, Harry Conway told us that his dead father-in-law had appeared outside the windows of their new home, even though he had never visited that place. The figure, easily recognisable to Harry, walked past the windows and out of sight. Furthermore the family were on the first floor, the ghost was walking outside the windows where there was no balcony – in thin air.

We must consider that such a ghost might have been the spirit of the father-in-law returning to the family. Although there was no interaction on this occasion, Harry told us of several times when he felt his father-in-law's presence. That this ghost was a projection from Harry's mind is also possible; perhaps Harry constructed a visual image to support the other, more interactive, feelings. Constructed visual hallucinations are examined below.

Quite different in character from 'recordings ghosts' are those which do interact with their environment, and often with the sighter. When ghosts act in this way they suggest presence and awareness, perhaps even purpose.

One example of an interactive ghost from our files comes from Sue. Her daughter, Sarah, saw the ghost of Sue's deceased boyfriend, George. George was not Sarah's father, but they had had a good relationship. One day Sarah saw George in their house. She had no doubts about identifying him and passed on messages from George to Sue, who was unable to see him.

Donald Campbell had several beneficial 'encounters' with his dead father, Sir Malcolm Campbell. On one well-known occasion, he took his father's assurance that all would be well on a dangerous record-breaking run in the Bluebird car. On other occasions he was convinced that Sir Malcolm took over the controls of his Bluebird boat. There are many other examples of such 'protective' encounters, airmen whose planes were 'taken over' by dead flyers, and the famous case of the ghosts of Flight 401 that crashed in the Florida Everglades, who vowed to protect similar aircraft in the future, and were seen by many people on several identical aircraft, many of which used parts recycled from the crashed plane.

Interactive ghosts are probably the most complex in explanation. Several possibilities need to be considered.

A person in stress, or danger, might 'create' an entity to help him or her out of the situation. Perhaps most classical is the lonely, lost mountain-climber who sees a guiding figure who leads him to safety, only to then disappear. Campbell's feelings of the presence of his father may come into this category. There is here the possibility of a needs-based hallucination; projecting the image to give comfort, company, and perhaps even encouragement.

But what if the hallucination also provides information not apparently known to the sighter? In some special cases perhaps there is genuinely information that comes from elsewhere. However in many cases it seems possible that the created hallucination embodies subconscious knowledge. As a way of accessing this data, and effecting a rescue, the subconscious may project an image which then relays the data back to the person's conscious mind, i.e. he sees it apparently through his eyes and hears the guidance apparently through his ears. And he follows the advice given – which is actually based on his own intuitive assessment of the situation – and then forever believes he was protected and guided by a ghost.

A ghost could also be considered as a projection by the agent of himself or herself to a place where he or she feels needed. Such a theory may explain doubles seen at a distance, or crisis apparitions (see 'Doubles', page 103; 'Crisis Apparitions', page 80). Such a ghost could then be a telepathic message perceived visually.

The motive for seeing ghosts might have to be considered in any attempt to understand them. Sighters might argue that they are victims, in the sense that they just happen to be there and see them. However, there is evidence that some people are more prone to seeing ghosts than others. Perhaps they have a need. We have considered above the needs of those in danger for whom the ghost might represent a lifeline. But we might broaden that considerably to the fact that we all face inevitable death. Perhaps ghosts for some represent the lifeline to safety when we die – proof that we shall continue in some way. That might be reason enough to see ghosts.

What this examination shows, as all ghost researchers know, is that the answer to the mystery of ghosts is not going to be supplied by one answer; it is probably a variety of several different phenomena all umbrella-ed under the term 'ghost' because of certain common characteristics. We must look more closely at the differences than at what the phenomena have in common if we are to unbolt this question.

H

HEXHAM HEADS
The Hexham Heads are a phenomenon in their own right, though probably representative of a number of objects, particularly skulls, that seem to attract a variety of paranormal effects. It is not any one particular feature of the Hexham Heads that makes them fascinating so much as their having collected what might be regarded as 'the full set' of paranormal effects.

The heads are carved stone, with rough shapes of eyes, nose and mouth visible. They are tiny carvings, only four or five centimetres in diameter. The one designated 'male' – for no obvious reason – is grey and speckled with quartz. The 'female' is slightly smaller.

They were found by eleven-year-old Colin Robson in 1972, in the garden of his house in Rede Avenue, Hexham, a village in the far north of England, not far from Hadrian's Wall. Poltergeist activity then started; the heads themselves were reported to move spontaneously, and objects were unaccountably broken. An apport of glass showering on to Colin's sister's bed disturbed the girl so much that she moved out of her room. Strange luminosity was reported in the garden, allegedly where the heads had been dug up. Almost immediately the Robson family reported hauntings; sightings of shadowy, inhuman shapes, half-man, half-animal. It could perhaps be argued that imagination was running wild in the family, and perhaps it was, but if so then it affected a neighbour. Ellen Dodd was in her own house, in bed with her son who was unwell, when he reported that he was being 'touched' by something. Mrs Dodd suddenly saw an animal-like shape on all fours walking around in the room, and even touching her. She described it as werewolf-like. Mrs Dodd demanded to be, and was, rehoused by the council. In the Robson house, the children were so disturbed that the family left the house. After the heads were taken away, and the house exorcised, the phenomena ceased.

Dr Anne Ross, at a Newcastle museum, took charge of the heads for study. She was not unaffected, feeling the presence of something she related to the heads. Considering her museum background, handling and studying ancient and strange artefacts should have presented no fears for her; we might assume that she was feeling something real, albeit unexplained.

While she had the heads at home she herself reported a shadowy figure six feet tall, half-man, half-wolf, not unlike the form reported by the family that had discovered them. Nor was it just shadows on the wall; she followed the figure down the stairs, across her hall, and into the back of her house. Her daughter, Berenice, also saw the figure, running the same route. Mother and daughter, together, also saw the figure, and Dr Ross claims she heard the padding sound of animal feet several times. Other visitors to the house apparently commented on bad feelings they were having there. The Ross's pet cat acted, they believed, anxiously. Poltergeist activity was reported; doors closed mysteriously, without cause.

Dr Ross was no doubt relieved to find a volunteer to take the heads off her hands. A chemist, Dr Don Robins, discovered that they had a high percentage of quartz in them, and believed that perhaps quartz crystals could hold energies that were, possibly, responsible for the effects reported. We have explored a section in this book of vehicle interference during paranormal experiences (see 'Vehicle Interference, page 330); the Hexham Heads provided an example of this. When Robins put the heads in his car the ignition failed and the car would not start. Robins shouted at the heads to 'stop it' and the car started! Robins reported none of the paranormal phenomena that others had witnessed, though he felt the 'uncomfortable' presence of, particularly, the 'female' head.

The heads were thought to be Celtic and nearly 2,000 years old. The Celts followed the Cult of the Head, believing the severed head to have magical qualities. If so, given their location, the Hexham Heads may have acted as guardians at the shrine of a Roman God; the Roman garrison contained many Celts. But a quite different origin was offered by Desmond Craigie, who was a previous occupant of the house. He claimed they were toys he had carved for his daughter. Dr Ross was not so sure of Craigie's claims, believing the heads to be too precisely Celtic. The heads were eventually buried, but they were dug up again after the area around the burial site became the subject of hauntings.

Coincidence arises in the stories of the heads. One might consider that if they are carrying a curse, as they seem to be, then it is coincident they should be discovered in Hexham ('hex' means 'curse'). More particularly, one of the Robson children had himself made a small carved stone head just before the Hexham Heads were found.

Poltergeists, hauntings, werewolves, coincidence, apports, anomalous lights, curses, electromagnetic disturbances: the reports come from a variety of people, and seem consistent enough to merit belief. Whether some of the reported incidents – the EM effects and coincidence particularly – guilt-by-association is possible, some of the reports – the wolf-man figure especially – seem genuinely associated with the heads.

The heads have at present been lost. Possibly when they turn up they will have proved to be the result of further disturbances as yet unexplained to their unsuspecting witnesses.

I

INCORRUPTIBILITY

Bernadette Soubirous of Lourdes, whose vision of the Virgin Mary in 1858 started a world-wide pilgrimage to the site that continues to this day, died in 1879 at the age of thirty-four in the Convent of St Gildard at Nevers. In 1909 her body was exhumed and, according to an eye witness, 'Not the least trace of corruption nor any bad odour could be perceived . . .'

Incorruptibility is a more commonly reported phenomenon than is perhaps appreciated. It tends to be examined in a religious light, presumably because of the special status certain religious figures achieve. This results in such figures being exhumed more than would be typical in the rest of the population, either to re-inter them in special places, exhibit them, or, occasionally, to protect the body from attack.

Incorruption is generally associated with saints, as in the case of St Bernadette. But even amongst saints it is a seemingly random event. Of forty-two saints listed by Father Herbert Thurston, twenty-two were found in a state of preservation that was better than would be expected considering the time since death. Yet we cannot assume that certain saints are any more worthy of a 'blessing' – if that is what it is thought to be – than any others. Some seem actively to have rejected it; St Thérèse of Lisieux hoped not to be incorrupt after her death, and was not.

Incorruption of the body of certain individuals might be the reason for whole beliefs about them to emerge in a few cases. St Catherine of Genoa is believed to have attracted a following, and canonisation, just on that basis. But as Thurston points out of several saints, 'No reasonable person can doubt that these servants of God would have been canonised even if the common law of dust to dust had prevailed . . .'

States of preservation vary. In some cases the whole body is preserved almost as if just asleep, with perhaps a darkening of the skin and shrinking of the eyeballs. In other cases parts of the body are preserved; St Anthony's tongue, for example, was discovered to be red, soft and whole despite the fact that the rest of his body had crumbled to dust.

Certain factors associated with preservation are considered part of the phenomenon: strong perfume emanating from the exhumed body; absence of rigor mortis; bleeding, even years after death; warmth after death; exuding body oils; movement of limbs.

Exuding oils are reported in several cases. The body of St Charbel, after being disinterred, was kept in a chapel. Very soon it was noticed that an oily liquid was oozing from the body. The oozing was so great that the clothes placed on the body needed changing twice a week. Eventually the corpse was placed in a zinc-lined coffin and bricked up. But the oil continued to flow.

It is claimed that Mère Marie Marguerite des Anges prayed to be burnt as a sacrifice to the Blessed Sacrament. After her death her body is alleged to have exuded so much oil that it kept the sanctuary lamp of her convent burning for years.

The question of post-mortem movement reaches extraordinary proportions. Movements of the limbs during the laying out hardly seems extraordinary, even if they are attributed special purpose by the devout. That the leg should move is possible, that it represents raising the foot to be kissed is another matter. But there are claims of extraordinary movements; the motions of giving a blessing for example.

Some bodies are preserved after years in conditions where we might expect a certain amount of preservation; sealed vaults and secure coffins for example. But that is not always the case. Several well-preserved bodies have been exhumed from where they were buried directly into the earth, for example St Thomas of Villanova. But there is some precedence for that in the rare finds of prehistoric figures found preserved. The bodies preserved in peat bogs and ice may not be truly incorruptible, given there is no suggestion that they would not have rotted in other circumstances. But they were in earth, and were preserved.

In Kiev there is a necropolis where seventy-three bodies lay in open coffins, all naturally mummified. At Palermo, Capuchin monks who have died are held in the catacombs, some have been there for up to two hundred years, yet none are skeletal although exposed to the air in the catacombs.

One problem in understanding this phenomenon is that there is very little work in evidence on how fast a body *should* decay, presumably because no one has thought of any practical use for the information. The conditions of burial, the conditions of the grave or vault, the condition of the body at death or burial, perhaps even lesser aspects such as what constituted the last meal and therefore what organic material is inside the body, could all play a part in the calculation of decay.

A second problem in understanding this phenomenon is that it has acquired religious overtones because of the 'sample selected', as pointed out above. There have been no comparable studies done. There have been no 'random exhumations', nor is there quite such an enthusiasm for exhuming evil people whose bodies, for all we know, are as incorrupt as those of the saints.

INCUBUS AND SUCCUBUS

The incubus is a demon that seduces or rapes women. The succubus is the female version, seducing or raping men. The claims of visits by these demons date to before the Bible. In the Middle Ages they were said to be sent to or by witches. An incubus or succubus was sometimes called on to 'make up the numbers' at a sabbat. It has also been thought that a witch can change into one of these beings in order to have sex.

Although these reports at first seem to be a thing of the past, there are reports of a comparable nature in the present day. One or two ghost reports must also be considered. Wesley Downes reports in *Haunted Clacton* the case of a local woman who claimed she had twice been attacked in her bed and raped by a ghost. Apparently she received bruising on her legs from the incident, which suggested to her it was more than a dream. She has apparently successfully warded off further attacks by wearing a crucifix around her neck at night. Downes also reports the case of what seems to have been a succubus. One night the vicar of Langenhoe church woke 'to find himself in the cold embrace of a naked female ghost'.

In an even more modern twist to the story, we now find many similar reports of sexual encounters made by alien abductees (see 'Alien Abductions', page 10).

L

LEVITATION

To levitate is to rise or float in the air in defiance of gravity. This is a much-reported, but elusive behaviour spanning most religions and creeds. Although levitation might arguably be regarded as a part of PK (see 'Psychokinesis', page 259), we have kept those sections in the book separate and examine here only cases of human levitation.

Levitation has been reported as part of religious experience by Christians (mostly Catholics), Muslims, Shamans and non-Western mystics, Eastern yogi, Spiritualists and practitioners of Wicca. It has been part of the paranormal claims of mediums and has arisen as a factor in poltergeist cases and claims of UFO abduction. It is also considered as a sign of demonic possession by the Church when considering the use of exorcism rites.

Many famous Catholics, and several stigmatics, have experienced levitation while in ecstasy. Some found it frightening and embarrassing. St Teresa described a 'feeling of sweetness' when she gave in to it; most of the time she would try to hold herself down and often asked others to help. She also asked these people not to talk about it.

Many reports of religious levitations exist. *La Levitation* lists 230 saints to whom this feat is attributed. Levitation is recorded in Hinduism and Buddhism. Milarepa, a great yogi of thirteenth-century Tibet, was said to have amongst his powers the ability to work, rest and sleep, all while levitating.

In the East the ability to levitate is said to come through secret breathing techniques and visualisations. Fakirs have often been reported to have the ability to defy gravity and levitate. They are often holding on to a stick pushed against the ground. Levitation is held by some to be part of the Indian rope trick.

Levitation is a part of New Age development practices. It is said to develop with the practice of Transcendental Meditation. Meditating, and slowly rocking in the lotus position, is held to eventually lead you to lifting into the air (yogic flying).

D.D. Home, one of the most famous mediums of Victorian Britain, was seen to levitate. In the forty years over which his paranormal abilities were witnessed, he was not detected as fraudulent. Journalist F. Burr, out to discredit Home's claims, ended up trying to hold Home down while the medium drifted up towards the ceiling. Home levitated in houses he was unfamiliar with, and to many audiences. One of his most spectacular feats was to levitate out of one window and back in through another. However, the fact that Home forbade examination of the feat, keeping his audience well away, and refused to let them look out of the window while he was 'in action' has caused considerable speculation – but no confirmation – that he was cheating.

Other mediums have been photographed while levitating, including Colin Evans (British), Amendee Zuccarini (Italian) and Carmine Mirabelli (Brazilian). The photographs of Mirabelli were shown to the SPR at a time of some disarray and the claims were not properly investigated. However, photo-analysis in the present day seems to indicate fakery.

Levitation has been reported in poltergeist claims. A witness at the Enfield poltergeist case reported that he was lifted out of his chair. He described feeling as if a cushion of air, not a draught, pushed him upwards. There was also a twisting motion, which rotated him a half turn in the process. In addition the principal focus, Janet, was photographed in mid-air in what is held to have been a levitation across her bedroom.

Levitation is recognised by the Church as a sign of possession. A schoolgirl said to be possessed levitated, then fell when sprinkled with holy water.

All levitations seem to take place during some form of altered state. Such states are brought on by different methods; visualisations, physical pain, food deprivations, and others. If you have an OOBE then you may believe you physically flew when you did not. Unless witnessed it would be difficult to determine.

The only thought-provoking laboratory analysis of levitation seems to have been undertaken by Professor John Hasted as detailed in his book *The Metal Benders*, but even that is far from conclusive. The best results were obtained with a Russian defector, Auguste Stern. Encased in a cube of mirrors at his own request (apparently the most successful method used in Russia) and videotaped, he failed to levitate. However, on just two occasions Hasted reports that there were weight losses that he cannot account for looking at the video-recording. This would have apparently have required Stern to push himself up from the surface that he was lying on, and that was also recording his weight, and Hasted is sure he did not do so. However, even if true, a slight loss in weight – half a kilogram for a few seconds – is far from proof of levitation.

Joseph of Copertino is perhaps the most famous Westerner to levitate. This seventeenth-century Franciscan monk scourged himself regularly with skewered needles and lumps of metal and was once described as 'one great open sore'. He starved himself in the hope of reaching a state of ecstasy, only eating roots and herbs which he dusted with an unknown powder. (We shall look again at his diet shortly.)

The reports of Joseph's levitations are incredible. He is reported to have flown over the heads of a congregation towards the altar and then back again, leaving the spectators filled with 'holy awe'. On another occasion, when ten men were trying to place a heavy cross in position, Joseph flew seventy yards to the thirty-six-foot-high cross, lifted it and placed it in position, apparently without difficulty. Levitation stories continued up to Joseph's death in 1663. The surgeon who saw Joseph's body reported it was raised a 'whole palm' in the air.

Joseph was, of course, convinced he could fly, and there

were many witnesses. But what is the likely position?

During the time Joseph was engaging in these feats there was, in use, a bread infected by the fungus ergot, which created hallucinations. The term 'bread-crazies' came into being. The effects were very similar to LSD 'tripping'. In addition, there were many additives Joseph may have used that could have had similar effects, and he was known to have a strange diet. His belief that he could fly is not unlike the claims of LSD users of the 1960s. Given Joseph's deliberately strange diet and the substances he put on his food perhaps it was his hallucination that he could fly.

What, then, of the many witnesses? Joseph is held by many today to be the case that proves the existence of levitation. He was known to be fit and athletic, with strength possibly enhanced by drugs. He could leap and jump high and long. Perhaps with a bit of 'showmanship' – reinforced by his own beliefs about himself – Joseph was able to create an illusion of levitation and flying. As John Cornwell points out in *Powers of Darkness, Powers of Light*, 'There is nothing so very unusual about leaping a height of six feet, nor a distance of twelve paces; it seldom happens in a church however, accompanied by a scream'. If a few of his devotees insisted he had flown, even above the claims of others who did not believe so, it is likely that the more extraordinary tales would have gone down in history. Over time, and perhaps given devoted belief by his followers, his feats may have become rather exaggerated. On the other hand we must weigh against that the claim that he was witnessed levitating by several cardinals and the Pope.

But the doubts might be true of many of the other claimants of levitation. In almost all cases either they, or their audience, believed they could do it and wanted them to succeed. That people might believe they can fly is one thing. That they can genuinely 'fly' within the altered states of 'leaving their body' (OOBE) is also possible. That PK might allow for uncontrolled, spontaneous apparent weightlessness is not easy to dismiss, even if it is far from proven. To that extent levitation might have some reality.

If there is such a thing as human levitation, we might have in

Copertino an example of that rare individual who could do what few others achieved so well, or in such control.

LEY LINES

In 1921 Alfred Watkins was travelling in the country and taking notice of Britain's sacred sites, the places where for whatever motive or reason our ancestors had set up their most important and usually religious based structures, early churches, burial mounds, earthworks, holy wells, standing stones, and so on. He observed (in his book, *The Old Straight Track*) that they seemed to be connected by trackways in straight lines. Watkins referred to these straight lines as ley lines or leys. Ley hunters, following up this work, use the alignments they chart on maps to then examine the detail 'in the field', studying the leys to locate the signs of their ancient use as trackways. The most sacred sites – Stonehenge or Glastonbury, for example – are often found to be at the junctions of several such lines.

Watkins appears to only have speculated that these tracks were, in the manner of the Roman roads, efficient means of crossing the country. However, speculation was quickly raised that the straight lines reflected lines of energy and that, intuitively or deliberately, earlier Man had built these sacred structures on these energy points. Many dowsers found they could dowse the lines of energy that were represented by the leys.

UFO researcher John Michell, in the 1960s when the 'new age' was dawning, suggested that UFO sightings were occurring at the crossing points of leys – and near sacred sites. Leys were drawn into the subject of 'flying saucers'. He, and those inspired by his work, speculated that the energies were magnetic, and used by flying saucers for either navigation or propulsion. Aime Michel, in *Flying Saucers and the Straight Line Mystery* had also indicated that he believed UFO sightings could be charted in straight lines. Even more recently crop circle researchers were speculating that crop circles were appearing along leys, and some even tried – with little obvious success – to predict the appearances of crop-patterns by reference to the leys.

The controversy over leys is based on the criteria needed to 'identify' a ley. Researchers believe there must be a certain number of sacred sites within a certain number of miles and so on in order to 'qualify' for investigation. There is, however, little or no consensus as to how many, or within what distance. Janet and Colin Bord, for example, have suggested that a ley is worth investigation if it has five valid sites within ten miles. Because of the ambiguity, there are those who dismiss leys as 'chance' alignments. Add to this the question of whether they arise because of 'meaningful' energies within the Earth, and the subject has sometimes been a fraught one.

Straight line trackways exist in Ireland, where they are called 'fairy lines', and other European countries. They are being charted all around the world; much work is being done to examine what are called 'spirit lines' in South America, Peru and Bolivia for example.

More recently researchers in Britain have concentrated on what are called 'dragon lines'. As one researcher, Mike Wootten, put it: 'If ley lines were the "A" roads, then dragon lines are the superhighways.' Glastonbury stands on one of the most intensely investigated 'dragon lines' running from Cornwall to East Anglia and taking in such sites as the Avebury standing stones.

LUCK

Is luck a purely random lightning strike – that person is lucky, this one is not? There is probably random luck of course, actually being hit by lightning for example.

But there is a considerable body of evidence arising from studies in the business world that the luck attributed to people's success or failure is far more a product of individual ability than is usually recognised. What is more the principal factors that generate that luck are beginning to be understood, and they apply to everyone in virtually all situations. Luck is therefore arguably becoming a subject of analysis. In this section we look at a particular type of perceived luck.

The value of luck has been noted many times. Napoleon is

famous for having declared that when he was looking for promotions to the rank of general, he was less concerned with a man's qualifications than whether or not he was naturally lucky. Stephen Leacock, a writer in the first half of the century, said, 'I am a great believer in luck, and I find the harder I work the more I have of it,' a sentiment later expressed by a golfer, Gary Player. He was congratulated for his luck on a particularly good shot and replied, 'It's interesting, isn't it – the harder I practise the luckier I get.' Leacock and Player are emphasising that their luck was the result of effort. Donald Campbell was told by his father, 'Never depend on luck, but you won't get far without it.'

In analysing those who are 'lucky' in business and those who are not the following traits are commonplace:

● *Knowing the rules*
We live in a complex society where certain conventions are expected of us: who we should greet, how we should greet them; when to stand firm as an oak, when to bend to the wind like bamboo; how to balance our own rights with the rights of others; where to cut corners and where not to; and a whole host of so called 'rules of life' which dictate our complex interpersonal relationships with those who influence us and those who we influence. Those who 'know the rules' and play to them succeed more frequently than those who do not.

There is evidence that the winners and losers in this game of luck are identifiable even at school or earlier. Watch groups of children 'egging each other on' and you can quickly identify the children who have a natural intuitive grasp of how far they can push their luck before adults will become censorious. Those with the intuitive grasp of what they can and cannot get away with are those who transfer that skill to their social and business relationships in later life and 'make their own luck'.

● *Natural skills*
Analysis of business successes shows that there are certain skills which are more likely to increase the chances of success, even though those skills may not be part of the business itself.

The successes are those where the principals are more naturally assertive and more easily communicative. Yet these skills are – at best – 'taught' in the infant-school playground, but are probably inherent from birth. Those with those skills are identified by their peers as 'lucky'. To this extent luck may be an accident of birth, but we are beginning to identify its components.

● *Knowing who to trust and who to be wary of*
Nobody is ever told the truth in life. That is not meant to be cynical, it is a reflection of the fact that there are few empirical truths. The truth is the truth as seen from one person's perspective. Judging the views expressed by others is mostly intuitive, but those who know who to trust and who not to trust are the 'lucky' ones.

● *Having a grasp of reality*
One psychologist explained to us that in his view everybody lived in fantasies. In order to get through our everyday life, we see the world to some degree modelled as we want to see it. One test with adjustable 'distorted mirrors', where the subjects used their own reflections to set the mirror to 'normal' indicated that over eighty per cent of people believe they are taller and slimmer than they really are. People boost their own courage by these fantasy images; for example, they may help a boy to make a pass at a girl that he would otherwise be afraid to approach.

The 'lucky' people in life are those whose grasp of reality meets the consensus reality of those around them, and who appear down-to-earth and realistic. For the high fliers who create fantasy situations which they are then able to turn into reality, the visionaries who create Disney Worlds and business empires that accelerate rapidly to success, their consensus reality is actually very good. They may not look down to earth but they have a down-to-earth knowledge of what can be achieved by a group of people well motivated and well led – and they know that they are the people that can lead and motivate a team.

● *Adaptability*

Whether it is your crisis or their crisis, or an external crisis such as recession, the 'lucky' people are those who know how to respond and adapt accordingly. Those who naturally have contingency plans built into their everyday lives are 'luckier' than those who do not. Some people have a very rigid forward plan of what they are going to try to achieve and if any outside or even internal influence throws that plan off, they become lost or depressed. The 'lucky' people in business are those who are constantly adapting their forward plans, however strongly they are committed to them.

This luck is similar to the difference between those who, playing card games, stay with a set of cards hoping for the right cards to turn up to 'complete' their hands and those who are constantly re-assessing the position and adapting their hands. Perhaps the former are just lazy. Certainly the luckiest looking people in business are never the lazy ones.

A famous phrase is that certain people are just 'in the right place at the right time'; there is no evidence whatsoever that that is the case. What is true is that a group of people 'in the right place at the right time' will respond to those circumstances differently and those with the in-built contingency plans and the natural ability to adapt will make the most of that situation while others will fall by the wayside. One definition of luck we found in one business training package was 'when preparation meets opportunity'.

● *Being a 'yes sayer'*

Experimental work in development classes with groups of businessmen has identified a division between people's reactions to challenge; into 'yes sayers' and 'no sayers'. The former accept all opportunities as challenges to be met and react to them by a version of, 'Yes – I will attempt that'. The 'no sayers' respond with lists of objections as to why a challenge cannot be met, why they believe they will fail. Training turning 'no sayers' into 'yes sayers' improves their achievement record and many have stated that they believe their luck has changed in all aspects of their life. It is, of course, their different attitude that is producing the effect.

The training reverses natural inclinations. Very often 'no' is a defence mechanism reflecting fear of the unknown, but once said it is hard to withdraw. All 'no sayers' are taught to first respond by saying 'yes' to any suggestion, no matter how silly. Then they can change their minds and say 'no' if they want to after reflection. Results indicate that once people are through the first hurdle of commitment they stay with that decision, taking more opportunities than they otherwise would.

Summary

These factors are not a matter of learning which would therefore be nothing to do with the question of luck. The evidence is that these talents – particularly in non-business, everyday situations – are character traits from birth. Their quantity and quality reflect on the amount of luck we do or do not have.

People also seem to have a fairly intuitive grasp of their own likely luck, however they define it. The expression often used in business is, 'Whether you think you can, or whether you think you can't, you are probably right.' Those who believe in themselves succeed more, but it is not just a matter of positive thinking. It is the constant reinforcement of success throughout their lives, often by factors they do not understand, but which when analysed are the factors described above.

Perceptions

Whether we are lucky or unlucky, the perception of luck probably arises from what psychologists call the 'locus of control'. Some people believe the locus of control to be within themselves, i.e. they are in control of their own world, their own environment and their own destiny. Others believe the locus of control is external, that they are subject to outside forces, the whims of others and so on. The person who feels that he is in control is more likely to succeed than the person who believes he is at the whim of others.

Those who believe they are at the mercy of forces beyond themselves are more likely to perceive themselves as victims.

The clearest example of this came to us in one-to-one counselling with one businessman who regarded himself as extremely unlucky. He had started many businesses, but they had all collapsed, leaving him with a continuous stream of failures and debts. We knew him to be intelligent and capable; so why therefore was he so unlucky when others were not? The answer we were certain was quite simple; he needed to lose. The analysis of the collapse of every one of his businesses was that just when it was becoming successful he would make irrational decisions, irrational changes. (Then he would pick himself up, dust himself off and start all over again.) We asked him what his attitude was to women, with whom he had had a large number of short-term and somewhat unsatisfying relationships throughout his life. He was quite happy to explain that he did not like long-term relationships; it was the chase rather than the conquest which thrilled him. He could not see that he was applying the same attitude to business, but we in the business group that was counselling him could see it very clearly. Yet his perception was very clear; the locus of control was external and he was very unlucky.

M

MAP DOWSING

In February 1994 Georg Horak used map dowsing to locate two British skiers who had been trapped in mountains above Oberammergau. He held a piece of wire over the map, letting it swing from side to side and predicted accurately to within 1,000 feet where they could be found. Rescuers from the rescue service took Horak's instructions and located the skiers quickly. Mountain rescue chief Alwin Delago said, 'We wouldn't have found them so quickly without the diviner's help.'

Map dowsing is a form of divining using, usually, a pendulum containing a stone or crystal, suspended over a map (see photo section) to locate people, objects or substances at a remote, real, location. Generally speaking, negative results are indicated by a sideways swinging of the pendulum and positive results by a circular rotation, though this varies from dowser to dowser. Countless experiments have successfully located a wide variety of targets.

Five basic rules are recommended for map dowsing (or 'field dowsing'), focused more on mental ability than on the physical equipment used:

- Ask a clear question
  For dowsing to produce accurate results the dowser must mentally 'ask' him- or herself a specific and clear question.

- Ignore preconceived notions.
  The pendulum may respond to your wishes, not your psychic senses.

- Ignore the five senses.
  Dowsing is essentially intuitive. Rational critical analysis blocks the intuition.

- Have confidence.
  'Success breeds success' is a common adage.

- Practice makes perfect.
  Dowsing is no different from any other human activity. The more you do of it the better you get.

Elsie Oakensen demonstrated 'question-dowsing' using these techniques and correctly identified the colour of paper concealed from her by us. She emphasised that focus on the proper question was, for her, the main key to success. The only failure we noticed was when she was aggressively challenged by a reporter. Presumably conditions of stress are as distracting to dowsers as to anyone else.

During further experiments we conducted more recently, the results strongly suggested that telepathy plays a part in this form of dowsing. A map dowser asked us to lay out a map of southern England on the floor and to locate a day in our diaries when we were in a particular place on that map. John Spencer undertook to do this. The diary was not brought into the room prior to the experiment nor was there the slightest likelihood that the map dowser could have seen the diary. John also knew not to get close enough to the map to indicate the location by looking at certain sections of the map and so on. Indeed he did not particularly look at the map and stayed several feet from it while the experiment was going on.

To continue in John's own words, 'This experiment was a direct hit. I had identified a day when I had been in a small town called Badshot Lea in Surrey. The dowser picked his way slowly through each square of the map and settled on precisely the correct location. He never once looked up from the job or made eye contact with me, or questioned me in any way.

'The second experiment was more fascinating. I chose a day when I had flown to Sweden. It is important to note that I was conscious of visualising the place where I had been; the tunnel leading into Heathrow Airport, the characteristic Queen's Building and control tower and the very busy, bustling terminals. Again the dowser put his head down and dowsed around the map in the same way and picked, with certainty, Heathrow Airport. Later I showed the group the entry indicating my flight to Sweden. On the page was the notation, which I had quite clearly missed, that I had flown from Gatwick Airport, not Heathrow. The experiment had accidentally become almost 'double blind'; I had believed I had flown from Heathrow and that was his conclusion.

'A similar result arose from the third experiment. I selected a time when I had been in Greenwich with a colleague, Tony Wells, with whom I was writing the book *Ghostwatching*. In my diary I had read (to myself) the notation 'to T. Wells' when selecting the entry. The dowser missed the location; and identified my location as Tunbridge Wells.'

That the same kind of energies or sensitivities that play a part in telepathy, clairvoyance or psychometry are involved is possible. We have to be open to the possibility that there are aspects of the brain which are constantly functioning, but for which we have not found appropriate measurement or analysis. These may be playing a part in what the dowser picks up.

MARIAN VISITATIONS

There is no other form of apparition or vision that carries such emotional charge as the sighting of the Blessed Virgin Mary. And of course, the specific types of vision examined here are complemented by other 'visions': most commonly weeping, bleeding or moving statues.

Visions of the Virgin Mary are widely attested to by individuals and whole communities around the world. A recent vision related to us was by a British stigmatic, George Hamilton. He has had frequent visions of a 'comforting light' in his home. On one occasion a figure 'started appearing in the light. She didn't have her hands in a praying position. She just . . . sort of put her hands out. I think she wanted me to say something. So it had to come from me. I don't know why it happened that way.' The same vision later appeared again, 'that's when she actually spoke, and I spoke to her. I asked her, "Could she take away the stigmata." "Sorry, that I can't do," she said, "I'll ask my son." When she said "my son", that's when the penny dropped. I'm afraid to use the word ["Mary"] because of the laughing of the sceptics. There's that many people have said they've seen the Virgin Mary I was afraid to open my mouth. They'd have thought I was another crank making it up. But even during a, what do you call it, a trance-like state, I knew straightaway at that point who she was.

'It wasn't her place to remove [the stigmata]. But I felt good afterwards. Rene [George's partner] noticed the difference [in me]. She said "Have you had a visitor or something?" I said, "It's funny you should say that . . ." '

We asked George if 'the lady' had colour, and whether or not he could see clothing. 'It's a funny thing,' he replied, 'through the bright light I could see she was wearing light-coloured clothes; I could make that out. I don't understand that: how could I see the colour of her clothes when this light was sort of blinding me?'

As George said, he kept the details of his vision to himself because he feared ridicule. Many such witnesses do the same. But there are many others around the world who have had visions and who have shared them widely, perhaps because of three main reasons: greater openness and willingness to accept within their community; the corroboration of other witnesses; and innocence – many of these witnesses are young children. These public announcements have often resulted in mass pilgrimages.

In Medjugorje, in Croatia (the former Yugoslavia), starting in June 1981, the Virgin appeared to children on an almost daily basis for eighteen months. She was described as a figure in a long, grey dress with a white veil. Many pilgrims visited the site. Although they did not all experience the vision the children reported, many saw other phenomena. They reported visions of the sun changing colour and spinning. There were reports of miraculous healings, rosaries changing from silver to gold and so on. The purpose of the messages and the attendant paranormal phenomena was, the children stated, to bring people to Jesus and spread his Word.

The pattern of these highly publicised visions has many similarities. There is one person, or a small number of people, who see the Virgin; most other pilgrims are treated to other paranormal phenomena such as burning bushes, heavenly music and visions of a rotating sun. Very often those who see the Virgin are children.

Bernadette Soubirous, aged thirteen in 1858, saw visions of the Virgin Mary at Lourdes. Her description was 'a girl in white no bigger than myself'. The vision spoke to Bernadette, and asked for the construction of a chapel. Although there were often others with her – even huge crowds – Bernadette was the only person who saw the Virgin at that time. Some curious miracles are associated with Bernadette and Lourdes, for example one that followed her being told to wash her face in a stream that did not exist. She scrabbled in the earth and succeeded only in smearing mud over herself, much to the amusement of witnesses, but the following day there was a clear stream running at that location, water from which apparently gave sight back to a blind man who bathed his eyes in it.

At Fatima, Mary appeared to three children. She told them only that she was 'from heaven'. The girls described her as a 'young lady, dressed in white'. The children were told there would be visions during the next six months, and were given a vision of hell that frightened them and several warnings to pass on about how mankind should stop offending God. Thousands of pilgrims went to Fatima to witness the visions. On the last day, 13 October 1917, an estimated 50,000 to 70,000 pilgrims were present. Most spectacular of the visions was the so-called 'dance of the sun'; the sun broke through clouds and seemed to rotate and dive towards the earth in a blast of multicoloured light, and with much heat. This lasted some ten minutes and was believed to have been seen as far as several miles away.

In Bearaing, Belgium, in 1932, the Virgin was seen by five children. The children first saw a light and one of them, Albert

Voisin, announced, 'This is the Blessed Virgin.' The children received thirty-two more visits. As in so many cases, although they were often accompanied by many other people, only the children saw the Virgin.

In 1961, at Garabandal in Spain, four children were witnesses. The Virgin is said to have appeared to the children over 2,000 times in over four years. As in other cases the children, when receiving the vision, appeared to be in ecstatic trance. The children were reported to march at phenomenal speeds – sometimes backwards – through and around the village. One of the children, Conchita, was said to have levitated and to have received a miraculous 'visitation' of the Host directly into her mouth.

In Lubbock, Texas in 1988, Mary appeared to three parishioners of St John Neumann Roman Catholic Church. As in other cases, she told the visionaries of the need for more prayer and more faith. She also told them that she would reveal herself at an August Feast of the Assumption. When this time arrived, 20,000 people attended near the church. Many of those attested to having witnessed a vision of Mary and Jesus' head. Miraculous healing was one of the other phenomena reported in this case.

A vision of a nun-like figure seen, and photographed, in Zeintoun, Egypt, in 1968 has been attributed to the Virgin Mary, but it differs from the most common pattern: the figure was seen by non-Christians and there is no evidence of any messages given.

Although there are unique aspects to almost all Marian visitations, these visions more than most have a great deal in common. Mary often appears first as a light, later taking human shape. (In Guadaloupe, in Mexico, she appeared to Juan Diego first as a woman 'standing in the luminous cloud of mist, iridescent with rainbow hues'.) She rarely identifies herself specifically, often just dropping hints. She appears mostly to children, often around the age of puberty, and shares messages for the world through them. The visionaries are usually from poor families living in remote villages and often encounter the Virgin while working in fields or other isolated places. Many pilgrims to the scenes of her appearances often do not see her, but are treated to paranormal 'spectaculars' such as the 'dance of the sun'.

In addition to these commonly identified characteristics, John Cornwell (in *Powers of Darkness, Powers of Light*) reports that social scientist Michael Carrol, working in the University of Western Ontario, isolated the fact that a great many of the sighters had suffered the death of their mother, or mother-figure, about eight weeks prior to the Marian visitation.

Quite why children should be more prone to these visitations is unclear. Since many of these children come from poorer, isolated Catholic communities it is possible that Mary is one of the few religious figures known to them other than Jesus. The evidence is that many of the children persuade themselves, or even are persuaded by others, that they have seen Mary. Another argument would suggest that children are most psychic and perhaps therefore able to see her, although attendant adults do see something. The argument that these adults are more exposed to the 'mysteries' of the world and therefore have wider expectations seems improbable. Most of the people, at least the elders in the villages, are likely to be more acquainted with religion that with the wider paranormal. And the 'dance of the sun' can hardly have been a well-anticipated phenomenon in 1917.

Catholic dogma states that religious apparitions are mystical phenomena permitted by God. However, the church is understandably cautious in granting official status to visions and miracles. Of the many reports of Marian visitations only a handful have been authenticated by the Church; primarily those at Guadaloupe, Fatima, Lourdes, and Knock in Ireland in 1852.

That the Mother of God actually makes visits to earth to convert people to the Church cannot of course be dismissed. But we can see in some of the Marian visitations many similarities to other phenomena, in particular, non-Catholics see strange sights but not the Virgin. This suggests that Marian visitation is, at least in part, the same as so much of our folklore and mythology; witnesses are seeing what they expect to see, conditioned by their pre-existing beliefs. In cases of ambiguity they are persuaded that what they have seen fits certain criteria.

But we must bear in mind that within the claims of Marian visitation are cases that must make us look again at the paranormal. Whatever happened at Fatima – and the spectacle was predicted accurately – tens of thousands of people surely cannot have been deluded into thinking something happened when nothing did. Something happened, and on a grand scale.

MARTIAN MYSTERIES

Mars, the nearest planet to the Earth, has, more than any other planet, fascinated mankind for centuries. Before space probes showed it to be a desert world it was the primary focus for Western people's belief in extraterrestrial life. Perhaps because it also represents the God of War, that life was often looked on as hostile, and a potential invasion threat. The term 'Martian' has at times been almost synonymous with extraterrestrial. Despite modern knowledge of the planet, it is still the focus of a continuing series of mysteries.

The variation in distance between Mars and the Earth is between around 56 million kilometres to 101 million kilometres. The next closest approach – always a time of renewed speculation – is in the year 2003.

What is fascinating about Mars is that almost every myth has been based on one presumption; intelligent life.

Canals

Probably the most famous early mystery is that of the canals. Early observers of the planet could see dark linear shapes criss-crossing the surface. The Italian astronomer Schiaparelli named the features '*canali*', simply meaning channels, but it was translated as 'canals' which implies an artificial origin. Other observers, such as Percival Lowell, became convinced that they too could see the latticework. Close examination shows no such structures; they had resulted from the visual 'connection' of dark areas, isolated geological structures and shadows; a product of wishful-thinking.

Maria

When observers saw that the polar caps on Mars expanded and contracted seasonally, they also noticed that dark areas within the *maria* (seas) changed size and shape. It was then thought that the dark areas were lichen supplied by water from the caps. This would suggest plant life and a basis for other life forms. In fact observation has shown that the dark areas are bedrock on to, and off which lighter sands are blown seasonally.

Moons

Mars has two moons, Phobos and Deimos. It was once believed that they were artificial, either orbited by intelligent Martians or 'parked' by visiting extraterrestrials. This theory was based largely on the fact that they were discovered by a little-known astronomer, Asaph Hall, in 1877, after many powerful telescopes in the hands of gifted and experienced astronomers had failed to detect them. The suggestion was therefore that they had only just arrived. The moons also seemed to be unusually light according to their orbital characteristics, which furthered the speculation that they were hollow. In fact Phobos, for example, has a density of only twice that of water, which accounts for the observation.

Moons: prediction

One mystery that is of interest is the moons' 'pre-discovery' in literature. They were first 'reported' by Jonathan Swift in his political satire-adventure story *Gulliver's Travels*, in 1726, 151 years before their discovery by Hall.

Swift refers to the astronomers of Laputa as having 'discovered two lesser stars, or satellites, which revolve around Mars; whereof the innermost is distant from the Centre of the primary Planet exactly three of his diameters, and the outermost five; the former revolves in the space of ten hours, and the latter in twenty-one and a half . . .'

His description is close. The suggestion, often made, that he got his information from 'ancient knowledge' is unlikely; there was a body of speculation available in his time for him to draw from. Johannes Kepler in the early 1600s had used mathematics and geometry to guess that Mars would have two moons. He wrote to Galileo, 'I long for a telescope, to anticipate you, if possible, in discovering two [moons] around Mars, as the proportion seems to require . . .'

Kepler had also published his third law which gave a basis for calculation of orbiting bodies; Swift could have used these speculations to make his fictional guess. In fact we can see that Swift was basing his ideas on mathematics when he goes on to add, 'so that the squares of their periodical times are very near in the proportion with the cubes of their distance from the centre of Mars . . .'

A good guess though, and a guess that has helped fuel the 'intelligent life on Mars' theories.

Martian face

Mars continues to mystify its observers. The observers nowadays are much closer than they used to be, with several space probes having landed on the planet or observed it from close proximity. Viking 2 landed on Mars on 3 September 1976 on the plains of Utopia, a secondary landing site chosen for safety after the initial consideration of the more unpredictable Cydonia region was abandoned. However, the photographs of the Cydonia region that were transmitted back by Viking 2 raised a mystery that persists to the present day; the image of a huge face staring up from the Martian surface. It has been estimated that the structure is about one mile long and 1,500 feet high. The image seems to be the product of rock structure and shadow, and the shadow conceals the answers as to whether or not the face is a simulacrum (an accidental arrangement that happens to look like a face) or a deliberate monument designed and built or carved out (see photo section).

The face has been the subject of considerable speculation. The 'eye' has been subjected to computer-based and other analysis and there are those who believe they can detect the carving of an eyeball within it. The opposite side of the face is all in shadow, but enhancements are alleged to have found corresponding details within the shadows that suggest symmetry and therefore design.

The question would be settled by further pictures from the site which would allow for stereoscopic study, but there are none available. NASA claimed that a second picture was taken and that it showed no face, but they have not released that picture.

Pyramids

Close to the face is a series of 'five-sided' pyramid-like structures reaching one kilometre in height, apparently having sharp edges, again suggestive of design. Complex mathematics and geometry have been applied to these arrangements by such as Richard Hoagland, who believes the face and the pyramids represent intelligent design. He states, 'We can begin to see geometry and numbers repeating themselves. They are arranged in shapes that bring out the same mathematical relationships over and over again . . . The conclusion must be that it was planned.'

Even Carl Sagan had admitted that 'they warrant . . . a careful look', but cautiously describes them as probably sand-blasted small mountains.

Mr Smiley

The resurgence in interest in Mars, and speculated intelligent life on Mars, will as ever be treated with great seriousness by its analysts from all fields of study. But as if to prevent the seriousness getting too deep, one photograph seems to show a 'smiley face' on Mars. A crater in Galle, on Argyre Planitia, has two prominent rocks where the eyes would be and a crescent-shaped ridge in precisely the right place for a mouth to be! (See photo section.)

The picture was promoted by *Fortean Times* (Aug/Sept 1994) on their front cover. They state that it was sent to them by 'Ralph Harvey, a planetary scientist in the Department of Geological Sciences, University of Tennessee' who confirms that he has not 'enhanced or changed any features in any . . . way from the original NASA mosaic'.

Only investigation of the Martian features will determine their natural or artificial origin; but those who believe in the latter should at least be cautioned by the errors of the past and the Galle crater that perhaps suggests 'someone up there is laughing at us'.

MARY CELESTE

The story of the *Mary Celeste* is well known, though surprisingly we still receive a regular number of enquiries about it from people who confuse the details with that of the fictional story based on the account. (Arthur Conan Doyle wrote a story called 'Marie Celeste' which in turn led to other fictional accounts; these included many details of exotic mystery; that the food in the galley was still warm, that candles were still burning, and so on.) Some stories seem never to lose their appeal; the sinking of the *Titanic* is another such event. Such is the thirst for information on this one account that even as recently as January 1993 *Fate* magazine ran a review of the known facts. We include it here also because one new theory deserves to be added to the list of possibilities; though we recognise that this is a mystery without resolution. What really happened will never be known.

In November 1872, Captain Benjamin Spooner Briggs set sail from New York on his cargo ship – the *Mary Celeste* – taking his wife and two-year-old daughter. His older son remained at home. Briggs had a crew of seven men with him and no passengers.

They were heading for Genoa with a cargo of crude (non-consumable) alcohol. The *Mary Celeste* left port travelled through good weather before meeting a 'moderate gale' after passing the Azores.

Also sailing from New York was the *Dei Gratia*, a British ship heading for Gibraltar. On 5 December, after journeying for nearly three weeks, the crew spotted the *Mary Celeste*. The ship appeared to be in trouble, veering from side to side.

Drawing closer they saw that the wheel was unattended. Captain Morehouse of the *Dei Gratia* sent three seamen in a boat to board the vessel and offer help. The sailors climbed aboard, finding the vessels' sails and rigging damaged by storm. On the whole, however, the ship was in good condition and unquestionably seaworthy. But the ship was deserted; they found no sign of the captain, his family, or his crew. The cargo was more or less intact. The food supplies were largely intact. The crew's clothing was aboard. The ship's log had been filled in; the last entry was dated 25 November, which suggested that the ship had been empty for up to ten days. Significantly, the boarding party found that a small sailboat, a chronometer, and a sextant were missing. The equipment is precisely what would be needed for navigation. This gives weight to the probability that the crew voluntarily left the ship. The mystery of the desertion remains to this day. Since the *Mary Celeste* was seaworthy, indeed in good order, why did the crew leave it for a small, less stable, boat?

Many theories have been put forward:

● *Murder*
It has been suggested that Captain Morehouse of the *Dei Gratia* and his crew turned their discovery of the *Mary Celeste* into a piratical attack and killed the crew of the *Mary Celeste* for the salvage value. Morehouse was forced to defend this allegation in court. An alternative is that someone on the *Mary Celeste* went mad (the bosun is often cited as a result of a 1936 film version of the story), killed the others, and then committed suicide. Lastly, that other pirates invaded the ship and killed the crew.

Against these possibilities is the fact that there were no signs of violence on the ship. This would seem to rule out pirates or ship-board insurrection. Pirates might have persuaded the ship's crew to leave the ship rather than fight, but if so why did the pirates then not retain the ship or at least steal the cargo. That Morehouse and his crew conspired is possible, but they would have had to remove all signs of violence, which seems improbable. In any case, Morehouse was a respected captain;

it is improbable that he would have committed such an act and even less likely that a captain of his stature would have had a crew that would all have agreed to comply, and then maintain their story in court hearings.

● *Captain Morehouse and Captain Briggs conspired together*
But for what? They did not steal the ship or its cargo. They might have wanted the salvage money, if so they were unlucky; the court considerably reduced it. Briggs was never seen again, but there is no obvious reason why he would have wanted to run away. It also seems improbable that he would have gained agreement to such a conspiracy from his wife, given that their son remained at home.

● *UFO attack*
It is almost inevitable that this suggestion would surface, despite not a shred of evidence in its support. And there have been no similar reports since that would make it any more likely.

● *Attack by sea monster*
There are few creatures likely to be able to threaten a ship the size of the *Mary Celeste*. Had it been attacked by anything large enough, the crew would presumably be safer aboard ship than on the sea in a tiny sailboat. Only in desperation would they have abandoned ship, but there were no signs of significant damage that would suggest they could have reached that stage of fear.

● *Whirlwind*
Was the ship hit by a whirlwind that resulted in everybody being blown off, or sucked off, the ship? It is unlikely that someone would not have been below decks and stayed there. The missing navigation equipment and boat would still have to be accounted for.

● *Poisoned food*
Did the crew go mad eating hallucinogenic drugs in the food on

board? Definitely not so; the salvage crew ate the remaining food on the voyage back to Gibraltar without ill effects.

● *Panic*

Oliver Deveau, at the hearing, put forward the most logical explanation for the desertion, though he could not offer a reason. He suggested that the crew panicked and left the ship, believing it was sinking. Any logical reason for panic must also take account of the following: that the ship was undamaged; that despite the lack of damage the ship was regarded as less seaworthy than the small sailboat; that the crew took navigation equipment with them; that they took no significant extra clothing; that although they may have left the ship quickly, they did not leave without planning and preparation; that the crew were never found.

One new compelling theory meets these points and should be considered.

In the section 'Bermuda Triangle' (page 41) we include a description of the work of Dr Richard McIver who believes that under the oceans are deposits of methane gas held in hydrate form. When the gas is released it bubbles up through the water to the surface. The effect on boats – experimentally proven – is that they start to ride dangerously low in the water and sometimes sink. If they do not sink before the gas disperses, they regain their buoyancy. When this happened to a floating drilling rig which sank, one survivor reported jumping into the water with a life jacket on and sinking when he expected to float, so unbuoyant was the water.

If the *Mary Celeste* was above a release of such gas, she may have started to float dangerously low in the water. The crew might have assumed she was likely to sink. At the time of their last log entry they had just passed the Azores (the entry allows for the possibility that they could have even been in sight of St Mary's Island). They might reasonably have expected to be able to make it back to the island in the little sailboat, so they might not have taken any large food supplies with them, or additional clothing. They took navigation equipment, suggesting that they had a plan of action in mind.

But they did not make it to the Azores, nor did they return to the ship, nor were they ever located. Why? The answer possibly lies in the original problem. If the *Mary Celeste* was riding low in the water because the ship had become unbuoyant in the gas-saturated water, then the sailboat was in similar danger. The crew may have boarded the sailboat already riding low in the water, but perhaps not too obviously so. Within a short time the lack of buoyancy would have affected the sailboat, now with ten people aboard. If so, the irony is that the boat probably sank within full view of the *Mary Celeste*. The crew might have tried to swim, even to swim back to the ship. But if a man in a modern life jacket can sink in gas-saturated water, then these crew members would have done the same. In a short space of time all ten may have gone to a watery grave, uncomprehending of the strange effects in the water that were drowning them. And as the buoyancy returned, after the gas seeped away into the air, the *Mary Celeste* would have regained her buoyancy and sailed on, deserted.

The *Mary Celeste* always was regarded as an unlucky ship. First known as the *Amazon*, on her maiden voyage she was damaged, gashed down one side in a collision. On later voyages she caught fire and ran aground. She ended her days being run aground again in a failed attempt to swindle her insurers.

MEDIUMSHIP

Mediumship is a tradition in all religions and cultures in one form or another. There is reference to mediumship in the Bible when Saul sought out the Witch of Endor. The tribal shamans act as mediums when they make contact with the spirits. In the modern day we generally think of mediums as independent communicators between this world and the spirit world. Most people visiting mediums go in an attempt to 'talk' to members of their family who have passed over.

Mediums are generally divided into two groups; physical mediums and mental mediums.

Physical mediums

Physical mediums are not as fashionable as they once were. They had a heyday around the turn of the century when the Victorian era was driving the train of technology forwards.

At one time they were the most sought-after form of contact with the spirit world. They demonstrated their abilities by producing ectoplasm extrusions, spirit photographs, levitations, apports, and rapping communications.

Many were unquestionably fakes. Many researchers spent a great deal of time and effort exposing fraud. Most of the early research into the validity of mediumship centred around 'catching' physical mediums producing fake effects. Almost certainly amongst the frauds were genuine mediums pushed to fake certain effects that were expected of them; some may have had genuine abilities however.

However, the 'special effects', whether genuine or not, do not advance any proof of the validity of mediumship or of the survival of spirit. For that we believe the only valid evidence likely is in the transmission of information that cannot come through any other means. The message is the substance of the claims of the mental mediums.

Mental mediums

Mental mediums act as channels to receive messages from the spirit world. They are no different to the physical mediums in that regard, except that the mental medium's own body becomes the receiver, no use is made of ectoplasm or other physical devices. Although there are many who hold that physical mediumship is valid and useful, there are many mental mediums who admit the possibility that all physical effects were produced to give confidence to the sitter that something real was happening. The only real effects, they argue, are the information channels.

The mental medium uses a spirit guide, or control, to act as go-between in the communication. The spirit guide is allegedly living in the spirit realm.

Mental mediums often receive impressions rather than clear information. This would seem to be an unnecessary complication, but many believe that it is inevitable as the spirit is struggling to deal with conveying meaning from a quite different environment, and using imperfect channels. Some mediums believe these impressions are also designed to stretch the thinking of the medium, and develop them. A typical impression given, where a straight comment might have been more obvious, was related to us by medium Barbara Wright.

She was telling a sitter that it was likely she would receive news of her son's continued life (he had lost touch with his mother who thought him dead) in the future. She thought it would be at Christmas, not because she had been told that, but because she could hear, in the background, carols being sung.

Some mediums do not appear to enter trance or altered state to do their work, though the 'warming up' period before they hold a sitting is suggestive of some level of altered state. These mediums remember the information they are given, relaying it in a normal voice to their sitters.

Other mediums, trance mediums, enter deep trances and allow the control, or the person in spirit, to enter their bodies and use their vocal cords. The voices that come out of the medium's mouth are therefore not his or her own voice. As the spirits use the medium as a channel in this way, the medium often retains no memory of what has been said. At the extreme end of the scale, trance mediums allow spirits to take over the whole body, a form of invited temporary possession. The spirits use their hands, eyes, vocal cords, and more to interact with the sitters.

An Irish-born woman living in America was probably one of the most famous trance mediums. Eileen Garrett started holding seances in the 1930s. She was thoroughly investigated by the American Society for Psychical Research and researchers such as Hereward Carrington. Like many mediums her greatest surprise in life was not discovering that she had special abilities, but in discovering that others did not; she had been making contact with deceased relatives, and having precognitive experiences, all her life. One of her most painful impressions was to 'see' her husband during the First World War, killed by a shell. His death was confirmed to her two days later. Her control was named Uvani, an oriental whose early origin was never identified. He claimed that his purpose was to prove the reality of life after death.

Another well-known, and thoroughly investigated, trance medium was Mrs Leonore Piper. Her career as a medium started when she was twenty-five and continued to the end of her long life. A sceptical and thorough researcher, Richard Hodgson, spent eighteen years studying her. To prevent her setting up fraudulent situations, he organised her sittings, and even engaged detectives to follow her to ensure she could not obtain information from normal but unexpected channels. Despite these constraints she performed impressively enough to convince Hodgson that she had special abilities. That said, he was not convinced she was contacting spirits of the dead, or that her abilities even indicated an afterlife; he recognised the possibility that she was receiving telepathic impressions from the living. Mrs Piper was also studied in England by Frederic Myers and Oliver Lodge of the SPR. Like Hodgson, they examined her thoroughly, checking her mail, following her, and so on, to ensure that she was not receiving information about sitters; she continued to perform well.

Mrs Piper used a spirit guide or control called Dr Phinuit; he could never be identified and many, including Hodgson, thought him a sub-personality of Mrs Piper. He was, Hodgson thought, thoroughly unconvincing. Nevertheless, she 'came through' with impressive results.

One sitting which also serves to demonstrate trance mediumship was the seance held for, and with, the Reverend and Mrs Sutton in 1893. They were trying to contact their deceased daughter, Katherine. When Katherine 'came through', Mrs Piper/Dr Phinuit picked up a button from the table and began biting it, exactly as the Suttons recognised their daughter used to do. 'He [a reference to the Piper/Phinuit combination] exactly imitated her arch manner,' Mrs Sutton noted. Katherine referred to 'Dodo'; Mrs Sutton noted this was a pet name for her brother George. Piper/Phinuit said, 'She calls herself Kakie'; Mrs Sutton noted this was correct, her pet name for herself. There were many other highly personal references made by Piper/Phinuit that the Suttons agreed related to their daughter. As Hodgson observed, however, it was not possible to say whether the information came from the deceased Katherine, or from the minds of the Suttons at the sitting. Either way, of course, Mrs Piper was demonstrating impressive psychic abilities.

This question of the search for unknown data that could only have come from the dead is a vexing one that has concerned researchers for a century. It would only take one provable item to confirm the existence of an afterlife – 'one white crow to prove not all crows are black'. However, that information is arguably impossible. Any information that can be checked for validity must exist somewhere. If it could be shown to be unknown to anybody at the time the information was given, eliminating telepathy, there would still be the question of remote viewing, premonition, and other effects.

We were impressed by a piece of information in one sitting we discussed with the subject, the information could not have come from anyone at the seance. The fact that someone alive at the time knew the information does not make it the 'one white crow', but it is, perhaps, the suggestion of 'one white feather'.

Carol had been sitting with a medium and had been very impressed with the information she was given. Most of it she knew to be correct. Some points that came through in the sitting she did not recognise, but agreed they were correct when she later discussed the sitting with her husband. But one piece of information was so wrong that it disappointed her to the point of her distrusting the medium's abilities, despite his other successes. In contact with Carol's brother in spirit the medium made reference to Carol's sister. Carol told the medium she did not have a sister. The medium was not apparently put out by this, nor did he suggest he had got it wrong and it was, say, her mother's sister; he simply insisted he was referring to her sister. Carol left the sitting puzzled by the blend of right and wrong information, and feeling a bit let down.

She talked about the experience with her parents, relaying information about deceased relatives. And she told them about the reference to a sister. 'There was a stunned silence. And they were obviously very uncomfortable,' she told us. Her mother then told her a part of the family history, that had been unknown to Carol. Carol had often played at school with a girl, called Laura, and indeed they had been told they were distant cousins. 'I think we had better tell you something,' Carol's mother said. 'Laura is your sister. We had to give her away at birth.' For reasons that even now Carol has not been told, her sister had been adopted by friends, and brought up separately.

MEN IN BLACK

'Men In Black' (MIB) as a generic term is an association with the modern UFO phenomenon. Almost certainly, in that context, its origins belong with a man named Albert K. Bender in 1952. However, there is an incident in 1947 which put on record what may have been the first trigger for a phenomenon so strange that it is today unclear how much of it is reality and how much is folklore in the making.

On 23 June 1947, the day before Kenneth Arnold's UFO sighting, Harold Dahl, his son, a friend and a dog were sailing near Maury Island, USA, when debris from the air fell around them, some falling into the boat, injuring the boy and killing the dog. The following day a large black car drove up to Dahl's house. A man in a black suit walked to the door, spoke to Dahl and invited him to breakfast. The man told Dahl everything that had happened in Maury Island Sound the day before and added a warning he should keep quiet and if he talked about the incident there would be severe consequences, not just for Dahl but also for his family. The Atomic Energy Commission was in charge of processing plutonium and was experiencing some difficulty in getting rid of its radioactive waste, so they frequently dumped it from cargo planes into water. Because this had been witnessed by Dahl, the Man In Black was almost certainly an Atomic Energy Commission agent attempting to cover up illegal dumping. The Atomic Energy Commission, at that time, was probably one of the most powerful government authority bodies in the United States, formed to protect atomic bomb secrets.

However, in this incident we see most of the elements of the Men In Black: the alarmingly quick appearance of the figure; the fact that he seemed to have very up-to-date and detailed knowledge; the mention of dark secrets and veiled threats.

The 1952 incident involving Albert Bender had different qualities. Since we are virtually totally dependent on Bender's own account, we are also subject to whatever projected fears, paranoia, exaggeration and so on he may have been prone to. Bender seems to have worked out a theory to explain UFOs which he communicated to another researcher. Shortly afterwards Bender was visited by three men wearing black suits and hats, one of them apparently carrying the very letter which Bender had sent to his correspondent. Their arrival and nature, according to Bender in his book *Flying Saucers and the Three Men* was extraordinary. Bender was lying down in his bedroom when he became aware of three shadowy figures appearing in or entering the room. 'All of them were dressed in black clothes, they looked like clergymen, but wore hats similar to Homburg style. The faces were not discernible, for the hats partly hid and shaded them . . . The eyes of all three figures suddenly lit up like flash-bulbs, and all these were focused upon me. They seemed to burn into my very soul as the pains above my eyes became almost unbearable. It was then I sensed that they were conveying a message to me by telepathy.' Bender was threatened, 'If I hear another word from your office, you are in trouble.' Later, Bender telephoned a friend and mentioned his visit and the discussion. Immediately after he had hung up the telephone it rang again and a voice told Bender that he had made a 'bad slip' and warned him not to make another one.

By visiting Bender and putting pressure on him to stop talking about his theory, they turned what was proposed to be an article in his flying saucer club's magazine *Space Review* into a full-length book with themselves in the title!

In subsequent years many UFO witnesses allegedly received visits from Men In Black. A typical report comes from Jim and Coral Lorenzen, founders of the Aerial Phenomena Research Organisation (APRO) in their book *UFOs over the Americas* (Chapter 2: 'Recent Firsts'.) Driving late one night, Robert Richardson saw a blue-white light in the road ahead of him, braked but thought he had hit the object. He found a small lump of metal which he believed had come from whatever it was he had hit. Richardson contacted the Lorenzens and gave their investigator the metal. As the Lorenzens described, 'One of the most interesting aspects of this case was the series of visitors received by Mr Richardson in the days following the incident.' Two young men visited Richardson's home. Richardson noticed, as they left, that they were driving a 1953 Cadillac with, as it turned out, a licence-plate number that had not yet been issued. A week later two other men in black suits arrived, seeking the material. Richardson pointed out he had sent the material to APRO and that it could not be recovered; one of the men said, 'If you want your wife to stay as pretty as she is, then you had better get the metal back.' As the Lorenzens point out, 'In view of the fact that the piece of metal was discussed only on the telephone between Mrs Lorenzen and Mr Richardson, and later in private between Richardson and Paquette (APRO's local investigator), those concerned are wondering how the information got out . . . It would seem that the telephone call from Mrs Lorenzen to Richardson was somehow monitored.' (APRO was singled out for surveillance by the CIA's Robertson Panel Report.)

In decades of the 'suppression' of witnesses by Men In Black, and UFO researchers being told time and time again to 'back off or you will regret it', they seem only to have elicited the inevitable response: publicity. And as Hilary Evans, in his analysis of MIBs (*Visions, Apparitions, Alien Visitors*) states, 'They do not appear to have the backing they claim to have: they threaten their "victims", there is no record of any serious injury or even physical assault.'

Men In Black as a phenomenon probably takes its most bizarre turn with the well-known story of Dr Hopkins's visitation. The fact that Dr Herbert Hopkins was a responsible MD and one somewhat sceptical of the UFO phenomenon adds credibility to an otherwise extraordinary case of MIBs.

He was drawn into UFOs after using hypnosis on a young man named Stephens who reported a UFO abduction one night. Hopkins was alone at home on Saturday 11 September 1976 in the early evening, his wife and son having gone to a movie show. The telephone rang and an individual indicated he wanted to visit Hopkins to interview him about the UFO abduction case. Within seconds a man was coming up the outside stairs; Hopkins was certain there was no way he could have made it to that position from any telephone box. The man was wearing a black suit, virtually black shirt, black tie and a black hat. When he removed his hat, Hopkins noticed he was completely bald, lacking even eyebrows or eyelashes and his skin was almost like plastic. Hopkins also noticed that his nose seemed very small, his lips bright red and his eyes slit-like with a dark pupil. Hopkins later indicated the lips were painted with lipstick. The man hardly moved, sitting upright almost like a mannequin. During the conversation the man seemed to be indicating to Hopkins that he knew as much about the Stephens case as Hopkins did. Hopkins noticed the man's speech was 'machine-like', no vocal tones, no accent, no contractions.

An extraordinary event then followed. The man asked Hopkins to hold a penny in his hand and look at it, which he did. Hopkins described the penny turning from silver to blue and said that he had trouble focusing; then slowly the coin dematerialised and was not there any more. Hopkins could actually feel the weight of the penny disappearing though he could hear, smell and feel nothing. Having frightened Hopkins with this display the man then instructed Hopkins to destroy his recordings of his sessions with Stephens. (Which he later did, he was so alarmed.)

More absurdity was yet to follow: the man's speech apparently slowed down rather in the way of a record player slowly grinding to a halt. The man indicated that his energy was running low and he must go.

The absurdity of some claims tempts us to consider that a particularly strange and uninformed bunch of extraterrestrials is charged with a mission to draw as much attention as possible to the subject in question and ensure a steady stream of literature and books on the topic. If they were sent to Earth to suppress stories of UFO sightings, their leaders would be well advised to 'beam them up' immediately before they make even bigger fools of themselves.

To try to make some sense of MIB reports probably forces us to take divergent pathways. Some MIBs, particularly such as reported in the Maury Island incident, probably were government agents. We can also be almost certain that some telephone calls and the occasional personal appearance were the result of practical jokes being played on people by mischievous or even malevolent locals. And some of the MIB phenomenon was almost certainly the projection of fear and paranoia on the part of victims.

MOTHMEN

Two men on a roof, hiding in the dark shadow. A tall, dark, humanoid figure descends to their level. Huge, leathery, black wings spread out from either side. One of the men is instantly disabled. The other confronts the creature face to face. 'I want you to do me a favour,' the creature says, 'I want you to tell all your friends about me. I'm Batman.'

Fiction imitates fact; fact imitates fiction. Whether it is Jules Verne and long duration underwater submarines, Michael Rennie in *The Day the Earth Stood Still* and UFO contactee and abduction claims, or a host of other imagery, researchers of the paranormal are all too well aware of how life imitates art, and art imitates life. The opening paragraph is from Tim Burton's 1989 movie *Batman*, the dark, moody portrayal of Gotham City's fictional Dark Knight based on Bob Caine's 1939 creation.

However, the image of a flying man has existed around the world as part of folklore and in more recent years has been reported as fact, particularly in the Americas, also in the

British Isles and in other places around the world.

Probably the classic image of what became known as the Mothman was the sighting in West Virginia, United States of America, in 1961. A woman from Point Pleasant was driving along Route 2 through the Chief Cornstalk Hunting Grounds. Suddenly a huge humanoid figure was in the road ahead. As she later related to researcher John Keel, 'As we got closer we could see that it was much larger than a man. A big grey figure. It stood in the middle of the road. And then a pair of wings unfolded from its back and they practically filled the whole road. It almost looked like a small airplane. Then it took off straight up . . . disappearing out of sight in seconds.'

Mothman became a phenomenon in 1966 and 1967. The 'triggering' case arose on 15 November 1966. Two couples, Roger and Linda Scarberry and Steve and Mary Mallette, both from Point Pleasant, were driving when Linda saw two large red eyes peering out from a deserted industrial site. The group saw that they were part of a humanoid figure perhaps seven feet tall with big wings folded behind it. It was grey and moved slowly. Steve voiced their fears, 'Let's get out of here!' he shouted and Roger, who was driving, accelerated away quickly. They could see the Mothman standing on a hill near the road. As they passed it spread its wings and took off directly upwards. They became convinced that it was following them and even at 100 miles an hour Roger was certain that the creature was keeping up with them without even flapping its wings. Deputy Sheriff Millard Halstead stated, 'I have known these kids all their lives. They have never been in any trouble and they were really scared that night. I took them seriously.'

The reports made the press and the name Mothman was created, according to John Keel, 'spun off from the Batman comic character who was then the subject of a popular TV series'. (The series had just become cult viewing at the time.)

Before the reader gets the impression that we are seeking to write off the Mothman reports as a fantasy generated on the back of a fictional creation, we should make clear that we can be fairly certain that is not the case. Its origins are deeper, whatever modern reinforcements there may be.

V. Arsenyev, walking along the Gobilli River in the Sikhote Alin mountains, in the far eastern former USSR, saw a footprint and heard the sound of a creature off the track in the bushes. After a time he threw a stone towards the creature. He heard the sound of wings flapping and something large and dark took off into the air and across the river. The creature was well known to local people.

On 27 July 1944 Father J. Johnson, the pastor of St John's Church in Hollywood, Maryland, saw in the night sky the shape of a huge man with wings sailing downwards towards the church. He described it as dismal and gruesome, a huge figure with an enormous head and gigantic wings. In his autobiography, *The Story of a County Pastor*, Johnson described it landing in the graveyard and disappearing.

In the 1950s two winged humanoids were seen in southern Brazil by Luiz and Lucy Real. The 'birdmen' came to the ground vertically, landing in a crouched position.

During the 1966/1967 wave of Mothman sightings, reports were coming in from all over Virginia. Five teenagers saw a human-sized, humanoid, bird-like creature standing in a rock quarry which turned and ran when their headlights picked it out. A business man found a Mothman on his front lawn which flew off leaving him so pale and shaken that his wife believed he was having a heart attack. As John Keel states in *The Mothman Prophecies*, 'All together, more than 100 adults would see this winged impossibility in 1966–1967. Those who got a close look at it all agreed on the basic point. It was grey, apparently featherless, as large – or larger – than a big man, had a wingspread of about ten feet, took off straight up like a helicopter, and did not flap its wings in flight. Its face was a puzzle. No one could describe it. The two red eyes dominated it.'

Indeed reports were not always consistent; many reports told of huge heads, others saw no head whatsoever. As the creature was often seen in the dark, and was dark itself, these impressions could be illusions, particularly given the fright with which many witnesses encountered the Mothman. Clearly the creature also had a haunting type of quality. It rarely flapped its wings in flight, giving it a glider-like silent eeriness and when it took off from the ground it would do so vertically upwards, in a manner no winged creature can actually achieve without artificial power.

In England there were several reports, usually classified as Owlman. In Cornwall in England in 1976, on 17 April, Owlman was reported by two children, June and Vicky Melling, who described the creature as feathered and hovering near a church tower. On 3 July two young girls reported Owlman as a figure standing in near-by pine trees. As one of them said, 'At first, I thought it was someone dressed up, playing a joke, trying to scare us. I laughed at it, we both did, then it went up in the air and we both screamed. When it went up, you could see its feet were like pincers.' After several sightings in 1976 Owlman reappeared in the summer of 1978 in the same area; there were several reports over a period of months.

Mothman, or something very similar, had earlier been seen in England. Following a UFO sighting by four teenagers at Sandling Park in Kent in the winter of 1963, the group are reported to have encountered 'a tall dark figure . . . it was completely black and had no discernible head. Mervyn Hutchinson described it as looking like a human-size bat, with big batwings on its back.' The group ran off without further investigation. However, there is some doubt as to what they saw. We spoke with Paul Harris, a local investigator of ghosts, who confirmed that the area is well known for anomalous phenomena including ghost hauntings and UFOs. He put us in touch with Chris Rolfe who had interviewed one of the four, John Flaxton, a few years after the encounter. Flaxton by then was apparently of the opinion that the group might have seen a scarecrow in a field. The apparent movement may have been caused by the lights of a passing train.

In 1980 a leathery-winged man was reported by Mrs Ruth Lundy over Woodbine, Maryland. Driving past a cornfield, near a cemetery, she saw a figure over six feet tall. It was like a man, but she described it as 'pterodactyl-like'. It flew up over her car, she believed scared by its approach.

Paranormal phenomena notoriously go in and out of fashion and for a time Mothmen seemed to be consigned, if not to history, then at least to unfashionability. However, while we were in Florida in 1994 we were put on the trail of what seems to be the resurgence of Mothmen. Perhaps this is a product to some extent of the success of the new Batman films with which we started this chapter. As reported in *Florida MUFON News* by Albert S. Rosales of Miami, Florida, a distraught woman telephoned the emergency services on 23 June 1994 after she saw 'a tall, broad, dark-winged, manlike figure stepping from behind [a tree in her garden] and seemingly gliding towards the east side of the house'. In April 1994 in Washington State a truck driver encountered a 'tall, hulking, winged creature'. Albert Rosales is cataloguing humanoid sightings; he already has almost 2,000.

Mothman, like so many similar mysteries, is still unexplained. The degree to which it is factual – and it has been seen by several reliable witnesses, sometimes many together – and the degree to which it is folklore and legend is unclear. It is difficult to imagine a species, or several species, of winged humanoids remaining so elusive from zoological study for so long, yet new species of creatures, some quite large, are occasionally discovered.

Because the creature is consigned by many to folklore and legend, or at least to witness interpretation, there have never been serious studies to locate its feeding grounds, its nesting grounds, its colonies. In the end, a zoological study is the only study which will satisfy such reports; if there is a corpse that can be examined then the full story can be written. However, it is highly likely that Mothman will turn out to be more akin to ghost than reality.

For the time being Mothman remains an unsolved mystery, an inhabitant of that twilight world between reality and legend.

N

NEAR-DEATH EXPERIENCES

'I was in hospital. Doctors and nurses were around me when – I don't really know how to describe this – but the atmosphere changed; it became peaceful and without a sense of time. I realised I was above my body. I could look down and see my body, I could see the hospital staff. I could hear the doctor saying, "We are losing her". I said, "I'm up here" but they could not hear me. I then heard a buzzing sound; it got louder and louder until I felt myself being drawn along a tunnel. There was a light at the end and as I got closer the light got bigger. I saw my Grandmother there, waiting for me. As I got to the light I felt a presence within it, I saw it displayed as if on a movie screen. Then in front of me I saw a wonderful landscape; flowers and horses in a field across a stream. I wanted to go there but the Being seemed to say, "Are you ready?" I thought of my husband and my children, then I found myself re-entering my body with a thud. I could once more hear the doctors. At first I did not want to be back and wished to go again to that wonderful place, but I know I have work to do here. I no longer fear death: it was a wonderful experience and I feel my life is happier now. I don't always talk about this, I find many people cannot understand or I cannot explain the brilliance of it. It really changed me.'

This report has been made up from the commonest factors in many accounts in our files and from other researchers to illustrate the sort of experience some people claim after recovering from near death or clinical death. It contains many of the elements first noted by Raymond A. Moody Jr MD in 1975 when he first introduced the concept as a possible medical reality. No two reports are ever the same, but certain themes do recur although each experience will contain only some of these core elements. This suggests that even if there is a core, real, experience, there is a personal element in the way it is appreciated or interpreted.

The term 'near-death experience', or NDE, was first coined by Moody to explain the mystical experiences often reported by people who have been close to death or even pronounced clinically dead for a time before recovery. From these reports Moody catalogued certain elements which recur.

- A difficulty in describing all aspects with language, perhaps because of not fully understanding the experience.

- Hearing the news of their own death.

- A sense of peace and tranquillity.

- Strange noises such as buzzing, loud ringing, or a gale-like wind.

- The feeling of travelling along a tunnel, or entering a cave.

- Out-of-body experience (OOBE): the sensation of consciousness being apart from the physical body.

- Meeting friends and relatives who have died previously. These deathbed visions are more likely to be populated with the deceased than any other form of vision.

- Seeing and perhaps talking with a 'Being of Light'; a brilliant but non-blinding light radiating love and peace. This Being is often thought to be God or an angel.

- A review of the individual's life; in a non-judgmental way.

- A border to cross; often visualised as a river, fence or bridge. It is thought that if the experiencer chooses to make the crossing, he or she is accepting death. This suggests that there is a choice to hand. (But of course we do not hear the stories of those who choose to cross!)

● The return of normality and reawakening of normal senses; often felt with a sense of disappointment.

● A significant effect on later life, usually positive. Less than three per cent emerge with negative feelings about the experience.

The 'boundaries' to cross can take varied forms. Peter and Elizabeth Fenwick in their book *The Truth In The Light*, published in 1995, describe the story of a choice whether to make a journey.

'At the time of his experience in 1961, David Whitmarsh was seventeen, and serving aboard a Royal Navy frigate.' Whitmarsh was accidentally electrocuted. 'He became a live circuit between the fan and the steel chains. Whitmarsh said: ". . . I seemed to be floating in a beautiful velvet-like darkness, feeling completely at peace away from the frightening flashes. I seemed to be going through a tunnel angled slightly downwards when suddenly I found myself standing in a field of beautiful yellow corn. The sky on the horizon was the deepest of sky blues I have ever seen and I felt even more at peace in this lovely tranquil place. The brightness was strong but not overbearing and . . . I appeared to be wearing a blue gown. Suddenly, on the distant horizon I saw something that appeared to be a train, in fact a blue train. At first I thought that there was no sound but the beauty of the scene had been so intense that I hadn't noticed . . . I could see people in the carriages beckoning to me and telling me to climb aboard . . . Then, again almost as if by magic, I was in the train compartment . . . I felt I was being pushed down yet I was going up. I didn't want to leave my new-found friends, who were begging me to stay, and how I wanted to stay." But he did not stay, he recovered. "My first emotion was one of anger: why did they bring me back? I was happy on that train. I wanted to know where we were going." Whitmarsh no longer fears death. "In fact I am looking forward to that trip on the blue train and maybe next time I will reach my destination," he states.'

Interestingly Whitmarsh has no memory of getting aboard the train, boarding 'as if by magic'. Doorway amnesia is commonly reported in UFO abductions; an absence of knowledge of how the subject gets aboard.

Since Moody published his book *Life after Life* in 1975, many thousands of cases have been reported. A number of independent researchers and study groups have looked into the phenomenon.

Several people report surroundings viewed during NDE. We have many cases in our own files where fairly normal surroundings, fields, streams etc. are reported, but there are a number where there was a real sensation of a 'special' quality to the geography. This case arose during a gas-anaesthetised dental operation that nearly proved fatal, 'I found that I was in the most fantastic place. The flowers were enormous. I have never seen such colours; they were wonderful. And the flowers were way above me. I seemed to be walking through these fantastic flowers. It seemed as if there was a light through every flower. Rather difficult to explain but that's the feeling I had. It was so wonderful. And then the dentist tried to wake me, the nurse was shaking me and I didn't want to come back. This place was so wonderful. Eventually, of course, I came back.'

Cardiologist Dr Michael Sabom was given a copy of Moody's book and at first was put off by the less than scientific collection of accounts. But he became curious and with his assistant Sarah Kreutziger interviewed about 300 hospital patients who had experienced a life-threatening crisis. They found that forty per cent had experiences similar to those reported by Moody. Their conclusion was that the NDEs are genuine occurrences, and they felt them different to the hallucinations produced by drugs, etc. Sabom became very interested in the fact that these patients could recount many of the things happening in the hospitals that they should have been unaware of. In particular he found that many of those who claimed to have seen their open-heart surgery operations from outside their bodies described their own hearts accurately. As a 'control' he interviewed a sample of people who had not seen their own hearts and asked them for a description of what they thought they would look like and most were quite wrong in their description.

Dr Kenneth Ring interviewed 102 people who had had a close brush with death. In his initial study he found that forty-one per cent had classical NDEs. He classified the NDE as containing five core elements:

- a feeling of peace at the onset of the experience

- a feeling that one has left the body

- entering into a darkness

- seeing a light

- entering into the light

Ring felt that these were progressive stages and that the closer one got to death the more stages would be experienced.

Paediatrician Dr Melvin Morse became fascinated by the subject after a seven-year-old girl reported her experience while in a coma. After this Dr Morse questioned hundreds of patients and found similar stories emerging. He set up a research team, the Seattle study; this group included neurologists and psychiatrists. Dr Morse wrote about children's NDEs in *Closer to the Light*. He later wrote *Transformed by the Light* in which he examines the powerful effects and resultant changes in people's lives following an NDE. The group examined the claims of NDE, and found that in the temporal lobe was an area that, when stimulated electrically, produced the sensation of being outside the body.

Most research has shown that the experience is perceived as a good one, and maybe life-enhancing. Some researchers, however, have found that this is not always the case. Dr Maurice Rawlings, a cardiologist, found when interviewing patients as soon as they recovered that some recalled hellish encounters. This finding has also been substantiated by Dr

Charles Garfield who studied over 200 coronary and terminal cancer patients, finding a small number who saw demonic figures and nightmare images. Rawlings also found that these bad experiences were soon forgotten by the patients and suggests this is why other researchers did not come across them.

Dr Susan Blackmore in her book *Dying To Live*, has suggested the 'dying brain hypothesis'. She believes that the breakdown of the brain's normal processes through lack of oxygen causes the hallucination interpreted as an NDE. The tunnel image, she argues, is the result of the physical structure of the eye and therefore is likely to apply to all experiencers.

It has also been found that experiences very similar to the NDEs can be induced with hallucinogenic drugs.

Most experiencers of this phenomenon feel that they have had a glimpse of the afterlife and many state that as a consequence they no longer fear death. It must always be remembered however that the experiencers have not died – and to that extent 'near death experience' may be a misnomer. The result of 'true' death may be quite different.

No sensible analysis questions that people have these experiences, but their meaning is the subject of considerable debate. Do NDEs prove the existence of life after death or is there a psychological or physiological explanation for them? Michael Persinger, in America, has done experimental work on the experiences of alien abduction and OOBEs, the latter an essential part of the NDE. His work suggests that a magnetic field generated around the head of a subject can produce all the sensations of these experiences. The tentative conclusion many have reached on the back of that is that the experience is a hallucination caused by brain malfunction rather than a 'real' experience of transfer to another place or dimension.

The phenomenon of NDE may seem to have arisen in recent years because of advances in medical work that have made it possible to revive patients from closer to death than would have been possible in the past. But the experience is not a new one. Plato, who wrote much on the subject of death, defined death as the separation of the soul from the physical.

NOAH'S ARK

A wide variety of ancient cultures have a 'great flood' story associated with their origins or with the origins of the world as they understood it. Given the possibility of these stories being mythology, it would be extraordinary if physical artefacts confirming one or some of these claims were found. Yet that is the claim being made for Noah's Ark; that it has actually been located. There have been many claims by people believing that they have seen Noah's Ark. Most relate to Mount Ararat itself, although the Bible only states that the Ark came to rest 'upon the mountains of Ararat', a wide region containing many peaks.

Survival of the Ark is itself a long-standing belief. A Babylonian writer in 275 BC claimed the Ark could be seen in the Armenian mountains and related then that people were taking bits of it for souvenirs.

In 1876 Lord Bryce discovered a piece of wood four feet long some 13,000 feet up the mountainside. He also cut off a piece as a souvenir, believing it could have been from the Ark.

On 25 April 1892 Archdeacon Nouri claimed he had found the Ark near the summit of Mount Ararat, apparently largely intact. He described it as a huge wooden ship which he and his companions were able to view from several angles. He regarded its discovery as proof of the literal truth of the Bible.

In 1916 Russian pilot Roskovitsky claimed he had seen a large ship lying near the top of Mount Ararat.

In 1956 Ferdinand Navarra published his book *Noah's Ark: I touched it!* claiming that he had found the Ark under ice high on Mount Ararat and seen a number of its woodwork structures. Some of the wood retrieved was carbon dated at between 1,500 and 5,000 years old.

One of the most famous claims of the three-dimensional, physical Ark being preserved was made by George Hagopian, an Armenian, who claimed he saw the Ark when he was a young lad. He claims that when he was about ten years old, around 1902, his uncle took him on a personal expedition to see the Ark up on Mount Ararat. He described it as an immense mass like a wall, as big as a building.

Mount Ararat, however, is not the only favoured location

for the final resting site of the Ark. Within 'the mountains of Ararat' are the peaks of Mount Nisir, which is named as a resting place in an early account in Babylonia, and, seventeen miles to the south, Mount Judi (or Djudi) is recorded as the location in the Koran. It is on Mount Judi that the most promising, and certainly the most photographed, possibility for the landing place of the Ark is located.

The imprint on Mount Judi

That story starts on 31 August 1949 when *France-Soir* recorded that an expedition on Mount Judi had found the remains of a vessel 500 feet long, 80 feet wide and 50 feet high. The report also claimed that they had found the bones of sea animals and Noah's grave. The claims gained an impressive foothold in probability when in 1959 a Turkish Air Force officer, photographing the area on Mount Judi from an aircraft, photographed the imprint of a boat-shaped object 7,000 feet up the mountain. The following year Turkish soldiers made an expedition to the location and took the first ground-based photographs. Many expeditions since have photographed the site and there have been some hi-tech investigations of it in recent years.

Archaeologists on the site indicated that if the imprint is the remains of Noah's Ark, the state of preservation is very poor and there will be little tangible evidence of proof in scientific eyes. The remains appear to be some sort of fossilised, or pre-fossilised, wood now turned to rock or silts in the shape of planking. There are apparently traces of the bitumen or plaster which held the Ark together in the locality and ground-penetrating radar has indicated a pattern of iron fragments which may have been nails or clips some twenty-five feet below the surface. These appear to be laid out in parallel lines converging at the bow and stern and conforming with the general shape of a boat structure.

We spoke with Greg Mills, a representative of Geophysical Survey Systems, whose operative Tom Fenner did the ground-penetrating work on the site. He commented, 'Based on Mr Tom Fenner's evaluation of the site . . . it was assumed by Mr Fenner that there was some type of target that would suggest perhaps a type of anomaly as would be produced by a seaworthy vessel. The data that was collected using GSS systems did show some remarkable changes in the ground contrast . . . that showed there could be a man-made structure below the ground.'

Whether or not the imprint is of Noah's Ark, there is compelling evidence to suggest that it is the imprint of a large boat. Together with other evidence from the site, the fact of a large boat being found 7,000 feet up a mountain in the location given in both the Bible and the Koran and other accounts, such as a Greek manuscript by a Chief Priest of Babylon, indicates the possibility that it is the boat once known as Noah's Ark.

Is it logical or likely that the imprint could be the remains of Noah's Ark?

The Ark probably started its voyage from Babylon around 550 miles to the south of where it allegedly lies today. The location of Mount Judi may have been the most convenient eventual resting place as the waters diminished. Mount Ararat is the highest peak in the area at around 17,000 feet; any navigator on flood-torn seas would be guided towards that location as the flood subsided, in search of a landing place.

Scholars are undecided as to what the Biblical reference to gopher wood refers to, it is possible that the Ark was a reed boat, given the style of boat-making of the time. At the most, it would have had to have kept the occupants afloat for about a year; the voyage started on the seventeenth day of the second month of Noah's 600th year and ended on the first day of the first month of his 601st year. A reed boat is quite capable of maintaining itself for that period of time in water as Thor Heyerdahl's Ra expeditions proved in the late 1960s.

For several miles around the Mount Judi site, huge stones have been found which appear to be oversized drogue stones. They have holes in them where ropes could have been attached. Drogue stones were used by ancient seamen to keep ships steady in very heavy seas by dragging them along in the water on ropes. The drogue stones found around the location of the imprint are similar to those found in and near Mediterranean shipwrecks, but are of a size relevant to a much larger boat. These drogue stones are of course on a mountain hundreds of miles from any present sea. There is some implication in the biblical account in Genesis that drogue stones may have been used by the Ark. The Bible states: '. . . the Ark came to rest upon the mountains of Ararat and the waters continued to abate until . . . the tops of the mountains were seen.' If the Ark came to rest before the tops of the mountains were seen is it possible that its drogue stones acted like anchors, securing the Ark at a particular place and that that is what is meant by 'came to rest'?

As archaeologist Vendyl Jones said, 'If the Ark of Noah rested in Eastern Turkey it tells us that civilisation started there and from there spread over the whole Earth.' Again the evidence for this is compelling; in 1968 Dr Koriut Megurchian of the Soviet Union found what he believed to be the oldest large-scale metalworks in the world in Armenia at Medzamor, fifteen miles from Mount Ararat. It is noteworthy that scientific verification of the imprint indicates metal as part of the structure.

The Bible states that one of the first things Noah did on setting up his home after leaving the Ark was to plant a vineyard. Modern sciences have indicated that Armenia was one of the countries where the wild vine was first successfully cultivated.

The implication of the flood story and Genesis is also, of course, that human and animal life would have begun from the survivors of the Ark; modern archaeology indicates that the area around the Ararat mountains has been continuously inhabited for at least half a million years and that many species of animals and plants found in Europe today originate in that region.

What if the imprint has natural origins?
The imprint on Mount Judi matches the biblical account of the Ark with accuracy. If the imprint is natural then consideration must be given to the possibility that some ancient sighting of the imprint, or a now-hidden natural structure which has caused the imprint, may have inspired the Ark story in the first place.

In 1992 the imprint was declared an official archaeological site by the Turkish government who plan to carry out an excavation in 1995.

O

OMENS

Psychologists refer to the 'locus of control'; the position from which individuals believe their destiny is determined. Fatalists believe themselves to be in the grip of forces outside their control; i.e. the locus of control is perceived as being outside themselves. Activists drive their own destinies, they see the locus of control as being within themselves.

How we view the way the world interacts with us determines at least part of our belief in omens. All people have a need to reach, mentally, into the future: if we do not think of ourselves as in control of our own destinies, we are forced to look for clues that might give us some idea of what is likely to happen to us. We look for omens. Depending on whether we are essentially pessimistic or optimistic the omens we decide on might be bad or good. People will tend to accept as omens signs which reinforce their predetermined, underlying beliefs, and reject those which do not fit. Cynics of astrology argue that this is the way astrology works; the astrologer sets out a bland set of proposals and each reader of a horoscope selects the evidence that seems to fit his or her already determined view of the world. It would be naive to write off astrology in such simple terms, but it would be hard to deny that this seems to be the technique of the tabloid astrologers.

Omens to which people commonly ascribe meaning have been astronomical events, such as the appearances of comets and the occurrences of eclipses, or they have a ghost or spirit nature.

The Irish traditionally have the banshee, the best-known of

ghost-omens (See 'Banshee', page 40). The Welsh have their own banshee called Gwrach-y-rhibyn, described as an ugly green hag said to fly around emitting terrible shrieking noises before a death.

Also in Wales as an omen of doom is the sighting of the 'corpse candle', a mysterious light that is seen in connection with a person about to die. The size of the candle gives an indication of the age of the person about to die, the longer the candle the older the person. The colour tells the sex of the doomed person, white for a lady, red for a man.

The sighting of a Roman soldier standing guard on a bridge at Plas Pren in Clwyd is believed to herald not just death, but violent death, for the sighter.

Other parts of Britain also have ghostly foretellers of doom. In the west of Scotland an old hag-like creature is seen washing the bloody clothes of those who are about to die a violent death.

The sighting of spectral animals is also said to foretell death in different parts of Britain, different families having their own individual kind. Mrs Edith Olivier, in August 1911, saw two white birds on Salisbury plain (a common legend there) which she later believed were an omen foretelling the death, which occurred, of the then Bishop of Salisbury. In 1885 they had heralded, to Miss Moberley, the death of her father. (See also 'Black Dog Phenomena', page 59.)

Arguably the most famous ghostly omen is the ghost ship, the *Flying Dutchman*. There have been enough sightings to suggest some level of reality of the apparition, which has also been regarded as a bad omen. (See '*Flying Dutchman*', page 138.)

The *Flying Dutchman* is not the only omen of its kind. A smaller version occurs in the story of the 'Spectre's Voyage'; a young woman is seen travelling in a small boat on the River Wye towards Hereford. A sighting of this vision is held to be a foretelling of the sighter's death.

Seeing your own double is also said to be an omen of death (see 'Doubles', page 103.)

Omens can be good as well as bad. In September 1994,

against reputed odds of more than ten million to one, a pure white buffalo was born, named Miracle. A white buffalo is sacred to all Indian tribes. Sioux shaman Floyd Hand said, 'This is like the second coming of Christ. The legend is that the white buffalo would return and unify the nations of the four colours, the black, red, yellow and white.'

OUIJA

The Ouija board is a device often used by spiritualists to contact people on 'the other side'. The Ouija board may be a special printed board with a free-moving planchette, or formed by using any polished table and an upturned glass. Either arrangement depends on a layout of letters of the alphabet, the numbers 0–9 and, normally, the words YES and NO. The name is made up from the French (*oui*) and German (*ja*) words for 'yes'.

A person, or more usually a group, sits around the table. Each rests a finger on the glass or planchette. Questions are then addressed to the spirits and the answer is spelt out by movements of the glass. Ouija became very popular after the First World War when people sought to contact the loved ones they had lost.

An example of the use of the Ouija board, and one which is interesting for its content, is offered in the account by John G. Fuller in his book *The Ghost of Flight 401*. Following a plane crash there were many reports of the return of two of the flight crew to protect other such planes. Fuller used a Ouija board to contact Don Repo, the deceased Second Officer. Many messages were received, mostly that would have been known to Fuller, but which nevertheless corresponded with what had been discovered about the crash of the aircraft. There was one suggestion of both humour and presence in the message; Fuller asked a question of Repo to try to identify him with certainty, he already knew the answer because he was holding a news clipping with it on. The Ouija board spelt out SEE NEWS CLIP IN YOUR HAND.

But one personal message puzzled Fuller. The board spelt

out TO GO INTO WASTE BASKET PENNIES SIT THERE BOYS ROOM. Fuller took that detail to Repo's widow to ask if it meant anything to her. She replied, 'This is amazing. You've got to tell me where you learned these things. Don used to collect Indian head pennies. There is a small barrel of them in my son's room.'

Some research into Ouija suggests that the responses may be coming from the subconscious of one or more of the sitters, rather than from 'the beyond'. One experimenter admitted to us, after a sitting that we took part in, that many of the answers we had been given to questions, and the description of the 'spirit's' earthly life, were from the persona and life-history of a character from a fictional story he had written some years earlier. Before the sitting he had been concentrating on that story, as a colleague had suggested making it into a film.

Joan Forman in her book *Haunted Royal Homes* relates the details of a 1948 series of seances by historian Tom Lichfield and another. They used Ouija at seances to investigate reports of hauntings around Barnwell Castle; two seances at Lichfield's home and one at the castle itself. During the first seance they apparently contacted the spirit of Marie Lemoyne who explained that she had died while imprisoned in the castle. Many of the details transmitted were found to be historically accurate. It was at the third seance, at the castle itself, that the Ouija produced unpleasant responses. A spirit identified as Bervengarius Lemoyne seemed to threaten the sitters, followed by a sharp cracking sound. The sitters saw the upper body of a monk framed in the doorway.

Tom Lichfield discovered later that the Lemoyne family crest was the upper torso of a monk carrying a folded whip in his hand. Lichfield told Forman that he wished he had not undertaken the investigation, which was abruptly terminated after the vision.

Joan Forman, in her narrative, goes on to warn against the use of the Ouija board, pointing out that quite often forces appear to be unleashed which cannot be controlled. She asks the question, 'Does one allow toddlers to play with naked electric wires?' We agree from our own investigations; the

Ouija board does seem to have the ability to unleash quite strong effects, and whether or not these effects are internal or external or even purely psychological in origin, they often leave a lasting psychological impression that is rarely pleasant. It seems that the danger in Ouija comes not from the device, but from the belief that one is in contact with, or open to, evil. In short, if you believe in demons, the Ouija board is as likely a way of getting possessed as any other.

People who use the board as a game, perhaps when drunk or at a party, may be unprepared, and may leave themselves open to psychic attack. The results of spontaneous fires that have started in houses where Ouija boards have been used recklessly are themselves suspicious evidence enough to be wary before misusing such devices. The user may, in reality, be misusing his own mind, a powerful device we believe.

Wicca practitioner Graham James sells Ouija boards as part of his services to other practitioners. He is very strict about their sale. 'The Ouija board is very good for intelligent, sane, normal people. But even then, I never sell them to young people who may misuse them, or party with them, or use them when they have taken alcohol.'

We used a Ouija board as part of an experimental seance. There were several objectives: to obtain answers to questions; to identify the source of several hauntings at that location (Charlton House in South London); and to lay down a basis for replication of table-tilting work done by Kenneth Batcheldor. None of these were achieved that night, but we did get an unexpected result from the Ouija board. It was identified when comparing notes afterwards that during the sitting (there had been five of us around the table), two had simultaneously identified the shape of a dark, hooded, monk-like form at the far end of the Long Gallery that we were working in. A third had seen a less clear shape. A fourth member felt 'something' but declined to turn around and look.

The evidence for the source of information coming through a Ouija board is unclear. Because the sitters are in contact with the glass throughout, there is not only the possibility of outright cheating, but of subconscious 'pushing' in response to deeper thoughts. We have seen examples of both at our own experimental sessions. We have also seen thought-provoking details spelt out where it is difficult to account for the information. As Alan Gauld states in *Mediumship and Survival*, 'I have come across a number of instances of Ouija . . . in which correct information was given which was prima facie unknown to any person present.'

OUT-OF-BODY EXPERIENCES

The essence of the out-of-body experience (OOBE) is that there is, within people and arguably all living things, an essence that is separable and that can perceive from outside the physical body. The following account is a simple description from one OOBE experience, 'I was laying on the bed. It was a warm day and I could feel a warm breeze blowing over my body from the open bedroom window. I started to get drowsy, but I am certain I never slept or dreamt. I became aware that I was 'rolling up' inside my body. I was gradually compressing into my head. Suddenly it seemed like I flew out of my head and upwards. For a while I drifted on the ceiling of the bedroom, looking down on my body laying on the bed.'

It is probable that OOBEs require an altered state in order to happen, or that they are a component of an altered state. Many are reported during near-sleep. However, there are cases that arise when the physical body appears to be not only awake, but highly active. Lorraine Parry described an OOBE she had when she was just five years old. 'I was at the top of the stairs and I looked down; and I wanted to fly down the stairs, I really wanted to fly. I jumped off the top of the stairs and I flew down and landed very gently just below the last stair. While I was flying down the stairs I was very close to the ceiling and I looked down and there was me, slowly holding on to the banister and very slowly going down the stairs. And when I landed just below the bottom of the stairs I entered into my body from above going in with a kind of a slight jolt.'

This is interesting as it suggests that the physical body is under some sort of control during OOBE, arguably from the 'self' in the 'astral body'. The autonomous functions are maintained of course – breathing, for example – but walking downstairs suggests a complexity of muscular coordination that requires more alertness. One lady reported how she had watched from above as her body took careful precautions while crossing the road, in another case a man saw himself holding a conversation.

Claims for the OOBE are largely anecdotal. However there are a few cases that, if they are being accurately reported, suggest that information is gathered while in the OOBE state that could not, or at least was not, obtained through normal channels. Graham told us his mother had suffered a cardiac arrest and was taken to the resuscitation room of a large hospital. Graham described how the Sister there would not allow him to stay in the room, although he argued the point. Eventually he went to join his partner in a waiting area. He was angry and upset; he kicked the chair and lit a cigarette. The hospital team was successful; Graham's mother recovered. Some weeks later they were talking together and Graham's mother told him what she had seen that day. 'She described looking down watching the staff ripping her clothes off. She remembered me standing at the doorway arguing with the Sister and she recalled me walking down the corridor – which was probably about fifty or sixty feet from the resuscitation unit – turning right into the waiting area, kicking a chair, Chris asking me if I was OK and me lighting a cigarette. There was no way she could have possibly known all these things that were so far from the room she was in.'

Cardiologist Michael Sabom found a case where a woman saw, while out-of-body, the Chief Resident present at her operation though she had been told her own doctor would be there. In fact it was the Chief Resident that had been present and although the woman had never met him, she recognised him immediately when they first met.

Not all OOBEs are pleasant; quite often the first experiences for any individual are unsettling. They can sometimes feel painful; burning sensations, racing heart, even painful separation from the physical body, described by one woman as though her heart was being ripped from her chest. There can be psychological fears also; the feeling that it will be impossible to re-enter the body, or that the person might accidentally slip into death. There are no reports of such deaths, at least from those who have deliberately set out to go OOBE (if it has ever happened spontaneously we would never know, of course!).

Spontaneous OOBE cases are generally irregular, and rare. But there are a few cases where it is reported as a regular occurrence. Three-year-old Ami Greenstead, according to the *Daily Mail* of 24 July 1993, has a heart condition which causes her heart to stop occasionally. Her mother describes what Ami has told her, 'She told me that she goes up to the ceiling and can see the room. Then she says she "clicks back in".' Within a minute or so Ami 'returns to her body' and announces, 'Don't cry, Mummy, I'm back now.'

Generally speaking, during OOBE perception continues from within the 'astral body', often reported as looking down on the physical body. But not always; a Ms Violet Tweedale reported seeing her astral body returning to the physical, apparently viewing from the latter.

The astral body is rarely seen by the OOBE experiencer, though there are a few reports of a vague, shadowy form, or of a glowing, luminous shape. But there are exceptions: S.E. Scammell wrote to *PSI Researcher* (Summer 1994) to report that his wife had told him she had seen his astral body floating above their bed, mirroring the physical form below it.

We must ask not just whether, but why, people should have such abilities. Most human attributes seem to have evolved as part of the natural selection that allows the best equipped to survive. That may be no less true of OOBE. A case that suggests this comes from Stanley Conway who suffered considerable poltergeist terrors in childhood. His OOBEs were a form of escape, 'At home (where these events happened) my greatest delight was not being in my body. I used to be out of my body looking down at everything else that was going on. I didn't want to be in the room but I was safe when I was out of my body, or so I felt. And at will I could get back into my body any time I wanted to. I remember I used to go into bed and I used to close my eyes. And if I didn't want to be in my body I could just turn myself out through my head and I could look down on my body. I could do it at will. This ability gradually stopped; I lost the ability as I lost the need to do it.'

Most of the reported cases of OOBE are spontaneous happenings. In the case above Stanley had learnt to control them; entering an OOBE when he felt the need. Others who claim to control their abilities have taken part in experiments to test the validity of the claims of OOBEs. One test undertaken to prove some sort of remote viewing effect was set up by Charles Tart. The subject was instructed to leave her body and read a number on a card that Tart had written there. Although she succeeded, after three failed attempts, the results proved very little; telepathy has been verified in many experiments and could easily have played a part here, the number was of course also 'written' in Tart's mind.

This work was replicated by Dr Karlis Osis, but with results that might overcome objections to Tart's work. Pictures were placed in a box suspended from the ceiling. The test subject, Ingo Swann, correctly described them. But he also described seeing some printing in the box that Osis was completely unaware of. On examination, Swann was found to be correct.

If OOBEs are a subjective experience only, with no objective reality, then any explanation for them must account for the similarity of reports from all around the world, and cross cultures. Dr Susan Blackmore suggests that the OOBE is a form of 'notional movement' compensating for the paralysis that protects us from hurting ourselves when we are asleep. This does not allow for the claims of those who believe they have acquired knowledge while in the OOBE state, but Dr Blackmore is not persuaded by that evidence. 'The successes [of tests] have been apparent rather than real, I think. I just think it probably doesn't work.'

Perhaps the ability to OOBE is inherent in all people; if it is a survival mechanism then it almost certainly is. As with all talents and abilities, there will be those who can 'do it' better than others. No doubt part of the reason many cannot do it is that they have little need to, we have a world that we believe we can adequately deal with using our normal five senses. But there has been an upsurge in recent years of claimants to OOBE and a wide range of paranormal talents. If those who believe the experiences are wholly subjective are correct, perhaps the reason for the increase in reports is that people are recognising underlying fears and needs as they believe their normal senses are not providing adequate safety. If the experiences are objectively real, the same fears may simply be unlocking real talents. If we increase our range of perceptions, we increase our chances of survival.

P

PANIC OF 1938
It is often said that when Orson Welles broadcast his famous version of H G Wells's *War of the Worlds* in 1938, placing Martian invaders on the outskirts of New York, there was extreme resultant panic.

The newspaper reports of the time support the notion of panic. Headlines and strap lines such as 'It's a Massacre' framed details of the hysteria. For example, 'The horror caused by radio's "end of the world" and "foreign invaders" as some listeners understood it, produced some strange repercussions throughout the country.' Messages on the Associated Press wire described 'weeping, hysterical women', and people 'gathering in groups and praying'.

Later, Major Donald Keyhoe in *Aliens from Space* described how 'tens of thousands fled their homes, setting off a frantic exodus in several eastern states. Many were hurt in traffic accidents, and others collapsed from heart attacks.' One recent television biography of Welles referred to reports of rape by Martian invaders being claimed. Even Jung in his analysis of UFOs *Flying Saucers – a modern myth of things seen in the sky* described 'the great panic that broke out in New Jersey, just before the Second World War, when a radio play . . . caused a regular stampede with numerous car accidents.'

But did the panic ever actually happen?

The answer seems to be: no, at least nowhere near the suggested scale. A dispassionate analysis of that night in America suggests a quite different picture. It seems that most people who quote the 'panic stories' are relying on the media and a study by

Hadley Cantril (see Bibliography); few people seem to have even listened to a recording of the broadcast.

The broadcast itself
(Our analysis is based on our own full recording of the original. The timings and other details we refer to are our own analysis.)

It is popularly held that the broadcast was presented 'as if live'. That is only partly true, Welles did not disguise the theatrical nature of the performance. The show opens to music and announces 'Columbia Broadcasting System and its affiliated stations and Orson Welles and the Mercury Theatre On The Air in *The War of the Worlds* by H.G. Wells.' The fact that it was a play was reiterated thirty-nine minutes into the broadcast, and again at the end.

It was the seventeenth in a long-running weekly series of plays broadcast by the station. Wells always took the lead part, in this case that of astronomer 'Professor Pearson'. Although Welles acted on radio anonymously – this was the first time he used his own name – his distinctive voice would have been familiar to listeners, as that of an actor. And the Mercury Theatre, created by Welles with John Houseman, was a high-profile operation, a recent stage broadcast of theirs having jammed the streets of New York for five blocks from the theatre.

However, these stage productions were costing dearly. The Mercury Theatre was in financial trouble and Welles needed a sensation, and some really good publicity. One true statement to arise from the analysis of the broadcast was 'the next morning the name of Orson Welles was headlines all over America.'

Welles 'warned' the newspapers ahead of time of the panic that 'might ensue'. And the tabloids took the hint, not for Welles's sake probably; they knew a good story when they were inventing one!

Of the broadcast itself: of fifty-six minutes, barely thirty-seven could be mistaken for reality, and even then only assuming a high gullibility factor unlikely to be present in 'tens of thousands' of listeners.

The section 'presented as live action' could only be barely thought of as such. The setting of the play is a broadcast of an orchestra, while several interruptions are 'news-flashed' into the programme. The extracts of music are too short and too theatrical; no broadcasting company covering a real news item would make so many small, annoying interruptions with so little to say.

The compression of time is also glaringly obvious. Pearson is speaking 'from Princeton'; after one minute thirty-nine seconds he is 'live' at Grovers Mill. The commentator states that he and Pearson 'made the eleven-mile journey from Princeton in ten minutes'. There are many such examples of compression that would have 'given the game away', including the speed of firefighting, and the time taken to move the dead to hospitals and identify them.

The later part of the broadcast makes no attempt to disguise its theatrical nature. Dialogue flicks between past and present tense. Welles compresses days – implicitly months, perhaps even years – into minutes. In one monologue he describes finding a farmhouse, then instantly describes the onset of morning, then his following the Martians ('for two days I wander in a vague northerly direction'), then meeting another survivor. Welles, as Pearson, describes his desolate loneliness – listeners must have wondered at how quickly he became lonely; three-quarters of an hour ago he was happily chatting 'live on air' from his office in Princeton Observatory!

Within just a few more minutes he describes seeing the disabled Martians and tells us how they died, from infection. (A very quick analysis!) Within a few further short breaths he is describing dissected Martian machines in a museum, and the re-born earth with children playing in the spring sunshine.

The listeners' perspective

The listeners in the 'panic zone' had just thirty-seven minutes during which they might – if they had tuned in just after the introduction – believe what they were hearing. That is the extent of the broadcast that might have been regarded as 'real'.

For the first thirteen minutes of the thirty-seven they were hearing mild speculations. The first probable cause for concern was when the first deaths were caused by the heat-ray (after seventeen minutes). From that point on they now had just twenty minutes before Welles again made it perfectly clear that they were listening to a theatrical performance.

At this point the radio announces that areas of New Jersey have been placed under martial law. Most people concerned about what might be happening would have stayed by the radio to hear the further developments rather than cutting off their source of information. And they had no reason to run; the 'strange creatures' were still confined to one small locality under the scrutiny of the military.

Twenty-six minutes into the section we hear the first indication of Martians on the move – herding the population ahead of them. Between now and eleven minutes time is the period during which some people, convinced they were hearing reality, might have left their homes to flee the locality. But tens of thousands? Many would not have heard the broadcast at all; many would know it was a play because they listened to one every week; many would recognise the familiar voice of Welles. Of the remainder, the majority would have checked the papers to see what they were listening to. Few who listened to it, even without the introduction, would have been taken in by it anyway – the broadcast is very theatrical.

Of course there would have been a few uncertain individuals who telephoned local press and media to make sure what they were hearing. Some of the media's reported hysteria will have come from those calls. Probably a few individuals, cottoning on to the 'gag', would have made 'hysterical' telephone calls as a gag of their own.

Of course there would have been heart attacks and car crashes in the Eastern States that night; there are every night, but were there unusual numbers? Investigation at this late time is difficult, but our enquiries to the hospitals and police departments in the area have produced nothing to substantiate those claims. The Department of Transportation (then the Department of Traffic) has no specific data suggesting a panic on the scale suggested, but is, thanks to our enquiries, now conducting a check of records of 'spotter cars' that cruise the city checking on congestion caused by hydrant bursts, fires, etc. The New York City Department of Health have replied that they have no data available, but they doubted the claims. Informally one 'old timer' (his description) we spoke to told us he remembered that night and knew well that the panic had been exaggerated. 'There might have been a bit heavier traffic on the bridges [that night],' was his only suggestion. A similar comment was made to us by an official of the Department of Transportation. Interestingly, he had first confirmed to us in a telephone conversation that there had been considerable panic that night, but when pressed he admitted he was going from the media reports only.

A very small number of people might have taken to their cars that night. One or two paranoid individuals may have run into the streets shouting. They would have mostly encountered people going about the normal course of their lives, not having heard the broadcast at all. The majority who were listening to the broadcast, knowing it was a play, were presumably still at home listening to it. And those people they did meet – and the normality they would have encountered – would have slowed them down for the few minutes it would take before Welles told listeners (for the third time) that it was just a play.

Anyone shouting and screaming in the streets after the play had ended would eventually have encountered someone who knew the truth, and told them so. There simply was not long enough for shotgun mobs to form, or for tens of thousands to surge through the streets. And the local police departments have no records of any such mob movements.

As for the probability of mass panic, there is in any case little likelihood. Studies of mass panic situations that resulted from incidents such as the Kings Cross fire in which thirty people died when fire broke out in the underground station in London in 1987 indicate that the typical image of panic requires very precise conditions. Robert L. Hall PhD, in a presentation to the MUFON 1990 International Symposium, set out the conditions as follows:

- A sense of urgent threat.

- Ambiguity about appropriate action. Lack of (or breakdown of) a structured, conventional way of dealing with the threat.

• Partial entrapment and interdependence. If escape is easy, panic does not occur.

• Limited communication with the collectivity. If there is no communication among those in the situation, they are unaware of one another's behaviour and cannot influence one another. If there is perfect communication, they are unlikely to exaggerate the danger and behave in a way that increases the danger to themselves and others.

None of these conditions arose during the broadcast. When we spoke with Robert Hall he confirmed that it was his belief that the panic not only did not arise, but probably could not have arisen in the conditions that night.

The question of the aliens being regarded as a serious threat is uncertain. In the 1930s the strongest influence on people's perception of aliens, particularly in America, was probably magazines such as *Astounding Science Fiction* which had started in the 1920s and which blossomed through the 1930s. The editor of *Astounding Science Fiction* in 1938 was John Wood Campbell Jr, and one of his most famous contributors, Isaac Asimov, has always emphasised that he liked his stories to emphasise the qualities of humans that made them superior over aliens. In these stories the Earthmen won in the end.

The social perspective
The broadcast was made in October 1938. It was a time of concern over the tensions that were shortly to generate World War Two. Such a social climate might have made fear of invasion all the more tense, Cantril's study (see later) certainly seems to suggest so.

But the key social factors are more likely to revolve around the radio itself. Radio was still very much the active medium of the people in America in 1938; they were used to it. The listeners who walked in during the broadcast and were unaware that it was a theatre production, had no need to panic. People today walking into a room where a television is showing a realistic film do not usually assume it to be a documentary.

Cantril's study

A study of the ensuing panic was undertaken. This confirmed
the reality of the panic, and it is the source document for the
belief in the panic that has existed for the past fifty-seven
years. But Robert Hall points out that Cantril's sample was a
flawed one. It was based on the news media coverage of the
time and those questioned in the study are thought to have
been those who reacted most strongly to the broadcast. If only
a few individuals reacted adversely, it is likely that Cantril
included all of them and extrapolated from there.

Hall suggests that 'the best interpretation appears to be that
news media at the time and many persons interpreting the
events later greatly exaggerated the amount of wild, panicky
behaviour that occurred.'

The only real 'panic'

Local to the site given by Welles on the radio there was,
obviously, a little more concern, but whether it justifies the
term 'panic' is doubtful. We spoke to several local police forces
in the area of Grovers Mill, Trenton and Cranbury (our thanks
to Lt Maxwell of Cranbury P D). Although most people 'knew'
of the panic it was by reputation rather than documented
report. None of those authorities, including the Museum
related to the Trenton Police Department (our thanks to Joyce
Allen), had any documentation which supported the rumours
of panic (though it must be said that many records would have
been destroyed by now). There had, it was thought, probably
been some 'frightened' calls to the local police departments
checking out what they had heard on the radio.

In the area immediately around Grovers Mill anyone not
hearing the start of the broadcast might have reacted more swiftly
– when the alleged Martians were in their 'projectile' for example. However, anyone 'panicking into the streets' would undoubtedly have met many people who had heard the start of the
broadcast and knew it was a play because there is evidence of
numbers of young people looking for a Halloween laugh heading
for Grovers Mill to see if Mercury Theatre had laid anything on.

Dr Gerald Miller, now in his nineties, remembers the 'Martian invasion' well as he had seven years before set up his local practice and from which he had only in recent years retired. He supports the belief in panic, but recalled as many people moving into the area as out of it. This ties in with the many descriptions we received of the gay atmosphere of a 'night out'. He recalled a local 'old timer', George Dock – over 90 years old then – who the papers photographed in front of Grovers Mill having given him an old musket; they captioned the picture 'George – waiting for the Martians'. The party-like atmosphere sounds – curiously enough – like that described at the sandpit in the original novel before the Martians began their attack.

Dr Miller had not been in the town that night, and had no first hand sight of any panic. He believed there was some panicking from his talk with 'five or six' locals the following day. Some were embarrassed by their concerns of the night before. Dr Miller pointed out though that in those days the roads were dirt tracks and if there were traffic 'jams' on those roads, it would not have taken many cars to cause them, particularly since numbers of 'sightseers' were moving in opposite direction to the few who were 'panicking'.

It is probably the extreme reactions of a few people in this area that Cantril extrapolated from. Those who have commented on the panic since have relied on that extrapolation – and many have shifted the scene into the bigger towns and cities, including New York, where panic was almost certainly not evident at all.

It might also be borne in mind that the local area is very jealous of what is now a significant tourist attraction. It was suggested to us that we would get no thanks locally for diminishing any belief in the panic. In fact just a few years ago a metal image of Orson Welles reading his script into a microphone was set up in the area.

Comparisons

There have been no sufficiently comparable events to the *War of the Worlds* broadcast that would allow for direct comparison. However, Hall compares the situation with the Swedish Barseback panic, taking account of the comparisons made by Rosengren in his 1975 study. A Swedish radio company broadcast a fictitious news programme suggesting there had been a nuclear accident. Almost immediately there were reports in the media of panic throughout southern Sweden. Investigation of these claims was easier than in the *War of the Worlds* case, this being more contemporary. Analysis showed that there was no evidence of any such response; 'panic' consisted of phone calls to the police, the media and the fire services. A small number of people adopted panic-type responses to the programme, but these consisted only of shutting windows, phoning members of the family, and so on.

As Hall suggests, 'if there was any panic, it was a panic of the news media, rushing to beat their competitors and to report the attention-grabbing story.'

Summary

The evidence is that even if deluded, people do not act in the way the news coverage suggested. There may have been people who believed the broadcast they were hearing and personally panicked, but it is unlikely it would have become a mass panic. The hysteria reported in the media was probably hype, with little or no substance. The analysis that suggested substance was probably flawed, and based on a few local hysterical people and the traffic congestion caused as much by a fun night out as it was by people in fear. The broadcast itself – which many people comment on, but few seem to have listened to – is unlikely to have fooled many people, certainly not the numbers needed to justify expressions like 'mass panic'.

And the most popular example of triggering mass panic is nothing more than a myth, and a tribute to the power of the media to influence belief over the long term.

PHANTOM HITCHHIKERS

Phantom hitchhikers are a type of ghost. However, hitchhiker stories also raise special questions relating to folklore and urban legend.

This class of ghosts can itself be sub-divided into three aspects: hitchhikers who 'hitch a lift'; figures that appear by the side of the road forcing the driver to slow down or stop; and figures that are near-missed or actually hit by road users. Sometimes hitchhikers in the first category issue warnings about dangerous bends or sections of road where deaths have occurred. The reason for all these manifestations is held to be that the victim of some past accident wishes to warn future road users.

In a high percentage of hitchhiker stories, particularly of the second type mentioned above, the ghosts seem to have some physical being, far more so than in a corresponding number of ordinary ghost reports. Cars feel the impact of hitting the figures on the roads, or jog as they seem to run over bodies on the road. Against that is the observation that despite sometimes quite high-impact collisions, there is almost always no damage to cars. Perhaps the illusion of impact, and therefore the illusion of substance, is just an aspect of the phenomenon to be studied.

A Mr Cedric Davidson-Acres reported picking up a hitchhiker on a forest road in Malaysia. The girl sat in the back of the car, saying nothing. When Mr Davidson-Acres turned to her, she had disappeared. He discovered he was not the first to have picked up this girl.

Roy Fulton in 1979 stopped for a hitchhiker in Stanbridge, Bedfordshire. The hitchhiker opened the car door and sat silently, unresponsive to Fulton's enquiries. Fulton chose to offer the hitchhiker a cigarette, but turning to him found that he had disappeared.

The same stretch of road is often home to numerous reports. The most famous is probably Blue Bell Hill, in Kent. In November 1965 two cars collided on Blue Bell Hill, one of which contained four girls on their way home after an eve of wedding party. The bride-to-be and two of her friends were killed. This is often held to be the origin of the Blue Bell Hill hitchhiker, though obviously that cannot be determined with certainty. Several reports have indicated a 'young girl of around ten years old' being hit, which would not seem to correspond with a bride-to-be, though some reconciliation of descriptions has been attempted by some researchers. The series of main reports include:

The *Kent Messenger* of 9 September 1968 indicated that a girl had been picked up and asked to be taken to Maidstone (where the wedding party had been heading). No witnesses could be traced for interview for this claim, which may therefore be legend building on the accident.

In 1974 Maurice Goodenough hit a 'young girl of about ten'. The man took the body to the side of the road, wrapped her in a blanket and alerted the police. On investigation, no body could be found, the blanket was empty. No injured girl was ever located.

On 8 November 1992 Ian Sharpe thought he hit a girl who went under the vehicle; no body was found.

Christopher Dawkins had a similar encounter, reported in the *Kent Messenger* of 27 November 1992.

Other roads are famous for repeated incidents, such as the A38 near Taunton in Somerset and the Frome – Nunney road near Warminster.

If ghosts can be seen, there is no reason why they should not be seen by drivers. But the stories of hitchhikers contain more than that. The apparent physical elements we have already mentioned. Such accounts are often attributed to local events or legends, as in the case of Blue Bell Hill, connecting the stories to one road incident there.

There is also a high incidence of 'complete' stories in hitchhiker accounts which suggest folklore or legend. For example, very often the hitchhiker has given an address which, when investigated, turns out to be the address of that very person (identified by a photograph offered by the grieving parents) who died in a road accident where she was picked up. But these have the characteristics of urban legend; generally, actual witnesses and families are untraceable by researchers, the stories are 'a friend of a friend who knew the driver it happened to'. Other ghost report categories rarely tie up their loose ends so conveniently.

The principal question to be asked, in addition to any relating to specific reports, is why should roads be subject to this type of phantom when other scenes of accidents are not? More accidents happen in the home than anywhere else, and plenty of accidents happen in factories and offices, yet there is no special type of protective phantom for those locations. There are cases of ghosts in both these situations of course, but not the high numbers we might expect if 'phantom protection' is a phenomenon in its own right.

What seems probable is that the phantom hitchhiker has become a special classification because of the 'cult of the car'. The special, almost sexual, attraction to cars for men in particular gives cars a special status in our society. Almost all those who encounter the hitchhikers are men; most of the ghosts are female.

Road use may itself offer some clues. In the case of seeing or even hitting figures we can consider the state of the driver. Some drivers may enter something of an altered state of consciousness when driving tired or in monotonous scenery. That alone, however, cannot explain phantom hitchhikers, or there would be a great many more impacts reported on motorways where those conditions are more frequently encountered. One other factor would seem to be the state of awakening, perhaps indicating that the hallucination of a figure is hypnopompic in origin. Many hitchhikers are seen at or just rounding a bend in the road; presumably there is a need to waken slightly to shift gears and manoeuvre the steering wheel to negotiate that bend. The condition of being forced from a doze to a more awake state could be the trigger for an hallucination. If that moment were combined with, say, a brief sighting of an unusual shadow or shape by the road, and even perhaps running over a rock or branch in the road, the conditions for an hallucination of an impact might be complete. The fact that no body is then found is explained.

Such a set of circumstances might explain many reports, particularly if the connection to a dead girl is later made – as is often the case – or if the local legend is already known. A deeper such state might even, at a stretch, offer some clues to reports of ghostly hitchhikers picked up and taken as passengers.

It does not, of course, explain situations where a body is found and even wrapped in a blanket. If there are 'real' ghosts involved in phantom hitchhiker reports, these few special cases might represent them. To study them for what they are, and identify their special characteristics, they first need to be separated from the confusing mythology of the phantom hitchhiker.

PHANTOM SCENERY

Sir Ernest Bennett reported in his book *Apparitions and Haunted Houses* a case typical of what has become known as 'phantom scenery'.

When Ruth Wynne, in the company of a young girl, Miss Allington, set out to look at the church at Bradfield St George, they were surprised to see a Georgian-style house, with Georgian windows, with large trees in the garden where they could not recall seeing one before. Starting some four months after their original visit in October 1926 they made several attempts to re-locate the house, but never could.

A similar report was published in the *Journal of the SPR* in 1961 when a brother and sister, Grace and Bruce MacMahon were walking in a wood near Hadleigh in Essex. They spotted a Georgian mansion they had never seen before, despite familiarity with the location. In later visits to the wood they sought out the mansion, but were never able to find it.

It is tempting to suggest that these witnesses simply got lost, or misinterpreted what they saw. Certainly other such cases that have been investigated have been at least tentatively resolved in this way. However, a few cases, such as the MacMahon's, offer no suggestion of either unfamiliarity or confusion, and they seem to have been followed up enthusiastically, suggesting some real phenomenon at work.

The suggestion is that the scenery viewed was from another time, temporarily visible to witnesses, and therefore this phenomenon is a close cousin of, or a part of, 'time slips' (see page 303).

PHILADELPHIA EXPERIMENT

If ever there was a highly fascinating, enduring mystery based on ridiculously suspect sources it is the Philadelphia Experiment. No amount of lack of substance in the claims for this mystery seem to deter ardent fans and believers who find it, presumably, both fascinating and entertaining.

(We are grateful to Jacques Vallee for assistance in this analysis, and particularly for permission to quote from correspondence and interviews with Carl Allen and Edward

Dudgeon which he sent us. Vallee has published his analysis in *Anatomy of a Hoax*. Vallee is not responsible for any of our own conclusions expressed here, though it appears we agree in most part on the analysis of these claims.)

The Philadelphia Experiment, as popularly believed, is the claim that the US Navy managed to make a ship, the USS *Eldridge* (designation DE 173) invisible in front of a number of observers in the Philadelphia Navy Yard, Virginia in October 1943. An extension of that rumour is that it was temporarily teleported to Norfolk, then returned to the yard.

The claims indicate that not only did the destroyer and its crew disappear in full view of observers, but that there were extraordinary after-effects; members of the crew disappearing at later times in front of other people during social functions and ordinary home life. There were claims of members of the crew reappearing physically enmeshed within the ship's physical structure.

The source of the rumours
In 1955 astronomer Morris Jessup published *The Case for the UFO*. Shortly after the publication of the book, Jessup received correspondence from a Carl M. Allen (also known as Carlos Miguel Allende). In the letters, Allen described the Philadelphia Experiment in some detail. He described the field which created the invisibility as 'an oblate spheroidal shape, extending 100 yards (more or less, due to lunar positions and latitude) out from each beam of the ship'. It has been suggested that magnetic or electromagnetic forces were used to create the field. Of the people involved, Allen stated, 'Any person within that sphere became vague in form but he too observed those persons aboard that ship as though they too were the same state, yet were walking upon nothing. Any person without that sphere should see nothing save the clearly defined shape of the ship's hull in the water.'

A paperback copy of *The Case for the UFO* was sent to the Chief of the Office of Naval Research (ONR), Admiral F.N. Furth, in late July 1955. The book was apparently annotated by three different writers in three different coloured inks. These notes on Jessup's book described knowledge of UFOs and their propulsion, and knowledge of the Philadelphia Experiment. In 1957 Jessup was asked to visit the ONR in Washington to discuss the book and its annotations. Jessup apparently handed copies of Allen's letters to one of the investigating officers, Commander George Hoover. In what seems a slightly bizarre move Hoover, apparently with the other investigating officer Captain Sydney Sherby, instructed the Varo Manufacturing Company, a Texas electronics firm, to publish a small run of Jessup's book containing both the Allen letters and the penned annotations.

Jessup apparently became obsessed by the whole mystery of the Philadelphia Experiment and frustrated by his inability to locate Allen, which he never succeeded in doing. He became depressed and full of self-doubts and in 1959 took his own life. Almost inevitably, rumours surrounding his death, such as that he was murdered, have been added to the Philadelphia mystery.

Much of the background of the Philadelphia Experiment was set out in Charles Berlitz' second book on the Bermuda Triangle, *Without a Trace* published in 1977, in which he speculates on a link between the effect used to create the invisibility field and the perceived effects inside the Bermuda Triangle of ship and plane disappearances. In 1979 Berlitz, together with William Moore, published the book *The Philadelphia Experiment* which entertained 'the possibility than an experiment sponsored by the US Navy may have accidentally managed to pass through a doorway into another world'.

What we have in essence then, when we ignore the various writers who have capitalised on the myth of the Philadelphia Experiment over the years, are the claims of one person, Carl Allen. What then of Allen, the key to the mystery?

Allen was not modest in his claims. He believed that Einstein had died after reading the Varo edition of the book, apparently shocked to discover how wrong he had been. But the Varo edition was published in 1957, indeed could not have been published before July 1955; Einstein died on 18 April 1955.

The researcher and author Jacques Vallee had himself received several letters from Allen starting on 28 June 1967 (as set out in Vallee's book *Revelations* published in 1991). Vallee reports that Allen offered to sell him the only true

17. Map dowsing. Mountain climbers have been found using this form of 'distance-dowsing'. The author's own experiments seemed to indicate a telepathy at work. *Credit: John and Anne Spencer*

18. George Hamilton. A stigmatic with many visible wounds, living in Scotland who has experienced visitations of the Virgin Mary. *Credit: John and Anne Spencer*

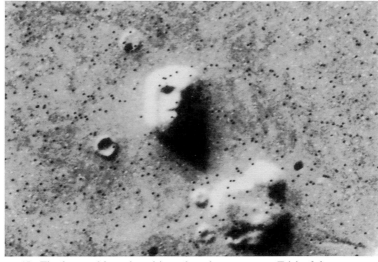

19. The face on Mars, the subject of much controversy. Trick of the shadows or message to Mankind? *Credit: NASA*

20. Mars has fascinated Mankind for centuries. 'Mr Smiley Face' – another face on Mars this time formed within a crater.

21. A stylized ouija board and planchette. Hand-drawn cards and a wine-glass will do just as well. But flippant use of ouija boards have been known to unleash unpleasant energies. *Credit: John and Anne Spencer*

22. H G Wells' walking Martians reportedly terrified the people of New York when a radio play version of the book was broadcast in 1938. *Credit: Martin J Bower (sci-fi model maker)*

23. Peddars Lane, Bedfordshire. The site of Roy Fulton's phantom hitchhiker report. Such reports come from far and wide: the UK, America, France, Africa, etc. *Credit: John and Anne Spencer*

24. Bradfield St George. Two women walking here believed they saw phantom scenery – a Georgian house – they could never again locate. *Credit: John and Anne Spencer*

25. Newark Street. The site of a frightening sequence of hauntings and poltergeist activities. *Credit: John and Anne Spencer*

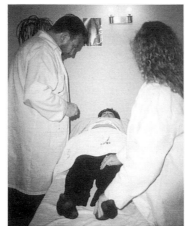

26. Jenny Bright about to undergo psychic surgery from Stephen Turoff ('Dr Khan'). *Credit: Jenny Bright and Dr David Cross*

27. Bent spoons, a modern mainstay of PK experiments. The centre spoon was bent effortlessly under hypnosis during experiments with the authors (the other two were tests for comparison). *Credit: John and Anne Spencer*

28. The 'Nine Ladies' ring of standing stones in Derbyshire. Three young girls, in the company of the authors, all heard their names called out whenever they touched the stones. Can psychometry trigger energies locked up by nature? *Credit: John and Anne Spencer*

29. SLI – Street Lamp Interference. Reports of PK-like interference with street lighting is collected by researcher Hilary Evans. Photo shows Harpenden Common where one of the authors had a SLIDE experience. *Credit: John and Anne Spencer*

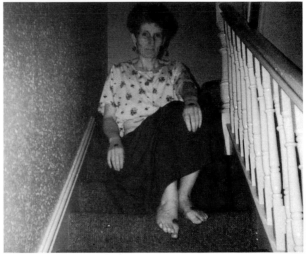

30. Heather Woods displaying her stigmata on hands, feet and sides. At other times a stylized cross appeared on her forehead. *Credit: The estate of Heather Woods*

31. 'Eleanor' looking in the window of the cottage where she had her timeslip experience as reported to the authors. *Credit: 'Eleanor'*

32. Frederick Valentich, a lone pilot lost over the Bass Straits in Australia during a UFO encounter. *Credit: Paul Norman, VUFORS*

33. Vampire legends, crystallised in the late 1800s, have a much longer history. And the claims of vampirism continue to the present day. *Credit: Hasan Shah (still from the film 'VAMPIRES' by Hasan Shah Ltd.)*

34. Mary Murray's statue of the Virgin Mary, seemingly weeping blood, has become a focal point of worship in Grangecon, Co Wicklow, Eire, as such statues have the world over. *Credit: Mary Murray*

35. The wolf, a much feared predator in Europe. Werewolf legends may have grown from a combination of fear of rabies and hallucinogenic fungus. *Credit: John and Anne Spencer*

36. Graham James of the 'House of Jupiter'. A thoroughly modern, hi-tech, business-advisor – using witchcraft. *Credit: Graham James*

original copy of this extraordinary book for a mere $6,000, though he later bartered himself down to $1,950, which Vallee still declined. Rather dubious correspondence from Allen, noted in Vallee's book, led Vallee to conclude, 'The man . . . was quite capable of twisting words to derive a personal benefit from his ability to convince or intrigue others. I felt I was corresponding with a con-man . . .'

Allen did not stop at one extraordinary story. He wrote to Vallee indicating that he had been a crew member of the SS *Maylay* in 1947 when it was attacked by a UFO 1,600 feet wide. Vallee was unable to find any listing for the SS *Maylay*.

Allen turned up in 1983 in a place where he could be interviewed by Vallee's companion, Linda Strand, who left her interview with the belief that Allen was 'an odd character who made off-the-wall statements'.

The mythology of the Philadelphia Experiment is strong. Stories relating to invisibility have crept into various mystery phenomena and of course feature strongly in Bermuda Triangle lore and UFO claims. No matter how insubstantial and uncorroborated the rumours for the Philadelphia Experiment, it is virtually impossible to attend a large gathering of devotees of the paranormal such as a national conference or lecture, without someone assuring anyone who will listen that the Philadelphia Experiment was real and that the American government has been continuing the research in the years since.

One interesting thought arises regarding the Navy Yard in Philadelphia. It might be that Allen created his ideas in the 1950s, when he wrote to Morris Jessup. But if he did have any contact with the Navy Yard earlier around the early 1940s, the time he gave for the actual experiment – then some of the personalities at the yard at that time might have been responsible for his ideas. (Jacques Vallee's interviewee, Edward Dudgeon tentatively states that Allen 'could well have been in Philadelphia at the time, serving in the merchant marine'). In early 1942 Robert Heinlein was working there; he was an engineer who had been trained at Annapolis, had retired from the navy due to ill-health, and had been retained as a civilian engineer at the Naval Air Experimental Station of the Navy

Yard at Philadelphia. L. Sprague de Camp joined him there shortly afterwards. Isaac Asimov joined them on 14 May 1942. They were doing emergency war work, nothing very exacting. Asimov describes his having 'punched a time clock' while he was there, and found the work nothing but a distraction from his writing. Nonetheless, three of the most influential science fiction writers of the twentieth century were all working there together. What must their coffee-break chats have been like . . .?

And what reality might there be?

By the outbreak of the Second World War in 1939, radar was in extensive use. For example, it is said to have been the major technological reason for the victory of the Battle of Britain in 1940, and it was radar-controlled fire from the *Bismarck* that sank the British battleship *Hood* in 1941. From the moment radar had been successfully applied, the military of several countries began looking for an 'anti-radar' shield. If the Philadelphia Experiment has any basis in reality, it might relate to an experiment to create radar invisibility rather than real invisibility.

But that seems not to be the explanation for the *Eldridge*. Jacques Vallee located a sailor who had been involved with work involving the *Eldridge* at the time of the alleged experiment, and who believes he knows the basis for the claims. Mr Edward Dudgeon was in the navy between 1942 and 1945; in 1943 he served on the USS *Engstrom* (DE 50). He stated, 'We were trying to make our ships invisible to magnetic torpedoes, by de-Gaussing them.' He added, 'The *Eldridge* and the *Engstrom* were in the harbour together. In fact four ships were outfitted at the same time . . . in June and July of 1943.' The de-Gaussing took place in some secrecy. 'They sent the crew ashore and they wrapped the vessel in big cables, then they sent high voltages through these cables to scramble the ship's magnetic signature.'

Of 'real' invisibility, there is probably no reality. If successful experiments in invisibility had been conducted in 1943, it is improbable that the work would not have been furthered in the years since. The idea that such an advanced and extraordinary capability could be kept under wraps for over fifty years is untenable in a Western society that has shown that honour and duty are out-priced by greed and glory. And the prize for a reliable revelation of successful invisibility would be great indeed! Given the involvement of private corporations in most Western governmental contracts, it is highly probable that spin-off technologies of this capability, were it to exist, would have surfaced in private enterprise ventures.

The fact is that the only thing that has disappeared without trace into total invisibility is any verification of the Philadelphia Experiment.

POLTERGEISTS

From the German *polter* = disturbance, or noisy, and *geist* = ghost.

It is the disturbances that differentiate the poltergeist from most other ghost reports. The nature of each case is unique; most cases contain some – if not all – of the following:

- Rapping noises and spontaneous noises with no apparent cause. In some cases people have been said to communicate with the poltergeist through these noises.

- Apparitions, ghostly appearances, or black shapes, even ghostly animals, have been seen by those affected by the poltergeist.

- Apports, the spontaneous manifestation of objects without apparent source, are often reported. These are often small stones falling on house roofs or small objects such as coins appearing within the house. A wide variety of different objects have been reported in cases world-wide.

- Levitations; people have been lifted into the air without apparent physical aid. In the Enfield poltergeist case, one of the best investigated and documented, Graham Morris set up a remote-controlled, motor-driven camera and caught several frames of film that appear to show the subject floating through the air.

- Moving objects; a common poltergeist report is that objects have been seen to move by themselves, even some very large and unwieldy items move around spontaneously. Chairs and tables have been seen to flip in the air (at Enfield a woman police constable called to the house watched a chair moving without visible cause). Commonly, sheets are described as ripped off beds (as was photographed during the Enfield case).

- Strange voices have been heard, sometimes coming from a person within the house, and often from the person suspected of being the focus of the poltergeist. These voices are often abusive and guttural. Experienced researcher Maurice Grosse listened to one girl speaking in a deep, guttural voice for far longer than he believed she could ever have done using her own, normal voice.

- Attacks; occasionally people have been attacked by the poltergeist. Scratch marks, bites and other skin markings appear. Some witnesses have suggested that the marks look as if they were being scraped on the skin from the inside.

- Small, apparently spontaneous, fires sometimes start around the poltergeist.

- Water is also often a part of the phenomenon. It may leak through walls, or fill objects with no apparent source. We have worked on one case where the two witnesses – the only two people in the house – stood side by side and watched a pair of shoes on the floor slowly fill up with water without apparent cause or explanation.

Poltergeist cases arising before the nineteenth century were usually considered manifestations of witchcraft. Occasionally they were thought of as spirits of the dead. It was when Sir William Barrett and Frederic Myers studied the characteristics of the reports that they concluded poltergeists should be viewed differently from other forms of ghost.

Nandor Fodor, a paranormal researcher of the 1930s, first suggested the possibility that poltergeists represented the repressed tensions and emotions of subjects. William Roll, an American researcher of the paranormal, believed this was the case when he studied recurrent spontaneous psychokinesis (RSPK).

Roll conducted interesting tests on a poltergeist focus. The focus was observed through a two-way mirror concealing two tape-measures in his clothing. He later threw them at a relative. After this, the subject was questioned and denied what he had been seen doing. The subject was then hypnotised and given a lie-detector test, but he still denied that he had thrown the tapes. The lie detector offered no evidence he was lying, suggesting a dissociated state of which the subject has no memory. While this might indicate something of the state of mind of the focus it does not, alone, explain all poltergeist activity, some of which has been seen by researchers when no other person was in the room. For example, Maurice Grosse at Enfield was hit on the head by a cardboard box which took off from a stationary position from where no person was standing. Perhaps the dissociated state, combined with PK abilities might offer some part of the explanation.

There is no consensus as to the origins of poltergeists. Present-day researchers are generally divided between those who believe poltergeists are a form of PK energy released, those who believe they are entities, and those who believe they are a combination of the two – an entity 'allowed in' by a certain state of mind.

A focus of the poltergeist activity can normally be found within an affected family. The focus might be unaware of his or her importance to the case. More women and young girls seem to be the focus of poltergeist cases than their male counterparts. This is a factor identified in many paranormal areas. Age has also been identified as a factor; many events happen around a person at puberty. However, both children and adults can be affected and it is perhaps the mind set of the foci rather than age that is important.

Poltergeist activity tends to strengthen and then diminish. It usually starts in a small way, often with scratching noises at first attributed to cats or rats in basements or attics. As time goes on the various characteristics listed above arise. At its peak, poltergeist activity can be extremely intrusive and very disturbing to the family or individuals affected.

We were the first, and to date only, researchers to interview the percipients of a prominent case of the 1950s. The family were effectively hounded out of their home in the Whitechapel area of London, and were never tracked down by reporters and researchers who covered the case from local newspaper reports of other people who had known the family. We located the family in 1993 and interviewed them as a group. It was a particularly interesting insight, as time had allowed the family to think through their experiences of forty years before. Even more unusually for poltergeist cases, it provided us with the opportunity to speak to its focus – a man of then forty-plus, who had been only five at the time of the 'attacks'. The case had the unusual property of seemingly being 'attached to the property'; most cases seem attached to a person or family and move with them. In this case the family got away from the poltergeist, and others who moved into the property were affected by it. To this extent it may either suggest a re-think of theories about poltergeists or, more likely, represent a case where the psychic activity contained a poltergeist, but more besides.

The case is, inevitably, a long and complicated one. We summarise it below.

Harry and Vera Conway, their son Stanley and his sister, the new-born Deanna, lived at 88 Newark Street, Whitechapel, London (see photo section). It was a four-storey house, the top floor used as a workshop. Stanley, who was certainly the main victim, and probably the focus, slept in his own bedroom on the second floor. This bedroom seems to have been a focal point and the scene of the most frightening occurrences. Vera told us she could never go into the room without feeling intensely cold.

Vera continued, 'From the very beginning Stanley used to wake up and scream. He claimed that someone used to touch him . . .'

There were many 'typical' poltergeist manifestations. The door to Stanley's room was always jamming closed; they pinned it open with a pressing iron at one point, but on another occasion the door had to be virtually broken down to gain entry. Harry entered the room on one occasion and was hit hard on the back of the head, though there was no one around.

Many noises were heard in the house, strange sounds of people running, or walking with a stick, were heard on the staircase. Noises in the upstairs workroom were so loud that the neighbours complained (it was only after the Conways left the house that the neighbours realised the noises were spontaneous). Other happenings included a mirror in the living room being cracked during the night, as also was a glass-topped coffee table, though no one had been near them.

Stanley recalled his nights of terror in the room. There were sightings of a 'ghost' cat. But worse than that was what Stanley described as 'being touched'. He was well into his adult life, and a long way from Newark Street, before he was able to sleep with his hands outside the bed covers. He told us that he spent a lot of his time OOBE; it was a defence mechanism. Out of his body he was safe, he believed. (See 'Out-of-Body Experiences', page 211.)

The whole family suffered during those years. As Vera said, 'We went through six years of hell in that house. We had nothing but bad luck from the moment we walked into that house. Everything that could go wrong went wrong; the children were always ill, we lost every penny we had in this business venture.'

Vera's opinion was that anyone moving to the house would have nothing but bad luck.

Stanley remembers the feeling of a different entity, 'It wasn't a kindly entity. It was a big, big, black entity, almost human . . . trying to grab me at the neck.'

Stanley reflected on his experiences, 'Whatever is locked in my memory is well and truly locked up . . . There are things locked up (in my mind) which are desperately trying to come out. And if I could handle it I would love to know what it is.'

There are many schools of thought on dealing with poltergeists. Some researchers such as Maurice Grosse, have advocated seeking the primary stress areas within a family and finding ways to reduce them. We ourselves have tried this with some success. Others have advocated rescue mediums to 'send the spirit to the light', again with many claimed successes. Banishment through exorcism has been used. (See 'Exorcism', page 120). It is not really known whether any of these approaches is effective; there is always the possibility that the activity would have stopped anyway. As a general rule, possibly connected with the emotional state of the focus, the activity dies away after about six months whatever approach is taken. Perhaps all people respond to reduced stress depending on belief; for example, perhaps those who believe in entities find exorcism more credible. That said, there have been some cases lasting for longer duration; we ourselves have been working on a case for over two years that shows no sign of abatement.

POSSESSION

Possession is the belief that outside forces can enter and control an individual. These outside forces commonly include the Holy Spirit, gods, demons, or spirits of the dead. Possession, within these contexts, can be either invited as part of a religious ceremony or belief, or uninvited.

The invited

Certain mediums, for example transfiguration or direct-voice mediums, or those mediums who practise automatic writing, may invite the spirits of the dead to use their bodies or a part of the body for a certain time, in order to contact, or pass messages to, the living. This is a form of invited possession.

Otherwise, invited possession is usually part of a religious ceremony. The practitioners of Voodoo (or Vodun), a hybrid religion of African and Christian beliefs, participate in ceremonies where they enter an altered state or trance. It is while in this state that a god may take control of – 'ride' – the devotee. From the moment of possession the subject takes on the god's character, voice and gestures. Such possession may last just a few seconds or until the end of the ceremony; the possession normally ends spontaneously. The participant will remember nothing of the time while possessed, and is not held responsible for his or her actions while possessed. Those possessed by gods in these Vodun ceremonies are seen as being worthy of the gods' attention and protection; such possession is therefore regarded as a blessing and an honour.

Christianity also has a tradition of voluntary possession by the Holy Spirit. In the Bible (Acts iv, 8) Peter is said to be 'filled with the Holy Spirit' and (Acts xi, 45–46) the Gentiles are similarly possessed, '. . . the gift of the Holy Spirit had been poured out even on the Gentiles. For they heard them speaking in tongues and extolling God.' Speaking in tongues is regarded as a characteristic of possession, and appears in this passage to be the identifying aspect that indicates the Gentiles are so possessed.

On day one of this century a group of worshippers in Kansas, under the leadership of Charles Fox Parham, claimed to have received the Holy Spirit after praying for a sign. 1 January 1901 has therefore become the date celebrated by Pentecostals as the birth of the Pentecostal movement. This follows clearly from the description of possession in the Bible on the day of Pentecost (Acts ii, 1–4), 'When the day of Pentecost had come they were all together in one place. And suddenly a sound came from heaven like the rush of a mighty wind, and it filled all the house where they were sitting. And there appeared to them tongues as of fire, distributed and resting on each one of them. And they were all filled with the Holy Spirit and began to speak in other tongues, as the Spirit gave them utterance.' Pentecostal churches offer the worshippers power through possession by the Holy Spirit, a power that may be used for healing. While possessed, the believers speak in tongues and writhe on the floor as the spirit fills them. A recent revival of this experience known as the Toronto Blessing which emerged in 1994 is covered separately in this book (see 'Toronto Blessing', page 307).

The uninvited
The most popularly known form of possession is the involuntary form; where a person seems to be infused with another personality or entity that controls his or her actions.

The possession that afflicted nuns in a convent in seventeenth-century France included many of the 'classical' aspects of possession. In the Ursuline convent at Loudun seventeen nuns and their students were allegedly possessed by demons. The prioress, Sister Jeanne des Anges, claimed she had seven demons within her body. Many of the nuns writhed in contortions, and blasphemed, but several priests who visited the convent were doubtful that the nuns were truly possessed; expected signs of possession were missing, extraordinary strength, levitation, and particularly the speaking in tongues on which the Church seems to place such store.

One Jesuit priest, Father Jean-Joseph Surin, did believe they were possessed however. He spent time exorcising the demons from Sister Jeanne, praying for the demons to leave the prioress and enter into him. Surin was successful, with the result that he found himself possessed. For the next twenty-five years he suffered great anguish and much physical pain. He was regarded as a lunatic and attempted suicide at least once.

On 17 May 1645 Surin attempted suicide while staying in a Jesuit house, built on a rocky ledge above a river near Bordeaux. He went to his room just before dinner, and saw the window was open. Without seemingly knowing what he was doing, he threw himself out of the window. Surin's body seems to have been obeying something other than himself. He also describes how he would attempt to do one thing and another part of his body would stop him; for example, he would move his hand only to have it bitten by his mouth.

However, through his torment Surin retained some hold on his mental state and was able to write of his possession, as he experienced it, to a fellow Jesuit. His description of his torment is enlightening, 'I find it almost impossible to explain what happens to me during this time, how this alien spirit is united to mine, without depriving me of consciousness or of inner freedom, and yet constituting a second "me" as though I had two souls . . . I feel as if I had been pierced by the pricks of despair in that alien soul which seems to be mine . . . I even feel that the cries uttered by my mouth come from both souls at once; and I found it hard to determine whether they are the product of joy or frenzy.'

On reflection, it seems highly probable that what Surin was describing was multiple personalities within him. Perhaps such potential had always lain dormant and the exorcism at Loudun triggered the release of his inner feelings, giving him permission and an excuse to allow his sub-personalities' exposure. This possibility would not have been recognised in his time. (Indeed, *The Diagnostic and Statistical Manual of Mental Disorders* only recognised multiple personality syndrome (MPS) in 1980, in its third edition.)

The most famous (or infamous) case of possession this century is that of a young American boy living near Mount Rainier in Washington State, USA. (In *The Possessed* by Thomas Allen, the boy is known as Robert Mannheim; other accounts have named him as Douglass Deen.) When the boy was thirteen, he was introduced to a Ouija board by a spiritualist aunt. Soon after this, rapping noises were heard around the house. When the aunt died, the rapping seemed to respond to questions addressed to her.

What must be regarded as poltergeist activity soon started; furniture and other items were seen to move. The family sought help from the Church. A priest took the boy to his home and watched as, first, the boy's bed shook. Then the priest saw the boy tipped from a chair and slide stiffly, still under his blankets, under the bed. There, the boy bounced up and down, finally scratching his face on the bed-springs. Soon spontaneous scratching appeared, looking as if the skin was being damaged from within. These scratches would later form letters, and then words. They seemed to answer questions in much the same way as a Ouija board would

The family were advised to consult the Catholics, they being the only Church group to perform exorcism. (Others use 'deliverance', prayers addressed to Jesus for help: the exorcist speaks directly to the demons.)

When the priests visited the boy it seems he was able to speak some Latin, regarded as a traditional sign of possession. Although it is true he would have heard a limited amount from the prayers of the priests, some phrases he used were not from prayers and involved a complex knowledge of the language that he almost certainly would not have had. The boy's possession developed. He sometimes spoke with a voice described as 'a deep gravelly voice'. This voice claimed to be the Devil, and continued to torment the boy and the priests. The priests spent much time with the boy, eventually performing the ritual of exorcism.

The Catholic Church would, and did, identify the boy's case as one of possession. They consider certain signs to be proof of demonic possession, including:

- Speaking in tongues

- Some comprehension of a foreign language (particularly Latin) unknown to the subject

- Clairvoyance, the knowing of secret matters

- Excessive physical strength

- Blasphemy

- Aversion to holy objects

- Levitation

Some of these were shown by the boy. Furthermore the case followed the pattern of the accepted stages of possession: firstly,

- Infestation: demonstrated by the scratching and rapping noises, then

- Obsession: tormenting the subject (the skin markings may be regarded as a sign of this), and finally

- Possession: the demon uses the body for himself (sees through the subject's eyes, speaks using the subject's vocal cords, and so on)

No commentary on possession can fail to consider the

non-religious alternatives. The *Diagnostic and Statistical Manual of Mental Disorders (DSM III)* describes multiple personality syndrome as 'involving the presence within the patient of two or more distinct personalities one of which is dominant at any particular time'. Psychotherapist and author Adam Crabtree, who encountered 'possession-type' cases in his practice decided that it was practical to treat them as possession, whatever the underlying mechanisms were. If the patient showed signs of possession, treating it as such was, he believed, the simplest and quickest way to effect a cure.

PREMONITION

Chris Robinson, of Bedfordshire, was reported on the ITV series *Strange But True?* as someone who has prophetic dreams. He dreamt of an image that he was convinced represented a terrorist attack on the RAF base at Stanmore in Middlesex. The RAF were sceptical, but took note of the comments of the Bedfordshire police that he had assisted them with his dream-images in the past. Just over one month later a bomb exploded at RAF Stanmore.

It is impossible to know how many premonitions are received, or how many receive them. After a major event has happened, many people claim they foresaw it; some may be hoaxing, others may be fooling themselves, but the evidence of premonitions is that they do happen, and so some of those claims will be genuine.

The problem is that because psychic abilities are unrecognised, it is embarrassing for some to admit to them. Someone might have a dream that a particular airliner is going to crash, but few would have the courage to contact the airline to tell them. Many would reason, probably correctly, that the airline is unlikely to halt the plane on the evidence of what might be a crank telephone call.

Nevertheless, any proof of the validity of premonitions hinges not on what people claim after the event, but on claims made before the event. The strongest evidence relates to situations where the person takes an alternative course of action because of the premonition.

A woman wrote to Tom Lethbridge, a researcher in various paranormal areas, telling of her dream of the collapse of a building; she heard a voice say, 'Collapsed like a pack of cards.' One month later a disastrous gas explosion wrecked the high-rise block of flats Ronan Point, which was described by one newspaper as having 'collapsed like a pack of cards'.

A well-known and impressive case, though one that did not save the child concerned and was reported by her mother after the event, is that of nine-year-old Eryl Jones. She attended the Pantglas school in the Welsh mining village of Aberfan. On 20 October 1960 she told her mother that she had dreamed about her school but that 'there was no school there. Something black had come down all over it.' The following day the school was engulfed by an avalanche of coal waste from an unstable tip that towered above the village. Over a hundred people, including Eryl Jones, died. It was a disaster that was foretold by many. A study of the claims of premonition associated with the disaster was made by London psychiatrist John Barker; he concluded that sixty of the claimed premonitions were genuine.

In 1978 a man described as 'an unemployed Welsh Prophet' was caught travelling on a train without paying his fare. He claimed that he wanted to warn the city of Glasgow that it was going to be hit by an earthquake. The press at the time reported the story as a 'silly season' item for which it seems to have all the ingredients. It must have come as a surprise to readers three weeks later when Glasgow and the west of Scotland was hit by an earthquake which damaged several buildings. Such earthquakes are very rare in the British Isles.

The most famous cases of premonition, where action can be shown to have been taken before the event, relate to the RMS *Titanic*. One William Klein was so impressed by his own premonition of the impending disaster of the ship that he cabled a friend, H.B. Harris, who was due to sail on it, pleading with him not to. Harris replied that he was unable to change his plans; he died in the disaster.

Blanche Marshall, watching the *Titanic* leaving Southampton, told her husband, 'That ship is going to sink before it reaches America.' She became almost violently agitated, asking 'someone' to 'do something', and described 'people struggling in the icy water'. Later, Mrs Marshall demonstrated her abilities yet again by switching her reservations on the *Lusitania*, convinced it was going to be torpedoed by the Germans. Her premonition was quite specific; she was happy to sail on the *Lusitania* providing it was not on the original voyage for which she and her husband were booked. They changed to an earlier voyage and completed it safely. During the voyage she had originally been booked on, the *Lusitania* was torpedoed and sank with the loss of 139 lives.

Not all premonitions are useful or accurate. Ernest Farenden had always been superstitious of the *Olympic*, on which he served, and was glad to know he was being transferred to the *Titanic*. He died with the ship. Mrs Joseph Leeford was apprehensive about her booking on the *Empress of Ireland* and transferred to the *Titanic*; and died there. We might have expected W.T. Stead, a well-known researcher of the paranormal, to have had some insight into the sinking, but in fact he ignored the warnings given to him by two psychics. Count Louis Hammon warned him that he would die in water and that April was a dangerous month. Clairvoyant W. de Kerlor described a vision of half a ship seemingly poised in the air and about to sink. Stead, however, posted a letter in Ireland at the first stop, written while on board, stating, 'This ship is as firm as a rock.' (De Kerlor later stated that Stead 'came through' to him in spirit and apologised for ignoring the warning.)

In all, there were well over a hundred reports of premonitions of the sinking, many impressively accurate.

Ken Phillips, a researcher of the paranormal and at the time working for ASSAP (the Association for the Scientific Study of Anomalous Phenomena) took action when a woman, Linda, had a premonition of the death of actor Roy Kinnear. We spoke to Linda and she told us she envisioned him in a dream 'on a film location, in a sunny climate'. She described Kinnear as 'on a boat' and then saw him fall. She saw the film cameras and set, and saw great consternation amongst the film crew. Previous laughter and gaiety turned into screams of horror. She had a feeling that 'something awful' was going to happen to Kinnear.

Ken Phillips told us that he took Linda's report seriously and wrote to Roy Kinnear via London Weekend Television warning him to avoid the situations described; he never received a reply and does not know if the letter was passed or regarded as a 'crank letter', or perhaps was passed on and still so regarded. He also lodged the report, many months prior to Kinnear's death, with ASSAP.

Kinnear died of a heart attack while filming *Return of the Musketeers* in Spain. He was, at the moment of his death, riding a horse over a drawbridge, over water.

Ken regards the premonition as ninety per cent accurate; Linda had named the right man, in the right scenario – a film set in a warm climate – and was fairly accurate about the situation. Her image of a boat is not so inaccurate; he was over water on a drawbridge.

PSYCHIC DETECTIVES

When *The Guitar Player*, a painting by Vermeer, valued at £2,000,000 was stolen by, as it turned out, the IRA, Nella Jones, one of the most prominent and successful psychic detectives in Britain, sensed clues towards the case. She was able to lead the police without hesitation to an alarm mechanism discarded in a lake and then to the picture's frame which had also been discarded. She later sensed that the picture would turn up in a cemetery, which it did. It was unharmed, as she had predicted it would be.

'There could only be two answers,' said former Detective Inspector Bayes. 'Either she was involved in the theft, or she was indeed psychic.' She was so successful, and so impressive, with her information that the police came very close to arresting her for implication in the crime. They soon determined without doubt that she could not have been involved.

In ITV's *Strange but True* former D.C. Neil Pratt and Bayes publicly confirmed that Nella Jones helped the police force. Nella had a letter from the Metropolitan Police confirming that she was turned to for help 'time and time again'.

Nella Jones had had many previous successes. Most famous was probably her identification of the Yorkshire Ripper. She spoke on several occasions to a *Yorkshire Post* reporter, Shirley Davenport. The story was not published, but after the arrest of Peter Sutcliffe, Shirley Davenport realised that many of Nella Jones' clairvoyant visions matched the true killer. She had kept her notes and was able to check back to them. Sixteen months before the arrest, Nella Jones had said that the Ripper was a lorry driver called Peter and that she could see a name beginning with C on the side of his cab. She had also stated that he lived in a big house in Bradford, No. 6 in its street. It was elevated above the street behind wrought iron gates with steps leading up to the front door. And he had committed other crimes. All these statements and more matched Peter Sutcliffe, and although other predictions were not recognisable, there was enough to prompt Shirley Davenport to say, 'It was the most weird experience. It went far beyond anything coincidence or guesswork could possibly have provided . . .'

In 1977 New York detective Rodney Roncoglio worked with Dr Karlis Osis a parapsychologist and his team of psychics to try to discover the identity of the killer known as 'the Son of Sam'. They were given limited help by the police, and not officially recognised. One of the psychics, a Canadian named Terry Marmoreo, told Dr Osis over the telephone of many details which, although not descriptive enough to catch the killer, were – after the arrest of David Berkowitz – near enough to be thought-provoking. For example, Marmoreo had said she believed that the killer was a postman; she marked on a map where she thought he worked. She reported that he drove a green Ford car, registration 366 XLA. David Berkowitz was a postman. The post office he worked at was close (but not the closest) to the mark on the map. He drove a cream (there is confusion as to whether 'cream' was misheard as 'green') Ford car, registration 561 XLB. Roncoglio thought that was close enough to cause a trained policeman to be suspicious of the vehicle and its driver.

Many psychics have visions of crimes, but very few become famous as a result of these visions. The two most famous psychic detectives are both Dutch. Amongst other achievements, they have both been able to help find missing persons.

Gerald Croiset, who was psychic as a child, first became aware of images when he held a ruler owned by a watchmaker; visions of the watchmaker's life came into his head.

Professor Willem Tenhaeff, a parapsychologist, met Croiset when he was thirty-six and spent many years investigating the Dutch psychic and his powers. Croiset refused payment for his services, but asked the people he helped to send a report to Tenhaeff. The Dutch police are more open to psychic predictions than their British or American counterparts (perhaps this helps the psychic) and often asked for his help.

Croiset was able to help people in America over the telephone. He was instrumental in finding the body of a murdered four-year-old girl and her killer in New York. On another occasion, in a phone call from Kansas, Croiset told Professor Walter E. Sandelius that his missing daughter would turn up after six days (she did) and was able to describe the girl's movements with accuracy.

In 1967 teenager Patricia Mary McAdam went missing after accepting a lift to her home in Scotland from a lorry driver. In 1970 a journalist, Frank Ryan, spoke to Croiset about the case. Croiset told Ryan that the girl was dead and described his visions of the surroundings. He described where the girl's body would be found, and gave other information such as that Ryan would find part of a car, a wreck, with a wheelbarrow leaning against it. The area relating to Croiset's description and the wrecked car with a wheelbarrow leaning against it were found – a host of extraordinary detail all correctly described. But the girl's body has never been found.

The second Dutchman who achieved fame as a detective is Peter Hurkos. Hurkos was not psychic while young, but after falling off a ladder and suffering concussion his powers came on very suddenly. Before he left the hospital he had impressed several staff and patients with his 'impressions'. Hurkos, like Croiset, had a lot of success locating missing people.

He was the first to connect what the police had thought were separate crimes in 1958. A cab driver had been shot in the Miami area and Hurkos was asked to help. He sat in the dead man's taxi and was able to tell the police of the impressions he had. He said the killer was tall, slim, with a tattoo; that he came from Detroit, his nickname was Smitty, and that he had committed another murder in Key West. The police found that another murder had taken place and that the bullets matched the same gun. After checking with the Detroit police they arrested a man called Charles Smith. He was identified and found guilty of both murders.

Hurkos was also involved in the hunt for the Boston Strangler. He was first given photographs contained in envelopes and was able to tell, without opening them, what the pictures were and which 'test' pictures had been falsely inserted. He was able to tell police many details of the stranglings which matched the crimes; details unknown to the public. He could describe the victims and how they died. He was, however, unable to identify Albert DeSalvo who, although never tried (he was a schizophrenic), is generally accepted to have been the strangler. Hurkos identified 'Thomas O'Brien' (a pseudonym) by psychometrising a letter of his. Although probably wrong in his identification, there was no doubt that the impressions he received related to 'O'Brien's' life, appearance, job and particular fetishes.

Part of the problem for the psychic when analysing his or her impressions is that telepathy from police officers or others with knowledge of the case, or other cases, can possibly cloud the impression received. Several psychometrists we have interviewed have indicated that it is not always easy to interpret the impressions received.

In *The Psychic Detectives* Colin Wilson describes the achievements of Suzanne Padfield. She was tested for her psychic gifts for many years in the Paraphysical Laboratory where she impressed the founder, Benson Herbert, with her abilities in telepathy, psychometry and psychokinesis. One of the most successful results of her detection came about when she was asked to help find a missing nine-year-old from near Moscow. Suzanne Padfield was sent a photograph and some of the girl's own writing. As soon as Suzanne received this parcel, the visions came very quickly. She saw the girl at a skating rink, talking to a thick-set, burly man, she saw the girl walk with the man to his home, saw the man strangle the missing girl, wrap the body inside 'something blue', carry it on a bus, and then dump the body in a river. Suzanne was able to return this information, along with a good description of the murderer, to Viktor Adamenko, a leading Russian parapsychologist.

The police had interviewed many suspects. One of them matched Suzanne's description. The police re-interviewed him and confronted him with such a detailed description that he confessed to the crime.

Many psychic detectives use psychometry as the access to the impressions that reveal information to them. By handling items relevant to crimes or to missing persons, the psychic 'sees' or 'senses' the visions. (See 'Psychometry', page 263.) For example, Croiset gained more information about Patricia McAdam after he was able to hold her Bible, sent to him by her parents.

Psychic detectives cannot, however, solve every crime. In 1980 and 1981 investigators of child murders in Atlanta, Georgia, received more than 19,000 letters from alleged psychics. The police took the trouble to analyse all the information, but concluded that none was instrumental in solving the case. Perhaps a major profile case simply brings out people who believe they have abilities that they do not, in fact, have.

Dr Osis believes that psychic detection has potential in the fight against crime, despite the fact that it is an immature and not well-understood ability. 'When methods of applying ESP become operational, there will be no walls for the criminal to hide behind, no location that could not be seen. Could there be a better deterrent than that?'

PSYCHIC, OR SPIRITUAL, HEALING

Psychic, or spiritual healing is practised around the globe, either as a part of religious belief or as an alternative and complementary therapy. Healers do not regard themselves as having any inherent abilities; they believe they channel them from other locations. Depending on their viewpoints and beliefs, they attribute these powers to Jesus, the spirit world, the cosmic consciousness, or nature.

One healer and Wicca practitioner, Graham James, explained how the 'mechanisms' work. 'We open a channel in order to receive power from the cosmic consciousness to channel energy into a patient. What I do is clear my mind, and work up a force field of energy between my hands for about four or five minutes.'

This is basically the description we have always been given in our work with healers, though the imagery differs according to belief. Heather Woods, a stigmatic whose purpose was, she said, to continue the healing ministry of Christ, opened herself to allow in 'the Holy Spirit'. Barbara Wright, a medium, opened herself to channel the power from the spirit world.

Graham had described part of the mechanism for healing being 'opening the aura'. He explained that, 'We are bathed or surrounded in an aura and it's almost like I allow a flap to open up above the crown of my head and allow energy to come down into my body. If you open up an auric channel you must close the channel in exactly the same way. It's like you pick up the telephone, you open a line, you've got to shut the line off. You mustn't leave it open.' Again, this seemed to be Graham's way of visualising his own mechanisms to make them work for him; others have different images, but they describe some form of dislocation from the everyday world at the start and end of the healing session. It may be a form of altered state of consciousness, though from our observations with many healers there is less evidence of this, or perhaps evidence of a less altered state, than in many psychic applications. Healers often go about their work chatting and joking, not unlike hairdressers!

We sat in on a programme of healing conducted by Graham. Our role was observational and to interview Graham, his team of three healers, and their patients, particularly two patients who were well known to us, and introduced by us to the healers.

The healers worked up a healing energy between their palms and transferred that energy to the patient by close proximity positioning and movement of the hands. In terms of observation there was little to see. Although they had apparently seen light effects on occasion which they were certain were visual impressions of the healing energy, we saw none. One of the patients reported seeing blue lights near Graham's hand during one session.

The correlation between the movements of the healers' hands and the feelings of the patients was high, even when they had no line of sight to what was happening. For example, one healer, working behind the patient's back, changed from moving her hand sideways to moving it towards and away from the patient's body. The patient immediately responded saying that she could feel a 'fluctuating' sensation inside her body; we asked her to call out when it was strongest and weakest – her calls matched exactly the movements of the healer's hands. When we tried to duplicate the movements, the patient felt nothing.

Throughout two months of repeated sessions, we recorded a high incidence of these correlations. The patients both reported significant improvement in their illnesses, one of which – a neck pain – had been a problem for several years.

Barbara Wright, a spiritualist medium, is also a healer, channelling healing energies through her body from the spirit world. She described healing a man with severe kidney problems. He was waiting for a transplant. 'He had been ill for a year. Couldn't keep down solid food, couldn't sleep at night.' Barbara gave the man healing by placing her hands directly on his back for some fifteen minutes. The following day his wife rang Barbara and told her that her husband had had the first good night's sleep for years, and had kept down a solid breakfast. He returned to Barbara and for four days she gave him spiritual healing. From that point on his life changed, he could drive, walk longer distances and live a more active life.

Brad Steiger, in *Mysteries of Time and Space* relates the case of Evelyn Monahan, who suffered severe problems with her sight following an accident in which she received a blow on the head. Her doctors attributed the onset of epilepsy at that time to the same accident. Seven years later she was injured when surgery went wrong and lost the use of her shoulder and arm. She believed in God, and in healing, and put her own beliefs to work. She and two friends channelled healing energy into her body. They used visualisation; their image was of white light changing the molecular structure of her brain. Despite the fact that her doctors had warned her to reconcile herself to a life of pain and disability, she fully recovered from all her difficulties.

This question of visualisation seems to be a crucial one. As a general rule, healers are as puzzled by the origin of their healing energies as anyone else. They realise that they cannot be certain where they get their energies from, nor exactly what they are. They cannot explain why these energies seem to work for some and not others. But by visualising some 'method' that explains it to their satisfaction, they know that they can make them work.

'I don't know if I get in touch with some sort of guide or spirit, I don't honestly know. What I do know is I have this ability to open up to receive an energy, to enhance the energies in my own physical side of me and to project that energy into the patient,' Graham told us.

Visualisation is a technique used in many conventional medical applications to assist patients. One patient being treated for 'furred arteries' was asked to visualise canoes travelling down her arteries with the canoeists scraping the walls clear. No one was suggesting the canoes were real, but the images apparently helped the patient to visualise getting better.

Whether or not the healer's patients need to visualise their cures is another question; in the cases we have witnessed, no such suggestion was made. The healers seem to take the responsibility for the cures.

However, while there is no doubt that many patients get well after psychic healing, there is some question as to the cause of the improvement. One school of thought on illness is that it is created by the mind, ulcers, cancers, and other ailments being psychosomatic responses, usually created by stress. If so, relieving the stress is probably all that is needed to reverse the illness and start the patient on the road to recovery. Perhaps the attentions of the healer, the caring closeness with the patient, reduces the stress.

No analysis of healing can ignore what conventional medicine has long taken into account; the placebo effect. Test groups of patients fed the correct drugs to deal with medical conditions often show no particular difference to groups unknowingly given sugar pills. The healing appears to be internal, perhaps based on the confidence that your doctor has given you something and therefore you are going to get better.

Perhaps there is also the question of faith; if you believe in what is happening, whether it is the administration of drugs or the application of psychic healing, then you get better. This seems again to suggest that the healers need only 'give permission' to the patients to heal themselves and they have the ability to do so. If stress – which is a non-physical effect – can create illness, there is no reason why 'anti-stress' should be less effective at curing it.

But healers and their patients believe that something real is transferring from the healer – energy channelled through them – to the patient. And there is some evidence to suggest that they are correct.

There is uncontrolled, anecdotal, evidence in work with animals, for whom presumably faith does not play a part. Graham James points to the successes he has had in this way.

'There was a dog called Bumble brought to me by a very sceptical owner. He had a golf ball size growth on the inside of his groin. His tummy area, normally pink on a dog, was black. I did thirteen healing sessions. At first the dog had to be carried up the stairs to my healing room. After around eight or nine healing sessions it walked fairly normally but with a limp up the stairs. On about the twelfth healing session I had this enormous build up of energy in my hand which I honestly couldn't explain; the only way I could explain the feeling that I had was if you hold an elastic band into your hand and close your fingers over it and pull it and let go, imagine it's quite painful in the palm of your hand. I put it over this growth. The following day the owner brought the dog back to me, its tummy had returned to its normal colour of pink, the golf ball growth had completely gone.' This case was covered in the local press, and the owner is quoted confirming Graham's descriptions.

Graham had several other equally impressive cases. He also described 'cancer-busting' in a woman, but no verification was possible as the patient's doctors refused to release her medical papers. The patient remained convinced that she was healed by Graham after the hospital had given her up, with three months to live.

Perhaps more important in the quest to discover if faith alone is responsible, or if there really is a transfer of energy, is the work of healer Oskar Estebany, working with Dr Bernard Grad of McGill University, Montreal, Canada.

Three groups of mice, totalling forty-eight had small areas of skin removed. Using only psychic healing Estebany 'healed' one group. A second group was warmed in case heat from the hands was the key (and in a second experiment a non-healer mirrored Estebany's movements in case something in the actions was responsible). The third group was ignored. The group healed by Estebany recovered significantly more quickly.

Perhaps even the mice, or Graham's canine patient mentioned earlier, can have 'faith' in the ministrations of humans. A second experiment by Estebany and Grad eliminated even that. Two groups of barley seeds were the 'patients'. One group was watered with 'healed' water, into which the healer channelled healing energy. The other group was watered with ordinary water. The group watered by Estebany's healed water grew much faster. Dr Grad concluded, 'I know of no other way to explain these experiments . . . I am inclined to feel that there was something from the hand that was being radiated and this penetrated the glass bottle and went in and altered the water.'

Ironically perhaps, Graham James discovered his healing powers while working as an air-ambulance paramedic. 'I picked up a lady in Greece who had had a stroke. I said to her daughter, "I am going to massage her legs and her feet, all right?" This was not in the formal medical work, but I felt intuitively that I had to do it. And by the time we got to Heathrow her condition was completely reversed from when we picked her up. Something inside my psyche helped me throughout the years in the ambulance service; it's kind of like I have been led.'

The National Health Service is cautious about claims of spiritual healing. However, it was reported in December 1991 in the *Mail on Sunday* that some forty NHS doctors were also spiritual healers, and a number more are engaging healers in their surgeries. They are popular with patients and regarded as an addition to, rather than a replacement for, conventional therapy.

PSYCHIC SURGERY

In the Philippines, many people are treated with a form of psychic surgery that cures their ills, but seems to have no ill effects. The witnesses to these operations see the surgeon use his bare hands to press on the flesh of the patient, blood appears, and the surgeon's fingers seem to enter and dip into the flesh. An object, or piece of tissue, is then seen to be removed. The surgeon removes his hands and cleans up the patient. There will be no wound from these operations, perhaps only faint markings on the skin.

Western investigators became interested in this form of practice in the 1960s and investigated many claims. A few of these so-called 'psychic surgeons' even came to the West to display their talents. Many of these investigations indicated that fraud and sleight of hand was taking place. Laboratory testing found animal blood and tissue.

But that was not the whole story of psychic surgery. The West looked at the subject with Western eyes and ignored any understanding of the spiritual beliefs of the Filipinos. What is more important must be that the treatment worked for the Filipinos, and even for those Western visitors who were able to suspend their belief system.

Perhaps the best-known psychic healer of all was the Brazilian Jose Pedro De Freitas, known as Arigo. Arigo worked in trance under the control of a Dr Adolphus Fritz, a German doctor who had died in 1918, very much in the way of a transfiguration medium, i.e. Arigo allowed Fritz to 'use' his body to do the work. Arigo became famous in 1956 after a Brazilian senator claimed Arigo had cured him by removing a tumour from his colon.

Arigo practised his surgery with unsterile instruments such as a penknife, kitchen knife, or rusty scissors. He wiped the patient's wounds with ordinary pieces of cloth or towel. Yet the patients never seemed to suffer from these unsavoury conditions; the wounds healed very quickly and never became septic. Throughout a career of nearly twenty years it was never claimed that he had caused anyone harm.

Andrija Puharich, a paranormal researcher from New York,

visited Arigo to witness and film him. Puharich described the operation on a woman with a large goitre, 'Arigo just picked up a paring knife, cut it open, popped the goitre out, slapped it in her hand, wiped the opening with a piece of dirty cotton, and off she went. It hardly bled at all.' Although Puharich described the scene as 'a nightmare' he asked Arigo to remove a benign tumour from his arm. The surgeon did this with his unsterile penknife.

At the height of his career, Arigo would treat as many as two hundred patients a day. Some would be treated with surgery, others would be given an instant diagnosis and prescribed medicines. He prescribed some known drugs sometimes in large doses and strange combinations, but they worked: the people felt cured.

It appears that Arigo did not work consciously, he was entranced and taken over by Fritz. When shown a film of himself operating, he fainted in shock.

Judge Filippe Immesi, investigating the surgeon, gave this testimony after he and the district attorney had watched Arigo treat a woman nearly blind with cataracts, 'I saw him pick up what looked like a pair of nail scissors. He wiped them on his sports shirt, and used no disinfectant of any kind. Then I saw him cut straight into the cornea of the patient's eye. She did not blench, although she was fully conscious. The cataract was out in a matter of seconds. The district attorney and I were speechless, amazed. Then Arigo said some kind of prayer as he held a piece of cotton in his hand. A few drops of liquid suddenly appeared on the cotton and he wiped the woman's eye with it. We saw this at close range. She was cured.'

There seems to be no doubt that Arigo made incisions and removed human tissue. His patients felt no pain, and many were cured. However, although he helped many people, Arigo's practices were illegal and he twice spent time in prison, though never for fraudulent behaviour.

There have been many other psychic surgeons over the years. We interviewed Jenny Bright, herself a medium and psychometrist, who underwent psychic surgery under the observation of her partner, Dr David Cross, who photographed the operation (see photo section). She was operated on by Stephen Turoff who is 'taken over' by a Dr Khan. She had been diagnosed as having intrusions into the bowel, had been admitted to hospital with bleeding, and had been told she might need a colostomy. We asked Jenny and Dr Cross to relate their own experiences of that surgery.

Jenny: 'The waiting room was full of people. Stephen was wafting in and out of the waiting room, and his wife was taking the details of our illnesses and problems. Very friendly, a nice atmosphere. David asked to take photographs and Stephen said "yes". Then Stephen came up to me, while he was in trance with Dr Khan, and he held his hand out in mid-air and started to rub something on my palm. He said "This will smell like your favourite flower" and it smelt just like freesias. Everybody was having a smell of it; to somebody it smelt like bluebells, to somebody else it smelt like roses. He did the same (to another lady) and the smell in her palm was completely different to the smell in my palm. Apparently this is something he does every so often where the ladies are concerned. It perks everyone up and makes them feel very happy.

'I got in (to the surgery) and took my clothes off. Stephen came in, and he put his hand exactly on the spot where I was having the problems. He said, "I'm just going to do an operation." He took the scalpel – David took photographs of it all – which looked just like a broken-off blade. I was not aware of the pain that I was going to encounter. Everybody I knew who had had it done had had no pain, I thought it was painless.

'I could feel him cut the skin, and I saw this scalpel disappear into my stomach. I could feel Stephen prodding around inside my stomach and then he grabbed something. I could feel it. Then he got the scissors in there as well, and with every snip it sounded like he was cutting bacon-rind. I could feel this thing he had gotten hold of loosen. Then he pulled it out, and I could feel it, and it seemed to dematerialise in mid-air. David said it was like a big white mass he had pulled out.' (David: 'I got a flash of it as he pulled something out, it was like a little ball of tight cotton wool, he flicked it into a bin.') 'Then he rubbed his hands over my stomach and I looked, and there was nothing there. No cut, just a small mark. He then put one hand on my stomach and one on my head and he said "This'll take the pain away," and it did. I had no more pain. I felt weak for about two hours; but the next day I was fine. The condition seems fine; I've not had any more problems. The mark lasted for about a fortnight, a tiny scar with bruising all around it.'

David confirmed all Jenny's recollections, and described watching the operation. Turoff had shielded the incision with his hands as he worked, but David said, 'What I did see was instruments like the scalpel, the forceps and the scissors . . . disappear a good two inches or so below the level where it would have been had it just been rested on her skin.'

A rational explanation of psychic surgery would suggest a sleight of hand being used. Even if this is the case, it does not of course explain why it works, and the positive healing effects it has. One explanation is that the surgery is more psychic than surgical. The alternative is that it creates a situation where the patients take control of their own illnesses and are given permission to heal themselves by believing some physical change has happened. Psychic surgery should be thought of not as an alternative to normal surgery, but perhaps as a complementary therapy.

Whatever the truth, and whatever the mechanisms, they should be studied with a positive attitude by the medical profession because, most importantly, the psychic surgeons are successfully healing people who feel that standard medical practice does not help them.

We asked Jenny for her conclusions. Jenny: 'I believe he did what he said he was doing. I believe he took some sort of growth or something out. The proof of the pudding is, I'm okay. I would go back again.'

PSYCHOKINESIS

Psychokinesis (PK) is the apparent ability of humans to influence other people, events, or objects by will, or mind-power alone, without the involvement of any known physical forces.

There appear to be two aspects to PK; the spontaneous and the planned. The spontaneous is often used to explain some poltergeist activity. Those who believe that poltergeist activity is the exteriorisation of energies in certain minds (individuals at puberty, most classically) believe that they are witnessing what has been termed Recurrent Spontaneous PK, RSPK. It is, however, the planned, deliberate, form that is open to testing.

Not all spontaneous PK arises in poltergeist situations. Probably the most dramatic example of it as exteriorisation (because of the individuals concerned) arose when Freud and Jung were arguing about psychic research generally. They were in Freud's study, and Jung was getting angry at the other's intransigent position. Jung began to feel a change come over his body; as if his diaphragm hardened and heated. Suddenly there was an explosive sound from a bookcase. Jung indicated it, 'There, that is an example of a so-called catalytic exteriorisation phenomenon.' Freud dismissed it, possibly angering Jung even further and there was a second sound. This time Freud admitted he was impressed. The sequel, however, is less well known and perhaps suggests something of the mechanisms or energies involved; the sounds occurred again when Jung was not there. If we assume that the fault did not lie coincidentally in the bookcase itself, then had Jung left an energy that could persist without him, or had Freud been angered enough to produce his own effects?

A similar effect is associated with the Russian, Nina Kulagina, following a bout of anger. As she described it, 'A picture moved to the edge of the shelf, fell, and smashed to bits.' She learned to control these abilities and was studied by Soviet researchers such as neurophysicist Genadi Sergeyev at the A.A. Utomskii Institute in St Petersburg. Probably the most spectacular result of the experimentation was her successfully separating the white and yolk of an egg without physical contact, all recorded on film. Equipment monitoring her physiology recorded loss of weight and pulse and blood-sugar responses consistent with stress.

There is some suggestion in this that individuals surrounded by spontaneous PK, perhaps reported as poltergeist activity, might be able to learn to control this force, which may lie within all people.

Of planned, deliberate, PK there have been many tests.

J.B. Rhine in 1934 studied PK effects on dice under controlled conditions at Duke University in North Carolina. Subjects were asked to influence the roll of a die. Early results seemed impressive, though they were challenged as being unsatisfactorily controlled. Results over an extended period showed that subjects were more effective when refreshed and that their abilities diminished as they became weary.

The work was updated in the 1960s by Helmut Schmidt, who produced an early 'random event generator' based on the totally random forces of radioactive decay. Test subjects were asked to influence the randomness of the output. There were successes beyond the range of normal probability.

Many of these tests seem to conclusively show that there is a phenomenon at work. But that conclusion has its detractors; and the mystery remains open.

Probably the most famous of PK subjects is Uri Geller. Stories of his spoon bending (at that time a new addition to PK claims) and other effects are well written up and easily available in the literature on the subject. Researcher, Professor Arthur Ellison said of Geller, 'For some strange reason [Uri] Geller has a different image of truth which doesn't quite agree about the strengths of materials taught in university. He believes that if he gently strokes a spoon between finger and thumb without putting a terrific pressure on it then it will bend. And sometimes it does. I had one child do that with a spoon I bought myself. I've seen Geller take a Yale key – it was Arthur C. Clarke's key – and he put his finger on it, Geller stroked it and the end came up. It rocked on the surface it was laying on. Arthur C. Clarke observed that, so did I, so did Arthur Koestler, so did Professor Hasted. Geller's image of truth just doesn't involve Yale keys being forever rigid.'

(Geller has been challenged by many, including magician James Randi who claimed to duplicate the 'Geller effects'. On the other hand Geller claims Randi ignores anything that does not suit his arguments. And so that particular debate continues . . .)

Ellison conducted his own experiments in PK. He explained, 'I am in no doubt whatsoever that the paranormal exists. None whatsoever . . . I've had scientists and colleagues from the university in my lab . . . and I presented them with a paranormal happening produced by Matthew Manning.' Ellison described a shielded meter with a needle, which Manning was able to make move without touching it, indeed from the other side of the laboratory. The demonstration was successful. However, the responses of the watching scientists were not consistent. Two accepted what they saw, accepting that they could not explain it in terms of their own experimental knowledge, but one refused even to consider the demonstration. His life's work designing electronic circuits was threatened if Manning could affect them in the way he had demonstrated, and he left declaring that there was no point looking at the evidence as there had to be a normal explanation. As Ellison so simply summed it up, 'He was unable to face the facts.'

Hasted conducted now-famous PK experiments. His attitude was one of empathy, not challenge. He felt that he would get better results if he was supportive of the subject. And he seems to have got impressive results. Most impressive probably was the 'scrunching up' of paperclips encased in a glass globe. These results have been challenged as the globe had a small hole in it, and no one saw the scrunching happen; but the subject was away from the globe at the time. Another similar experiment that seems to have shown some agency at work was when Hasted left small aluminium strips alone in a room, went outside and stayed with the subject, re-entered with the subject and found the strips 'concertina-ed'.

The highest number of claimed results comes from a team in America called SORRAT, the Society for Research on Rapport and Telekinesis. They reported many experiences of PK activity and sometimes that the PK energy was so great that the whole room would shake. One experiment shows the quality of the results they achieved. A stainless-steel spoon was hung by its neck inside a sealed glass bottle. Two members of the team stroked the bottle, willing the spoon to bend. Although they believe the bowl of the spoon flattened slightly, they were not overly impressed with their first result. They kept the unit intact however. The following month four members of the team put the bottle on a table and stroked it, repeating the words, 'Bend, bend'. The handle twisted, and the bowl flattened. The unit was photographed during this experimentation. Gradually the spoon 'jammed' in the bottle, unable to swing freely. All the observers concluded that the movement had taken place. Two seals on the bottle broke, but three were still intact as were other controls to prevent tampering.

A colleague of ours attempted to spoon-bend while hypnotised. The subject, Tony Wells, held the spoon which then began to bend and twist without apparent effort on Tony's part. While the spoon was bending, Tony looked down to his hands – saw what was happening, shouted 'F*** me, I'm doing it!' Immediately, he stopped doing it. As Tony described it, as soon as he started to analyse what he was doing, he could not do it. His hands jammed as if seized, and the spoon never moved again.

The question of those effects being possible at a distance, without contact, is much more difficult. We believe that Hasted, Ellison and the like have provided sufficient evidence for a tentative belief that it can occur without trickery.

The best results of PK – assuming that the name properly applies – are the observations of poltergeist activity. No one under laboratory conditions has yet reproduced to order such 'macro-effects' as moving furniture or lifting cars. That degree of force of energy, under controlled observation, will settle the question once and for all.

PSYCHOMETRY

Once called grammerie, the term 'psychometry' comes from the Greek, literally translated meaning 'measuring the soul'.

A sensitive person holds an object and is able to give descriptions of past events, and people of the past, alive or dead, associated with the object.

During the nineteenth century Dr Joseph Rodes Buchanan, of the Covington Medical Institute, supervised experiments that to him indicated that some people in his test sample had some form of psychic ability. They could identify chemicals in glass phials, just by holding the phials. Other experiments included holding chemicals in paper to their foreheads and identifying them, and 'reading' the character of letter writers by holding their letters. A professor of geology, William Denton, tested the work with his own students, and found supporting results. Buchanan stated, 'The past is entombed in the present . . . The discoveries of psychometry will enable us to explore the history of Man as those of geology help us explore the history of the earth.'

T.C. Lethbridge realised that if psychometry was a possibility then it would be of value in the field of archaeology. He describes in *Ghost And Ghoul* that he was warned by his friends that he might lose his reputation dabbling with such ideas. Lethbridge ignored these warnings, saying he had no interest in his reputation.

He investigated the claims of psychometry with a psychic and concluded that what was happening was a form of telepathy: the object is like the switch in an electrical current. He added, 'The answer, however, must surely be that there is no magic memory stored up in, or around, inanimate objects.'

What Lethbridge believed he found and Buchanan and Denton missed in their enthusiasm, was that the sensitive was picking up details telepathically.

Psychometry has played a major part in 'psychic detection'. (See page 246.)

Michael Crichton was a post-doctoral fellow at the Salk Institute in La Jolla, California and a highly successful writer. He had the healthiest of sceptical approaches to the paranormal, questioning and open-minded. In his autobiography *Travels* he relates the stories of his visits to psychometrists, and the successes they scored against his determined attempts to test them thoroughly. His essays in his book are amongst the best we have read, not for their content particularly, but for the way in which his scientific mind was able to acknowledge what he was seeing. When he saw the psychics, whether mediums or psychometrists, he obeyed certain home-made rules: he withheld his name, said very little withholding even his accent and clues to his nationality, withheld body language gestures, and blanked his mind as near as he could achieve. Onc psychic impressed him with her reading of his occupation, despite her own lack of understanding of it. He had been editing a film he was making; her description of the room she 'saw' him in was clearly related to that. His second visit was to a psychometrist who touched his watch. The psychic related his impressions, a mixture of the precise and the bland. Crichton concluded he was pretty accurate. Crichton's acceptance of the 'hits' scored is even more impressive because of his inclusion of the 'misses'; one psychic was wrong in every detail.

Crichton's summary was his conviction that there was indeed something going on, that these people had access to some information source that ordinary people did not.

Jenny Bright is a psychic who uses psychometry, and has made many appearances on television programmes such as the 'Magic and Mystery Show'. She explained how psychometry works for her, while cautioning that she realised the impressions 'came' in different ways for different people.

'The thing I do is still my mind. The first thing with psychometry is the impressions you're feeling from the object; warm, dead, or flat, for example. Whether you like the object, or not; whether you feel heavy with it, perhaps tired with it. All logic has to go out of the window; you have to feel your way. Override your conscious mind; once your conscious mind begins to analyse the object all is lost.

'The next thing is I close my eyes and start talking immediately, getting my impressions out. The way I see pictures are like photographic negatives, in black and white. I see pictures, maybe symbols. I usually see the person doing what they were doing at a certain time.'

Jenny related the time she was asked to psychometrise an 'Hawaiian death doll' for a university. She had no idea what one was, but instantly did not like the look of it and was reluctant. She was asked to do it because they felt the impressions she gained would help them evaluate whether or not the item was genuine. She touched it and saw 'this object being pushed between two sheets, and going into a cave, deep down into the ground'. They were satisfied; they explained that the death doll is placed between the winding sheets of a corpse before burial, often in caves.

On the 'Magic and Mystery Show' she was given dog tags to psychometrise; she felt going down into water. She felt it as her own experience, what turned out to be an accurate description of the way the owner of the tags had died during the war.

Emotion seems to play a part. Jenny explained that if she takes, say, a watch the impressions gained are often 'something that has been playing on (the owner's) mind, recently'. Images of dying, or of very pleasant experiences, are common. Presumably mundane actions and activities leave as little impression in our items as they do in our minds. This may be why there have been some strong successes in psychic detection; the crimes 'examined' by this technique – murder in particular – or the finding of lost, often drowned, children are all presumably of high emotional intensity.

Jenny believes that objects absorb energy, and it is this energy that is being read. She believes, perhaps for that reason, that constant reading and re-reading of objects drains the energy until those impressions cannot be picked up any more. For that reason her highest 'hits', she feels, come from old objects that have been buried – and have therefore been untouched – or from new objects only owned by one or at least a small number of people.

Jenny took part in a demonstration of psychometry at Loughborough University in August 1992, as part of a course given by Professor Arthur Ellison. A report of the session was published by 'PSI Researcher' in Winter 1993. Jenny psychometrised items belonging to seventeen complete strangers, and scored 125 correct 'hits' out of 160 statements, confirmed by all but two of the seventeen people confirming by correspondence (two did not reply to enquiries). There were some statements made that were accepted as bland, but as Ronald Kay (who wrote up the demonstration for the publication) states: 'such general statements were usually accompanied by correct particular statements made about the same person' and went on to add, 'so many of the facts produced were known only to individual members of the group (all highly responsible people who have explicitly denied any previous contact with Jenny) that collusion or fraud must be ruled out.'

R

REINCARNATION

Reincarnation is the embodiment in flesh in (normally) human form of the soul of a person now dead.

The return of the soul to another body is a fundamental proponent of many people's beliefs and religions. To many people, especially those of Eastern cultures, reincarnation is a 'known fact' and does not need to be tested or proven. But to Westerners without this inherent belief, it is an intriguing puzzle.

Reincarnation was probably first embraced, within the major religions of the world, by Hinduism. Oral traditions take the basis of this religion back five thousand years; it is uncertain at what point reincarnation was regarded as a part of the beliefs. Hindus believe that each soul is reborn in a continual cycle. The law of karma is played out partly through reincarnation. Good deeds are rewarded by a spiritually happy and rewarding life in the next incarnation, bad deeds by a life of impoverishment or suffering.

Buddhism also embraces reincarnation; rebirth follows death unless the soul has achieved the state of Nirvana, mastery over individuality and base needs and desires.

A native American Indian, before he dies, asks a couple if they will allow him to reincarnate into their family. In some tribes a pregnant woman will sit by a corpse and plead that its spirit enter her child.

The early philosophies of the Western world, particularly of the Greek civilisation, embraced reincarnation. Plato believed if you lived a bad life you could be reincarnated as an animal.

The Second Catholic Congress in AD 553 ruled reincarnation out of Christianity. It was decreed that death was the end of life, and that at that point the person, depending on his or her life, would go to Heaven or to Hell.

Only in recent times has reincarnation made an impact in the West, but not as a part of established religion, rather as a part of modern, paranormal studies and beliefs. When 'the sleeping prophet', Edgar Cayce indicated that he believed many present-life difficulties arose from past-life traumas, he opened up the question of past lives, and created considerable debate. In the wake of this, Morey Bernstein published *The Search for Bridey Murphy*, an astonishing account of a detailed, almost contemporary, past life.

A young American woman, Virginia Tighe ('Ruth Simmons' in the book) told of her former existence as an Irishwoman, Bridey Murphy. These memories came out through regressive hypnosis. The book paved the way for many similar recollections, often drawn out in the same manner. Because regressive hypnosis seems to bring out these memories (and it was then thought that a person could not lie under hypnosis) the interest in reincarnation soared. By 1980 newspaper polls showed that twenty-eight per cent of British adults believed in reincarnation. In America in 1982, the Gallup poll organisation stated that nearly one in four Americans believed in reincarnation.

Not all past-life memories come through hypnosis. Some report spontaneous and fleeting memories in the form of dreams (flashes of *déjà vu* are thought by some to be suggestive of hidden memory).

Frederick James told us of his 'flashback' memories of what he believes are past lives. He recognises that some of his dreams have a style and quality to them that suggests to him they are memories rather than normal dreams. They never differ in detail, or progress.

'There is the sea on the left-hand side. Behind me is desert. There is, on the edge of the sea, a stone-built quay or unloading bay. About a hundred yards from where I am standing there is a deck-loaded ship. I have a feeling that it was probably a Phoenician ship. There are stevedores, obviously slaves by their dress, unloading it. Standing over them and occasionally using a heavy whip he holds is a large man wearing a rough, leather-like skirt or kilt.

'I am about a hundred yards away from this on the other side of this stone quay and peering just over the top of the top stones. It looks as though, by my dress, I am one of the gang who are unloading this ship and I have got away from it. Obviously the foreman, or overseer, has missed my presence – presumably by counting the number of people there now and again – and he comes walking down towards me flourishing his whip and shouting. That is the moment when I finish; I have never managed to get past that point. I wish I could, I have tried many times without any success.'

If reincarnation is factual and memories can be released in this way then Frederick James's account may be valid, certainly it is for him. But it falls short of proving the case for reincarnation simply because it is unverifiable.

Proof of reincarnation demands that something, information or ability, is brought from one life into the next in a way that no other mechanism can explain. It has been suggested that gifted children and child prodigies may represent previously learned talents being brought into the present life. Mozart is as famous for composing at the age of four as he is for his life's work.

Author Frank De Felitta's son played the piano for the first time when he was six years old, superbly playing ragtime music. This is complex music which requires speed and dexterity as well as learning. The boy exclaimed, 'Daddy my fingers are doing it by themselves.' De Felitta was inspired to write the novels *Audrey Rose* and *For Love Of Audrey Rose*, fictional stories based on reincarnation.

The memories that surfaced in the Bridey Murphy case fell short of proof of reincarnation, suggestive though they were. Some recollections did not match the historical period, some were confused, some undoubtedly were affected by the 'overlay' of Tighe's present life, using obviously American expressions even when speaking as 'Bridey'. But this is not always the case and often corroboratory evidence can be found. It is these cases that are of great interest in the search for proof. The apparent memories of children are often the easiest to research as the memories are often near-contemporary and the evidence is more likely to be traceable. The memories have also had less time to decay.

Dr Ian Stevenson of the University of Virginia has spent over thirty years investigating, and has files of 2,500 children and of these has a nucleus of twenty where reincarnation seems the likeliest explanation. (*20 Cases Suggestive of Reincarnation* by Ian Stevenson, MD). His strongest cases are based on children with pre-natal memories that can be verified often in considerable detail, and in circumstances that make it highly unlikely that the children would have sourced the information. For example, one boy – Ravi Shankar – described in detail all the toys he had played with in his former life; when Stevenson investigated the 'former' family he was shown the toys, just as described. The same boy remembered that his former life – as Munna – had been ended by murder, and he recalled the details with a high degree of accuracy, including details unlikely to have been widely publicised.

Other evidence that Stevenson finds of interest are birthmarks that match marks on previous suspected incarnations, particularly where they might relate to the death of the former individual; for example, where the reincarnation of a gunshot victim has birthmarks which match the entry holes of bullets in the victim.

Stevenson is the most cautious of researchers. He emphasises that, 'I consider these cases suggestive of reincarnation and nothing more . . . Neither any case individually nor all of them collectively offers anything like a proof . . .'

In fact no matter how good the evidence, it cannot prove reincarnation. Even if we accept that a person has memories that at one time belonged to someone now dead, we still cannot prove how they travelled from one to another. An interesting point here is the story of Jaspir, also one of Ian Stevenson's twenty 'best cases'.

Having apparently died, Jaspir was prepared for burial. In fact, he revived, but he now believed he was no longer Jaspir. He described a former life, in some detail. Further investigation showed that Jaspir seemed to have the memories of a now deceased child, Sobha Ram. This would be a case highly suggestive of reincarnation if it were not for the simple fact that both had been alive at the same time, Jaspir being born before Ram's death. The suggestion is that the deceased Ram took over the body of Jaspir. There are several other cases that have the same implication.

One case that demonstrates not just the possibilities but the 'grey areas' between possession and other aspects of the survival spirit is that of Lurancy Vennum that arose in Watseka, America in 1878. It is the story of a 'deal' struck between the living Lurancy and the deceased Mary Roff.

Lurancy claimed to have contacted the spirit of a dead child, Mary Roff. Mary had died thirteen years earlier and it seemed that Lurancy was now possessed by her spirit. Mary asked to go home (to the Roff home) and while there recognised and interacted with family and friends. She revealed details of the home and family history that should not have been known to Lurancy. The possession was 'invited'; Mary Roff and Lurancy had struck a deal for Mary to possess Lurancy's body for a short time, and to return it to its rightful owner in due course. After that time was over, Mary walked back to Lurancy's home; by the time she got there she was Lurancy again.

These cases raise questions which may play a part in understanding the mechanisms. In the case of Jaspir, and other cases like his, why did Jaspir die? His body was apparently racked with smallpox, causing his death, yet the new persona was able to occupy it for some time, apparently in good health.

In this context possession becomes a potential explanation for all cases of reincarnation: a body, even at birth, possessed by the spirit of a former person rather than naturally 'owning' it. The evidence for some paranormal process of transfer of memory is high, but identifying its mechanisms is very difficult.

S

SAVANT SYNDROME
What is the cube root of 941,192?* In other words, what is the number which multiplied by itself, and the result then multiplied by itself again, produces that figure? Having trouble? Not surprising really; but one savant could give the answer, with no calculator or notepaper to work on, in around six seconds.

There are a small number of people, called savants, for whom the world works in a quite different way to the majority. They are regarded as mentally challenged, and suffering from some sort of deficiency. This is true inasmuch as they do not have the character and make up to effect normal social interaction. In extreme cases they need considerable care, as they are unable to deal with their own needs.

However, they have extraordinary talents that have puzzled doctors and psychiatrists for decades. The puzzlement is not whether they can do what they claim, they obviously can and they can be observed doing it; the question is, how do they do it?

In fact it is the same situation as with studying, say, psychic healing; it can be observed, but it cannot be explained. But presumably since the medical profession have confirmed the existence of savant syndrome, the focus is on the abilities rather than on the question of whether or not they exist. Even sceptics do not seem to feel obliged to insist that savants are cheating.

There are many references to savant syndrome in literature; probably the best is *Extraordinary People* by Darrold A. Treffert which contains a comprehensive analysis of savant cases.

Savant abilities vary. Calendar calculating is probably the best known of such claims. Charlie and George, twin brothers, were born prematurely. Tests indicated they were probably monozygositic (identical twins, from the same fertilised egg). They showed signs of mental impairment from an early age, banging their heads self-destructively, fighting, hand-biting, rocking and swaying motions. Their IQ was low, somewhere between 40 and 70. The twins could only read simple words; and they could just about add up to 30. But they can calendar count with extraordinary accuracy through 80,000 years. Ask them what day of the week 26 June will be in the year 31,995 and they can correctly reply in an instant. Ask them in which years Easter will fall on 23 March and they will reel off the list immediately. They are as fast as a computer, and as accurate. They were first presented to the American Psychiatric Association in Los Angeles in 1964 by psychiatrists William Horwitz, Clarice Kestenbaum, Ethel Person and Lissy Jarvik.

The studies on Charlie and George indicated that theirs was not entirely a feat of memory, it had to involve calculation. They had not learned the dates, they calculated in response to questions. This was particularly observed because they did not understand the change-over between the Gregorian and Julian calendars; their answers had to be adjusted by ten days whenever they calculated back beyond AD 1582. Horwitz suggested that they had learned by rote the 400-year complete calendar cycles and then subtracted blocks of 400 to arrive at the present date-range where they would search for the answer. Their general memory was not, however, very adept; they could not remember the names of the US Presidents.

No one yet really knows how Charlie and George, and those like them, do what they do. Horwitz believes memory plays a part. Oliver Sacks, Professor of Clinical Neurology, states they have an 'immense mnemonic tapestry' at their command. A colleague, Dora Hamblin, simply says she has no idea how they do it. George himself threw little light on the subject, 'It's in my head and I can do it,' is all he knows.

Blind Tom was a savant with quite different abilities. A

slave, he was sold with his mother in 1850; no charge was made for Tom as he was regarded as valueless. He gained little education, not surprising for a slave, and he was aggressive, needing supervision. But Tom could play an estimated 5,000 pieces of music of almost any complexity faultlessly. Any music he heard, he could reproduce. It was thought that he could even weave in his own interpretations. He was taken on a concert tour, and earned $100,000 in his first year, an incredible sum of money for the time. His relationship with his owner, Colonel Tom Bethune, was such that when the Colonel died, Blind Tom sank into introspective despair, never played again and died, sullen and alone.

In 1987 a BBC programme called *The Foolish Wise Ones*, promoted the effects of savant syndrome to a wider audience than had probably ever realised the full extent of these specially talented people. It centred on a British subject, Stephen Wiltshire, whose talent was to draw with astonishing accuracy, from memory. He drew several prominent London landmarks having seen them for the first time only briefly. One leading architect explained that Wiltshire's talents were such that without shading he could reproduce the effect of depth and contrast, no easy task.

The nearest to analysis of savant syndrome that has produced results – and extraordinary ones at that – is the work of Benj Langdon. He studied with Charlie and George to see if he could learn to calendar calculate as they could. He tried hard, but could not match the abilities of the brothers. But almost without warning, he suddenly found that he could! He matched their speed, apparently having memorised the table that was the key to his calculations, and found he could access the table intuitively, without calculation. Unfortunately, despite attempts to explain what he had done, it seemed that he had only learned to do it, not how it was done. He seemed to have no more idea how he did it than the brothers. Rather as learning to tie shoelaces goes through a process of intense concentration and then suddenly becomes 'you just do it'. Dr Bernard Rimland in *Psychology Today* (August 1978) states that he believes Langdon switched from using his left brain functions (scientific, calculating) to right brain functions (artistic, intuitive, creative).

Natural talents seemed to be housed in the right brain; the left brain is where we have to work to produce results. The implication seems to be that our standard learning processes teach us – perhaps restrict us – to learning certain types of skills in a 'left brain way'. Perhaps savants intuitively learn these functions in 'the right brain way'.

(*The answer is 98)

SHAMANISM

Shamans are the wise men and healers of 'primitive' peoples, set apart by their intense spiritual experience. With their mystical abilities, they are said to have access to, and influence on, the spirit world.

Shamans may be male or female. (Sometimes the term shamaness is used, but more often the term shaman is used for both sexes.) Shamans are found in native peoples in North America from Alaska to Hawaii, Central Asia from Siberia to Tibet, and Australasia.

There are various accounts of how shamans came to be. In legend, at least, it is said that the first shamans descended directly from heaven with great knowledge and abilities. These early shamans were said to have amongst their powers that of physical flight and great speed. Since that time the numbers of shamans has increased, but their powers seem to have faded. Shamanism has been said to be on the decline.

The traditions and teachings of the shamans are passed down one to another and involve self-study and meditation. Some people are born to be shamans; others find direction in dreams or altered states. The ability to enter a trance state is fundamental, as it is during this trance state that the shamans perform their functions and receive knowledge from the spirit world. During this altered state the shaman has access to three zones: the earth; the sky; and the underworld. The shaman remains lucid during his altered state and is able to recall what transpired.

There are different techniques used to enter these altered states including drumming, chanting, dancing, fasting, isolation, contemplation, suffering and sometimes psychedelic drugs. The most powerful shamans are said to be those initiated by being struck by lightning, or being subject to a near-by lightning strike. It is a sign of direct contact from the realm of the gods.

Shamans go through intensive training. A major part of this is the 'Vision Quest', normally taking place at puberty. The would-be shaman leaves the village and sets himself up in isolation, perhaps in a cave, a tent or a small shelter he builds for himself. During his isolation the initiate will fast – not eating or drinking until he meets his spirit healer, or guide. This would normally happen in four days. These helpers appear as animals. The initiate may chose the first he sees, then he can give up his fast and return to the village. However, if a stronger spirit is required, the would-be shaman politely explains this to the spirit and continues his quest until he meets a suitable guide.

This is very similar to the modern search for 'teachers'. In modern quests to explore the inner self, or psychic self, individuals are taught to find themselves a teacher, perhaps an animal, plant or inanimate object, that can teach and guide them. Michael Crichton, in his book *Travels*, devotes a chapter to 'Cactus Teaching' describing how he spent time in contemplation and discussion with a cactus at a desert retreat.

Crichton at first tried to talk to the cactus, which did not respond to him and then he thought, 'Of course it didn't answer – it was just a cactus. I thought, I am talking out loud to a cactus, which is bad enough. But, worse, I am feeling annoyed that it won't answer . . . They lock people up for this.'

But Crichton 'learnt' from the cactus. It seemed the teacher acted as a focus for his inner thoughts, and for releasing the subconscious. At one point after several days of absence from the cactus Crichton went back to it and feels that he heard it speak aloud, 'Where have you been?'

During training a would-be shaman may go through a symbolic death and dismemberment. He is then reassembled, resurrected and given a new name. (In the modern West similar quests are the equivalent of losing the ego.)

These various experiences are very akin to near-death experiences (see page 196); they give knowledge and answers to the shamatic student.

The magical powers of the shamans are held to allow them to foretell the future, affect the weather, even perform extraordinary feats such as stopping a bullet in mid-flight. The powers the shamans use are not good or evil, neither white or black; they are neutral, and can be used to kill or cure.

The shamans are also great healers. However, before healing patients the shamans (sometimes known as medicine men, or even witch doctors) first heal themselves. To train for this they may take on the illness of the patient, and then heal themselves. This presumably gives them a better understanding of illness and patient complaints than any medical school. Heal the culture, heal the people, then heal the illness. Healing can include a variety of techniques, even travelling astrally to pursue the lost souls of patients. As with so-called New Age healing, shamans seek to heal the holistic complex that is mind, body and spirit.

Writers on shamanism have taken great pains to distinguish between shamans and sorcerers. To quote Dr Stanley Krippner of the Saybrook Institute of California (*PSI Researcher* Spring 1993), 'Sorcerers look for power and keep it to themselves, while the shaman looks for power and uses it for the patient and the community.'

The powers of the shamans have been ignored by Western society since the Church dismissed these mysteries as heathen, but now with a more accepting outlook Westerners are becoming interested and are attempting to find the skills themselves. A great deal of modern business training, evidenced in corporate training programmes, is shamanistic in all but name.

SPECTRAL ARMIES

A current belief in ghost research involves the idea that past events are somehow 'recorded' within local surroundings. It is believed that we see or hear such 'ghost recordings' when certain appropriate conditions cause a 'replay' of these past events. This is based only on anecdotal accounts and observation; no experimental work has yet produced the conditions for either recording or replay. This theory is held to explain those ghosts that are non-interactive with the present surroundings, or with the sighter. It is analogous to showing a video recording on a TV in your living room; the replay contains only visual and auditory recordings of those on the screen – there is no real 'presence' or 'spirit' of the people on the screen in the room. The recording always 'unfolds' in identical sequence; the players cannot alter their actions, or the outcome.

In searching for the conditions which might be necessary to 'embed' the images, it has been suggested that emotion plays a part in making the recording. Individual emotion might account for the 'ghost recording' of, say, a suicide, but there are certain 'ghost recordings' that suggest a more complex possibility. Fights and battles are often experienced many years after their happening. However, the emotions of those in the battle must be varied; there will be those who were afraid, those for whom war was ecstasy, and those less moved by the events. In that case we might have to consider that the quantity – rather than the quality – of the emotions may be a factor.

A further possibility exists in a theory of T.C. Lethbridge's. He suggested that a sighter of the original scene embeds the recording by experiencing it, presumably under certain other special conditions. The sighter would act as a sort of 'psychic camera'. The soldiers at the battle would themselves therefore not be responsible for embedding the recording, and their individual emotions would not have to be considered.

On 16 April 1746, on Culloden Moor, the English army massacred the Scots in sixty minutes of frenzied battle. Since that time there have been many reports of ghostly armies; their battles seen to be replayed in the sky.

On the cliffs above Worbarrow Bay, near East Lulworth in Dorset, is an Iron Age fort called Flower's Barrow. In 1678 a spectral army was seen there, marching from the Barrow over Grange Hill. The sounds of 'clashing of arms' was reported.

When Henry IV fought to save his kingdom, there was a bloody battle at Bramham, near Leeds. In recent years there have been many reports of the sounds of horses where no horses can be seen; held by many to be an echo of the battle.

The story of the ghosts of the Battle of Edgehill is of particular interest. Although the reports come from many years ago, the witnesses were numerous and were investigated at the time. Furthermore, at least one of the identified 'ghosts' had not died in the battle.

In 1643, on 23 October, the first battle of the English Civil War took place at Edgehill, Warwickshire. There were 1,400 fighting men; at the end of the battle 500 of them were dead on the battlefield.

One month after the battle, shepherds witnessed what they thought was another battle. They saw the cavalry and gunsmoke, and heard sounds of beating drums and the screams of the wounded. Only when the noises, and the men and their horses, disappeared did the shepherds realise they had seen something very strange indeed. On Christmas Eve the following month the battle was again re-enacted. This time a report was written which came to the attention of King Charles I at Oxford. He sent six army officers to investigate the phenomenon.

On their return, these men not only reported that they had spoken to the witnesses but that they had themselves seen the event on two occasions. At least one of the investigators had fought at Edgehill and was able to recognise a number of the men who had died amongst the spectres. He also recognised Prince Rupert who – although he had taken part in the battle – was still very much alive.

With the passing of time this spectral battle has ceased to be reported, but perhaps it will replay again when the conditions are right. The fact that among the ghosts was at least one person who was alive at the time of the sightings underlines the reasoning that this form of image is simply recorded and has no connection to the survival of spirit beyond death.

On the night before the Battle of Marston Moor, a troop of phantom horsemen was seen galloping over the heights of

Helvellyn where no ordinary horse could pass in safety. This claim opens more questions: can a recording be played before the event? We could speculate on the mechanisms which might help account for precognition, or even time slips. However, since here it is stated 'where no ordinary horse could pass', we might have to look for another explanation. Perhaps a clue is given in the case of a ghost army from Oxfordshire. A regiment of soldiers was seen marching in the sky, complete with drum and fife band. Upon inquiry it was found that such a regiment had been passing at the time along a road near Bicester, six miles away. It was concluded that the apparition in the sky was probably a freak reflection.

A more recent, but similar, report comes from A.H. Griffin in *In Mountain Lakeland*. He recounts the experience of F.S. Smythe and a fellow climber while they were climbing in the Alps. 'He and his companion both saw what appeared to be a line of ships floating over the Black Forest. They looked like battle-cruisers and the two climbers could see every detail of the masts and funnels. For a quarter of an hour they watched this strange, heavenly armada and then it disappeared. An interesting correspondence followed in *The Times*. It was suggested, for instance, that the ships had been taking part in exercises somewhere near the junction of the English Channel with the North Sea and that the image had been magnified, as well as refracted, by different layers of air – over a distance of something like 400 miles.' Griffin states that he believes the explanation to be an unconvincing one.

So here we find another theory suggesting a sort of mirror or reflected image in a manner similar to a mirage, perhaps. If there is validity in these theories, we might have at least two phenomena producing the same effect.

Such battlefield ghosts are not entirely confined to the distant past. The 381st Bomber Group of the United States Army Air Force was stationed at the American Airbase built at Ridgewell during the Second World War. The group flew many daylight bombing raids across France and Germany, taking off in the early morning. It was rumoured that local residents never used alarm clocks; the noise of the airfield beginning early morning operations was sufficient! In the winter mornings, bright lights on the airfield did the same job. The airfield has long been derelict, but locals claim many ghostly sightings of the lights and the airmen themselves, and they report hearing the sounds of the engines of jeeps and planes.

A modern case offering the potential of new evidence arose in a report of a ghost army seen at Otterburn in Northumberland. In 1388 the Scots defeated the English; their phantoms were seen in 1960 by Mrs Dorothy Strong, who was in a taxi at the time. Many other sightings of the ghost armies had been reported in the area. 'Suddenly the engine died, the fare-meter went haywire and the taxi was as if it was being forced against an invisible wall. The soldiers seemed to close in on us and then fade into thin air.' (Electrical effects associated with paranormal research are also covered in Vehicle Interference, page 330.)

SPONTANEOUS EQUIPMENT FAILURE
A German film crew was filming in a crop circle and, seeing John Spencer with a group of researchers, asked if they could do an interview. The equipment was set up but the audio-visual technician announced that all the batteries in the equipment had failed. The crew were not too surprised, as they had been working all day filming. They knew they had fully charged batteries in their car, which they collected. Having fitted the replacement batteries, they confirmed the power was full, began recording and almost immediately all the power drained away. The interview never could be filmed.

A similar case was described to us by Mike Lewis, head of investigation for ASSAP, the Association for the Scientific Study of Anomalous Phenomena, while conducting a vigil at the Ancient Ram Inn in Gloucestershire. A perfectly functioning video camera light always failed every time he took it into one particular room, reputedly the most haunted room in the inn.

Nor are such reports restricted to involvement in the paranormal. It was reported that everywhere President Johnson went lights would fail.

Another case of a haunting where we find equipment failing at the vital moment arose when a nurse and headmaster saw the New Year's Eve Nun at a girls' school in Cheltenham (see 'Ghosts', page 144). They shone a torch at the apparition and after the beam of light 'touched' the ghost, the torch went out and could never be made to work again.

A researcher of the paranormal, Bertil Kuhlemann, a Swedish colleague of ours, recorded speeches around a table without touching either the tape recorder set in the middle of the table or the tape within it. Nonetheless just one voice did not record on the tape, though voices either side of it recorded clearly.

Several cases of UFO encounter have involved effects on equipment. Betty and Barney Hill's watches were stopped when they got home, presumed affected by their encounter. But what do we make of Charles Hickson, who was abducted at Pascagoula? He never wears a watch. 'People said I had electricity,' he states. Every watch he tried to wear would lose or gain time, or stop altogether. Even pocket watches were no use.

In the cases of equipment malfunction during paranormal investigation such as ghost vigils, the investigators are not always surprised by the experience, indeed that is why they are there in the first place. But there is a recognition that in researching the paranormal, things go wrong. No more specific expression is possible; the problems are random and varied. But they occur so frequently, and with the appearance of deliberation, that it is becoming viewed as a phenomenon in its own right. Viewed in a wider perspective, and occurring as they do at vital moments, these events are close cousins of 'the phone rings just when you get in the bath'.

When there are cases of repeated failure, often in the presence of several witnesses and in what almost amounts to test conditions (walk in the room, the light goes off, walk out of the room, the light goes on, walk in the room the light goes off again, etc.) there seems little doubt that some mechanism is at work. The question is whether the mechanism is a force or influence affecting the equipment or, as must be considered, whether the person using the equipment is at some level affecting it.

Since several cases involve equipment not being touched, out of sight, or even at a remote location miles from the operators, the explanation of subconscious interference alone does not explain all cases. We would suggest that since there seems to be evidence that people can affect equipment using some sort of mechanism we presently call PK (see 'Psychokinesis', page 259), we feel it is not necessary at this stage to look beyond that to an external force. By the same token we would not rule another possibility out.

We might suggest that what we have here is a sort of anti-PK (APK). Just as 'lens-cap effect' makes us clumsy when we need not to be (the term comes from leaving the lens cap on when you need to take an important picture) so perhaps the stresses caused by desperately wanting something to work at a significant moment may perversely cause APK to be directed at the equipment. If we can be clumsy with our physical abilities, there is no reason to assume we cannot be clumsy with our mental abilities.

It is also cautious to remember that the same mechanisms may not be causing all the effects.

SPONTANEOUS HUMAN COMBUSTION

There are reports of humans burning, often to death, without apparent or obvious cause. Often the bodies are found burnt beyond all recognition, apparently burnt with a heat more intense than that used in a crematorium. There have been many well-documented cases from around the world, though we note that coroners tend not to use the term spontaneous combustion, possibly because of its paranormal overtones, and therefore many more cases may be missed.

People have been witnessed bursting into flames with the power of a blow-torch, as did Pastor Lueger, in November 1986, dramatically and in full view of his congregation. While he was giving a sermon, a bright flash was seen to come from the pastor's chest, he screamed, slumped forwards, then exploded in a ball of flame.

In Los Angeles, in May 1990, Angela Hernandez spontaneously exploded in flames while on an operating table at UCLA.

Strange Stories, Amazing Facts, published in 1975, described the case of a nineteen-year-old secretary who was dancing with her boyfriend at a nightclub in the late 1950s. She suddenly burst into flames. Within a few seconds she was described as a 'human torch', and she was dead before the flames could be beaten out. Her boyfriend testified at the inquest, 'I saw no one smoking on the dance floor. There were no candles on the tables and I did not see her dress catch fire from anything. I know it sounds incredible, but it appeared to me that the flames burst outwards, as if they originated within her body.' These statements were confirmed by other people on the dance floor. The verdict of the inquest was 'death by misadventure, caused by a fire of unknown origin'.

Part of the mystery is that the immediate surroundings are often left with very little damage: sheets on a bed may be undamaged, even when a person has burnt to death on them; clothing, although scorched, will not be burnt and yet the person wearing the clothes is completely burnt. One man's genitals were described as 'fried to a crisp', yet his underwear was no more than scorched.

There have been apparent survivors. Jack Angel awoke to find first-degree burns on his legs, groin, back and hand. His hand was so badly burnt it needed amputating. Yet nothing in his motor home seemed damaged, not even his sheets.

Spontaneous human combustion (SHC) was thought to be brought on by alcoholism, as many of the victims seemed to be from 'down-and-out' situations. The suggestion was that alcohol-soaked flesh was prone to ignition. More recent analysis has shown this to be false. It has now been proposed that SHC victims share a common personality type, often of a lonely and depressed disposition, perhaps feeling neglected. Some are described as 'no hopers'. In line with the original hypothesis is the likelihood of a higher number of alcohol abusers within a group of depressed individuals.

The emotional states, or at least intensities, of the victims seems significant. The priest mentioned earlier was said to have worked himself up into a frenzy just before bursting into flames. A groom giving his speech after his wedding – surely an emotional time – burst into flames and was reduced to ashes in less than a minute in full view of the whole wedding congregation of a hundred people.

Michael Harrison's work *Fire from Heaven* describes two victims planning, and actually in the process of committing, suicide. Glen Denney in September 1952, in Louisiana, seems to have attempted suicide but died, it seems, from smoke inhalation from his own fiery destruction. Billy Peterson seems to have successfully committed suicide by connecting a car exhaust to a hose and feeding it into the window of his car; he was found dead from carbon monoxide poisoning. But there was severe burning to his arm, genitals, nose, mouth and ears, although there was no indication of where the fire could have started.

There are cases that suggest a deeper mystery. One suggests a mechanism difficult to even guess at, though it could arguably include telepathy or some cousin of that process. Authors Jenny Randles and Peter Hough, in *Spontaneous Human Combustion*, set out the case of two sisters, Amy (aged four) and Alice (aged five) Kirby who both died after bursting into flames at exactly the same time – 11 a.m. – on exactly the same day, even though they were living a mile apart, each with one of their separated parents.

The fire that engulfs these victims seems to have special qualities. A blue flame is often noticed. Another oddity is that the fire cannot be put out by water. In fact water seems to intensify it. There is one case of a girl bursting into flames while taking a shower.

We spoke to Ron Campbell of the London Fire Service, who is a specialist consultant on fire and fire-prevention; he indicated that in his experience the only fires made worse by water were those where magnesium or titanium are involved, as in the framework of aircraft. Aircraft fires are attacked by foams rather than water precisely because water will exacerbate the flames. It is the intensity of the heat that creates the problem; magnesium burns with such heat that it releases hydrogen which is itself highly combustible. SHC then would seem to involve fires of intense heat.

One victim, a male professor, felt a pain on his left leg and, looking down, noticed a blue flame which he extinguished by smothering it. It can only be speculated what the results would have been if he had tried pouring water on it.

Dr D. Gee, a lecturer in forensic medicine, investigated the case of an elderly lady found almost totally incinerated. He suggested that the body had burned in its own fat in the manner of a candle.

There seems to be a case for considering two types of manifestation for SHC. Some of the reports indicate an incredibly rapid speed of burning; the secretary in the night club mentioned earlier, for example. On the other hand we have Dr Gee's suggestion of slow burning over a long period. Whether these represent two different phenomena, or the same phenomenon under different conditions, is impossible to analyse with the present level of understanding of the subject.

Poltergeist phenomena often includes fire-starting of a spontaneous nature. We must consider the possibility that the SHC victim is tapping into the same energy force as the poltergeist. SHC victims on the whole tend to be older people, whereas poltergeists seem to focus on young people near puberty. If SHC is an expression of emotion, perhaps younger people 'let it out' while older people 'bottle it up'.

Women outnumber men as psychics, mediums, stigmatics, poltergeist foci, and also as SHC victims according to the present global summaries by all researchers. Perhaps something in the female attributes of emotion makes them more susceptible to all forms of sensitivity. Michael Harrison has suggested that the intensity of the heat in males is higher than that in females, generally speaking.

Randles and Hough's book contains a most useful catalogue of 120 cases for anyone interested in the subject. They have produced interesting bar-graphs which we shall not repeat here, but we have used the listings for two analyses of our own.

(We have not attempted to evaluate the merits of any of the cases, or to distinguish between likely or less likely cases of SHC. Randles and Hough make clear that they apply the same caveats in producing the list.)

Firstly, we analysed the sex/time progression of the cases. There is some tendency towards more men becoming victims in recent times. Randles and Hough's global statistics indicate that fifty-eight per cent of victims are female, but we calculate that since 1980, of twenty-six cases, fifteen were men (fifty-eight per cent male). We were interested in that statistic because we had noted in our analysis of stigmatics that original statistics of approximately eight females to one male were diminishing, with a trend seemingly heading towards equality (see 'Stigmata', page 289). The changing statistics of SHC and stigmata might reflect that in the modern day it is more acceptable for men to allow their 'feminine' qualities to come to the surface. As such, if emotion plays a part in the production of these paranormal effects, perhaps men are being affected more because of this.

The second analysis was a more detailed time/event study that shows very clearly that more cases arise in the winter months. Using Randles and Hough's 120 cases as the sample, this is very clear. Of the 120 cases listed, 25 have no known month-date. The majority of these arise pre-1900, not unexpectedly. Of the 81 cases from 1900 onwards, 7 have unknown dates. Of the remaining 74 cases, 27 (36.49 per cent) arise in just the two months December and January (16.67 per cent would be average). If we take in November's 6 cases then of the 74 cases, 33 (44.6 per cent) arise in those three months (25 per cent would have been average). We have not taken into account multiple deaths; for example, in case 71, 5 charred bodies were found in a car. Assuming SHC we cannot be certain if one person 'ignited' catching the others alight, or if there was more than one case of SHC. For the purposes of our crude statistics we have treated the case as one only. While a high number of heat-related deaths might be expected in the winter months, because people use heat to keep themselves warm, it must be noted that what often leads to an inclusion of a case as one of SHC is that there is no known heat source in the vicinity. What may turn out to be more relevant is the belief in Seasonal Affective Disorder (SAD). Some psychiatrists have noted that people seem more depressed in winter for no obvious, personal cause. There is a growing belief that the absence of sunlight and warmth simply leaves the body feeling less well. As we have already suggested, emotional state, and depression, evidenced for example by the suicides, seems to be a part of the cause of SHC.

SPRING-HEELED JACK

The Victorian tales of Spring-Heeled Jack (or Springheel Jack) seem almost legendary, but as researcher Stephen J. Gamble points out, 'There are so many reports . . . over a number of years and a variety of locations that it seems unlikely that the reports are totally baseless.'

The first reports probably relate to 1817 when a shadowy figure was seen on Barnes Common in South London, but the story is generally held to date from January 1838 when Sir John Cowan, the Lord Mayor of London, officially recognised Jack by reading out a letter from a Peckham resident of her frightening encounter with the figure. It triggered a flood of claims from people who had also seen the figure, but had been too mystified, or uncertain of themselves, to report their sightings.

In February 1838 Lucy Scales and her sister spotted a giant, shadowy figure near Green Dragon Alley in the East End of London. The figure, reportedly seen spitting flames, apparently leapt a fourteen-foot wall to elude capture. In the same month he was seen by Jane Alsop when she answered her door. Jack ripped at her clothes before she escaped and he ran off. She said, 'His face was hideous. His eyes were like balls of fire and he vomited blue and white flames. His hands were like claws, but icy cold.'

In 1845 Jack was blamed for the murder of a prostitute, Marie Davies, throwing her to her death from a bridge over Folly Ditch in Bermondsey. As before, the report had Jack spitting flames.

Jack was reported for many years, the last reports being in 1904, in Liverpool.

It has been suggested that Henry de la Poer Beresford, Marquis of Waterford, was Jack, at least in the first period of reports. He was a well-known prankster and eccentric, with a brutal, vicious streak. While he might have been responsible for some attacks, it seems hardly likely he could account for the more exotic ones. Black-caped (or winged?), gleaming-eyed, and leaping and bounding: the reports sound unlikely and exaggerated. But there is similarity in the reports of Jack's description and manner to the more modern reports of the Mothmen (see page 191). Viewing Jack alongside those accounts may throw light on these early British claims.

STIGMATA

In 1224, two years before his death, St Francis of Assisi reported that he had received on to his body marks representing the wounds of the suffering of Jesus Christ. In the 770 years since that time it is estimated that some 300 people have reported this phenomenon. It is thought that there may be more, that some recipients of the marks might have kept them secret believing them to be for the eyes of the devout only. Certainly one recent case, Heather Woods of Lincoln, only made her marks public when she was told in a message from the Lord that they could be made public. The vast majority of the claimants have been female; one estimation indicated a figure as high as eighty-five per cent.

We note that original statistics of approximately seven or eight females to one male are diminishing; at present the figures are nearer three females to one male. Part of the reason would seem to be that originally women had rejected the churches that had in effect disenfranchised them, and had sought their own path to Christ. The path they chose was one of concentration on His suffering for our sins, rather than – as the Church emphasised at that time – his miracles and origins. We note in our analysis of spontaneous human combustion (see page 287) that there is a similar trend away from an excess of women to, in that case, an excess of men. We suggest that part of the reason, in both SHC and stigmata, is that in modern times it is more acceptable for men to allow their 'feminine' qualities to express themselves. Perhaps these paranormal phenomena, and others, need the feminine emotions and other characteristics that are present in some balance in all humans, rather than the male side.

In the case of St Francis, the stigmata were described as the appearance of the nails themselves; the points and the nail-heads showing through the skin on both sides of his hands. They were alleged to have existed after his death; with many pilgrims filing past his body witnessing 'not the prints of the nails, but the nails themselves formed out of his flesh and retaining the blackness of iron . . .'

Other stigmatics have reported similar marks; for example Giovanna Bonomi in 1670 and Domenica Lazzari in 1848. The marks are not, however, consistent. Some reports are of red patches that do not bleed, deep holes that in some cases are alleged to go right through the limb, circles, ovals, oblongs and so on. The marks can include a representation of the spear-mark in the side and marks representing the crown of thorns on the forehead. Recently Heather Woods displayed all of these marks over two Easter periods in 1992 and 1993.

Georgette Faniel of Montreal has reported, in addition to the usual marks, a pain that she believes represents the wound caused by Christ carrying the cross on his shoulder as he walked to Golgotha.

Some stigmatics have wept blood; Teresea Neumann is probably the most famous of these. In the case of St Teresa of Avila, whose heart is preserved as a sacred relic, there are marks which are believed by some to represent the piercing of her heart by a spear. There have been other cases of post-mortem marks on the heart attributed to the stigmata; for example Caterina Savelli in 1691, and Charles of Sezze in 1671.

The most famous stigmatic was Padre Pio. After eight years of pains he received the stigmata at the age of thirty-one, on 20 September 1918; his wounds opened up and wept a great deal of blood. For him, as for many stigmatics, his marks were painful. He wrote, 'I saw before me a mysterious person . . . his hands and feet and side were dripping with blood. The vision disappeared and I became aware that my hands, feet and side were dripping blood. Imagine the agony I experienced and continue to experience almost every day . . . I am dying of pain because of the wounds and resulting embarrassment . . .' He remained a stigmatic for fifty years; even his shoes were specially made to accommodate the bandages that were a normal part of his life.

There were those who believed they could put their fingers right through the wounds; others claimed he was a fraud. Such extremes of views are normal in paranormal subjects, usually reflecting the viewpoints of the investigators more than those of the subject.

Padre Pio and St Francis of Assisi have many close parallels. From an early age Padre Pio – born Francesco Forgione – wanted to be a Franciscan priest. St Francis received his stigmata after a pilgrimage to the shrine of St Michael at Gargano in Italy; Padre Pio lived in a monastery in the small town of San Giovanni Rotondo, just a few miles from that shrine. Padre Pio's stigmata appeared three days after he had celebrated the Feast of the Stigmata of St Francis. However, when Padre Pio died, on 23 September 1968, there were no signs of the wounds on his body, as there had been with St Francis.

Those displaying the stigmata often have associated paranormal experiences, in particular: visions, receiving channelled messages, writings and drawings. Padre Pio was frequently reported in bi-location – seen in two places at the same time.

Generally speaking, those displaying the signs of the stigmata indicate that they believe them to represent a sign from Jesus. Certainly there are few stigmatics who are not obviously religious, with a belief in Christ as a centrepiece of their conviction. There are no reliable claims of the stigmata in non-Christian religions. Heather Woods indicated that she believed they were given to her at a time when a suffering world needed a symbol of faith.

Another currently active British stigmatic, George Hamilton

(see photo section) in Scotland, whom we interviewed several times in 1994, has a slightly different interpretation of the meaning behind the phenomenon. He believes the marks are a sign of his being protected by Christ; just prior to the appearance of the marks, he had suffered several poltergeist-like attacks including a wood chisel thrown at him when he was alone in his house. After the marks appeared, he found peace and security. Unlike Heather Woods, who felt she knew her mission in life was to continue the healing ministry of the Lord, George Hamilton constantly asks the question, 'What is it you want of me, Lord?' In interviewing both Heather Woods and George Hamilton, we were astounded by the similarity of their histories; both having similar visions of Christ's baptism and crucifixion, both having visions of a light that brought for them a tranquillity they had never known. Heather died before they could meet (though they had both wished to meet each other, they told us), but when George read Heather's biography – which we had just written – he was amazed at the points of similarity.

Analysis of the phenomenon indicates that internal beliefs and imagery may explain the markings. Prior to the claims of St Francis of Assisi, religious art – including depictions of Christ on the Cross – were highly stylised. They were graceful, artistic, beautiful and did not show blood, wounds or suffering. Religious art changed around the thirteenth century to a more realistic image; the suffering was depicted in all its detail – and the claims of the stigmata followed. When the Turin Shroud (see page 316) – whatever its authenticity – showed that the nail wounds might have been made through the wrists rather than the palms of the hands, claims of stigmata in the wrists followed. In fact, studies of the stigmata indicate that the marks seem to follow the imagery of the suffering as believed by the claimant.

This verges on suggesting that claimants actually want to display these signs; in fact we can be sure that this occasionally happens. Two years before St Francis of Assisi reported his stigmata, one man allowed himself to be crucified and therefore bore the marks, and in recent times a court prosecuted two men for crucifying a third on Hampstead Heath, even though the 'victim' admitted he had requested the crucifixion.

Apart from those who will have faked the marks – most paranormal subjects have their frauds – the majority seem to be displaying a psychosomatic response to their religious fervour. That the body can will itself to produce such marks has evidence outside of the realm of stigmata claims, and has even been put to the test. A Swedish girl known as Maria was badly beaten up when she was twenty-three; after that time she would, every few weeks, produce bleeding from head, ear and eyelids. A doctor examining her concluded that she could produce bleeding at will, from no visible wounds, when she picked arguments and reached a certain emotional state.

This ability, known as hysterical conversion, is a close cousin of a form of extreme hypochondria as exhibited by a woman known as Elizabeth. She could manifest the symptoms of any illness she heard about. On one occasion she went to see a slide show of the Passion – the crucifixion of Christ. She left feeling pains in her hands and feet. A Doctor Lechler, using hypnosis, suggested that she – like Christ – had been pierced by nails in her hands and feet. Nail-like wounds appeared. Using suggestion, he also induced tears of blood and bleeding wounds on her forehead. Lechler was also able to use hypnosis to heal the wounds, and he could eventually re-manifest them without hypnosis.

Whether the stigmata are God-given is, of course, a matter for conviction rather than research. Research seems, however, to have identified a mechanism by which the body can – in certain extreme emotions – manifest strange markings, producing a truly extraordinary, and highly visible, mysterious phenomenon.

STREET LAMP INTERFERENCE

After various people had independently spoken to researcher Hilary Evans, he set up and continues to organise SLIDE, the Street Lamp Interference Data Exchange.

He is collecting data relating to a specific claim which appears to have similar characteristics to both PK and associated electrical effects.

The claim made is that certain people, usually unknowingly and usually spontaneously, affect the operation of street lighting. Evans chose this category for special study because of certain characteristics which give it advantages over other forms of PK claim.

Firstly, a great many people, at least in the initial sample, made their claims without realising that there were other people making similar claims. In many cases it is clear that the claimants felt that the claims they were making were unique. Therefore these people were not fitting their beliefs about themselves or their reports into a pre-existing framework.

Secondly, when they discover that their claims are not unique they do not seem to be disappointed. Indeed the claims are for the most part without any obvious bias or prejudice and made only on the basis of 'an interesting point to relate'.

Thirdly, some of the events have been witnessed by others. Since street lighting is less likely to have been 'rigged' for fraudulent purposes than, say, household appliances, this allows for greater reliability than the reporter who makes similar claims of interference with devices within his control such as computers, house lighting, kettles and the like.

Lastly, there is very little kudos attached to the claims of street lamp interference. The ability to affect such an object is in its own way virtually meaningless and does not confer on the reporter the 'importance' that might be granted by others to someone claiming to be, say, in contact with extraterrestrials. There is therefore a less obvious motive for making fraudulent claims.

The numbers of street lamp interferers is low at present; fewer than 100 were included in the initial study. Evans points out that, 'Considering that the number of people who know of SLIDE's existence must be an infinitesimal percentage of the human race . . . it is reasonable to suppose that those . . . must be representative of a very substantial population.' This point may at this stage be arguable: as Evans himself points out, 'Considerable interest was aroused by a short piece by the respected Texas journalist Dennis Stacy, published in the American popular scientific magazine *OMNI* in September

1990. This brought in a substantial response, and accounts for a high proportion of American cases in the SLIDE files.' The interference is that many reports have come from people who are themselves already interested in or reading reports of paranormal or mystery subjects and the data base may not yet have a representative sample. Nevertheless it is early days yet and larger numbers of reports, should they arise, will serve the statistics better.

The basic claim of street lamp interferers is that, on coming into near proximity to street lamps, they cause them to turn off (or occasionally on). By their very nature, most reports relate to hours of darkness, but there are one or two claimants who also make similar reports for equipment in their homes or offices during daylight hours, suggesting that the time of day is not the relevant factor.

There appear to be no common factors. People can be alone, or with witnesses, driving or walking. It can happen frequently or rarely, for a brief period or for an extended period, from once or twice a year to 'at least 140 plus in the past year and a half'. Various types of lamps are affected, including mercury vapour and sodium vapour.

Proximity to the lights does not appear to be a major factor, as many people report the lights going out as they approach them, some when directly beneath them. Distances from the lights vary from immediate proximity to over 200 metres away. (If the light went out when the person had passed it, it would probably go unnoticed.)

A few people believe that they can deliberately turn off the lamps, though most claim it happens spontaneously.

There appears to be no particular background for claimants; Evans lists engineer, artist, draughtsman, geologist, account-ant, mathematician, nursing student, radio announcer, teacher and so on. Neither age nor sex appears to be a factor, though the samples are still too small for any definitive statement in either case. State of mind seems varied with reports including: 'concentrating', 'elated', 'fed up', 'happy', 'irritated', 'serene', 'stressed', 'terror', 'worried'.

Among the most extraordinary accounts is the following

(witnessed by the police), '. . . as I turned on to a lighted street, each and every lamp went out as my car reached within three metres of it. I looked back and nearly six lights or one and half city blocks of street lamps were darkened! . . . I drove again on that street in the opposite direction and once again the far side street lamps went dark as I approached all the way through the city approximately eight kilometres.'

Or this, 'One night I was walking past an apartment building and the yard light turned off. After I had walked past it a few metres, it spluttered back on. I didn't think much of it until the next night, when the same thing happened. Now I began to wonder if perhaps I was doing this somehow. I made a game of it – actually concentrating on turning off the light – and found much to my surprise that I could do it consistently. I found that I couldn't turn off just any light, but that one was a snap. I discounted oncoming car headlights and even observed the light from a distance for a few minutes one night to make sure it wasn't just going on and off at random.'

Occasionally witnesses are available, 'SLI has been happening to me for years. Recently my mother and I stopped at a highway rest stop just north of Springfield, Illinois, to stretch our legs after many hours of driving. The previous day I had showed my mother that I made street lights turn off and she thought this was really odd. While stopped at the rest stop, we both walked towards the rest-rooms and the light above us went out. This was the perfect opportunity to prove it to her. When we had come out of the rest-rooms, the light was back on again. So I walked toward the light and it went out again. We spent about twenty-five minutes individually walking towards the light pole and it went out every time on both of us. We stayed around and watched other people walk under it, but nobody else had an effect on it.'

A provisional assessment of SLI was issued by Hilary Evans in 1993. In it Evans comments on the synchronisity of SLI by relating an account of his own, 'This is perhaps the moment to report something that happened to me while transcribing this report. I was writing out on my computer the incident . . . where a SLIder says how he always knows when his computer was about to die when, at precisely that passage in the text, my computer – which has given me no trouble for more than a year – died on me.'

Hilary published provisional conclusions based on the collection of data to date as follows, 'In so far as a meaningful model can be constructed on the basis of anecdotal testimony, the body of case history so far accumulated does seem to constitute a case for regarding SLI as a phenomenon in its own right. Like so many other anomalous phenomena, its existence must remain in question until some conclusive evidence is forthcoming; for the apparent evidence is persuasive.' And, 'It is justifiable to proceed to construct the hypothesis on the basis of their testimony, with the implicit caveat that our speculations are contingent on the good faith and accurate reporting of those who supply the testimony.'

Hilary Evans confirmed in 1995 that reports of SLI have continued to come in regularly, 'not a week goes by without a report,' he commented to us. Nothing in those recent letters yet changes the comments from the original study.

The SPR, under the guidance of Professor Arthur Ellison, is taking over an experimental programme on SLI. Reports will continue to be collected by Evans, an address for whom is given at the back of this book.

T

TELEPATHY

Telepathy is communication from one mind to another without the use of speech or sign language. The word comes from the Greek (*tele* = distant and *pathos* = feeling). It was chosen by F. Myers (SPR founder) to replace the expressions 'thought transference' and 'thought reading'.

Einstein saw a possible contradiction between the claims of telepathy and known physics. Experimentation seemed to indicate that distance was no object to telepathy, but Einstein believed that all transmissions diminished over distance.

Freud thought that telepathy was an ability, or sixth sense, people once had but lost with over-dependence on the other five senses. In infrequent cases the ability comes to the fore. Freud suggested that dreams might even be recordings of extra-sensory communication.

Close family members often have visions of each other, particularly in times of stress (see 'Crisis Apparitions', page 80). Telepathy is frequently reported between twins. In one case we interviewed twins Jan and Sue who described several occasions of knowing what the other was doing. On one occasion Sue, living in Australia, had a miscarriage causing her great pain and distress. Jan, in England, felt the pain so physically that she burst out crying, much to the distress of her husband. She knew where the pain was coming from, and telephoned her sister to be told the sad news.

There is a great difficulty in differentiating between clairvoyance and telepathy. Clairvoyance is the sensing of events or objects in a paranormal way, but if the event is known to someone, it is possible that the information has been picked up in a telepathic communication. The same problems apply when mediums claim to have obtained information from the dead in a spirit world; if the information can be checked, it is usually known to someone – could that someone be in telepathic communication with the medium? (Some few extraordinary cases do not seem explainable by that theory – see 'Mediumship', page 182.)

F. Myers raised similar doubts about the overlap between apparitions and telepathy. He suggested that apparitions may be a telepathic message given embodiment by the percipient.

In 1934 Dr Joseph Rhine detailed the results of experiments into telepathy and clairvoyance in his monograph *Extrasensory Perception or ESP*. Rhine, working in the newly-formed Parapsychology Department of Duke University, North Carolina, showed that some people were able to predict the order of cards and gain a score that was considerably above that of chance alone. The subjects were first able to name a card held by a sender. This may be evidence of telepathy, but some subjects were also able, again above levels of chance, to predict the card to be turned over next. In this way the experiment suggested that something more than just telepathy was being used.

Rhine had used playing cards, but went on to use cards designed for him by Karl Zender (an expert in the field of psychology of perception). The cards that became known as Zender cards consisted of a pack of twenty-five cards containing five cards in each of five designs; circle, square, star, plus sign, and three wavy lines. The Zender cards are still frequently used, but it is common today to use electronic random-event generators, which produce a higher number of possibilities. These experiments, and refinements of them, were taken up by other universities and colleges.

Several telepathic experiments have centred around a sender viewing a picture or physical object, and the receiver attempting to draw that object. Mary Craig Sinclair was successful in these experiments. She attempted to draw images originated by her husband, his secretary and her brother-in-law. Of 290 images 65 were held to be 'hits' and 155 'partial hits'. Uri Geller had several successes in this way. For example, he duplicated the drawing of a bunch of grapes so accurately that he even drew the same number of grapes as in the original. It was pointed out that during experiments at the Stanford Research Institute Geller's score was much better when the experimenter knew what image was being tested. When Geller had to examine images from a random pile that the researchers themselves had not seen, his scores went down. These factors suggest telepathy was being used rather than, say, remote viewing; ESP without telepathy.

But perhaps the telepathy was an easy way out for Geller. When tested specifically for remote viewing his score again became impressive. For example, a die was placed in a closed box and shaken at random, yet Geller guessed the correct upsided face every time. The two areas of research cross frequently; remote viewing was experimented on with Pat Price, a retired police commissioner, as the subject. He claimed he had used psychic powers to catch criminals during his career. Physicist Russell Targ conducted the tests. Harold Puthoff and Dr Bonnar Cox were to drive somewhere and then Price would describe where they were. Before the couple had even got to wherever it was they were going. Price recorded his description of what the scenery would be when they got there ('. . . a boat jetty . . . motor launches . . . feeling of Oriental architecture . . .') The couple – their destination known only to their driver – stopped at Redwood City Marina near an Oriental-looking restaurant. Remote viewing seemed not to be the explanation. Either Price was picking up a telepathic image from Puthoff and Cox's driver of where he was envisioning they would be, or some premonition was in evidence.

It has been found that some children with a disfunctioning brain, or who have suffered brain damage, have fairly high telepathy scores in tests. Perhaps they have a greater need to use all their innate abilities; to retain a close bond to their mothers, for example. Telepathy is also known quite often in those of advanced years; perhaps as a result of the decline of the normal senses

Terry White in his book *The Sceptical Occultist* summarises the tests done on 'the Cambridge boy', who had been born with mental and physical disabilities. While having his eyesight tested, the boy identified letters on a wall chart much more effectively when his mother was in the room than when she was not. It seemed to indicate that he was picking up the correct identification telepathically from his mother. Later tests were conducted which showed that his 'hits' were way above chance. Using the letters A to Z and numbers between 1 and 10 randomly presented to his mother, the boy, on his first guesses, correctly guessed with almost twenty-five per cent accuracy.

Dream experimentation done in the 1970s at the Maimonides Dreamlab suggested telepathic transfer during dreams. One group looked at art prints while a sleeping group reported the images they saw in their dreams. It appears that for about eighty per cent of the time there had been some 'pick up' of the images being looked at.

These results certainly show that some people have abilities that cannot be explained by statistics alone. It is generally accepted by fair-minded analysts of paranormal phenomena that telepathy has been shown to exist as a real ability, though it is also accepted that this is based on the results of tests rather than an understanding of the underlying mechanisms, which still remain a mystery.

Certain factors however were identified as possibly having some effect on the results. Mood-state seemed to be one such factor. The best results seemed to come from subjects who were encouraged. In one case Rhine offered a subject $100 for every success; the subject took $2,500 on a streak of hits of twenty-five cards against odds calculated at 298,023,223,876,953,125 to 1.

The research also showed that results were suppressed by boredom, tiredness and self-consciousness; for example the same subject that got the $2,500 scored measurably less well after his fiancée jilted him.

This reaction to mood might well account for why test subjects in a range of paranormal areas often fail to perform to the standards they themselves expect when in confrontational situations with sceptics.

THOUGHTOGRAPHY

The imprint of a mental image on to photographic material is known as thoughtography.

The first spontaneous images to appear on film were noticed by Tomokichi Fukaria, the President of Psychical Research, Japan in early 1900. While working with medium Mrs Nagao and others, he obtained images on film. It was he who created the term thoughtography.

Ted Serios, investigated by Jule Eisenbud, is probably the most famous of those claiming the power of thoughtography. In 1955 Ted Serios was first noticed as being a good hypnotic subject and as possessing remote-viewing abilities. Following his discovery that he could imprint on to film in a camera, he became the subject of examination. In 1964, Serios met Jule Eisenbud, who then went on and studied him and his pictures for the next three years, after which Eisenbud wrote the book *The World of Ted Serios*. During these years Serios produced hundreds of images on film by staring into the camera. Some of the most interesting are the 'near-miss images' such as a thoughtograph showing a hanger, but with the name on the front, 'Canadian' misspelt as 'Sainadian'!

Unfortunately Serios insisted on holding what he called a 'gismo', a small tube covered at one end with transparent material, while the photographs were being produced. Two reporters, Reynolds and Eisendrath, constructed a device that could be hidden in a gismo and which gave results similar to those of Serios.

But investigators who watched Serios stated that they had not observed him acting suspiciously. And images would also appear while others were holding the gismo.

Serios was never caught cheating and never admitted it either, but because he would not allow the gismo to be examined there must always be doubt.

A Japanese psychic, Tenshin Takeuchi, claimed successes in

this field as did fellow-countryman Masuaki Kiyota. Willie G. and Willie Schwanholz are two modern claimants.

While most paranormal photography involves the imposition of images on a photograph, there are occasionally exceptions. Brad Steiger, in *Mysteries of Time and Space* reports the case of David Graham, who took a photograph of his wife with the wife of a well-known spiritualist. The woman claimed he would not be able to photograph her, and indeed in the photograph her face is obliterated by a white blur. According to Steiger the camera had no faults and pictures taken before and after that one were normal. (See also 'Anomalous Faces', page 22.)

TIME SLIPS

Vera Conway arrived in a London building for a music lesson. She went to the first floor, mistaking directions she entered a door between the two cloakrooms. She found herself in a theatre, but realised that the audience were all in period dress, possibly from the Regency period. A man approached her wearing breeches and powdered hair. There were no electric lights, just lanterns. Vera felt strange, but no one appeared to notice anything amiss about her. Realising all was not right, she left the theatre and returned to the reception to ask again for directions. She later returned to that corridor and determined for certain that there was no door between the two cloakroom doors.

Vera's account is what is classed as a 'time slip'; a perceived fold or bridge in time that brings the present in contact with another time. The vast majority of time slips refer to a bridge with the past, though there are some indications of occasional bridges with the future. Sometimes the time slip seems to be just a vision, on other occasions – as in Vera's case – there is the suggestion that the sighter is 'within' the scene.

The most celebrated such time slip is probably that of Charlotte Moberly and Eleanor Jourdain, who in the early 1900s, visiting the Palace of the Petit Trianon at Versailles witnessed scenes apparently from the 1700s. They published their account, which included many scenery changes and possible visions of Marie Antoinette and the King, in 1911 in the book *An Adventure*. This time slip has been adequately discussed in many publications including our own *Encyclopaedia of Ghosts and Spirits*.

'Eleanor' reported to us directly the story of her own time slip which she underwent with a friend, 'Sally' (both pseudonyms). (See photo section.) They were holidaying in Burra, Australia and stayed in recently refurbished cottages that dated back to 1849. They chose No 15, which was small and cosy. After a day's sightseeing they returned to their cottage, Eleanor got out of the car and looked in at the window. She could see a woman of slight build sitting on a couch talking to someone just out of view on the other side of the room. The woman looked towards the window, towards Eleanor and smiled directly at her, giving her the embarrassing feeling of being rather like a 'peeping Tom'. Embarrassed, Eleanor checked that it was the right cottage; it was. She looked back again, but then realised that the curtains were drawn. Indeed she had closed them herself before they had left the cottage earlier that day. Eleanor and Sally checked for reflections that could have accounted for the image, but that was not a plausible explanation. She said, 'I felt humble and certainly privileged that her spirit had revealed itself to me and I had glimpsed a scene from the past.' Eleanor regretted not doing more in the way of investigation. She said, 'No one, but no one, will ever convince me that I did not see her . . . The whole scene was so vivid. I am mad that I felt so embarrassed, I should have been a Nosy Parker and had a really good look into the room. If only . . .'

A slightly different suggested time slip is that of Mrs Dorothy Norton and Miss Agnes Norton, sisters-in-law, who were on holiday in 1951 in France near Dieppe when they apparently heard the 'replay' of the Allied raid of 19 August 1942. In view of the theory we suggest below it is interesting to speculate what they would have seen had they gone to the beach. Moberly and Jourdain saw scenes inside Versailles; would the Nortons have seen anything at all?

A man staying with friends near Colchester looked out of his bedroom window and saw in a near-by field a pond with what appeared to be a woman's body floating face downwards. He rushed downstairs and into the field, but could not locate the pond. Assuming that he had lost his sense of direction, he returned to the bedroom window and again could see the pond and the body. He returned to the field again, but could see no such vision. His hosts later told him that there had many years ago been a pond in the field, but the farmer had had it drained and filled in after a woman had been found drowned in it. As Wesley Downes, who reported the case in his *Haunted Colchester Area*, states, 'What he must have seen was a re-enactment of the scene from years ago, but why could he only see it from the bedroom window?'

Lethbridge suggests that apparitions are a recording embedded by a previous sighter, then seen by a later visitor to the locality. In time slips, the scenery seems to change, not reported in the case of apparitions, but could this not be just that the original sighter took in the scenery whilst observing? The analogy might be that of a photographer; sometimes he shoots portrait, and sometimes landscape.

Did the woman sitting in her cottage look up and see a friend at her window who recorded the moment, a recording that Eleanor then saw? When we consider the case of the Dieppe raid, we can speculate that someone may well have stayed in the same place on the night of the actual battle who listened to the sounds of war, but perhaps because of blackout or fear did not look out of the window and so recorded sounds to be heard, but not sights to be seen. In this way perhaps 'audio-ghosts' become a possibility to be considered. Interestingly, the person who laid down that recording in 1942 might still be alive today.

This could also explain why the Colchester man saw a body lying in a pond from his window, but could not see it when he shifted his own location. Perhaps the recording was laid down from the same window.

In 1982 Lorraine Parry was walking in a suburban road in Wembley, north of London, when she felt a distinct change of surroundings. She describes seeing it as desert-like, though she perceived herself as standing in a lake. She could 'feel' the wetness against her skin. While looking at the desert she saw, '. . . a craft going through the air. It was like an oblong shape. I think it must have been some kind of metal, it was silvery in colour and it had some windows . . . I had the distinct feeling it was like a bus.' She could see faces staring back at her, reminiscent of descriptions of aliens in several UFO reports. 'They were all excited, and pointing, and I thought, "they are pointing at me".'

Lorraine's report is very similar to the case of a British family travelling on a autobahn in Germany. They saw, passing on the other side, a long, silver, cylindrical vehicle with round portholes in the side out of which four apparently equally startled faces were looking. They were not sure that the vehicle had wheels and they heard no sound of engines.

A likely reason for the lesser number of claims of sightings of the future may be simply that visions of the past may be more instantly recognisable as such, whereas visions of the future may not be. For example the silver object seen on the German autobahn could have been reported as a UFO and Lorraine's was so reported. If one was prepared to consider time slipping far enough into the future when the human race had evolved unrecognisably, even the claims of meeting aliens could arguably be fitted into that context.

The belief that the time slip represents a window between times of which neither time is any more intrusive into the other is suggested by both Lorraine and the autobahn case with the parties on both sides of the possible time slip apparently mutually startled by, or interested in, what they were seeing.

This mechanism is speculated upon, but not understood. The conditions for either record or replay can only be guessed at. We suggest that part of the replay mechanism may be in a process similar to psychometry (see page 263). There is some suggestion of this in the case of Mrs Anne May who (according to researcher Joan Forman – probably the foremost expert on time slips in Britain) experienced a time slip on 29 May 1973. She had a vision of ancient people setting up monolithic stones at the exact moment that she herself touched the stones. Had the contact with the stone triggered the memory?

One or two cases even involve tactile impressions. A Mrs Philip Hester, standing in St William's College in York, felt herself being dressed in the robes of an earlier time while she appeared to be seeing a period in the building's earlier history and a Mrs C. Maddison travelling in a bus and wearing heavy winter clothing suddenly felt herself as if in a horse-drawn carriage and described 'I no longer had trousers, coat and boots on but a bonnet, cape and long dress.' A possible implication of these accounts is that the experiencer of time slips temporarily 'remote views' through the eyes of a person who was actually there at the time. On that basis, the people in the past seeing them are seeing a perfectly normal scene.

TORONTO BLESSING

'I was leading worship, but I'd hardly begun before I fell down. I didn't, or couldn't, get up again for an hour and twenty minutes. The meeting went on until 11 p.m. People were laughing, crying and shaking.'

'Thousands of professing Christians are being hoodwinked by a psycho-religious phenomenon that is completely unrelated to genuine Christian spirituality . . . harmful to the emotional and spiritual health of those who fall under its compelling power . . .'

These two quotations are typical of the division within Church circles surrounding an extraordinary, recent, revivalist phenomenon known as the Toronto Blessing. The first quotation comes from Malcolm Kyte, assistant pastor of the Queens Road Baptist Church in Wimbledon. Like many pastors and congregations touched by the Toronto Blessing, Kyte believes the phenomenon is indeed a blessing. Others, such as Professor Arthur Pollard of the Church of England's General Synod Board of Education, the author of the second quote, believes the phenomenon is not connected with genuine Christianity.

The Toronto Blessing takes its name from its origins in the Airport Vineyard Church in Toronto, Canada. Several observers have pinpointed the starting date as 20 January 1994. Certainly a special meeting at the church on that date, organised by Pastor

John Arnott and St Louis Vineyard Pastor Randy Clark, was the scene of 'wildly Pentecostal' activity with 'literally dozens of people falling "under the power" and laughing uncontrollably'. However, this revival has slightly earlier origins, as Marc Dupont, a member of the pastoral team at Airport Vineyard Church explained in an interview with Dave Roberts, editor of *Alpha* magazine in September 1994.

In both 1992 and 1993 Dupont had prophesied about revival in Toronto, believing 'there would be a sovereign outpouring of the Holy Spirit on Toronto and that it would flow like a river out into the rest of Canada'. In 1993, at Karl Strader's Carpenters Home Church, what was to become known as the Toronto Blessing attracted a great deal of press coverage because of the so-called 'holy laughter'.

John Arnott himself has explained that he had spent some of 1993 on a quest searching for spiritual revival. He had visited Argentina in November of that year. He met evangelist Benny Hinn, a healer based in Florida, and met with Randy Clark. Clark's own St Louis church had seen revival after being prayed for by another leading figure in Toronto Blessing lore, Rodney Howard-Browne. Howard-Browne is a South African evangelist who moved to the United States in 1987.

The Toronto Blessing takes the form of surrender to or invitation of the Holy Spirit into the Church community and into the individual. Infused with the Holy Spirit, members of the congregation fall down, lie immobile, burst into uncontrollable laughter, occasionally have periods of crying or 'talking in tongues' – the so-called language of the angels. This is the charismata in action – the gifts of the Holy Spirit, traditionally talking in tongues, prophecy and physical sensations – which were granted to the disciples on the first Pentecost.

Many effects of the Blessing in each church are reported. Gerald Coates of the Pioneer network of charismatic churches said, 'People are talking of a heightened awareness of God, a personal revival of faith and devotion to Jesus.' There has been an increase in self-reported prophesy and visions. Those hurt by pain such as that of bereavement feel uplifted and 'cured' by the Blessing. Congregations have multiplied, soaring in some cases to record levels. The Blessing is even being thanked for healings: two pregnant women with breech babies were prayed for and the babies were held to have 'moved to the correct position almost instantly'.

The Blessing appears to be contagious, and has been described as a religious virus. It seems that it only appears within a congregation when someone visits it from a church already affected. The Blessing has, throughout 1993 and 1994, spread around the world in this way to Sweden, Switzerland, Ireland, Canada and the United States, Argentina, India, South Africa and the United Kingdom.

It appears to have entered the United Kingdom after UK Church leaders visited the Airport Vineyard church in Toronto. The Blessing 'hit' churches such as Holy Trinity Brompton in Central London, Church of Christ the King in Brighton and Queens Road Baptist in Wimbledon in May 1994. In the months following it spread throughout the UK. The chief accredited source of bringing the Blessing to England is Eleanor Mumford, wife of the pastor of the South-West London Vineyard church, who had recently returned from Toronto. On Sunday 29 May, Mumford spoke at Holy Trinity Brompton; soon the whole congregation was reported to be affected by the crying, laughing and collapsing. She reminded the congregation that the Blessing was about Jesus, that the visible effects were secondary. 'There were scenes that few had ever seen before' as it was described in *Renewal*, a Christian magazine. This was the scene that attracted prominent press coverage in *The Times*, the *Daily Telegraph* and the *Daily Mail*.

For those who believe the Blessing is the sign of revival, an effect of the presence of the Holy Spirit, no further analysis is necessary. Marc Dupont states, 'I believe this will lead to major, major revival in the Western world nations, I believe it's going to come between the year 2000 and 2005.' Evangelist Billy Graham has said of the revival, 'This is a wonderful day to be alive. It is a day in which God has allowed us to live to see a new dawning for evangelism.' In 'Directions' within the *Church of England Newspaper* Michael Harper describes his visit to the Airport Vineyard Church in Toronto; he was discomfited by the airport noise, loud music and a hot temperature, but 'from the moment I stepped inside the door I knew God was there . . .'

Press coverage has, predictably, been sceptical. The 13 June edition of *The Times* described it as a hysterical fad. In the *Daily Telegraph* the religious affairs correspondent Clifford Longley pointed out that 'the laughter seems to have a sharp emotional edge to it, and little to do with humour'. This reflects a limited view of laughter and if anything adds to the veracity of the claims. People do not only laugh at humour, they laugh at death and funerals sometimes and feel very embarrassed about it. Laughter is a release of tension within, and that tension can arise from many sources.

A more cautious scepticism is voiced by some who point out that the Blessing can cause pain in those who feel 'passed by'. Some members of congregations are asking why they have not been filled with the Holy Spirit. Caring pastors are keen to avoid elitism of the 'God came to me and not to you' variety.

But what is it that these people are experiencing? If we put aside the belief that it is the Holy Spirit, something that can only be felt rather than proved, then what the Toronto Blessing amounts to is a 'permission-driven' experience. Most of the churches affected are those of a charismatic nature, high-intensity emotion churches. During the singing, shouting passions of the services, members of the congregations appear to enter altered states of consciousness. (A state such as ecstasy would, it could be argued, also be necessary to receive the Holy Spirit.)

It is surely significant that a principal entry point for the Blessing in England was Holy Trinity Brompton. That church publishes *Alpha News*, a supplement to *HTB in Focus*, its own church newspaper. Holy Trinity Brompton is at the forefront of the Alpha Course which is presented by the vicar, Sandy Millar, and Nicky Gumbel. As the course outline states 'laughter and fun are a key part of the course, breaking down barriers and enabling everyone to relax together'. These conditions might well be just those that reduce the inhibitions and 'give permission' for the physical manifestations of the Blessing to appear in the congregation.

The Toronto Blessing is not a new phenomenon; like most religious or for that matter pseudo-religious phenomena, it is a new version of an old experience. Revivals are not uncommon. In 1740 a revivalist mood swept through New England. In 1804, in Kentucky, there were outbreaks of revival characterised by 'falling down'. In 1904 Wales was overtaken by similar effects; over 20,000 people joined church congregations in five weeks. William Gibson examined the 1859 revival in Ulster commenting on those touched, 'strong men have staggered and fallen down under the wounds of their conscience . . . the whole frame trembles'.

Whatever the mechanism, whatever the source in fact, the primary question should be 'Is it doing good or harm?' There is no evidence it is doing harm. Virtually all the effects are positive, particularly to those 'touched' by the Blessing. If there is a God then He is touching people through many signs and visions that do harm to no one unaffected. People are 'using' the Toronto Blessing as a way of finding their own way back to the path they seek, or of getting on to that path in the first place. It is a positive path, religious or not.

Rodney Howard-Browne, who visited England in December 1994, was interviewed on ITV's *Sunday Matters*. It was pointed out to him that there had been revivals before, but they had died away, leaving people unsatisfied. Howard-Browne was clear that responsibility for the success of revival lay with the individual. 'It will only fizzle out if people stop being hungry for the things of God . . . you have to maintain that hunger in your own life.'

And did he believe that the Toronto Blessing was really a force for good?

'I think it is,' he asserted, 'because we've seen marriages put back together, churches that were on the brink of closing now busting at the seams, lives totally turned around and changed . . . I can see the fruit in people's lives. It's for good, yes.'

TUNGUSKA EXPLOSION

At 7.17 a.m. on the morning of 30 June 1908, a tremendous explosion destroyed an estimated 40,000 trees in the Tunguska region of central Siberia and devastated an area of some seventy kilometres radius from the focus point of the basin of the River Podkamennaya Tunguska. The resultant shock waves were detected in various points around the world; several locations in England, Germany, Washington, Jakarta and so on. Shock waves had been recorded moving at 323 metres per second, even faster than the 314 metres per second that had been recorded following the volcanic eruption of Krakatoa in August 1883.

In northern Siberia the night of 30 June to 1 July was known as the 'White Night' because of glowing silver clouds reported by many. In fact night skies did not return to normal until August. In London it was possible to read clearly at midnight and other reports from around the British Isles indicated similar phenomena. Photographs could be taken at midnight in Europe without the aid of flash lighting.

There have been a number of speculations since that time as to the cause of the explosion:

- A crashing extraterrestrial vehicle

- The impact of a black hole

- The impact of anti-matter

- The impact of a meteorite/bolide

- The impact of a comet

- *Crashing extraterrestrial vehicle*
Given a huge explosion as far back as 1908, it is almost inevitable that someone would suggest the possibility of an advance propulsion system malfunctioning on an extraterrestrial spacecraft, causing impact and explosion. The first suggestion was made by Soviet science fiction writer Alexander

Kasentev. In *Visitor from the Cosmos* in 1959 he suggested that the nuclear power source of an extraterrestrial vehicle had exploded. Kasentev was supported by some, such as Soviet aircraft designer Monotskov and university professor Felix Zigel. He also received considerable criticism for his theories in such publications as the *Soviet Astronomical Journal* in 1961.

There are natural events which could have created the same effects as those Kasentev observed and reported; his theory of an extraterrestrial craft was mostly based on the claim that the object prior to explosion had manoeuvred in the atmosphere. This manoeuvring was apparently concluded to be the result of the various eye-witness reports, not all of which were consistent. Rather than accepting the probability that some of the witnesses may not have been fully accurate in their recall, Kasentev appears to have reconciled all reports by assuming the manoeuvring of the object.

Traces of nickel and cobalt found in the soil in 1957 were explained as being from the spaceship's structure; traces of copper from its electrical equipment. Kasentev's theory slightly predated the birth of the modern era of flying saucers in June 1947, but by that time speculation about life in the universe was rife and a good deal of science fiction in literature and films had been concerned with this.

The problem with the theory of a crashing extraterrestrial spacecraft is that it is an extremely exotic suggestion not required by the facts.

● *Black hole*

It has been suggested that the object causing the Tunguska explosion could have been a small black hole with a massively powerful gravitational field and the mass of a small asteroid. The explosion of a black hole would not leave a crater, nor would it leave behind physical matter. As such therefore this seems closer to reconciling the facts at Tunguska. The black hole would penetrate the Earth and indeed would pass through the planet exiting, in this case, somewhere in the North Atlantic. The exit would have been some ten to fifteen minutes after the first explosion.

This theory falls down simply because there were very accurate microbaragraph records of the shock waves which do not show a second set of waves resulting from any exit.

Nor would the black hole theory account for the bright nights experienced throughout the world after the explosion.

● *Anti-matter*

Anti-matter was first proposed in 1930 by physicist Paul Dirac. It is based on the positron, which is in effect an anti-electron within each particle. The positron exists for an instant, being annihilated when it encounters its positive counterpart, the electron. Indeed this is the foundation on which the atomic bomb was created.

According to the anti-matter theory the anti-matter object would have carried with it a very strong radiation shock which would have heated the air ahead of it, thereby making its entry into the Earth's atmosphere possible. At a point when it was deep inside the atmosphere the over-heating would then cause an explosion.

However, witness reports of the fireball that passed through the sky ahead of the explosion indicated that it had only been visible for a few seconds, whereas the anti-matter would have needed over half a minute according to the best calculations available.

In fact much of the analysis of the Tunguska region indicates that the increase in radiation around the 1908 period of time was negligible, if measurable at all. The lack of a massive increase in radiation probably rules out the anti-matter theory.

● *Meteorite/bolide*

The Tunguska explosion cannot have been the impact of a simple meteorite – like the one that created the famous Arizona crater at Winslow, for example – for the obvious reason that no crater is in evidence in the Tunguska. If the explosion was caused by that kind of physical matter, it would have to have been a bolide, a meteor that explodes in flight. This is caused by the speed with which the outer surface is heated by the friction of entry into the Earth's atmosphere, as opposed to the coolness of the core of the object. It fractures violently, creating an airborne explosion. The meteor concerned would need to be big enough to allow for depletion of much of its mass on entry, but still leave enough material for the explosion. Such an event might explain the airborne explosion, but it would not account for the huge dust clouds that were in evidence in the atmosphere around the world in the subsequent days and nights. It is not thought that a meteor could have put enough dust into the atmosphere.

A more likely alternative not only exists, but was in the right place at the right time . . .

● *Comet*

A comet has been described as a dirty snowball. It is essentially ice, rock and frozen gases. Most comets – known as short-period comets – orbit the sun within the solar system on predictable paths – like the famous Halley's Comet that visits the Earth every seventy-six years. When comets are heated – as in an approach to the sun – they become more conspicuous. They have a dust trail that would have sufficient matter to have caused the extraordinary lighting effects around the world following the Tunguska event.

On entry into the atmosphere, a comet would heat up, and create a powerful 'bow wave' ahead of itself until the pressure of its push into the atmosphere and the heat it created caused a huge airborne explosion. No physical matter of significance would be deposited on the ground, yet the damage to the trees and surroundings would be exactly as seen at Tunguska.

In 1994 the world was treated to twenty-one comet-collisions into the atmosphere of the gas giant planet Jupiter, which showed the huge effect such an impact could have.

Comet Encke was in the right position on 30 June 1908, passing across the Earth's orbit. It is highly likely that a piece of that comet – Carl Sagan has speculated a chunk of ice 100 metres across and weighing 1,000,000 tons, moving at 70,000 miles per hour – entered the Earth's atmosphere, heated and exploded above the Tunguska. Its tail debris would have covered the Earth sufficiently for the observed effects, and the lack of debris left would be accounted for by the almost total destruction of the comet's matter.

Tunguska was almost certainly a comet-collision, and a salutary warning of our mortality. If something the size of the Levy-Shoemaker comet that hit Jupiter was to hit the Earth, there is every possibility that all human life would be eradicated in a manner akin to the speculated death of the dinosaurs some sixty-five million years ago.

TURIN SHROUD

The Turin Shroud is a fourteen foot by four foot piece of linen, depicting a full-sized, front and back image of a scourged and crucified man. The image shows a naked man, five foot ten and a half inches tall and thought to weigh approximately twelve and a half stone. The cloth is linen with a three-to-one twill weave similar to fabrics from first-century Palestine and not known in medieval Europe. It is held to contain pollen fossils from plants that grew only in Palestine at the time of Christ.

The Shroud is believed by many to be the cloth in which Christ's body was wrapped for burial after the crucifixion. The image is believed to be a miraculous picture of the face and body of Christ Himself.

The Shroud's known history dates back to its possession by a French family in 1353. Geoffrey de Charny, Lord of Savoy and Lirey, had built a church in honour of the Virgin Mary within which he kept the precious relic. The Shroud is further associated with the family by a medallion commemorating an exhibition in the church in Lirey in 1357; it depicts both a carving of the Shroud image and the coat of arms of Geoffrey de Charny.

The Shroud was mentioned in a memorandum to Pope Clement VII in 1389, written by Bishop Pierre D'Acis (or D'Arcis). The Bishop stated that it was a fake, painted around 1350, and that the artist had confessed. The letter itself has been the subject of controversy and is alleged by supporters of the authenticity of the Shroud to be fraudulent.

In 1443 the Shroud came into the possession of Marguerite

de Charny who, after exhibiting it in 1452, presented it to the Duke of Savoy. In September 1578 the then Duke of Savoy transferred it to Turin, and it has been known as the Turin Shroud since that time.

In 1532 it was housed in a chapel at Chambery when the building was destroyed by fire. The cloth was contained in a silver casket and suffered several burns and water damage, visible on the Shroud today.

On 18 October 1983, following the death of the last of the Savoy family, ex-King Umberto II, his executors formally handed over title of the Shroud to the Holy See.

The earliest claim of fraud – Pierre D'Acis's memorandum – probably proves very little at this late date. The de Charny family may well have wished the Shroud to be known as a fake within Church circles to prevent it being taken from them by the authorities. Relics at that time were good money-spinners and there were many notorious fake relics on display. Verification procedures were relaxed, to say the least. In any case, the Church was in some state of disarray at the time; the memorandum was written to the anti-Pope Clement VII; 1389 was the year of the death of Pope Urban VI and the appointment of Boniface IX. Such a situation would have created many hidden agendas that could account for claim or counter-claim.

The question of fraud continues to the present day. For example Lynn Picknett and Clive Prince have suggested that the Shroud is a fake created by Leonardo da Vinci.

The Shroud cannot be positively dated to a time earlier than 1353, but several authors, including Ian Wilson, believe it can be traced to much earlier times. There are many references to images of Christ miraculously created. At the end of the sixth century there was a translation of a document relating to King Abgar at the time of Christ. The reference is to Jesus having sent a picture of himself, miraculously created. In 944 a picture of Christ known as the Mandylion surfaced in Constantinople. These and a myriad of other references have been held to be early references to the cloth now known as the Turin Shroud.

The Shroud is today kept in Turin, locked in a casket in the Cathedral, and seldom taken out for public viewing. The last time this was done was in 1978 when three million people made the pilgrimage to view it. The Church has withheld making any pronouncements on the Shroud's authenticity. Whatever belief the Church officially holds, it protects the Shroud as a treasured relic, and creates devotion by generating demand through scarcity of public appearances.

It was in 1898 that Secondo Pia, a keen amateur photographer, took the first photograph of the Shroud. Its negative image was seen for the first time; this gives a much clearer picture of the figure. This has led to the question of how difficult it would have been to forge an image that would stand the test of time under the scrutiny of a photographic technology then unheard of.

Controversy surrounds all aspects of the Shroud, and in particular the way the image was formed. Between 1978 and 1979 several scientists studying samples lifted by sticky tape concluded that the cloth's image was formed of blood and other body secretions. In 1982 an American group STURP – the Shroud of Turin Research Project – declared, 'We can conclude for now that the Shroud image is that of a real human form of a scourged, crucified man. It is not the product of an artist. The bloodstains are composed of haemoglobin, and also give a positive test for serum albumin.'

However, an American microscopist, W.W. Crone, spent a year making spectroscopic tests examining 40,000 fibres and loose particles. He concluded that the marks were made by paint pigment – red ochre, an iron oxide. He dated the Shroud's beginnings to 1356 or slightly earlier, a date consistent with the claims of D'Acis and later carbon-dating.

In 1988 three samples of the Shroud were carbon dated using the technology of the tandem accelerator mass spectrometer. This meant that reliable work could be done on small pieces of the Shroud. The testing was done independently in Oxford, Zurich, and Arizona. Each laboratory concluded that the Shroud was a medieval forgery. They concluded, 'There is a ninety-five per cent probability that the flax was harvested between 1260 and 1390.'

That should have been the end of the debate. However,

controversy still surrounds the Shroud.

Some, like author Rodney Hoare, believe the carbon dating to be wrong because of pollutants and the handling the Shroud has suffered over the hundreds of years. It is also believed that the fire damage of 1532 would affect the dating.

Perhaps the most controversial suggestion for 'upsetting' the carbon testing is that the process used to form the image – perhaps a radiation surge from the resurrecting Christ – itself affected the cloth.

Elmar Gruber and Holger Kersten believe that the carbon dating process is faultless, but that the scraps of material used were not from the original Shroud. The Vatican, they suggest, deliberately gave out false samples for testing. The reason they give for the Vatican's conspiracy is that they think the Church knows that the image is genuinely that of Christ, but that the Shroud shows he was alive when taken down from the Cross. If Jesus did not die, then he was not resurrected; a cornerstone of Christian faith would crumble.

Rodney Hoare suggests that when taken from the Cross Jesus was in what would now be recognised as a coma. His body was left without proper burial because of the Sabbath and later on Sunday it may have been found still warm and secretly taken away to be cared for.

Gruber and Kersten agree that Jesus was alive when taken off the Cross, but go further in suggesting this was planned by Joseph of Arimathea (the man who claimed the body for burial). They suggest that some narcotic, or anaesthetic (possibly opium) was mixed with vinegar and given to Jesus on the sponge that was lifted to his lips during his suffering on the Cross. This would render Jesus immediately unconscious, and he might then have been presumed dead. Then Joseph could remove the body and hide it away for later care.

Even amongst those who believe the Shroud genuinely shows the image of Christ created shortly after the crucifixion, there is debate as to the method of formation. One school of thought, perhaps most clearly stated by John Jackson at an international symposium in Paris in 1989, is that the resurrection created the image miraculously; as Jesus 'dematerialised' passing on to heaven, so the process irradiated His image into the cloth. The second school of thought, reasonably successfully tested, is that a combination of elements could have caused the image to form. The perspiration and body oils following crucifixion, combined with an excess of ammonia, created by urea resulting from the excessive beating and whipping suffered prior to crucifixion, could have generated the markings on the cloth.

What the image depicts is as much a controversy as how it was made. Much of what is written in the Bible is represented on the Shroud: scourging, the crown of thorns, the spear wound that cascaded blood and water, the nail wounds of the crucifixion, and so on. However, any forger with a knowledge of Christ would have been aware of these factors. The Shroud breaks new ground also; it was the first popular depiction of nails driven through the wrists, rather than, as previously supposed, through the palms of the hands. The image is surprisingly anatomically correct; the thumbs are missing on the image, but tests show that nails driven through the wrists would automatically pull the thumbs into the palms and out of view. Gruber and Kersten have pointed out that the blood flows on the Shroud match those of a crucified body laid to rest (though, as already stated, alive when laid out).

In 1995 Canadian portrait artist Curtis Hooper released his computer-generated enhancements of the Shroud.

Full-sized photographs and other evidence, also a life-size model of the Shroud Man, can be seen on display at the Centro Romano di Sindonologia, near Vatican City.

U

UFOS

UFOs – Unidentified Flying Objects – have been a high-profile mystery since 1947. In the decades since then, many mysteries have been 'bolted on' to the central question of identifying unknown lights and objects seen in the sky; in particular, the claims of abductions, close encounters, and contactees, all covered separately in this book. (See 'Alien Abductions', page 10, 'Close Encounters', page 61; 'Contactees', page 71.)

Some UFO researchers have suggested that these distant sightings are the only true UFOs; that analysis of the 'higher strangeness' experiences is perhaps only distantly related, if at all.

When examining UFO reports, it is vital to understand that around ninety to ninety-five per cent of all investigated reports are solved, even to the satisfaction of the witnesses. The most common answer is an astronomical one; sightings of planets and stars, even the moon behind clouds. Nearly as frequent are reports of aircraft lights. Other explanations include lenticular cloud formations, weather conditions causing glare and reflection, meteor showers, man-made satellites and laser and searchlight shows.

One early group of UFO reports was the 'Foo Fighters' reported during the Second World War. British and American pilots reported orange, red or white lights around their aircraft, often keeping pace with them in flight. It was believed at the time that these might represent some sort of German weapon. However, after the war ended it was discovered that there were reports from German pilots as well. 415 Fighter Group had several such reports to offer such as: on 23 November 1944

Lieutenants Schluter and Ringwald watched a formation of around ten red lights at speed over the Vosges mountains, and four days later Lieutenants Giblin and Speyer saw a huge, orange, glowing sphere south of Mannheim.

But throughout these times, these reports of mystery lights were without a common identity. That identity arose in 1947 in America. It gave the phenomenon a name that the public took to its heart, and which embraced the public's – and the media's – hopes and fears, 'flying saucer'.

On 24 June 1947 Kenneth Arnold was flying near Mount Rainier in Washington State USA, when he saw nine objects in formation and estimated their speed at between 1,300 and 1,700 miles per hour, their distance from him at 23 miles, and the individual object sizes to be approximately 45 to 50 feet . . . This sighting coined the phrase 'flying saucer'. These estimates are unreliable; size and distance can only be calculated in such circumstances if one or the other is already known. However, while Arnold's analysis may have been wrong, his sighting was respected. J. Allen Hynek, then working for the US Air Force's UFO study group, Project Sign (Arnold's was Case 17), stated, 'It is impossible to explain this incident away as sheer nonsense . . .'

Such UFOs have been reported by a wide variety of people, all around the world. Many pilots have reported such sightings: Flt Lt Saladin over the Thames estuary in 1954, Bentwaters Lakenheath in 1956, Goose Bay, Labrador 1954, IL-14 over the Ukraine in 1967, Shanxi airport, China in 1978, Captain Barker over Queensland in 1965. UFOs have been detected on radar, photographed and even filmed. They have been seen by large groups of people: in 1993, in Bristol, England, a whole street full of people were spending their summer nights in deckchairs on the pavements watching lights wheeling overhead, a phenomenon that lasted several nights.

No one knows how many such sightings there have been around the world; one recent estimate put the figure at forty million. A small selection of key cases suggest a real, and important, phenomenon.

On 11 May 1950 farmer Paul Trent and his wife twice

photographed an object that passed over their farm at McMinn-
ville, Oregon. The Condon Committee, dedicated to rejecting
UFO claims, found this one pair of photographs compelling.

On 16 January 1958 a Brazilian naval vessel was in the south
Atlantic. A group of military personnel from the ship saw a
'Saturn-shaped' UFO. Four photographs of it were taken and
developed in a darkroom on the ship. The case had its
detractors, and Project Blue Book listed it as a hoax, assuming
the photographs to be faked. However, the testimony of the
witnesses so impressed the President of Brazil that he vouched
personally for the authenticity of the pictures.

From the mid 1960s to the mid 1970s in Warminster, England
there were many reports of UFOs. Typical of such reports: on 17
August 1965, between 1.55 a.m. and 2.05 a.m. over the Boreham
Fields council estate, Mr and Mrs D. Pinnell saw a huge orange
flame 'like an electric light bulb', Mr and Mrs J. Plankernhorn
described a huge orange ball and several others heard loud
sounds. The following month Mr P. Fletcher saw a 'solid, silvery,
round object, sharply outlined and the size of a sixpence held at
arm's length . . . (travelling) . . . from NW to N soundlessly.'

In October 1973, Captain Coyne, 1st Lieutenant Jezzy, and
Sergeants Healey and Yanacsek were flying a helicopter to
Cleveland Hopkins Air Force base. It was a clear night. About
eighty kilometres from the base, Jezzy saw a bright red light to
the left which he thought was unusually brighter than the navigation lights of an aircraft. Just a few minutes later Yanacsek saw a
red light to the right which seemed to be following, and closing in
on them. Coyne contacted Mansfield Flight Control for identification of the object, but they were unable to assist. As the bright
light got bigger and closer, it appeared to be on a collision course
with their helicopter. However, it stopped abruptly, hovering in
front of the helicopter. Coyne, Healey and Yanacsek saw a grey,
cigar-shaped, metallic object filling the helicopter's entire front
windows. From the base of the object a green cone of light swept
over the helicopter as if scanning it. The object hovered for a
while more and then flew away, manoeuvring. The report was
corroborated by five people on the ground.

Almost exactly five years later another green light, and

another aerial encounter, was to have a more serious result, and leave little doubt that whatever UFOs are, they are real and can be deadly serious.

The Frederick Valentich encounter occurred in October 1978 during one of the most concentrated periods of UFO sightings in Australian history. And there were many other witnesses to aspects of the event, as there were to the Coyne case.

At 6.19 in the evening, Valentich flew his single-seater Cessna 182 (designation DSJ) from Moorabbin Airport in Melbourne to King Island. He was in radio contact with the ground, and at 7.06 radioed an enquiry which was the start of an extraordinary story. 'Melbourne, this is Delta Sierra Juliet. Is there any known traffic below five thousand?' Melbourne Flight Service reported they had nothing on radar. Valentich reported a large aircraft with four bright lights. A few seconds later Valentich reported that the object had passed over him 'at least a thousand feet above'. The object stayed in the vicinity of DSJ, and at 7.08 Valentich reported, 'he's playing some sort of game, he's flying over me . . .'

At 7.09 Valentich reported, 'It's not an aircraft, it is . . . a long shape . . .'

Shortly afterwards Valentich reported that the object was relatively stationary above him; He described it as '. . . sort of metallic . . . all shiny on the outside' and with a green light.

At 7.11 Valentich first reported his aircraft 'rough idling' and 'coughing'. Unless it was an extraordinary coincidence, it appears that the proximity of the UFO was affecting the plane's performance. Many drivers of cars and pilots of planes have reported engine cut-outs in the vicinity of UFOs.

At 7.12 Valentich gave his call sign, there was an open microphone for seventeen seconds, and then strange, 'metallic' sounds.

Valentich has never been heard from again.

Theories abound of course; the loss of the plane guaranteed speculation that aliens had captured the lost pilot. Perhaps he encountered a natural, but rare and unclassified, energy or meteorological phenomenon. Whatever the cause, the serious outcome demands that UFO research be conducted.

Throughout the early 1980s anomalous lights in the Hessdalen valley in Norway gave UFO researchers an opportunity to study such strange reports over an extended period of time. Project Hessdalen was set up by a joint group of Scandinavian researchers on 3 June 1983. One survey of witnesses in the area indicated: seventeen witnesses reported a yellow, spherical light; twelve witnesses reported cigar-shaped objects; eight reported egg-shaped objects; and six reported objects with consistent light-patterns (two yellow, one red).

Project Hessdalen investigated the reports using a variety of equipment; radar, a seismograph, a magnetometer, a spectrum analyser, infra-red viewers, Geiger counters, and many cameras.

It has been argued that the lights may have been the result of tectonic strain, a natural but unclassified energy released by heavily geologically faulted areas during shifts or movements. The Norwegian fjords are still regaining balance (isostatic readjustment) following the melting of the ice-cover after the last ice age. Such movements might have 'bursts' that could cause such energy releases.

Lights at night, disc-like shapes seen in daylight hours: they do not have to be flying saucers. The shapes and lights reported are quite capable of being produced by natural pressures and energies, in the case of these types of UFO reports – the bulk of the core of the subject since 1947 – there is little evidence to tie the witness reports in to exotic claims of extraterrestrial visitation. If we 'unbolt' the mishmash of claims that have been tied together under the umbrella of UFO (and examine them under separate headings, as in this book) then here we should be considering strange, unclassified, natural energies as a possible cause of these UFO sightings. If those energies can crash aircraft, they need to be understood. UFOs are a subject worthy of the full programme of scientific study that it has to date been denied.

V

VAMPIRES

'Vampires issue forth from their graves in the night, attack people sleeping quietly in their beds, suck out all their blood from their bodies, and destroy them. They beset men, women and children alike, sparing neither age nor sex. Those who are under the fatal malignity of their influence complain of suffocation and a total deficiency of spirits after which they soon expire.' So wrote theologian Heinrich Zopfius in 1733.

The vampire is an ancient figure of mythology. Vampires are the embodiment of terrors of the night and their mythology varies widely round the world and over time. Originally they were a form of spirit that fed off the living. Various vampire legends include the drawing off of 'life forces', milk from women, tearing out foetuses from pregnant women and, of course, drinking blood. Attacks by vampires can include sitting on the chests of victims causing feelings of paralysis and suffocation and as such are part of the 'old hag' beliefs. They are parallel to the legends of birth demons; slighted or spiteful female entities that prey on pregnant women or new mothers, tearing open their bodies to feed on entrails, foetuses, milk or blood. In Africa they are cannibals. The Penanggal of the Malay forests (the revengeful head and entrails of a woman who died in childbirth) suck the blood and life forces of men. In Eastern Europe and parts of Russia they have the ability to transform their shape, most commonly into that of the wolf. In Eastern Europe vampire and werewolf legends merge closely.

Vampires were said to be alive, in a dead body. Because it was believed that vampires were caused by the improper burial of the dead, exhumation and further treatment of suspected corpses was regarded as the method of eradication of a vampire. Remedies such as driving a stake through the heart, so popular in modern fiction, were designed to pin the body into the grave from which it could not then escape. Alternatively bodies could be treated with magical substances to prevent movement; the best known is probably garlic. Alternatively, since the vampire seemed to need a whole body, bodies were often cut up or even totally destroyed by fire.

A particularly persistent vampire was that of Weinrichius, a Silesian man in 1591, who committed suicide but was wrongly buried in consecrated ground. It was thought that as a punishment for this, the spirit was sent wandering at night when it attacked people in their beds; suffocating, sexually molesting and draining them of their energies. Weinrichius's body was exhumed and reburied under a hangman's gallows, but the vampire reports continued. Finally the body was hacked to pieces and the head, arms, legs and heart were burnt. Finally the vampire had been laid to rest.

The vampire, then, can be described as the embodiment of the fears of the night and the fears of the dead. But in the late nineteenth century the vampire myth took on such a specific guise that the older vampire legends became disassociated from the new 'vampire proper'; incubi and succubi, birth demons, the Strigae and Lamiae (demons in Greco-Roman lore) all became viewed as entities in their own right. Indeed many scholars believe that these never were part of the vampire legend. While it seems highly probable that these earlier legends contributed to the creation of the vampire, there is no question that from the nineteenth century onwards, a definitive model of the vampire was created.

The influence of Gothic horror, 'penny dreadfuls', and a tabloid cartoon called *Varney The Vampire*, should not be understated. Almost all Gothic horror owes allegiance for its origins to *The Monk* by Matthew Lewis, published in 1796. The story was of a young monk obsessed with sex and demonology selling his soul to the devil. *Varney The Vampire* ran to 220 chapters and something like 1,000 pages over the year 1845 to 1847. It was illustrated and all the classic images can be seen in the illustrations; hordes of angry villagers exhuming Varney's coffin and finding it empty; body-snatchers running for their lives when they find the coffin full, but with the occupant sitting up; Varney terrorising women wearing a long, black coat billowing out in a cloak-like way, Varney laid to rest with a stake through his heart, and so on.

It should also be remembered that two main themes were running through all Gothic stories; Gothic horror and Gothic romance. The vampire legend merged the two. In the nineteenth century, Goethe and Baudelaire produced romanticised images of the vampire. Another romantic image was created by John Polidori in *The Vampire* in which he created Lord Ruthven, who preyed on the upper class.

But the beginnings of the definitive vampire image came in 1897 when Irish writer Bram Stoker wrote *Dracula*. It was a work of fiction concocted from a mixture of the folklore of the Slavs and tales of a vicious fifteenth-century Wallachian General called Vlad Tepes, also known as Drakula ('Devil's son'). The story was set in Transylvania and drew on a great many images of vampirism from that region's mythological history. The connection between the vampire and the image of a bat was also established by Stoker's novel.

Although the vampire films depict the vampire as physically leaving the grave, the 'true' vampires were always found inside their coffins during periods of their attacks. Indeed it was the discovery in the coffin of a body fresh with blood (probably the vampire's own blood) and not as decomposed as was expected that led people to 'confirm' vampire rumours. Once destroyed, usually through fire, the vampire's spirit was laid to rest. There are many such accounts. In the *Visum Et Repertum* there is an account for example, of Arnod Paole, who haunted several people and allegedly killed four in the month after his death. His body was exhumed and found to be not decomposed and leaking fresh blood. The body was burnt.

The implication is clear: 'true' vampires were thought to be psychic, attacking victims in an astral, out-of-body, way. The reports such as the one mentioned above, many of which are authoritative and signed by experienced doctors, refer to the vampire in two ways: a report on a physical body, and stories of ghostly attacks on individuals. These medical analyses do not specifically link the vampire body in the grave with the vampire victims, other than by implication, belief or mythology.

Dracula, the novel, and later the film spin-offs as they progressed through the decades, identified the vampire with a number of characteristics. He is generally tall and distinguished and fatally attractive to women; no longer using the rape-like impositions of the incubus, the new vampire relies on seduction. He lives by drinking the blood of, primarily, women, keeping them alive in order to provide him with nourishment. He can change into other creatures, most commonly now the bat. He uses a form of hypnotism rather than strength or aggression to manipulate victims or would-be attackers.

If film and literature is the way in which our modern folklore mutates, then these images of the vampire are becoming highly attractive to modern-day individuals with a particular mind set. Fatally attractive to women, super-powered, immortal, a creature of the mysterious night ('mad, bad and dangerous to know' as was once said of Lord Byron), are all features that have conspired to make being a vampire highly attractive. Particularly in modern, politically correct times the image of being in control of one's own destiny is a powerful one.

As such there are now cults of people across the world who believe they are vampires, and they act out many of the images creating, as it were, a vampire reality. Whether it is a mental or physical condition, or a combination of both is uncertain. After Rosemary Ellen Guiley, a leading authority on vampires, published *Vampires Among Us* she received a great deal of mail from would-be vampires. Her correspondents were varied: they asked where they could contact real vampires; they claimed to be real vampires, one even claimed to be 500 years old; and so on.

Philip Hine acquired his taste for blood following a friend's accident where blood spattered on him, triggering his fetish.

He described his taste for blood in *Chaos International* in 1992 in which he reported just wanting to see the blood trickle, and to taste it.

Following the release of the film *Interview with the Vampire* starring Tom Cruise, it was estimated that some 700 Americans were claiming to be vampires. There are apparently thirty-six registered human blood drinkers in Los Angeles alone.

Jack Dean, in November 1994, told his story of vampirism. Dean describes it, 'I don't know why, but I need to drink human blood. It gives me a rush of energy and just fills me with excitement.' Like Hine, he appears to have developed his need for blood after a crash, in this case his own. He also claims he now no longer enjoys sunlight. Dean claims his girlfriend is sympathetic to his problem and provides him with some blood by allowing him to 'cut her in the back with a knife and drink her blood'. He says of her, 'She is kind of intrigued – but at the same time she is a little scared. She won't let me cut her neck.' When he can get blood no other way, he cuts his own body and sucks his own blood.

VEHICLE INTERFERENCE

In 1979 the British UFO Research Association published *The Vehicle Interference Project*, compiled by Geoffrey Falla. It is a valuable catalogue of cases of close proximity to perceived UFOs and simultaneous electromagnetic effects on vehicles, primarily cars. Four hundred and twenty cases were sampled, while acknowledging that there were a great many more available. Two hundred and fifty cases described temporary engine malfunction, one hundred and twenty-five cases reported a malfunction of the lights, usually of a temporary nature while twenty-five per cent of the cases also showed some kind of other effect on the witness; paralysis and fainting amongst others.

Interestingly, other effects included watches slowed or stopped and involuntary movements of the car such as violent rocking or being thrown off the road. We have summarised two typical cases from the report.

On 3 November 1957, Newell Wright was driving towards

Levalland, Texas on Route 116 when his car ammeter began jumping, the motor gradually died and the lights went out. Having got out of the car and found nothing wrong with the battery and wires, he noticed an oval object on the road ahead. The object appeared to be over 100 feet long and was glowing a bluish-green colour. The witness tried to start the car without success. After several minutes the object rose 'almost straight up', veered to the north and disappeared almost instantly. The car then started without difficulty.

On the Lake of the Ozarks, Missouri, two men were starting out one morning to fish when the outboard motor of their boat died. A heavy humming sound was heard in the fog and when the fog parted briefly a shiny, disc-shaped object was seen about five feet above the still water of the lake. The object was oscillating slowly and both men noticed that directly beneath the object the water was dancing in thousands of tiny, sharp, pointed waves. The fog closed in again and the men then paddled their boat back towards the shore.

The catalogue took cases from all over the world, it studied a great many reports in detail and found that electromechanical interference with vehicles in close proximity to perceived UFOs is commonly and widely reported.

Aircraft are similarly affected. In September 1967 a Russian aircraft flying over the Ukraine encountered a UFO above it. At that moment the engines cut out, only restarting after a fateful plummet and when the UFO could no longer be seen.

In other areas of the paranormal we find some very similar reports: When Mrs Dorothy Strong, driving in a taxi near Otterburn in Northumberland, saw the ghost 'replay' of a phantom army (see 'Spectral Armies', page 277) 'Suddenly the engine died, the fare-meter went haywire and the taxi was as if it was being forced against an invisible wall. The soldiers seemed to close in on us and then fade into thin air.'

In September 1960 six people were travelling together in one car. Out in an empty landscape the car showed signs of overheating and they were forced to stop. When investigating the cause, the car and its occupants found themselves victims to a poltergeist-like attack; stones began to fly around and to hit both the people and the car. Later they had to hold very firmly on to the doors when they felt them being pulled open. A vague form was seen outside the window, but when they tried to shoot at it the gun they were using jammed.

While flying over the area known as the Bermuda Triangle, Charles Lindbergh in *The Spirit of St Louis* reported in his log, in 1928, 'Both compasses malfunctioned . . . the earth indicator needle wobbled back and forth. The liquid compass card rotated without stopping . . . kept rotating until the *Spirit of St. Louis* reached the Florida Coast.'

We find therefore that electromagnetic effects are not restricted to the UFO field by any means. One woman reporting to the Street Lamp Interference Data Exchange, SLIDE, included in her report that she had to drive a very simple car because cars with complex electrical systems failed too frequently for her. (See 'Street Lamp Interference', page 293.)

The incident/perception relationship becomes linked here. Street lamp interference may suggest that PK is part of the mechanism of such electrical interferences. But there may be a genuine energy in the atmosphere that can become visible (hence UFOs) and can affect the workings of electrical equipment. We note that it seems to be active in many fields we call 'paranormal' (see 'Spontaneous Equipment Failure', page 281) and may be related to the phenomenon.

However, if the energy can affect not only the equipment but the human brain, as speculated by Michael Persinger, then the details of the UFO or other paranormal effect or experience may itself be a hallucination. This may be particularly relevant when considering close proximity events such as alien abductions overlaid on UFO sightings.

W

WEEPING, BLEEDING, MOVING STATUES

In May 1994 in Grangecon, a small town in Wicklow, in the Republic of Ireland, a small statue was seen by its owner, Mrs Mary Murray, and her daughter, Attracta O'Hara, to have altered. The statue is an image of the Virgin Mary; a representation of the appearance of the Virgin at Fatima. Its eyes had become wet as if filled with tears, drops of which then seemed to be blood. The tears then spread down from the left eye. Later, both eyes were running with the brown substance.

The appearance of these tears from her statue was thought to be a sign from the Virgin Mary. Mrs Murray opened her house to allow people to enter and pray. When the news spread, many people did come and visit. By the end of the month there were so many people visiting that Mrs Murray's house was open between eight in the morning and eleven at night, with queues outside.

Many pilgrims saw the statue weep. At least one saw its hands move as if to pray. Mrs Murray herself said, 'I am not making any claims . . . But my door is open and people can see for themselves. It's not my house now, it's Our Lady's.'

Mrs Murray, described as 'an incredibly religious person' keeps the statue in the back room of her post office, in what has been described as a shrine. Mrs Murray has led prayers in the room, and sometimes outside her home, where the statue has become the focal point of the meetings.

Tom Dowling of CKR Radio stated that the statue had focused attention on the town. 'There are those that maybe don't accept that the statue has much to do with the miracle,' he said, 'but a lot of people come away from it feeling that something is happening. Probably that people's devotion and prayer and the various visitors are part of maybe a small modern miracle.'

The local parish priest, Father Garry Doyle has pointed out that the manufacturers of the statue have stated that the eyes are held in place with a substance that may have melted, causing the staining and wet appearance. According to a television documentary, Mrs Murray has not allowed forensic investigation of the statue, wishing to keep it in the box it always stays in. 'I wouldn't have her tampered with,' she said.

Father Doyle stated that he believed in miracles, but he took note of the statements made by the manufacturers of the statue, 'For me that is a reasonable, possible explanation,' he said, 'I don't look for God in this, in moving and weeping statues and apparitions, or whatever. I look for God in people. I think that's where God reveals himself to me.'

This may well be true and maybe the melting would have occurred wherever the statue was positioned. But it did happen in the house of a woman who gave out the message and went on to lead others in prayer and perhaps convert some to Christianity. If any of the reported messages from Mary have any truth, then this is her mission working.

We confirmed with Mrs Murray in January 1995 that the statue was continuing to weep.

Such an explanation would not in any case account for a case that arose in Italy in 1971. A picture of the Virgin wept blood, it was sealed overnight in a locked safe by the police, but when opened was found to have exuded more blood. Analysis showed that the blood was human.

Many other such reports come from around the world. Spain is home to many. Also Italy, where in 1951 at Syracuse a plaque of the Virgin Mary wept profusely for four days. Thousands of pilgrims and devotees were able to wet handkerchiefs or cotton wool. The plaque is now kept in a safe, but has not wept again.

Japan has a weeping statue of the Virgin Mary kept in a convent. 101 incidents have been noticed, not only by

Christians. One of the witnesses is the Buddhist mayor.

But the Republic of Ireland probably beats any other country in numbers of different occurrences. In one year, 1985, at least forty-seven different locations reported phenomena connected to the Virgin Mary.

The first and main report came from Ballinspittle in County Cork. In 1954 a grotto to the Virgin Mary was erected containing a life-size concrete statue of the Virgin standing at the entrance of an artificial cave. The cave and statue are positioned on a hillside some twenty feet or so above the road level. On 22 July 1985 a seventeen-year-old girl, Clare O'Mahoney, was walking past the grotto just after dusk when she saw the statue move. Clare reported that the statue was rocking towards her, going backwards and forwards as though someone was pushing it.

Three days later, as word had spread, the number of visitors was up to several thousand. One of these was a member of the 1954 committee which had erected the statue and is quoted as saying, 'I thought I had better go and see what these nutcases were up to. I joined about forty other people saying the rosary. Then I saw the statue move. I got a terrible fright. I thought it was going to fall on some youngsters below.'

Very soon reports of moving and bleeding statues, and other phenomena, came from other towns and counties around the country.

One explanation offered for visions of moving statues addresses the lights around the figures. Many statues of Mary are surrounded by a ring of small, bright lights. The reports of movement seen at night might be accounted for by the bright lights against the dark background causing the optical effect of movement as the retina in the eye opens and closes to try to adjust to light levels. One survey of the witnesses to one moving statue indicated that many people in the crowd saw it move, but all at different times even though they had stood together for a period as a group. Such explanations probably account for many reports, but they would not account for one report where the percipient became so concerned he grabbed on to a statue and had difficulty holding it in place. Optical effects combined with religious fervour might be offered as a possible explanation here.

The importance of Mary as a figure cannot be overstated. She is the most important figure in Catholic worship after Christ and there have been periods when more churches were dedicated to her than to Jesus. Mary was a human, cousin of John the Baptist's mother Elizabeth, but one different to any other human. She was chosen by God to look after His Son and ascended to heaven at her assumption, undead. Mary, like the saints and martyrs, went straight to heaven with no stop-over at purgatory. It is prophesied that she will fight the great Battle of Armageddon.

The focus of attention on Mary is not without logic; it is possible that, as she was a human, some people find her more 'approachable' than Jesus.

WEREWOLVES

Stories of man's ability to change into animals, or beings half-animal and half-human, come from all around the world, but the werewolf seems the most lasting of these claims. The stem of these beliefs is in the belief of some tribes that dressing up in an animal's skin grants the wearer the strength of that animal. Dressing up in bear skins was a Nordic habit, as in the case of the Berserkers, a fierce class of warriors immortalised in the word 'berserk'.

The werewolf was a common legend in Roman times; written about by Virgil, Petronius and Ovid amongst others.

The people of the northern hemisphere, and especially Europe, have historically had a fear of wolves which is perhaps out of proportion to the truth. It is presumably the semi-nocturnal habits of wolves that connect them to evil doings. Healthy wolves do not generally attack humans, although rabid wolves might. Such attacks as there were might have furthered the werewolf legend. A person bitten by a rabid animal can contract rabies. The bite of a rabid wolf was certainly something to fear, almost always resulting in the painful death of the victim. Perhaps a few witnesses to these presumed transformations, when they were underway, failed to stay around long enough to observe the outcome. Even Pasteur, after trying to treat some of the afflicted, realised their agony and the men were painlessly put to sleep.

The most detailed account of a werewolf is that of Peter Stubb who lived in Germany in the sixteenth century. Stubb apparently made a pact with the Devil, who gave him a wolf-skin belt. In order to metamorphose, Stubb had only to put on this belt. For the next twenty-five years Stubb terrified the countryside around the towns of Cologne and Bedburg, killing and eating cattle and sheep. He is also said to have killed many people; the women and girls would be raped before being murdered, and then eaten. Amongst his victims were thirteen children and two pregnant women who had their babies ripped out for Stubb to feed on. There are similarities in these claims with some vampire legends; the werewolf is often regarded as a close cousin of the vampire. Stubb's most heinous crime would seem to be the murder of his own son, though it is a crime that shows the depths of his desires. His love for his son seemed evident, but Stubb's need for gore resulted in his luring his son into the woods where he killed him and then ate his brains. Stubb was said to have many concubines, including his sister, his daughter – who had a child by him – and a succubus sent by the Devil.

Eventually Stubb was caught. While being chased in his wolf-form, he removed his belt and returned to human form; the belt was not found but his sudden appearance along with his other sins was enough to convince his captors. Stubb was tortured on the wheel and confessed to a series of villainous acts (most people interrogated on instruments such as the wheel confessed; they probably rightly concluded that they were going to die anyway, and better sooner than later). His confession included the murder of sixteen persons. He also admitted his pact with the Devil. Stubb was decapitated and his body burnt at the stake alongside his wife and mistress; his head was put on display as a warning.

To change into a werewolf was said to involve casting spells, rubbing the body with a salve and the wearing of an animal skin or girdle.

In the fifteenth and sixteenth centuries werewolf lore became widespread, and the reality of the stories was accepted. The highest number of reports comes from France, where in the records of werewolf trials between 1520 and 1630 there are an incredible 30,000 cases. Werewolf hunting, just like witchhunting, was a religiously driven craze, and one that gave the hunter great local political power.

In 1598 Jacques Rollet, believing himself to be a werewolf, was caught eating a child victim. He was incarcerated for life in an asylum. In this case the legend of the werewolf may have intertwined with reality; those who caught Rollet found him after they had been chasing wolves from the scene of another murder. However, there may have only been an implied connection in the coincidence, or even an elaboration on the part of the captors.

Whether people physically turn into wolves is a matter for conjecture, and seems hardly likely. However, there is no doubt that there have been many people who thought that they could and did. For example, in the seventeenth century there was the case of thirteen-year-old Jean Grenier. He had a malformed jaw that gave him a canine appearance and no doubt he was tormented by other boys for it, and this was made worse by the fact that he appears to have been mentally retarded. He was caught attacking a shepherdess and afterwards confessed to fifty killings, to eating children, and to making a pact with the Devil. The evidence suggests he did kill and eat his victims, and even indicates that he thought himself a werewolf.

Grenier was convicted and sentenced to be hanged and burnt. But by 1603 a different view of werewolfism was beginning to emerge. When Grenier's case was reviewed, although it was agreed that Grenier was a murderer, he was considered incapable of rational thought and it was said that 'the change of shape existed only in the disorganised brain of the insane' and 'Consequently it was not a crime which could be punished'. Grenier was then ordered to be cloistered for life within the walls of a Franciscan monastery in Bordeaux, where it seems he did not give up his lycanthropy. When visited a year before his death, he was said to move about on all fours, his teeth were long and his hands claw-like.

Grenier was very lucky. Although not the first to be given clemency, his case showed a changing view away from the belief in pacts with the Devil, shape-changing, and magic pelts. Although werewolf claims in other parts of Europe continued, it seems the trials and executions that took place in France were soon to come to an end. The lycanthropic claimants were now treated not as criminals and occultists, but with more compassion; with regard for the lycanthrope as a victim of his delusions rather than a predatory animal.

In the seventh century the illness of 'melancholic lycanthropia' was described by Paulus Aegineta, from Alexandria. Amongst other things the sufferers were said to have ulcerated legs, as a result of moving on four limbs. They felt the compulsion to wander about at night and howl until dawn. This illness was blamed on an excess of melancholy, or black bile, one of the four elements that were then believed to make up the human body.

So the illness of lycanthropy had been known for a long time, but during the werewolf hunts reason was set aside and the claims were accepted at face value. At the end of the werewolf hunt craze, judges, after pressure from doctors, became more and more convinced that the werewolves were in fact suffering mental delusions, perhaps enhanced by drugs and incantations.

In modern times, Mr H, a twenty-year-old patient, became deluded that he was a werewolf after taking the hallucinogenic drugs LSD and strychnine. He had been serving in the United States Army in Europe at the time, and took the drugs in an isolated forest. The man claimed he saw hair appearing on his hands and thought it was forming on his face. He acquired the compulsion to eat live rabbits. After two days he returned to base, but on seeing the sign 'Feeding Time' in the mess, he was sure those around him knew he was a wolf.

If drugs such as LSD can make a man believe himself a wolf, or if a mental disorder causing delusions can create the same belief, then it is likely that cases can reach back through time. Many potions and drugs were available in medieval times, extracts from the skins of toads and plants like belladonna or mandrake could be used to cause delusions. These specialised drugs were available to those who looked for them, but on the 'mass market' there was bread made from ergotised (diseased) grain, this too would cause delusions.

There have been other cases of werewolves in modern times; in America in 1946, in Rome in 1949, and in the Far East in 1957. In 1975 in Britain a man committed suicide because he believed he was turning into a werewolf.

Werewolves are the most common form of these shape-changers, but also reported are weretigers in India, were-leopards, werejackals and werehyenas all in Africa and a variety of creatures in Russia and France such as werebats and werefoxes. Bridging claims of lycanthropy and posses-sion, one sixteen-year-old girl in Brazil became convinced she had been possessed by the spirit of a wolf.

In 1977 an American woman also claimed to be possessed by the Devil. During this possession she believed she became an animal, and described what she saw in the mirror as 'the head of a wolf in place of a face on my own body – just a long-nosed wolf with teeth, groaning, snarling, growling . . . with fangs and claws, calling out "I am the Devil." '

She was treated by her doctors as suffering acute schizo-phrenic psychosis and responded to the treatment.

It is not hard to imagine the outcome of claims such as these in a time of belief in the supernatural and fear of those soliciting with the Devil.

WITCHCRAFT INTO THE MODERN DAY

Witchcraft, or Wicca, is based on an understanding of nature, arising as it does from early pastoral peoples such as the Celts. Wicca practices are said to be traceable to prehistoric times, with evidence of certain Wiccan imagery visible in cave paintings. Certainly the earliest cave-dwellers would have been closely in touch with nature.

It is also a religion that demands self-development of its adherents, without obedience to a set of fixed rules, or a code of living governed by one book. It is akin to the way of the shamans of the native tribes of central Asia, Australia and North America. Indeed, there is evidence that the learnings of the Native Americans derive from witches who fled Wales, and Christianity.

The onset of Christianity created some of the greatest challenges to Wicca. The first Christians took on a lot of pagan beliefs, and built their churches on sites of ancient rituals and importance. They also used the pagan holidays as their own holy days. Pentacles can be seen in some churches, for example over the door of the Holy Trinity Church, Rothwell, in Northamptonshire. There are also carvings on the outside of some churches which show pagan figures.

The Christian Church in the thirteenth century went through quite a dramatic change when many criticisms were brought against it. The Church, under pressure, turned the attack outwards. Heretics and witches were sought out and killed for their beliefs. The Church confused witchcraft with devil worship and believed all witches to have joined with the Devil with some evil intent. In order to show its power to the people, the Church needed a powerful enemy; if it could attack the Devil himself through his presumed followers – and defeat them – it could show its own strength. This also explains why the Church promoted the belief that witches were more powerful than they themselves claimed to be.

In reality Satanism and witchcraft are not directly associated. The Satanist, although using rituals and ceremonies taken from witchcraft, is not a pagan, but a renegade Christian. Satanists accept the Christian duality between good and evil (and choose to follow evil).

1951 saw the repeal of the Witchcraft Act and the practice of witchcraft was no longer a crime. Many leading lights 'came out of the closet': Gerald B. Gardner and Alex and Maxine Sanders were probably the best known. The two main modern branches of witchcraft are known as Gardnerian and Alexandrian.

The modern witch is a practitioner of white witchcraft. He or she can act as a sole practitioner or join a coven, usually of thirteen members. If membership of a coven reaches beyond this number, it is natural for some of the group to break away and form another coven. The witches are worshippers of a dual deity; the Lady and the Man. The female deity's closest parallel would be Artemis (Diana) or Aphrodite (Venus). The male is a horned god, symbolic of power rather than evil, and closer to the Greek Pan than to Satan.

The only true witches in the West today seem to be good witches; 'black magic' as such being largely restricted to Satanism. Witches make the point that the powers they use are neutral; neither good nor bad. They are used for whatever purpose the witch chooses. One witch we have interviewed extensively, Graham James, believes however that there is a balancing force in the cosmos – akin to the law of Karma – that demands the powers be used for good. 'If you use the powers for wrongdoing it will rebound on you tenfold,' he said.

A typical coven of today has six couples and a leader, most likely a female high priestess. A circle is drawn on the floor, this is to focus the power (perhaps psychic force). This power arises from the witches' own bodies, and this is one reason why some covens meet in the nude because clothing dissipates the power. They do not indulge in sex orgies; the nudity is a desire for oneness with nature. Many participants in a coven, in any case, often wear robes. After the circle has been drawn, the priestess or priest will invoke the Goddess and God with incantations, perhaps reading ancient writings. After a symbolic feast the coven members may dance, sing or chant, this may be the start of bringing on the altered state needed for their magic.

There is no 'witch bible' any more than there is one 'chief witch'. Each witch has a Book of Shadows into which he or she makes notes, and records spells. These books are not printed but copied out when joining the coven, and developed throughout the witch's life.

Witchcraft today, more properly referred to as Wicca, is getting back to its natural origins. As such, it is becoming more acceptable as it casts off the mystique and rumours that have abounded. At the same time it is adapting to the modern day, and to the needs and problems of the modern day. Typical of recent press coverage of witches:

- In September 1992 Salem's Chief Witch, Laurie Cabot, commented that there were 2,400 witches in Salem alone. They demand their proper legal protection under the US constitution which recognises witchcraft as a legitimate religion, a fact which was fully supported by Captain Paul Murphy of the Salem police department. 'Anybody who tried to harm the witches because of their beliefs will find me coming after them,' he said.

- In 1994 Ms Susan Leybourne, a white witch, was appointed a chaplain at Leeds University. Ms Leybourne is a pagan priestess, ordained in Louisiana. She will offer guidance on magic and rituals. She is, therefore, on a par with the other chaplains from other recognised religions. She stated, 'Witchcraft can play a positive role in people's lives. It emphasises how an individual's needs and ambitions can be influenced by magic and how such beliefs can bring personal rewards, such as academic success.'

- Also in 1994, the town council of Milton Keynes voted to grant permission to the Milton Keynes Wiccan coven to use local land for worship.

Graham James has, for over a decade, been at the forefront of bringing Wicca into the modern era. He uses his skills in modern business applications and is consulted by leading industrialists and financiers for assistance with decision making. He has a total of 25,000 clients world-wide who call on him for a variety of 'products'; talismans, spells, spell pouches, oils, protection talismans, and others. He supports pagan supporters in New York, practitioners of Kahuna magic in Peru, and others in virtually every country of the world. He recently received two letters from clients attributing their wins on the National Lottery to his Ethos Pyramid, a scale reproduction of the Great Pyramids using holographics.

We commissioned responses to Graham's work from his clients, with his permission. One such unambiguous response is reproduced here, as a measure of the impact modern Wicca is making:

Dear Graham,

As you know my Company, The Lancashire Steel Fabrication Co Ltd, has made an offer to purchase larger (60,500 sq ft) industrial premises surrounded by 5.4 acres of spare land for further expansion when needed.

When I first read about you in the Sunday Express many years ago and wrote to you asking if you would supply one of your magic 'Talismans' and 'Power Pouches' little did I realise how truly powerful these were. When you provided these my Company had a 'serious' overdraft with its Bankers and was barely surviving on an annual turnover of £750,000. Today we have an annual turnover of £4,650,000, no overdraft and, in fact, are 'cash rich', operate three factories employing a work force of 94 and have more work than we can handle.

A few weeks ago we engaged the services of leading management consultants, Arthur Andersen and Co, to advise us on our intended relocation to much larger premises. The attached graph, provided by Arthur Andersen, confirms our continual annual growth.

It is, perhaps, unusual for the Chairman and Managing Director of a British manufacturing Company to attribute his Company's business success to his belief in the phenomenal 'power' of a specially prepared magic talisman and 'power pouch' or in simple terms, 'witchcraft'. But, as your Records show, I do honestly believe this to be true. Obviously, you must work hard in believing that what you want to happen will happen, also you need the power of 'belief and honestly use the 'power' of your 'talismans' to create only good works and not, at any price, use their power to harm others.

So strong is my belief, and faith, in what your talismans can achieve that, as you know, I will not make an important decision, both personal and business, without first contacting you for protective advice. Always the advice you have given has been helpful and very beneficial.

There are many who would scoff at what I have now written. However the proof is given in our professionally audited, financial Accounts which the world at large are entitled to examine.

Thank you for your continuing help and may your efforts be always successful.

Yours sincerely,

J.C.H. Roberts
Managing Director.
17th October 1994

Y

YETIS

The most famous of the stories and legends surrounding unknown 'man-beasts' is that of the Abominable Snowman, or yeti, in the Himalayas. The creature was first described to the West by B.H. Hodson, the first Briton to take up residence in Nepal in 1832, when he described a creature which 'moved erectly, was covered in long, dark hair and had no tail'.

Westerners have reported footprints since 1889. In 1921 an officer of the British army 20,000 feet up Everest reported footprints. This witness added some credibility to the tales, but no further evidence. It was the photographs of the footprints first taken in 1937 by F.S. Smythe and the more famous photographs taken by Eric Shipton in 1951 during an expedition on the Menlung Glacier that began to generate real interest in the man-beast. Shipton was with mountaineer Michael Ward, who examined the tracks and commented, 'They were really well defined . . . we could see the toes of all the feet . . . There was absolutely no blurring round the edges.' The pictures indicate the footprints were thirteen inches long and eight inches wide.

There are several indications of the existence of the creature in 1955. Abbé Bordet of the Paris Geological Institute followed three sets of tracks during an expedition in that year, one set for over half a mile. In the same year an RAF expedition in the Himalayas resulted in photographs of footprints taken by Squadron Leader Lester Davies.

In 1978 Lord and Lady Hunt, in Nepal to commemorate the Silver Anniversary of the 1953 conquest of Everest, photographed a series of tracks. In 1979 a British expedition found footprints in the Hinken valley, their leader John Edwards stated, 'I think our pictures will prove to be the best taken yet. What is more we heard this high-pitched scream and our Sherpa said it was a yeti.' In 1980 a photograph was taken by a Polish mountaineer of a footprint fourteen inches long and seven inches wide.

The photographs are the subject of debate. Do they represent a real unknown species or are they the product of normal footprints, enlarged by melting snow? Almost certainly they are not the product of deliberate fraud, though there may have been individual frauds in the claims. Reputable people such as Lord and Lady Hunt with everything to lose and nothing to gain by their claims have made reports, and if several of the sets of tracks are over half a mile in length, and in other cases even longer, then outright fraud would seem to be improbable.

So what other evidence for the yeti is claimed?

While there is evidence to indicate the possibility of an unknown species of animal in the Himalayas, much of it is anecdotal. John Napier, a writer on such creatures, comments, 'Sherpa reports are suspect because Sherpas do not distinguish between the reality of the real world and the "reality" of their myth-ridden religious beliefs.'

An expedition sponsored by the *Daily Mail* newspaper discovered droppings which suggested that the creature had omnivorous eating habits, i.e. meat and vegetation.

There have been many claims of scalps, individual hairs, bones, skins and so on, but nothing that certainly points to an unknown species. It has been suggested that the yeti could be a Langur monkey, which is known to live in the area, but analysis by zoologist W. Tschernezky suggested that the footprints were unlike those of either a bear or monkey. He concluded, 'All the evidence suggests that the so-called snowman is a very huge, heavily built, bi-pedal primate, most probably of a similar type to the fossil Gigantopithecus.'

The question cannot truly be solved until a live yeti or a

carcass in a reasonably preserved state is located. Given the remoteness of the region and the relatively few Westerners who might by chance encounter a yeti and be in a position to retrieve it for examination, it is hardly surprising that one has not yet turned up. There may have been cases of the locals locating such carcasses, and these may well be the foundation of many of the local legends, but it is unlikely that they would willingly display them. The yeti, to the local people, is also an almost god-like creature and certainly one about which there are many superstitions.

Don Whillans in 1970 had the privilege of seeing a yeti, announced to him by his Sherpa. He stated, 'What was really strange to me was the behaviour of the Sherpa. If it had been a bear . . . that would have been the end of it. But they were subdued for a couple of days and if I ever tried to mention the subject or was looking at the track through the binoculars during the day I would hear them passing comments to one another.' Some Sherpas believe that if they encounter a yeti they should never look at it and should immediately move away down the mountain out of either respect or fear.

Whillans described the creature as ape-like, bounding along in the snow and apparently eating from the branches of trees. Tracks located where he had seen the creature were human-sized though, as he stated, 'I suppose yetis, if such a thing exists, come in different sizes, the same as people.' This is borne out by the local legends which indicate three classifications of yeti of which the smaller (*yeh-teh*) gives the creature its popular name. Larger than *yeh-teh* is *meh-teh* and it is the largest of all, *dzu-teh* which is thought to be the giant man-beast of the local folklore.

Another name used by the local inhabitants for the creature was *metoh-kangmi* which means 'foul-smelling man of the snows'. A corruption of this translation led to the popularist phrase 'Abominable Snowman'.

In 1974 a Sherpa girl, Lakhpa Domani, was near a stream tending her yaks when a yeti seized her. She described it as having large eyes, and prominent cheekbones and being covered in black and reddish hair. The creature carried her to the stream, but her screams appear to have disturbed it and it dropped her.

A seemingly important breakthrough came in March 1986 when Anthony Wooldridge was making a solo run in the Himalayas for charity. His report was contained in the *Fortean Times* of Spring 1987. He located and photographed several strange tracks, and later that day saw a large, hairy figure which he was able to photograph. Various analysts including anthropologists and zoologists, in company with mountaineers familiar with Everest and the locality, have been impressed by the picture. The dark, hair-covered creature was standing, legs apart, looking down the slope with its right shoulder towards Wooldridge. Wooldridge indicated that the creature remained motionless for at least forty-five minutes, possibly watching him. Forty-five minutes or more is a long time for a creature to stand motionless. If Wooldridge did not photograph an inanimate bi-ped shaped object (he never saw it move), perhaps it was aware of being watched, or given that there had just been an avalanche in the area, it might have been concentrating on ground vibrations, to which it would presumably be attuned, before risking being engulfed by any follow-up snow movements. There is also the possibility that a sadhu, a reclusive holy man, could have been in contemplative prayer at the time; the figure photographed could be a man heavily swathed in warm skins and a hat.

The yeti is not unique in the world; there are reports of yeti-like creatures from almost every area of the globe. There is the North American Bigfoot (See 'Bigfoot and Sasquatch', page 51). There are many reports of man-beasts in China, where one was apparently shot in 1913. In 1954 Russians visiting Yunnan province were told of a sub-human hairy race of people living there. In Russia these creatures are referred to as '*alma*' and in the Urals, as *yag-mort*. In the far north, in the Siberian region, a creature known as the *chuchunaa* is reported as much more human-like than beast-like and even wearing clothes. He has been described as over seven feet high, with a dark face and shaggy hair. In Australia there are reports of a creature called *yowie*.

What would be required for the yeti to be a proved reality?

The yeti would require open space for safety and, for its anonymity to have remained for so long, few approaches by humans interested in its capture or study. This would certainly be true of the high Himalayas and locations around the world where yeti-like creatures are seen.

Secondly, the creature would need a supply of food. The high Himalayas would not appear to provide a suitable food supply for a large creature, but this may only mean that it successfully forages at lower levels. The fact that footprints are found in the high snows may only reflect a place where footprints are imprinted; the creature might spend a great deal of its time at lower levels.

Thirdly, there needs to be a reasonable sized population in order to maintain stability. However, such a population could still be measured in relatively small numbers and in sufficiently isolated places need not be easily discoverable.

Another question regarding the yeti is whether it is more man or more beast. Most of the reports indicate a creature acting in an animal-like way; protective, fleeing discovery, foraging for food and wary of approaches by other creatures. However, the human-like gait and often overall appearance of the creatures suggests a closer kinship to Homo sapiens than most apes or bears.

The mystery will not be resolved to final satisfaction until such a creature is studied closely. Should the opportunity arise, it is unfortunate, but inevitable, that the creature will be captured and contained. We hope that any such treatment and subsequent study is done with consideration and humanity.

Z

ZOMBIES

'Battalions of "zombies" have been formed in Haiti – to halt the threat of an American invasion. The military junta claims to have created a force of men once dead, but brought back to half-life to serve voodoo priests.' This was the description given in the London *Daily Mail* just prior to the American invasion of Haiti in 1994. The idea was, of course, to instil fear into the US marines who were poised to invade the island.

The belief in zombies is based on the premise that a voodoo priest, a *bokor*, can revive a dead body that has not started to rot. The awakened body, or zombie, walks, eats, hears and can speak, but has no memory of the past. It also seems to act like a robot demonstrating no ability to think or process thought. The zombie is under the control of the *bokor* who employs it as a slave, perhaps in the fields.

The Haitians have a great fear of the zombie, but the overriding fear is of becoming one. Many graves have large, heavy stones placed on them to stop the *bokor* reaching the corpse. Relatives watch over graves until the body starts to rot. If the fear of a relative becoming a zombie is great, the body is sometimes 'killed' a second time, and usually mutilated. Slightly less obvious techniques are sometimes employed; for example thousands of tiny seeds and lines of string are left around the grave in the belief that the corpse will be so involved in trying to thread them into a chain that it will not hear the call of the *bokor*.

Despite the image of the zombie, promoted mostly by horror movies, of a creature used to dominate, threaten and kill, most zombies are supposedly created as slave labour. They either work on the *bokor*'s farm, or they are created to be sold to other farmers. The *bokor* has to keep a watchful eye on his zombies. If they eat meat, or salt, then it is held that the zombie will realise his plight and return to the grave, and proper death.

French anthropologist Alfred Metraux studied zombies and was sceptical of the evidence, particularly when one supposed zombie turned out to be a mentally retarded woman known to be alive. He seemed more impressed by the case of a woman who, after death, had her neck twisted to fit into a wrong-sized coffin, and whose foot was badly burned in an accident during the burial. She had rejected the overtures of a would-be lover, but some years later her zombie was seen working in menial tasks for that same man. The deceased's brother identified her, and took note of her badly twisted neck and burned foot.

The Duvalier dictators of Haiti – 'Papa Doc' Francois and 'Baby Doc' Jean-Claude – promoted the image of zombies. Papa Doc let it be known that he was a powerful *bokor*; his personal mafia were named *tontons macoutes* – after the powerful voodoo sorcerers. Belief in his zombie-backed power would have been a powerful tool of rule in superstition-ridden Haiti. Although the Duvaliers were finally deposed in 1986, the myth of the zombie continues, as the opening paragraph of this chapter indicates.

Research indicates that the sorcerers' powers may stem from a knowledge of medicines rather than supernatural energies. Ethnobiologist Wade Davis suggested that the deep coma of zombification was being brought about by certain poisons that can be found in puffer fish and a type of toad. A hospital might well recognise the condition, but in the superstitious, tribal surroundings the victim might well be presumed dead. After a time in this 'dead' state the *bokor* would administer an antidote to the poison and the dead would appear to come back to life. A side effect of the drugs would be some brain disfunction; the zombie would have lost his memory, act as if in a drugged state, and those that witnessed him alive after seeing him dead would believe in the power of the *bokor* and his voodoo magic.

Arguably, without a functioning memory the zombie would rely heavily on the guidance of the *bokor*.

Article 249 of Haiti's Criminal Code recognises this possibility and has specifically outlawed it. 'Also shall be qualified as attempted murder the employment which may be made against any person of substances which, without causing actual death, produce a lethargic coma more or less prolonged. If, after the administering of such substances, the person has been buried, the act shall be considered murder no matter what result follows.'

THE VALUE OF SCIENCE, SCEPTICISM AND COMMITMENT

The mysteries of the paranormal provoke fierce reactions in those who take an interest in it. There is often a polarisation of viewpoints; 'believers' willing to believe anything and 'sceptics' not prepared to examine any evidence no matter how compelling. These standpoints often reflect predispositions, an unwillingness to adapt belief to changing evidence.

Scepticism is important. In examining subjects where the mechanisms and effects are unknown, difficult to quantify or difficult to replicate, there is a wide margin for error. A sceptical approach to claims made by witnesses, researchers, test subjects, experiencers and so on is wise. This is as good a point as any to remind the reader that the word scepticism comes from the Greek word *skeptikos*, meaning 'thoughtful'. All people are subject to error, misinterpretation and wishful-thinking and these can colour belief in tests and evidence.

However, a dismissive approach to these mystery subjects is unhelpful. Even if the interpretation of evidence is incomplete or inaccurate, there is often an underlying truth to be sought for. From that truth, understanding progresses. If we consider the claims of alien abduction, for example it is easy for the sceptic to dismiss the claims out of hand; physical evidence is rare and always ambiguous. However, some process is happening that is affecting witnesses and creating a belief that is largely consistent across the world. A truly sceptical approach – by which we mean an open-minded enquiring, review of the evidence – will at least offer insight into why that global belief exists. Something of use is learned.

There was a time when the energy we now call lightning was thought to be a manifestation of the gods; at some point a challenge to that thinking must have been proposed and the new theories examined. When it seemed likely that lightning might be a natural effect of certain atmospheric conditions, that theory was tested and found to be correct. But there are possibly other energies around the earth that still require understanding, such energies might create the effects we interpret as 'ghosts', 'alien encounters', and so on. Like the 'lightning gods', those interpretations may be only personifications of a natural force, or they may represent something more deeply important to mankind. Open-minded study will eventually offer new truths, but only if the research is allowed to continue in an open-minded fashion. Sceptics – cynics – of today would probably have dismissed stories of lightning flashes as delusions in the minds of witnesses, and would never have come to understand them.

There is a gulf between open-minded enquiry, the true scepticism, which is healthy and necessary, and the closed minded 'make-it-go-away-I-am-not-prepared-to-look-at-this' attitude of some who have usurped the use of the term 'sceptic' and who might more properly be referred to as cynics. There is a world of difference in the quality, and resultant value, of the comments of, say, Arthur Ellison or Michael Crichton who we know have approached the subject eager to learn, and, say, the comments of an individual or organisation which seems eager only to dismiss. When Michael Crichton was preparing to address a meeting of CSICOP (Committee for the Scientific Investigation of Claims of the Paranormal) he read through a selection of essays from their magazine the *Sceptical Inquirer* and commented, 'in several essays I was disturbed by the intemperate tone of many writers I admired; there was a tendency to attribute the basest motives to their opponents. In fact, there seemed to be a good deal of personal animosity and name-calling on all sides.' Perhaps much of this will change, or even is changing; just as constructive scepticism has in recent years come from within organisations that might formerly have been branded 'believer cults' or 'unbeliever cults' may be forced to incorporate constructive attitudes also. The tone of correspondence between the two sides will indicate that progress.

We have always believed we must be doing something right

when we are challenged from within the subjects we work and research in. We are frequently called sceptics, not always politely, by the 'believer cults', and almost as often called believers (presumably also not always politely) by the 'unbeliever cults'. In a climate of intemperate correspondence, perhaps that is the best sign of steering the fine line between the two opposing views!

Of the introduction of the scientific method, believers can be very dismissive of a scientific challenge to what they believe in, while cynics can be overly dependent on the scientific approach. These are attitudes which further reflect a polarisation of views, and almost certainly a distorted mistrust or belief in the scientific method.

Understand the way in which we come to understand the world. We perceive something with our senses. We build a representational model of it in our mind. For example we see an object driving on the road, with four wheels touching the ground, and we construct an image of it which we call 'car'. We then compare that in the 'card index' in our mind made up from all our experiences and we conclude that it was a car. But we can make mistakes. We might hear the sound of a car and jump back on to the pavement in fear, then see a pedestrian walking round the corner with a CD player playing the sound of a car engine. We built a model from the evidence, but we interpreted it wrongly. Although the car was not the right interpretation, the experience was still real, and there was a real phenomenon – a sound in this case. Science can measure the size of a car, or the decibel level of a sound, but it has to know which it is dealing with before it can make any useful contribution.

Consider that science is just a measuring tool and it can only measure something for which certain parameters are already known. Where the unknown is concerned, science cannot make a useful contribution until there are data to examine, and theories to test. Once the opportunity is there, science makes an invaluable contribution. Scientific challenge is being brought to bear on some beliefs too early, as a club with which to oppress rather than a rule with which to measure.

Those who are dismissive of claimants of paranormal

experiences point to the errors and failures of some claimants. Not unfair, but rather distorted. The list of scientific errors is equally significant. Lord Kelvin made something of a habit of such errors with statements such as 'X-rays will prove to be a hoax', 'heavier-than-air flying machines are impossible' and 'radio has no future'. Analysts do not use Lord Kelvin as proof that all science is nonsense; nor should the case of a man who believed himself guided by aliens living inside his television set be used to 'disprove' claims of telepathy. Each subject, each test, must stand alone. Some of the so-called paranormal will turn out to have no valid claim to being a phenomenon in its own right; some will, however.

Finally, there are aspects of the world to which science has not found a way to apply itself, yet no one seriously challenges their existence just because they cannot be measured, replicated or their cause and effect fully documented. For example, few people would deny the existence of love; yet what is love? A response to a stimulus certainly, but no scientist has yet replicated the stimulus so that it will guarantee to affect any test subject in the same way as any other. It is a collection of physical, physiological and psychological responses to a situation also; but measuring heart-rates, blood pressures and breathing rates do not tell us very much about love. It is accepted that it is irrational, unpredictable, unmeasurable – yet real. Another example, art. Is there some measurable difference between Michelangelo and a man who cannot draw a straight line? One or two tests relating to hand and eye coordination might tell us something about the test subjects, but will it enable us to replicate art from any test subject? The intuitive, right brain, creative abilities are real, but beyond scientific analysis.

Nothing seems to upset scientists and sceptics alike more than the claim by 'doers' of paranormal feats that they cannot 'do it' to order; that they have to be in the right frame of mind. Nothing more surely creates an atmosphere of mistrust, and cries of 'Fraud'. And there may be some justification for that. Fraudulent claimants, or just the misguided, may well hide behind this as an excuse, or even as a way to set up situations in which they can fool an audience. But the fact that there are fraudulent claimants does not mean there are no real ones. The fire brigade is called out on false alarms, but there are still real fires. Steven Spielberg can create 'fraudulent' dinosaurs for us all to see; but there were still real ones.

The question of being in the right frame of mind should be set into a context where that is acceptable without challenge. An artist cannot be creative if the mood is not there, for painters some days produce a passionate, almost unstoppable, flow of beautiful work, and on other days produce nothing. Salesmen have good and bad days selling, and they recognise that their mood, which governs their interaction with others, accounts for it. A man, in particular, will find sex almost impossible if he is not in the right frame of mind. So if frame of mind is necessary to unlock certain talents, psychic talents should not be excluded from that list. As we said in the section on 'Luck', 'Whether you think you can, or whether you think you can't, you're probably right.'

There is evidence that psychic powers do respond to attitudes of mind. In telepathy experiments there was a noted difference between the results of happy, alert people and those of tired and depressed individuals. Professor John Hasted found that he got more impressive PK results from test subjects when he himself believed in them. That sounds like an unscientific sort of approach, and so it probably is, but it is also a truth we acknowledge in, say, child education. Believe a child will do well, create an expectation of high achievement and the child often responds. Put people down, tell them they are 'good for nothing' and there is evidence that they come to believe it. Why should psychic abilities be excluded from that educational process?

We do not understand how psychic abilities work, where in the body they are housed, or what makes them more or less effective. We should not be dismissive of varying results until we understand the mental processes of people – in their normal lives – better than we presently do.

We should also be wary of predisposition to stereotypes. The learned journals and the learned associations place a lamentable dependence on the academic, the scholarly, and the respectable. These are the qualities which we traditionally value in our everyday life. But they may not be the best attitudes of mind to produce psychic phenomena. Ted Serios (see 'Thoughtography', page 302) was known to be a drunk, but perhaps he had that special something that allowed him to access a part of his mind that others cannot. Stigmatics produce spontaneous physical wounds on their bodies – even under thorough test conditions – but not without a belief system that can hardly be said to be rational within our 'traditional' framework. Most of the great artists had their unrespectable moments too; but they produced great art.

It is a fine line working with 'unacceptable' people, knowing that one slip and the scientists and sceptics will use the excuse to bay for blood, but it is one that needs to be walked by any serious researcher. An attitude change would move us all further down a road we all want to explore.

We are always interested to receive accounts of experiences of and contacts with the mysteries described in this book.

If you have a personal account to offer we can be contacted by letter at the following address:

The Leys
2C Leyton Road
Harpenden
Herts
AL5 2TL
England

or by fax: 01582–461979

John and Anne Spencer

SLI reports can be sent directly to Hilary Evans at:
59 Tranquil Vale
London
SE3 0BS

Recommended Reading
And References

'A Piece Of Cloth, The Turin Shroud' Investigated By Rodney Hoare, Aquarian Press, 1984.

'Afterlife' By Colin Wilson, Grafton Books, 1985.

'Alien Liason' By Timothy Good, Century, 1991.

'An Angel On Your Shoulder, Angel Encounters And Everyday Life' By Kelsey Tyler, Berkeley Books, New York, 1994.

'Arthur C. Clarke's Mysterious World' By Simon Welfare And John Fairley, Harper Collins, 1991.

'Arthur C. Clarke's World Of Strange Powers' By John Fairley And Simon Welfare, Collins, 1990.

'Beyond Earth' By Ralph Blum And Judy Blum, Corgi, 1974.

'Beyond The Impossible' By Richard Lazarus, Warner Books, 1994.

'Beyond The Light Barrier' By Elizabeth Klarer, Aquarian Book Centre Publishers, 1980.

'Child Possessed' By David St Clair, Corgi Books, 1982.

'Confrontations' By Jacques Vallee, Souvenir Press, 1990.

'Crash At Corona' By Stanton T. Friedman And Don Berliner, Paragon House, 1992.

'Crop Circle Apocalypse' By John Macnish, Circlevision, 1993.

'Deliver Us From Evil' By David A. Yellop, Macdonald Futura, 1981.

'Deliverance' Edited By Michael Perry, SPCK, 1987.

'Dictionary Of Fairies' By Katharine Briggs, Penguin, 1977.

'Dimensions' By Jacques Vallee, Souvenir Press, 1988.

'Dying To Live' By Susan Blackmore, Grafton, 1993.

'Encyclopedia Of Ghosts And Spirits' By John And Anne Spencer, Headline, 1992.

'Encyclopedia Of Mystical And Paranormal Experience' By Rosemary Ellen Guiley, Grange Books, 1991.

'Evidence For The Bermuda Triangle' By David Group, Aquarian Press, 1984.

'Extraordinary People' By Darrold A. Treffert, Black Swan, 1990.

'Fire From Heaven' By Michael Harrison, Scoob Books Publishing, 1990.

'Flights Of Fancy' By Lynn Picknett, Ward Lock Limited, 1987.

'Flying Saucers And Modern Myth Of Things Seen In The Sky' By C.G. Jung, Ark Paperbacks, 1959.

'Flying Saucers Have Landed' By Desmond Leslie And George Adamski, Neville Spearman, 1953.

'Folklore, Myths And Legends Of Britain' By Reader's Digest.

'Gifts Of The Gods?' By John Spencer, Virgin, 1994.

'Ghost And Ghoul' By T.C. Lethbridge, Routledge And Kegan Paul, 1961.

'Ghosts And Legends Of The Lake District' By J.A. Brooks, Gerald Culler Publications, 1988.

'Ghostwatching' By John Spencer And Tony Wells, Virgin, 1994.

'Gods, Spirits, Cosmic Guardians' By Hilary Evans, Aquarian Press, 1987.

'Great Mysteries Of The Past' By Reader's Digest, 1991.

'Haunted England' By Christina Hole, Fitzhouse Books Limited, 1990.

'How About Demons' By Felicitas D. Goodman, Indiana University Press, 1988.

'Human Personality And Its Survival Of Bodily Death' By Frederick W.H. Myers, Longmans, Green And Co., 1927.

'In Search Of The Dead' By Jeffrey Iverson, BBC Books, 1992.

'James Randi, Psychic Investigator', Boxtree Limited, 1991.

'Larousse Encyclopedia Of Mythology', Paul Hamlyn, 1959.

'Life After Death' By D. Scott Rogo, Guild Publishing, 1986.

'Life After Life' By Raymond A. Moody, JRMD, Phantom Books, 1976.

'Modern Mysteries Of The World', By Janet And Colin Board, Grafton Books, 1989.

'Mysteries, A Guide To The Unknown, Past Present And Future' By Colin Wilson And John Grant, Chancellor Press, 1994.

'Mysteries Of Time And Space' By Brad Steiger, Sphere Books, 1977.

'Mythology And Illustrated Encyclopedia' (Ed.) Richard Cavendish, Littlebrown & Co., 1992.

'Paranormal – A Modern Perspective' By John Spencer, Hamlyn, 1992.

'Perspectives' By John Spencer, Macdonald Futura, 1989.

'Phantasms Of The Living' By Edmund Gurney, Frederick W.H. Myers And Frank Podmore, Kegan, Paul, Trench, Trubner & Co., 1918.

'Phantom Encounters', Time Life, 1987.

'Phenomena' By John Michell And Robert Rickard, Thames & Hudson, 1977.

'Poltergeist' By Colin Wilson, Llewellyn Publications, 1993.

'Possessed' By Thomas Allen, Doubleday, 1993.

'Powers Of Darkness, Powers Of Light' By John Cornwell, Viking, 1991.

'Psychic Voyages', Time Life, 1987.

'Revelations' By Jacques Vallee, Souvenir Press, 1991.

'Secret Life' By David M. Jacobs, Simon & Schuster, 1992.

'Secrets Of The Inner Mind', Time Life Books, 1993.

'Shamans, Healers And Medicine Men' By Holger Kalweit, Shambhala, 1992.

'SORRAT, A History Of The Neihardt Psycho-Kinesis Experiments 1961–1981' By John Thomas Richards, The Scarecrow Press Inc, 1982.

'Spirit Within Her' By John And Anne Spencer, Boxtree, 1994.

'Spontaneous Human Combustion' By Jenny Randles And Peter Hough, Bantam Books, 1993.

'Stigmata' By Ted Harrison, Harper Collins, 1994.

'Strange Creatures From Time And Space' By John Keel, Neville Spearman, 1975.

'The Beast Of Exmoor And Other Mysterious Predators Of Britain' By Di Francis, Jonathan Cape, London, 1993.

'The Beast Within' By Adam Douglas, Avon Books, 1992.

'The Bermuda Triangle Mystery Solved' By Laurence David Kusche, New English Library, 1975.

'The Boston Strangler' By Gerald Frank, Handbooks Ltd, 1966.

'The Case For Reincarnation' By Joe Fisher, Diamond Books, 1993.

'The Case Of The Cottingley Fairies' By Joe Cooper, Robert Hale, London, 1990.

'The Coming Of The Saucers' By Kenneth Arnold And Ray Palmer, Privately Published, 1952.

'The Devils Of Loudun' By Aldus Huxley, Penguin Books, 1973.

'The Ghost Book, St Albans Favourite Haunts' By Beryl Carrington And Muriel Thresher.

'The Ghost Of Flight 401' By John G. Fuller, Souvenir Press, 1978.

'The Hynek UFO Report' By Dr J. Allen Hynek, Sphere Books, 1978.

'The Jesus Conspiracy' By Holger Kersten And Elmar R. Gruber, Element, 1994.

'The Persecution Of Mr Tony Elms (The Bromley Poltergeist)', By Manfred Cassirer, Privately Published, 1993.

'The Power Of Gems And Crystals' By Soozi Holbeche, Piatkus, 1989.

'The Psychic Detectives' By Colin Wilson, Pan Books, 1984.

'The Reader's Digest Book Of Strange Stories, Amazing Facts', The Reader's Digest Association Limited, 1975.

'The Sceptical Occultist' By Terry White, Century, London, 1994.

'The Secret Of Atlantis' By Otto Mark, Bookclub Associates, 1978.

'The SLI Effect' Compiled By Hilary Evans for ASSAP, 1993.

'The Supernatural' By Douglas Hill And Pat Williams, Aldus Books Ltd, 1965.

'The Truth In The Light, An Investigation Of Over 300

Near-Death Experiences' By Peter Fenwick And Elizabeth Fenwick, Headline, 1995.

'The Warminster Mystery' By Arthur Shuttlewood, Neville Spearman, 1967.

'The World's Greatest Mysteries' By Joyce Robins, Chancellor Press, 1993.

'This House Is Haunted' By Guy Lyon Playfair, Souvenir Press, 1980.

'Transformed By The Light' By Dr Melvin Morse With Paul Perry, Piatkus, 1993.

'Travels' By Michael Crichton, Pan Books, 1988.

'Twenty Cases Suggestive Of Reincarnation' By Ian Stephenson, M.D., The University Press Of Virginia, 1974.

'UFO Contact At Pascagoula' By Charles Hickson And William Mendez, Privately Published, 1983.

'UFO Encyclopedia' By John Spencer, Headline, 1991.

'UFO Exist!' By Paris Flammonde, Ballantine Books, 1976.

'UFO Silencers' By Timothy Green Beckley, Inner Light Publications, 1990.

'UFOs Over The Americas' By Jim And Coral Lorenzen, Signet Books, 1968.

'UFOs – The Definitive Casebook' By John Spencer, Hamlyn, 1991.

'UFOs 1947–1987', (Ed.) Hilary Evans And John Spencer, *Fortean Times*, 1987.

'Undiscovered. The Fascinating World Of Undiscovered Places, Graves, Wrecks And Treasure' By Ian Wilson, Chancellor Press, 1987.

'Unsolved Mysteries Past And Present' By Colin Wilson And Damon Wilson, Headline, 1993.

'Visions, Apparitions, Alien Visitors, A Comparative Study Of The Entity Enigma' By Hilary Evans, The Aquarian Press, 1984.

'Wesley's Essex Collection' By Wesley H. Downes, Published 1993.

'Wicca' By Vivianne Crowley, Aquarian, 1989.

'Witchcraft For Tomorrow' By Doreen Valiente, Robert Hale, 1978.

'Whales And Dolphins' By Vic Cox, Ted Smart, 1990.

'Wolves And Werewolves' By John Pollard, Robert Hale, 1964.

Videos: 'Crop Circle Communiqué', Circlevision Production, 1991.
'Crop Circle Communiqué 2, Revelations', Circlevision Production, 1994.
'Undeniable Evidence', Ark Soundwaves, 1991.

Sundry:

Referenced within the text: Various magazines and newspapers with particular reference to *The Daily Mail*, *The Unexplained*, *OMNI*, *UFO Times*, *MUFON journal*.

Index of Names

Adamenko, Viktor 250
Adamski, George 61, 71
Aegineta, Paulus 339
Allen, Dr Robin 86
Allen, Thomas 241
Allington, Miss 228
Andreasson, Betty 13
Angel, Jack 284
Angelucci, Orfeo 71
Anthony, St 153
Arnott, Pastor John 307
Aristotle 32
Arnold, Kenneth 187, 322
Arsenyev, V 193
Asimov, Isaac 221, 232

Baba, Sai 25
Barclay, John 8
Baring-Gould, Reverend Sabine 114
Barker, Captain 322
Barker, John 244
Barlow, Edna 22
Barnes, Robert 101
Barnett, William 234
Basedow, Dr Herbert 95
Batcheldor, Kenneth 210
Baycs, Detective Inspector 246
Bayliss, Raymond 118
Bender, Albert K. 187
Bennett, Sir Ernest 228
Berkowitz, David 247
Berliner, Don 76
Berlitz, Charles 43, 76, 230
Bernal, Dean 99

Bernstein, Morey 268
Bethurum, Truman 71
Biggs, Jemima 101
Blackmore, Dr Susan 214
Blavatsky, Helena P. 30
'Blind Tom' 273
Bloecher, Ted 61, 76
Blunsdon, Norman 116
Boniface IX, Pope 317
Bonner, Gerogc 118
Bonomi, Giovanna 290
Bord, Janet and Colin 161
Bordet, Abbé 346
Boston Strangler, (see DeSalvo Albert)
Bozolli, Jean-Luc 101
Bower, Doug 87
Brashear, Craig 54
Briggs, Captain Benjamin Spooner 178
Bright, Jenny 257, 265
Brown, Rosemary 38
Bryce, Lord 202
Bryne, State Trooper 55
Buchanan, Dr Joseph Rodes 263
Burr, F. 157
Bux, Kuda 128

Cabot, Laurie 343
Cadorna, General Luigi 55
Caidin, Martin 41
Campbell, Donald 95, 147, 162
Campbell, Malcolm 147
Campbell, Ron 285

'Cambridge boy, The' 301
Cantril, Hadley 217
Carnarvon, Lord 94
Carrington, Hereward 184
Carrol, Michael, 173
Carter, Howard 94
Cassirer, Manfred 24
Catherine of Russia, Empress 104
Catherine, St 152
Cayce, Edgar 30, 268
Charbel, St 153
Charles I, King 279
Charles of Sezze 290
'Charlie and George' 273
Cheepen, Maurice 129
Chorley, Dave 87
Christ, Jesus (see Jesus Christ)
Christmas, Captain 114
Clark, Randy 308
Clarke, Arthur C. 261
Clarke, Ray 45
Clement VII, Pope 316, 317
Clinton, A.C. 7
Coates, Gerald 308
Collier, Mrs 84
Collins, Matthew 101
Conway, (family) Harry, Vera,
    Stanley, Fleur 105, 146, 213,
    236, 303
Cornwell, John 159, 173
Cowan, Sir John 288
Coyne, Captain 323
Cox, Dr Bonnar 300
Cox, Lt. Robert F. 133
Craven, John 101
Crichton, Michael 35 264 276, 356
Cringle, Captain 114
Croiset, Gerald 248
Crone, W.W. 318
Crookes, William 116
Cross, Dr David 257
Crowley, Aleister 92, 94

D'Acis, Bishop Pierre 316, 317
D'Esperant, Madame Elizabeth 25
Da Vinci, Leonardo 317

Dahl, Harold 187
Darling, Charles 129
Davenport, Shirley 247
Davidson-Arcres, Cedric 225
Davies, Lester 346
Davies, Marie 288
Davis, Kathie 13
Davis, Wade 352
Dawkins, Christopher 226
de Camp, L. Sprague 232
de Charney, Geoffrey 316
de Charny, Marguerite 316
De Felitta, Frank 269
De Freitas, Jose Pedro 256
de Kerlor, W. 245
de la Poer Beresford, Henry 289
Dean, Jack 330
Delago, Alwin 167
Denney, Glen 285
Denton, William 264
des Anges, Sister Jeanne 19, 240
des Anges, Mère Marie Marguerite
    153
DeSalvo, Albert 249
Despatures, Mgr. 131
Deveau, Oliver 181
Dickson, Peter 112
Diego, Juan 172
Dirac, Paul 314
Dock, George 223
Dobbs, Dr Horace 100
Dodd, Ellen 149
Domani, Lakhpa 348
Donnelly, Ignatius 32
Doone, Barbara 67
Dowding, Air Chief Marshal Lord
    20
Dowling, Tom 333
Downes, Wesley 127, 154, 305
Doyle, Arthur Conan 126, 178
Doyle, Father Garry 334
Dudgeon, Carl Allen and Edward
    229, 231
Dunning, John 70
Dupont, Marc 308

Duvalier, 'Papa Doc' and 'Baby Doc' 352
Dyke, Sally and Nick 50

Eades, Father Eric and Betty 39
Eckart, Alan W. 43
Edison, Thomas A. 7, 119
Edmunds, O.R. 52
Edwards, John 347
Einstein, Albert 230, 298
Eisenbud, Jule 302
Eiscnhowei, President Dwight 77
Ellison, Professor Arthur 26, 261, 297, 356
Espie, Mr 57
Estebany, Oskar 255
Evans, Colin 157
Evans, Hilary 104, 125, 189, 293
Evans-Wentz, J. 11

Falla, Geoffrey 330
Farenden, Ernest
Faniel, Georgette 290
Fenner, Tom 203
Fenwick, Peter 58
Fcnwick, Peter and Elizabeth 198
Festinger, Leon 88
Flaxton, John 194
Fletcher, P. 323
Fletcher, Albert 51
Fodor, Nandor 235
Foltz-Stearns, Edith 20
Ford, Chris 48
Forman, Joan 209, 306
Fort, Charles 141
Francis, Di 47
Francis of Assisi, St 289, 291
Freud, Sigmund 104, 260, 298
Friedman, Stanton 76
Fry, Daniel 71
Fuentes, Corporal Juan 64
Fukaria, Tomokichi 302
Fulfer, John G. 12, 208
Fulton, Roy 225
Furth, Admiral F.N. 229

Gaddis, Vincent 43

Galanapoulos, Professor A. 34
Galileo 176
Gamble, Stephen J. 288
Gardner, Gerald B. 341
Garfield, Dr Charles 201
Garrett, Eileen 184
Gasparetto, Luiz Antonio 38
Gauld, Alan 211
Gee, Dr D. 286
Geller, Uri 261, 300
George, Prince, (later King George V) 139
Gettings, Fred 126
Gibson, William 311
Gill, Reverend 62, 63
Gimlin, Bob 52
Giffard, Henri 6
Glenn, John 71
Goethe, Johann Wolfgang 105, 328
Goffe, Mary 83
Goodenough, John 49
Goodenough, Maurice 226
Goodman, Felicitas D. 121
Gotowski, A. 110
Grad, Dr Bernard 255
Graham, Billy 20, 309
Graham, David 303
Gratton, Colonel Harry 110
Greenstead, Ami 213
Greenwell, Russell 64
Grenier, Jean 338
Grieve, Dr D. 52
Griffin, A.H. 280
Griffiths, Frances 126
Grosse, Maurice 27, 123, 234
Groth, Arne 36
Gruber, Elmar 319
Guiley, Rosemary Ellen 329
Gumbel, Nicky 310
Guppy, Agnes 25
Gurney, Edmund 80

Hagopian, George 202
Hall, Asaph 175
Hall, Richard H. 61
Hall, Robert L., PhD 220

Halstead, Deputy Sheriff Millard 192
Hamblin, Dora 273
Hamilton, Alexander 8
Hamilton, George 16, 291
Hammon, Count Louis 245
Haraldsson, Professor Erlendur 26, 85
Harper, Michael 309
Hams, H. B. 244
Harris, Paul 194
Harrison, Michael 285
Hartland, Edwin 11
Harvey, Ralph 177
Hasted, Professor John 158, 261, 359
Haut, Lt. Walter 75
Healey, Sergeant 323
Hearst, William Randolph 9
Heinlein, Robert 231
Henry IV 279
Herbert, Benson 249
Hernandez, Angela 284
Hester, Philip 307
Heyerdahl, Thor 138, 204
Hibbard, Robert 8
Hickson, Charles 282
Hill, Betty and Barney 11, 282
Hine, Philip 329
Hinn, Benny 308
Hinton, Rohan 13
Hoagland, Richard 177
Hoare, Rodney 319
Hodgson, Richard 185
Holzer, Hans 145
Home, D.D. 157
Honorton, Dr Charles 85
Hooper, Curtis 320
Hoover, George 230
Hope, William 23
Hopkins, Budd 13
Hopkins, Herbert 190
Horak, Georg 167
Horwitz, William 273
Hough, Peter 285
Houtkooper, Dr Joop 26

Howard-Browne, Rodney 308, 311
Hudson, W. 25
Hughes, Howard 72
Hunt, Lord and Lady 346
Hurkos, Peter 248
Hussain, Ahmed 129
Hutchinson, Mervyn 194
Hynek, J. Allen 65, 322

Immesi Judge Filippe 257
Inglis, Brian 70

Jackson, John 319
Jacobs, Professor David 10, 13
James, Frederick 268
James, Graham 90, 210, 212, 251, 342
Jarvick, Lissy 273
Jeffrey, Lt. Walter 135
Jessup, Morris 229, 231
Jesus Christ 17, 72, 111, 120, 171, 241, 251, 289, 308, 316, 336
Jezzy, 1st Lieutenant 323
Joan of Arc 73
Johnson, Father J 193
Johnson, President Lyndon B. 281
Jones, Eryl 244
Jones, Nella 246
Jones, Vendyl 205
Joseph of Copertino 158
Jourdain, Eleanor 303
Jung, Professor Carl 70, 216, 260
Jurgensen, Friedrich 117

Kane, J. P. 32
Kasentev, Alexander 312
Keel, John 43, 192
Kelvin, Lord 358
Kennedy, President John F. 68
Kerridge, Roy 50
Kersten, Holger 319
Kestenbaum, Clarice 273
Keyhoe, Major Donald 216
Kilner, Walter J. 36
King, George 72
Kinnear, Roy 245
Kirby, Amy and Alice 285

Kiyota, Masuaki 303
Klarer, Elizabeth 72
Klein, William 244
Koestler, Arthur 70, 261
Kreutziger, Sarah 199
Krippner, Dr Stanley 277
Kuhlemann, Bertil 282
Kulagina, Nina 260
Kyte, Malcolm 307

Langdon, Benj 274
Langford, Eric 62
Lankford, Mrs 63
Larkin, Lt. James 83
Lazar, Bob 77
Lazarri, Domenica 290
Leacock, Stephen 162
Lechler, Dr 293
Leeford, Mrs Joseph 245
Leidenfrost, Johan 129
Lennon, John 38, 67
Leslie, Desmond 74
Lethbridge, T.C. 108, 145, 244, 264, 278, 305
Lewis, Mike 281
Leybourne, Susan 343
Lichfield, Tom, 209
Liddell, Dr, Dean of Christchurch 24
Lidfors, Lennart 101
Lincoln, President Abraham 68
Lindbergh, Charles 42, 332
Lodge, Oliver 185
Longley, Clifford, 310
Lorenzen, Jim and Coral 189
Lowell, Percival 174
Lueger, Pastor 283
Lundy, Ruth 195
Luukanen Kilde, Rauni-Leena 38

M'Connel, Lt. David 83
Machen, Arthur 21
Mack, Dr. John E., MD 13
MacMahon, Grace and Bruce 228
MacNish, John 86
Maddison, C. 307
Mahalek, Cathy 69

Mallette, Steve and Mary 192
Mannheim, Robert 241
Manning, Matthew 262
Mansell, Nigel 100
Marmoreo, Terry 247
Marsh, Ngaio 56
Marshall, Blanche 244
Mary, Virgin 18, 152, 169, 333
Maupassant, Guy de 106
Maxwell of Cranbury, Lt., P.D. 222
May, Anne 306
McAdam, Patricia Mary 248
McCollum, Eileen 67
McDowell, Clayton 110
McElrow, John 131
McGowan, Dr C. 115
McIver, Dr Richard 45, 181
McIver, Mrs 57
McLenore, Deputy Sheriff 6
McPherson, Robin 73
Megurchian, Dr Koriut 205
Mehrez, Dr Gamal ed-Din 94
Melling, June and Vicky 194
Menger, Howard 71
Metraux, Alfred 352
Michel, Aime, 160
Michell, John 160
Millar, Sandy 310
Miller, Dr Gerald 222
Mills, Greg 203
Mirabelle, Carmine 157
Moberley, Charlotte 303
Mogyorossy, Bonnie 84
Moi, Stephen 62
Moiser, Chris 48
Monahan, Evelyn 252
Moody, Raymond A. Jr., M. D. 196
Moore, William 76, 230
Morehouse, Captain 179
Morris, Graham 233
Morse, Dr Melvin 200
Moynagh, Digby 129
Muck, Otto Heinrich 33
Mumford, Eleanor 309
Murphy, Bridey 268
Murphy, Captain Paul 343

Murray, Arlene 100
Murray, Mary 333
Myers, Frederic W.H. 56, 80, 145, 185, 234, 298
Myles, John 22

Napier, John 54, 347
Napier, Sir William 103
Nathanson, Dr David 99
Navarra, Ferdinand 202
Neihardt, Dr J.G. 28
Neumann, Teresea 290
Newton, Silas 62
Nixon, Roland 114
Noonan, Allen-Michael 73
Norris, Dr Kenneth 102
Norton, Agnes and Dorothy 304
Nouri, Archdeacon 202

O'Hara, Attracta 333
O'Mahoney, Clare 335
O'Sullivan, Dave 48
Oakensen, Elsie 168
Olivier, Edith 207
Ono, Yoko 67
Osis, Karlis 26, 214, 247, 250
Ostman, Albert 52
Owen, Sir Richard 113

Padfield, Suzanne 249
Palladino, Eusapia 23
Paole, Arnod 328
Parham, Charles Fox 239
Parry, Lorraine 211, 305
Pasteur, Louis 337
Patel, Farida 121
Pauli, Wolfgang 70
Pennington, E.J. 7
Pereira, Maria 23
Persinger, Michael 201, 332
Person, Ethel 273
Peterson, Billy 285
Phillips, Ken 245
Picknett, Lynn 317
Pia, Secondo 318
Pinnell, Mr and Mrs D. 323
Pio, Padre 55, 291

Piper, Leonore 185
Plankernhorn, Mr and Mrs J. 323
Plato 32, 201, 267
Player, Gary 162
Podmore, Frank 80
Polasky, Stephen 54
Polidori, John 328
Pollard, Arthur 307
Porcelain, Sidney 96
Powers, Captain 133
Pratt, D.C. Neil 246
Price, Elvet 146
Price, Harry 128
Price, Pat 300
Prince, Clive 317
Puharich, Andrija 256
Purdy, Henry J. 105
Puthoff, Harold 300

Rai, Mona 122
Raleigh, Sir Walter 144
Ram, Sobha 271
Randi, James 261
Randles, Jenny 285
Raudive, Dr Konstantin 117
Rawlings, Dr Maurice 200
Real, Luiz and Lucy 193
Reeves, William 68
Reinhardt, Kathryn 106
Repo, Don 208
Rhine, J.B. 261, 299
Rhodes, Rosemary 49
Rich, Lady Diana 103
Richards, John Thomas 28
Richardson, Douglas 50
Richardson, Robert 189
Rimland, Dr Bernard 274
Rines, Robert H. 115
Ring, Dr Kenneth 200
Roberts, Dave 308
Roberts, J.C.H. 345
Robinson, Chris 243
Robins, Dr Don 150
Robson, Golin 149
Roff, Mary 271
Rohman, Delilah 118

Rolfe, Chris 194
Roll, William 235
Rollet, Jacques 338
Roncoglio, Rodney 247
Roosevelt, President Theodore 51
Rosales, Albert S. 195
Ross, Dr Anne 150
Rostron, Arthur 114
Roszak, Theodore and Mrs 67
Rowland, Ian 129
Rupert, Prince 279
'Ruth' 58, 107
Ryan, Frank 248

Sabom, Dr Michael 199, 212
Sacks, Oliver 273
Sagan, Carl 177, 315
Sagee, Emilie 104
Saladin, Flt. Lt. 322
Sandelius, Professor Walter E. 248
Sanders, Alex and Maxine 341
Sanderson, Ivan 43
Santos-Dumont, Alberto 7
Savelli, Caterina 290
Scales, Lucy 288
Scamell, S.E. 213
Scarberry, Rober and Linda 192
Schatzman, Dr Morton 58, 107
Schiaparelli 174
Schmidt, Helmut 261
Schopenhauer, Arthur 70
Schultheis, Rob 16
Schwarz, Karl 7
Scott, Sir Peter 66
Scully, Frank 62
Sergeyev, Genadi 260
Serios, Ted 302, 360
Shackleton, Ernest 20
Shandera, Jamie 77
Shankar, Ravi 270
Sharpe 226
Shattenkirk, Captain R. 45
Shaw, Glynis 67
Shelley, Percy 103
Sherbroke, Captain 81
Sherby, Captain Sydney 230

Shipton, Eric 346
Simon, Dr Benjamin 12
Sinclair, Mary Craig 299
Smith, Charles 249
Smith, Jason 101
Smith, Margo 145
Smith, Dr Willy 64
Smythe, F.S. 280, 346
Socrates 32
'Son of Sam', (see Berkowitz, David)
Soubirous, St Bernadette 152, 171
Spencer, John Wallace 43
Springfield, Leonard 76
St Clair, Sheila 40
Stacy, Dennis 294
Stead, W.T. 23, 245
Steff, Philip 83
Steiger, Brad 96, 303
Steiner, Rudolph 30
Stern, Auguste 158
Stevenson, Dr Ian 270
Stoker, Bram 328
Stone, Kathy 67
Stoop, Cor 69
Strader, Karl 308
Strand, Linda 231
Strong, Dorothy 281, 331
Stubb, Peter 337
Surin, Father Jean-Joseph 240
Sutcliffe, Peter 247
Sutton, Lucky 63
Sutton, Reverend and Mrs 185
Swift, Jonathan 175

Takeuchi, Tenshin 302
Talloy, Captain Joe 42
Targ, Russell 300
Tait, Charles 214
Taylor, Billy Ray 63
Taylor, Lt. Charles 132, 133
Tenhaeff, Professor Willem 248
Tepes, Vlad 328
Thalbourne, Dr Michael 26
Teresa, St 156, 290
Thérèse, St 152

Thomas, St 153
Thurston, Father Herbert 122, 131, 152
Thynne, Lady Isabel 103
Tighe, Virginia 268
Treffert, Darold A. 272
Trent, Paul 322
Tryon, Admiral Sir George and Lady 81
Tschemezky, W. 347
Tumer, Reginald and Kathryn 70
Turoff, Stephen 258
Tweedale, Ms Violet 213
Tyler, Kelsey 20

Umberto I, King 68
Umberto II, King 317

Valdivia, Luigi 5
Valentich, Frederick 324
Valinziano, Giuseppe 5
Vallee, Jacques 65, 79, 228
van der Decken, Hendrik 140
van Tassel, George W. 72
Vaughan, Dean of Llandaff 24
Vennum, Lurancy 271
Verne, Jules 191
Villas Boas, Antonio 10
Virgin Mary (see Mary, Virgin)
Voisin, Albert 171
von Szalay, Attila 118
von Wrangel, Antonie 105
von Zeppelin, Count Ferdinand 7

Walker, Canon Dominic 120
Walker, Dr Jearl 129
Walker, William 23
Walters, Ed 66

Walton, Philip 28, 130
Ward, Michael 346
Warner, Pat 49
Watkins, Alfred 160
Weinrichius 327
Welles, Orson 216
Wells, H.G. 9, 216
Wells, Tony 169, 263
White, Terry 124, 301
Whitmarsh, David 198
Williams, Robin 100
Wilson, Colin 249
Wilson, Ian 317
Wiltshire, Stephen 274
Woodfield, John 48
Woods, Heather 37, 251, 289
Woods, James 99
Wooldridge, Anthony 349
Wright, Barbara 184, 251
Wright, Elsie 126
Wright, Machaelle Small 126
Wright, Newell 330
Wyllie, Timothy 100
Wynne, Ruth 228
Wynyard, George 81

Xavier, Francisco Candido 39

Yanasek, Sergeant 323
Yorkshire Ripper, (see Sutcliffe, Peter)

Zamorra, Lonnie 65
Zender, Karl 299
Zigel, Felix 313
Zopfius, Heinrich 326
Zuccarini Amendee 157